Wise Choices, Apt Feelings

WISE CHOICES, APT FEELINGS

A Theory of Normative Judgment

ALLAN GIBBARD

Harvard University Press
Cambridge, Massachusetts

Library of Congress Cataloging-in-Publication Data

Gibbard, Alan.
    Wise choices, apt feelings : a theory of normative judgment /
Allan Gibbard.
        p.   cm.
    Includes bibliographical references.
    ISBN 0-674-95377-0 (alk. paper) (cloth)
    ISBN 0-674-95378-9 (paper)
    1. Ethics.   2. Judgment (Logic).   I. Title.
BJ1012.G53   1990
170'.42—dc20

89-28705
CIP

To Mary, in loving memory

Preface

My thoughts for this book began with a straight piece of philosophical problem-solving. The problem was perplexing enough: what the term "rational" means. We can ask what is the rational thing to do on one occasion and, more broadly, we can ask how it is rational to conduct our lives. What are we asking? It seems the widest question in life: how to live. Yet the term "rational" is beset with all the problems of moral terms like "ought" and "good" and "right", and these problems engaged whole swarms of moral philosophers for the first two-thirds of this century. Might some of their techniques work, then, for rationality? Could I exploit devices pioneered by such ethical non-cognitivists as A. J. Ayer, Charles Stevenson, and R. M. Hare? Hare's theory of conditional imperatives started me off, and after I had developed a version of my theory, Isaac Levi suggested a way to get to the heart of what I was saying. I put my theory in terms of norms and their acceptance, and this book was the eventual upshot.

Rationality, I became convinced, figures in all aspects of human life and thought. The term "rational" itself crops up rarely in everyday thinking, but using the term we can explain thoughts of morality, of what is worth having, of whether a claim merits credence, of what is shameful and what is cause for pride—and indeed all the other kinds of thought that philosophers call normative. Rationality was a crucial notion to analyze.

As I developed my theory, though, I found I was glimpsing far more than the meaning of a term, however crucial. We are special animals, and we find it easy to regard ourselves as special—but hard to conceive of ourselves as special animals. How can we understand ourselves as members of an evolved species, we humans who can think about rationality and justification and morality? I became convinced that new work in evolutionary theory could provide an answer. Broadly moral strands pervade human life, and by thinking about the evolution of a highly social, linguistic species like ours, we can start to see why. My speculations on this score are at best the roughest approximations to the truth. Still, I try sketching a naturalistic picture of human normative life, and enough in it coheres and fits the phenomena to make me think the truth may lie somewhere in its vicinity. If so, the old philosophical problems now come in new forms. What place do rationality and morality have in this naturalistic picture? What place do our thoughts about these matters have? A new theme emerged in the book: how we can think as self-understanding members of an evolved biological species.

Philosophers have stockpiled an extraordinary collection of devices of thought, and various of these devices promised to help with the grand set of problems I was addressing. Throughout the book, I cling to the shoulders of giants: I apply various of their philosophic inventions, and at times I work to improve those inventions.

It was Richard Brandt who, more than anyone else, led me to my present understanding of ethical theory. I follow him in starting out with questions of rationality, and interpreting moral questions as special questions of rationality, somehow connected with moral emotions. I am influenced by his account of the social workings of morality, and I follow him in looking to these workings as the key to moral theory and moral justification. Brandt was my teacher at Swarthmore when I was an undergraduate, and he and my other teachers held out shining examples of how to pursue philosophical inquiries. (My special thanks go also to Jerome Shaffer, who ignited my love of philosophy.) Coming to Michigan allowed me to profit from ongoing philosophical conversations with Brandt. I have always hoped to emulate his insistence on clarity, his rigorous honesty, his refusal to be swept along by trends, and his determination to press to the heart of matters.

In graduate school at Harvard, I found in John Rawls another brilliant teacher of a far different cast of mind. Rawls more than any other teacher I can think of treated his students as partners in philosophy. He listened carefully and responded creatively, perhaps even over-acknowledging our contributions. This was a heady role for students to play. Rawls exposed me to philosophical visions quite unlike any I had encountered before. In some ways I found these visions less congenial than Brandt's, but wrestling with them taught me new holds on deep philosophical issues. It was Rawls who convinced me of many of the themes I develop in this book: that problems of reciprocity have been crucial in shaping human moral capacities, that reciprocity gives rise to questions of fairness, and that consequently judgments of fairness and sentiments of fair reciprocity are central to our moral experience. Late in the book I grapple with Rawls's treatment of compromise and toleration.

In this work I disagree both with Brandt and with Rawls at many points, but always with thoughts I could not have had but for them. In criticizing them I intend to honor them: both marvelously encouraged questioning and criticism from me as a student, and each develops a profound view of the place of moral thought in the world and its bearing on moral justification—views greatly worth study. I might say schematically that Brandt sets the agenda of the book, and Rawls provides some of the moral psychology.

This book has been long in the works, and during this time I have received extensive support, financial and institutional. I began the writing in 1982–83 as a Fellow of the Center for Advanced Study in the Behavioral Sciences in Stanford, California. There I was supported by a National Endowment for the Humanities Fellowship for Independent Study and Research, and by the Andrew W. Mellon Foundation. Later work I did in 1985–86 as a Visiting Fellow at All Souls College, Oxford, with support from a Rockefeller Foundation Humanities Fellowship and a sabbatical from the University of Michigan. My own university has supported me with released time, facilities, and chances to teach seminars on this material. I am very grateful for all this generous support.

Some parts of the book have appeared elsewhere, in different form. I draw from two articles written before I began work on the book itself: "Human Evolution and the Sense of Justice," in P. A. French, T. E. Uehling, Jr., and H. K. Wettstein, eds., *Midwest Studies in Philosophy*, no. 7 (Minneapolis: University of Minnesota Press, 1982); and "A Non-Cognitivistic Analysis of Rationality in Action," *Social Theory and Practice* 9 (1983). Parts of this book coincide extensively with the following articles: "Moral Judgment and the Acceptance of Norms," *Ethics* 95 (1985); "Normative Objectivity," *Nous* 19 (1985); "An Expressivistic Theory of Normative Discourse," *Ethics* 96 (1986); "Rationality and Human Evolution," in N. Garver and P. Hare, eds., *Naturalism and Rationality* (Buffalo: Prometheus Books, 1986); "Normative Inquiry and Its Evolution," in Peter Koller, Alfred Schramm, and Ota Weinberger, eds., *Philosophy of Law, Politics, and Society: Proceedings of the 12th*

International Wittgenstein-Symposium (Vienna: Verlag Holder-Pichler-Tempsky, 1988); and "Communities of Judgment," *Social Philosophy and Policy* 7 (1989). I am grateful for the publishers' kind permission to reuse this material.

While writing the book I received an immense amount of philosophical help from many people; their comments, suggestions, and arguments have importantly affected the book in many places. Alas I have kept poor track of all this help, and I am bound to omit people. Those who gave me extensive written comments include Simon Blackburn, Thomas Carson, Daniel Farrell, Patricia Greenspan, Donald Herzog, Shelly Kagan, Ralph Lindgren, Don Loeb, Joseph Mendola, Adam Morton, Adrian Piper, Peter Railton, Donald Regan, Richard Rorty, Nicholas Smith, Sigrún Svavarsdóttir, David Velleman, Nicholas White, and three anonymous readers. These commentaries were often copious, and with most of these people I have had long conversations too.

I presented material for the book in well over thirty forums, and was helped greatly by the discussion. I should mention especially the joint class that Simon Blackburn and I conducted at Oxford, and the marvelous commentaries written and delivered by Michael Bratman, Ian McFetridge, Nicholas Sturgeon, and Zeno Swijtink.

As for conversations about the book and its topics, here especially I despair of adequate acknowledgement. Much of my stimulation the first year came from a series of conversations with Michael Bratman. Apart from people already mentioned, others with whom I have discussed aspects of this project at length include Christopher Achen, Kenneth Arrow, Annette Baier, Paul Boghossian, Jennifer Church, Sarah Conly, Stephen Darwall, William Frankena, Thomas Hurka, Don Locke, Rodney Needham, Derek Parfit, Samuel Sheffler, Amos Tversky. Two discussion groups at Oxford, the Michigan Philosophy Department faculty colloquium, and our informal Michigan ethics lunch deserve special mention.

Mary, Stephen, and George Gibbard cheerfully accompanied me to far places where I could work and talk with fresh people; they put up with my neglect and philosophical preoccupation. Mary has been my greatest support, Stephen my most avid interlocutor, and George my sternest critic.

Contents

I · ANALYSES

1 · The Puzzle

Why ponder our lives? At one extreme, the question is not a live one. We are a pondering species—and not each by himself; we are conversants. Silence is a discipline; too much is torment, as children learn in school. Sometimes we discuss earnestly, and in any case we banter and tease, quarrel and sulk. We gossip and tell stories, with verve if we can. Do these things engage us because they have point? Are they ways of working matters through with each other, or playing them through? Even when we are not pondering outright, we are caught up in equivalents.

With human beings it has always been so. The !Kung of the Kalahari are hunter-gatherers, and perhaps in them we can see what our hunting-gathering forebears were like. "Conversation in a !Kung encampment is a constant sound like the sound of a brook, and as low and lapping, except for shrieks of laughter. People cluster together in little groups during the day, talking, perhaps making artifacts at the same time. At night, families talk late by their fires, or visit at other family fires with their children between their knees or in their arms if the wind is cold."[1] The !Kung criticize each other, they gossip, they make oblique hints; they tell about events, about comings and goings, and about past hunts. They plan their hunts, and the successful hunter may consult on the proper distribution of his kill. Occasionally they quarrel, and frequently they talk about gifts and their suitability.

Conversation, then, is far more than a carrier of information. In talk we work out not only what to believe about things and events and people, but how to live. We work out how to feel about things in our

---

1. Marshall (1976, 351–352). The !Kung San live in Namibia (South West Africa); the San (or Bushmen) are among the few remaining hunting-gathering peoples.

3

lives, and in the lives of others. Not that we strive always to get to the root of things: we think not so much how to live and to feel on the whole, but about one thing or another, as it catches our attention.

Socrates was different. Plato has him saying to the jury, "If . . . I tell you that to let no day pass without discussing goodness and all the other subjects about which you hear me talking and examining both myself and others is really the very best thing that a man can do, and that life without this sort of examination is not worth living, you will be even less inclined to believe me. Nevertheless that is how it is" (*Apology*, 38a). When Socrates spoke of a life without such examination, he warned of a way a person might really live, that most people perhaps do. Socrates drank the hemlock for pressing too far these questions of how to live. What he did, and the Sophists before him, was start from the materials of common thought and speech, and refine them. Euthyphro could speak of piety, and he could reason about it; he could not have lived the life he did without reasoning. We can be tripped because we walk, and Euthyphro could be tripped because he reasoned, and had to.[2] Socrates' path is avoidable, and yet not always with ease. We think and talk by nature, and whoever thinks and talks can be led, unless he is careful, into wider questions. That may not be what makes everyone's life worth living, but it grows out of parts of our being we could not be without. The !Kung are not Socratic, so far as I know, but Socrates and the !Kung both are of our species.

In this book I ask about Socrates' quest. To ponder how to live, to reason about how to live, is in effect to ask what kind of life it is *rational* to live. I offer no special answer to this question; my first worry is what the question *is*. What does it mean to call an alternative rational, or another irrational? That is the puzzle of the book, and my hope is that from working on it, we can learn things worth learning about ourselves and about our questions.

In part the question how to live is moral—perhaps in whole. What kind of morality, if any, would be worth heeding? Or does the rational life do without morality? Here again my puzzle will be what the questions are. Again I want to know what 'rational' means, and in addition I want to understand this talk of morality. What are moral questions;

2. Euthyphro, as Plato presents him, is also a self-righteous fool, bent on a shocking course of action (prosecuting his father). Still, it is not this abnormal foolishness that leaves him vulnerable to Socrates's techniques. Euthyphro is abnormally foolish but normally prone to be tripped in his reasoning.

what do they mean? What, if anything, do they have to do with rationality?

The tie of morals to reason supports the whole of moral theory— perhaps. In any case, moral theories abound that say what the tie is or what it is not. They tell us whose good, if anyone's, reason commands we promote, but different theories tell us different things. Hume said that "Reason is, and ought only to be the slave of the passions, and can never pretend to any other office than to serve and obey them" (1740, bk. 2, part 3, sec. 3). Kant said the commands of morality are categorical demands of reason, and "reason issues inexorable commands without promising anything to the inclinations" (1785, 405). Sidgwick said the good is happiness, and that "as a rational being I am bound to aim at good generally,—so far as it is attainable by my efforts," and not at one's own happiness in particular (1907, 383). He thought also, though, that an egoist could evade this claim, and that in a "recognized conflict between duty and self-interest, practical reason" would be "divided against itself" (497, 508). Recent writers are divided against each other. Philippa Foot writes, "if justice is not a good to the just man, moralists who recommend it as a virtue are perpetrating a fraud" (1959, 100). David Gauthier maintains that reason demands maximally satisfying one's own desires, but under constraints that would be agreed to in certain ideal conditions (1986, esp. chap. 6). Thomas Nagel argues for pure impartiality between oneself and others. "In any situation in which there is reason for one person to promote some end, we must be able to discover an end which there is reason for anyone to promote, should he be in a position to do so."[3] Thinking about reason leads people to claims that are sharply at odds. It would be good to see what might be at issue.

My puzzle, then, is about Socrates, but it is also about the !Kung. I ask about moral philosophy, but also about everyday, non-philosophic life and thought and talk. The two kinds of talk are not the same, but one grows out of the other. As part of a human way of living, we think and discuss what it makes sense to do, and how it makes sense to feel about things. This thought and talk nudge us toward refinement. Wise choices and apt feelings figure in talk at both extremes: in refined, self-

---

3. Nagel (1970, 90). The list could be carried much further. See, for example, Grice (1967) for many claims about reasons. Parfit (1984, 313) argues at length against the claim that a rational person is "*equally* concerned about *all* the parts of his future."

conscious philosophizing and in everyday banter and quarrel. I want to know what is at stake in normative talk of both kinds.

A Glance Ahead

My proposal goes like this: Start with morality. We can understand the term broadly or narrowly. Broadly the moral question is how to live. Narrowly, we might try saying, morality concerns moral sentiments: the sentiments of guilt and resentment and their variants. Moral wrongs are acts to be avoided on pain of these sentiments. Morality in this narrow sense is a narrow part of life, but still, perhaps, something we need as a set of constraints. It seems worthwhile examining these constraints and asking whether they should matter.

To feel guilt or resentment is not in itself to make a moral judgment. A person can feel guilty and yet think he has done no wrong. He then thinks it makes no sense to feel the way he does, that his feelings are irrational. Narrowly moral judgments are not feelings but judgments of what moral feelings it is rational to have. Feelings, we think, can be apt or not, and moral judgments are judgments of when guilt and resentment are apt.

Saying this requires that we understand rationality. We must talk not only of wise choices, but of apt feelings too. What would a theory of rationality tell us? What does it mean to call something rational or irrational, a choice wise or foolish, a feeling apt or off the mark? My question shifts, then, from morality specifically to rationality in general.

To call a thing rational is to endorse it in some way. That suggests a scheme for getting at the meaning of the term. Instead of trying to define a property "rationality" by giving conditions under which a thing would have that property or lack it, start with the use of the term. Fix on the dictum "To call a thing rational is to endorse it," and search for a sense of 'endorse' for which the dictum holds true.[4]

The word 'rational' has a learned flavor, but the notion I have in mind is familiar. It is the one we use when we talk about "what it makes sense" to do or to believe, or when we speak of "the wise choice" in a situation. It is the one we use when we ask what we

---

4. My single and double quotation marks need a quick word here. Single quotes I try to use in the strict logician's way, to construct a name for the expression the marks surround. In the sentence this footnote tags, I name the word 'endorse'. Double quotes I use in the many looser ways quotation marks can be used, often to mention a word and use it in the same breath.

"ought" to do, or search for the "best thing to do", in a way that does not already presuppose we are talking morality. With feelings, it is the notion we use when we talk of anger, say, as warranted, or of pity as apt or misdirected. There does seem to be a common thought involved in all these turns of phrase, even if shades of meaning differ; one test is that to apply one phrase to an action or feeling while denying another is to invite puzzlement. I shall be using the learned term 'rational' in this broad way. It carries a kind of direct and flavorless endorsement, taken from the point of view of the person whose acts or feelings are being assessed. The rational act is what it makes sense to do, the right choice on the occasion. A rational feeling is an apt feeling, a warranted feeling, a way it makes sense to feel about something.[5] The term 'rational' may carry narrower suggestions, but this broad, endorsing reading is the one I need.

What is it, then, for an act or a way of feeling to be rational? In what way does a person who calls something rational endorse it? Cryptically put, my answer is this: to call something rational is to express one's acceptance of norms that permit it. This formula applies to almost anything that can be appraised as rational or irrational—persons aside. It applies to the rationality of actions, and it applies to the rationality of beliefs and feelings. We assess a wide range of things as rational or irrational, and it is puzzling how this can be. The analysis offers an answer.

"To call something rational is to express one's acceptance of norms that permit it." This is only a first sketch, and it raises many questions. What is it to accept norms? Acceptance is a state of mind, and a good way to identify this state of mind might be to exhibit its place in a rough psychological theory. The capacity to accept norms I portray as a human biological adaptation; accepting norms figures in a peculiarly human system of motivation and control that depends on language. Norms make for human ways of living, and we can understand our normative life as part of the natural world.

Normative talk is part of nature, but it does not describe nature. In particular, a person who calls something rational or irrational is not

5. The phrase 'it makes sense to' strikes my ear as carrying the right kind of endorsement, but there may be dialectical differences. If I say "It makes sense to read the footnotes later," some of my informants hear only a weak and grudging admission that postponing the footnotes would not be utterly crazy. For them I can say "It makes *most* sense to read the footnotes later," and that does carry the meaning I want. Alas it also carries an unwanted claim of uniqueness, that it makes more sense to read the footnotes later than now.

describing his own state of mind; he is expressing it. To call something rational is not to attribute some particular property to that thing—not even the property of being permitted by accepted norms. The analysis is not directly of what it is for something to *be* rational, but of what it is for someone to *judge* that something is rational. We explain the term by saying what state of mind it expresses. In this sense the analysis is *expressivistic,* and in too big a mouthful, I shall call it the *norm-expressivistic analysis.*[6]

The analysis is non-cognitivistic in the narrow sense that, according to it, to call a thing rational is not to state a matter of fact, either truly or falsely.[7] None of this leaves normative language defective or second-rate. The analysis explains why we need normative language, and as it takes shape, it ascribes to rationality many of the features on which theories of normative fact insist. In many ways, normative judgments mimic factual judgments, and indeed factual judgments themselves rest on norms—norms for belief. Normative discussion is much like factual discussion, I shall be claiming, and just as indispensable.

Part of my concern, then, is to understand morality, but my total concern is much wider. Morality narrowly glossed is a part of broadly normative life in general. Diverse aspects of life are governed by norms: action, and also belief and feeling. A good account of humanity will include a story of norms, a story of psychic mechanisms that make for their acceptance. The story will show these mechanisms in inter-action and exhibit their adaptive rationale. We need, however, more than a theoretical account of ourselves as a part of nature, an account as if from afar. As we lead our normative lives we need a sense of what we are doing, a picture of ourselves that can guide us. The ways we see norms should cohere with our best naturalistic accounts of normative life, and it is here that an expressivistic analysis becomes useful. We experience our lives in normative terms, in terms of things it makes sense to do, to think, and to feel. The analysis joins this experience to the detached, scientific perspective. It tells what we can see ourselves as doing as we engage in normative inquiry and discussion.

6. Ayer (1936, chap. 6) and Hare (1981) are both expressivists in this sense. Ayer thinks that moral utterances express feelings or moral sentiments. Hare thinks they express preferences of a special kind: preferences, all told, that are universal, in that they do not depend on who occupies which position in the situation to which they pertain (1981, 107).

7. Non-cognitivistic treatments of moral language emerged as a distinct alternative with Barnes (1933), Ayer (1936, chap. 6), and Stevenson (1937). Later Hare's version stood out (1952, 1963, 1981).

The analysis is non-substantive, in that one could accept it and yet have no idea how to go about inquiring into what sorts of things are rational. In some ways that is a virtue, for the analysis is not itself meant to capture a substantive view on the nature of rationality. It is meant, rather, to capture the common element in dispute when people disagree about the nature of rationality. To address substantive questions, we should know what the questions are.

The analysis has worth, though, chiefly if it does help us with normative inquiry. It should help us say what sorts of things really are rational or irrational, right or wrong. In this book, however, I take up substantive normative questions only cursorily, and only at a high level of abstraction. I do have substantive hopes for the analysis, but they are indirect. The analysis will not yield a mechanical procedure for answering normative questions; I doubt even that it will lead us to think about good lives in ways that are strikingly novel. It should help us make sense of ways we already inquire, when those ways are reasonable. It should help us sort ways of inquiry that make sense from ways that do not. My hope is that if we proceed with a clear, plausible view of what we are doing, then we can progress—not automatically, but with less murk than otherwise.

Above all, I hope, the analysis will help us understand why it matters which acts and feelings are rational. Deciding what sorts of things are rational is deciding what norms to accept in various realms. The point of the book is to ask what this involves. We can picture human normative life as a part of nature, but that might leave us at a loss as to how to engage in that normative life. My first step toward engagement is to try to puzzle through what normative questions are. The eventual goal is to address normative questions with a better sense of what addressing them consists in.

Substantive Analyses

According to any expressivistic analysis, to call something rational is not, in the strict sense, to attribute a property to it. It is to do something else: to express a state of mind. It is, I am proposing, to express one's acceptance of norms that permit the thing in question. There is a special normative element in talk of what it makes sense to do, to think, and to feel, and that element resides in a special state of mind.

This may seem perverse. Surely a descriptivistic analysis would be better; that is to say, if a person calls something rational, it would be best to hear him as describing it, as ascribing a property to it. Then we could assess what he has to say and have clear grounds for judging it true or false—whereas on an expressivistic analysis, we can only react.

My broad response is that any such descriptivistic analysis leaves a puzzle. It misses the chief point of calling something 'rational': the endorsement the term connotes. More specifically, we find that even the best descriptivistic analyses fail. They yield meanings that are inadequate to the basic purposes to which the term 'rational' can be put. They leave the puzzle of what it could mean to call something rational—a puzzle we can solve if we bring in endorsement.

This is not something I can prove conclusively. New analyses may appear, and I have no general proof that they all must fail. The most promising current contenders do fail, though, and on a plausible diagnosis of their failure, others will fail as well. On that diagnosis, what descriptivistic analyses miss is a general element of endorsement—an element an expressivistic analysis can capture.

Some analyses are substantive: They start with a theory of what rationality is, and then say that that itself is what the term 'rational' means. They take the characteristics that go to make something rational, and have them constitute the meaning of the term. For action, the most sophisticated theory of rationality might be called the *Hume-Ramsey theory*. It is now orthodox among economists and decision theorists, and we might look to it for a substantive analysis. The Humean element is that instrumental rationality is all of rationality. The content of one's ultimate ends cannot be assessed as rational or irrational. Rationality lies in adopting appropriate means, in an uncertain world, to whatever substantive goals one may have. *Instrumental rationality* here means rationality in the pursuit of ultimate ends which are accepted as given. Ramsey's contribution is to interpret instrumental rationality as a kind of formal coherence among preferences and actions. The conditions of coherence are such things as that one's preferences form an ordering, and that one always does what one most prefers. On the Hume-Ramsey view, in short, rationality demands no more than a formal coherence of preferences, in a way that can be expressed by a set of axioms.[8]

8. Hume (1739, bk. 2, part 3, sec. 3) thinks that reason, strictly understood, yields only beliefs, chiefly about cause and effect. An irrational action, then, could only be an action founded on unreasonable belief—or, as Hume adds in his discussion of "unreasonable passions", one that chooses a means insufficient for its end. (See Sturgeon 1985a, 27–28.) The more adequate, axiomatic view of rationality in the pursuit of goals was developed by Ramsey (1931). Ramsey's theory at first got little notice, but Savage (1954, 1972) elaborated a similar theory, and was highly influential.

Now my purpose here is not to assess the Hume-Ramsey theory as a substantive account of what makes an act rational. My question is rather, could Ramsey's axioms, or some similar set of axioms, be taken as giving the very meaning of the term 'rational'? Could they constitute, in the strict sense, a definition or analysis of the term? The answer, I claim, must be no, and for reasons of the very kind that Moore put forth in his attacks on various "naturalistic" definitions of 'good'.[9]

Take first the Humean component: that instrumental rationality is all of rationality, that one's intrinsic ends, wanting the things one wants for their own sake apart from what they bring, cannot be substantively irrational. According to Hume, reason must be the slave of whatever intrinsic preferences one may have. In his oft quoted words, " 'Tis not contrary to reason to prefer the destruction of the whole world to the scratching of my finger. 'Tis not contrary to reason for me to chuse my total ruin, to prevent the least uneasiness to an *Indian* or person wholly unknown to me. 'Tis as little contrary to reason to prefer my own acknowledged lesser good to my greater, and have a more ardent affection for the former than the latter" (1739, bk. 2, part 3, sec. 3). It is no less rational to seek pain than pleasure, it is no less rational to seek destruction than to seek cooperation, and it is no less rational to devote one's life to the collection of bottle caps than to the composition of symphonies—if one's ultimate preferences run that way. Now these are matters of controversy, to say the least. If, however, the Humean thesis is built into the very meaning of the word 'rational', then all these controversies are settled by the meaning of a word. What can the controversies be about?

Perhaps they really are about words and usage. People seem to be claiming something more substantive, though, when they quarrel with Hume. They seem to be making claims about how to live. Hume's own point may well be about words: he himself does not seem to be talking about which things are ultimately worth seeking; he is debunking the question. Still, his opponents do try to make claims of substance. They claim that there are things—accomplishment, for instance—that it is rational to want whether or not one does happen to want them.[10] They

---

9. Moore (1903, 10–21, esp. 10–12). Moore seems to have thought he had a blanket argument that all such definitions stemmed from a "naturalistic fallacy". It is hard to see quite what the argument is supposed to be; see, for example, Frankena (1939). What I imitate is his pattern of attacks on specific examples of naturalistic analyses.

10. Griffin speaks repeatedly of accomplishment as a chief prudential value. He lists

claim there are other things—vengeance, say—that it is irrational to want, for their own sake at least, even if one does in fact want them. These people use the word 'rational' in a way Hume finds unintelligible. It would be good to see if we can interpret what they could mean.

Any difficult analysis will be controversial, and so the point is not just that there are controversies. An analysis can be questionable and still be right. To refute an analysis by counterexample, we need a case in which a person not only doubts it, but accepts something inconsistent with it—without linguistic or logical confusion. Here is such a case: Octavia thinks reason demands that anyone give weight to his own future happiness. It makes this demand, she thinks, even on a person who is now indifferent to the future. Now whether or not she is right, if her thought is intelligible, if it is unconfused linguistically and logically, then the Humean thesis is wrong as a claim about meaning. Future happiness is no goal of Cassius's, imagine, and so by the Humean thesis, it is rational for him to give it no weight. According to Octavia, he rationally must give it weight. If the Humean thesis is right as a claim about meaning, then Octavia has meanings wrong or else she is logically confused. If her opinion is intelligible, then the Humean thesis is wrong as a claim about meaning.

No such counterexample will be airtight. It can always be asked whether the opinion put forth as intelligible really is intelligible. Is the thinker really free of all linguistic and logical confusion? The point, though, is this: An opinion seems intelligible; we seem to understand what the person is claiming. There is pressure, then, to interpret the opinion as intelligible—or at least to explain the appearance of intelligibility.

In short, then, the Humean thesis fares poorly as a claim about meaning. People think some things worth wanting whatever in fact one wants, and other things not worth wanting even if in fact one does want them. We seem to understand these claims, and it would be good to have an analysis that counts them as intelligible.

Instrumental Rationality

Perhaps the Humean's point is something like this: Instrumental rationality seems unproblematic. We quarrel about facts and we quarrel

---

as other prudential values understanding, enjoyment, deep personal relations, and such components of human existence as autonomy, basic capabilities, and liberty (1986, 67–68). His account of what makes something a prudential value is partly a full-information account. In addition, prudential values must be widely shared among people (113–120).

about ultimate goals. In disputes about ultimate goals, though, is talk of rationality anything more than a rhetorical bludgeon? Why not disarm, and confine the term 'rational' to talk of means? Rationality then is rationality of beliefs: beliefs about what means will reach what ends. So Hume seems to have thought, and so perhaps ought we.[11]

Instrumental rationality, though, is more than rational means-end beliefs. Any account of instrumental rationality must cope with interactions of reasoning agents one with another. It must cope with uncertainty. We need something like Ramsey's theory to capture these complexities.

Ramsey treats rationality as a kind of formal coherence. His axioms require more than sheer logical consistency in belief. They require that one's preferences form an ordering. They require as well a "sure thing principle" that goes like this: Let A, B, and C be prospects, and let p be something that might happen—say, a coin's landing heads—about which, in itself, one cares not at all. Suppose one prefers A to B: then one prefers the compound prospect

A if p and otherwise C

to the compound prospect

B if p and otherwise C.[12]

Ramsey's account is widely accepted, but it is controversial—even for instrumental rationality. Proponents claim that an action is rational when and only when its agent satisfies Ramsey's formal conditions of coherence for preference. That incorporates Hume's thesis, but even for instrumental rationality, the claim is hotly disputed. Now if Ramsey's axioms give what 'rational' means, it is puzzling what the controversies could be. They appear substantive; they seem to be over whether a person can be rational without satisfying the axioms. They do not seem mere disputes over English usage, as they would be if Ramsey's axioms defined the very meaning of the term 'rational'.

Here, at length, are two current examples of controversy.

You and your twin are arrested and placed in a prisoners' dilemma. The district attorney has isolated you from each other, and now con-

---

11. Don Loeb proposed this line of thought to me, and convinced me that it, or something like it, explains some of the attraction of Humean accounts of practical rationality.

12. I speak of Ramsey's axioms loosely. The points I want to make are not about Ramsey's specific formulation, but about the general form of theories like those of Ramsey (1931) and Savage (1954, 1972).

fronts you each with this proposition: You get a year off your sentence if you implicate twin in a robbery. Specifically, if twin implicates you, you get ten years in jail unless you have implicated him, in which case you get only nine. If twin keeps mum, then you get one year, on a trumped-up charge, unless you yourself have implicated him, in which case you go free. Twin is faced with the same proposition, and you both know it.

	Twin rats	*Twin keeps mum*
You rat	9 years for you	Freedom for you
	9 years for twin	10 years for twin
You keep mum	10 years for you	1 year for you
	Freedom for twin	1 year for twin

You want to minimize your own time in jail, and you care not at all about how long twin spends there. Twin and you are very much alike, and so if you rat on him, that is bad news for you: it indicates that probably twin is ratting on you, making you spend nine years in jail. Likewise if you keep mum that is good news for you: it indicates that probably twin is keeping mum, giving you just one year in jail.[13]

How is it instrumentally rational for you to pursue your goal—your goal of spending as little time in jail yourself as possible? Some say it makes sense to rat. What twin does is now beyond your influence, and whatever he does, you save yourself a year in jail if you rat. This is the standard view of game theorists, yielded by systems like Ramsey's: ratting "dominates" keeping mum.[14]

Others say it makes sense to keep mum. That indicates twin is keeping mum, and twin's keeping mum will save you nine years in jail.[15] Others even say it would make sense to keep mum if the other prisoner were not your twin—at least if you each can expect the other to keep

13. The prisoner's dilemma is attributed to A. W. Tucker; see Luce and Raiffa (1957, 95–97). Nozick (1969) introduces twins, and points out that doing so makes the problem into an analog of Newcomb's paradox, the topic of his paper.

14. Gibbard and Harper (1978) and Lewis (1979b) are among the people who accept this argument. There is some dispute over the interpretation of dominance in systems like Ramsey's (see Levi 1975), but I take the interpretation favored by Nozick (1969) and Gibbard and Harper (1978).

15. This argument would be recognized as sound in the decision theory developed by Jeffrey (1965); see Gibbard and Harper (1978). Levi (1975) and Eells (1982) defend Jeffrey's kind of decision theory from attacks based on examples like this one, but they may want to deny that it has the consequences I am claiming for it.

mum. It cannot make sense, they say, for both of you to act in a way that jointly frustrates the goals of each.[16]

Now my puzzle is not which of these sides is right, but what is at issue. Those who think it rational to keep mum may know perfectly well that keeping mum violates axioms like Ramsey's; they think the axioms mischaracterize rationality. 'Rational' as they use the term cannot mean "satisfying the axioms", or these people would be trivially wrong. Do they mean something different by the term from their opponents? Then there is no real disagreement, just a word used in different senses. There seems, though, to be real substance to the dispute: hypothetically taking on egoistic goals, the two sides disagree about what to do.

Here is a second controversy, active among economists.

You are forced to play Russian roulette—but you can buy your way out. One bullet is placed in a six chamber revolver, and you must spin the cylinder vigorously and shoot yourself square in the head. Here is a question: What is the most you would pay to have the bullet removed? (Pay in installments over a lifetime if you survive. The payment is excused if you die.)

Next the scene shifts to a second version of the problem. You are forced to play Russian roulette with four bullets in the revolver. Answer a new question: What is the most you would pay in this version to have *one* of the four bullets removed, leaving three? More? Or less?[17]

Most people answer less. Standard decision theory says to answer more. Indeed it tells you to pay as much to reduce the bullets from four to three as you would pay to reduce the bullets from two to none.

The second scene, after all, is as if you were forced to play in two stages as follows: First you must play with three bullets. Then, if you survive, you have to play again, this time with two bullets—but you

---

16. See Baier (1958, 308–315) for reasoning that appears to support this conclusion, and Rapoport (1960, 174–178) for such a treatment of the prisoner's dilemma itself. Parfit attacks this conclusion (1984, 87–92). Gauthier (1986, chap. 6) takes a position something like this for certain circumstances. The circumstances are these: that the prisoners agree beforehand to keep mum, that each is disposed to keep the agreement so long as he expects the other to, and that each can tell fairly well that the other is so disposed. Then, Gauthier maintains, each acts rationally in keeping the agreement. This in effect is a claim about instrumental rationality, and others disagree.

17. Kahneman and Tversky (1979, 283) give this example and credit Richard Zeck-hauser. The structure is that of the Allais paradox.

can pay to have them both removed. Work it out: All told, in both versions, if you don't pay, your chances of killing yourself are four in six. If you do pay, your chances of killing yourself are three in six—again in both versions. The two versions, then, are equivalent.[18]

How much are you willing to pay? In the two-round version if you die in the first round, it makes no difference what you are to pay on survival. Your question, then, is how to treat the second round: how much at most to pay to have both bullets removed, when they are the only ones in the cylinder. You would pay more, presumably, to have two sole bullets removed than to have one sole bullet removed. Therefore in the two one-round scenes, you should pay more to reduce the bullets from four to three than to reduce them from one to zero. So goes the argument.

Some people accept it. Others understand it but reject it. They stick with their initial claim that it is worth more to rid oneself of a one-in-six threat to life and get safety, than merely to move one's chances of safety up from two-in-six to three-in-six. The argument depends, they say, on a dubious principle. Take the stage with two bullets in the cylinder. How much do you pay to have them both removed? The argument assumes that this should not depend on what risks lead up to that stage. It should not depend on whether the choice is faced all by itself or whether another stage leads up to it. If that yields counterintuitive results, so much the worse for the principle.[19]

What is at issue between those who accept the principle and those who reject it? Those who reject it cannot mean by 'rational' what axioms like Ramsey's say. They know the principle is one of the

18. David Lewis has argued along these lines.

19. The appeal here is to the sure-thing principle. It says that if two lotteries are equally undesirable, then when one is substituted for the other in a compound lottery, that makes no difference to how undesirable the compound is. The principle looks appealing, but the Russian roulette case shows it wrong, its detractors say.

A little more carefully, the argument is this. Take the most you would be willing to pay to have two bullets removed if they are the only bullets. Call living having paid that much being *poor*, and living having paid nothing being *rich*. By stipulation, you are indifferent between *poor* and what I shall call the *plunge*: namely, four chances in six of being *rich* and two of being *dead*. Now take the two-round game. This is a lottery with even chances of two prizes: *dead* and the *plunge*. The buyout substitutes *poor* for the *plunge* in the compound; the result is even chances *dead* and *poor*. By the sure-thing principle, that should make no difference: you should pay as much to have one of four bullets removed as to have two bullets removed if they are the only ones. But clearly, opponents argue, it is not worth as much to have one of four bullets removed as to have a bullet removed when it is the only one—and so much the worse for the sure-thing principle.

axioms[20] and they think rational choice violates it. Do its opponents and its proponents simply mean different things by 'rational'? Then there is no real dispute. There seems in fact to be a dispute of substance: The two sides differ on whether to pay more in the one case or in the other.

It is easy to think that instrumental rationality, at least, is unproblematical. The problems seem to lie with the substantive rationality of goals. Instrumental rationality seems just a matter of beliefs about consequences, and of doing the thing whose consequences one most wants. The two examples—prisoner's dilemma with twins and Russian roulette with buyouts—each show that things are not so straightforward. In both cases the facts are clear enough; they are given by stipulation and known to the agents. The puzzles of instrumental rationality lie not just in the facts. Agents seek their goals in interaction with other agents who have different goals. Agents pursue their goals knowing they are ignorant. Instrumental rationality includes coping with both these features of life, and there are disputes about how it makes sense to do so. In a broad sense, Ramsey's decision theory treats rationality as a kind of coherence, but this coherence is not just logic narrowly construed, and it is not just straightforwardly choosing what one most wants.

We need, then, something as complex as Ramsey's axioms to characterize instrumental rationality. Such characterizations are controversial. Choosing sides in these controversies is not a simple matter of saying which axioms are satisfied and which are violated. People who agree on that can disagree on which acts are instrumentally rational. Choosing sides consists, it seems, in a kind of hypothetical endorsement: we hypothetically adopt certain ultimate ends, and then settle what to do.

The Ramsey axioms may, of course, be offered as something other than a definition of 'rational' in the sense I am after. In that case, nothing I am saying speaks for or against them. The axioms may be offered as a substantive account of the nature of rationality. My puzzle then becomes, What is the account claiming for actions that satisfy those axioms? The axioms may, on the other hand, be used to stipulate a

---

20. Again, the reference is not specifically to Ramsey's formulation, but to systems like it. The principle is one of the axioms or it follows from the axioms, depending on how the particular set of axioms is formulated. The name "sure-thing principle" comes from Savage (1954) but his formulation is somewhat different.

meaning for the word 'rational', as mathematicians stipulate what shall constitute a "group" or a "well-ordering". In that case, there is no great room for controversy: nothing is at stake in a mathematician's appropriation of a term but suggestiveness, clarity, and fecundity. What I am asking is what the term 'rational' means in genuine controversies, if such there be, on the nature of rationality.

Full Information Analyses

On a view widespread among philosophers, rationality is somehow a matter of full awareness of the facts. Brandt elaborates a view of this kind. He announces that he will "pre-empt the term rational to refer to actions, desires, or moral systems which survive maximal criticism and correction by facts and logic" (1979, 10). Brandt's account could be put as follows. First, we characterize the intrinsic desires that it would be rational for a person to have. They are the ones the person would have after repeated representation of all relevant, scientifically available information, in an ideally vivid way, at appropriate times (11, 113). Brandt calls this vivid, repeated representation of facts *cognitive psychotherapy*. Second, we define the rationality of an act as a means, or its "instrumental rationality". Take some system of intrinsic desires as given. An act is *instrumentally rational* as a means to the fulfillment of those desires if and only if the following holds: if a person had those intrinsic desires, and he had all relevant scientifically available information "present to awareness, vividly, at the focus of attention, or with an equal share of attention," then he would be willing to perform that act (11). An act, then, is *fully rational* if and only if it is instrumentally rational as a means to the fulfillment of the intrinsic desires it would be rational for the agent to have (149).

One problem for any "full awareness" account such as Brandt's is that rationality, in the ordinary sense, often consists not of using full information, but of making best use of limited information. Acting in full awareness of all relevant facts suggests not rationality, but something more like "advisability". Whereas rationality is a matter of making use of the information one has, advice can draw on information the advisee lacks. Suppose, for instance, I am lost in the woods without a map or compass. With full information, I would take the shortest, easiest route out of the woods and to where I want to be—but I don't have full information. The rational thing for me to do, then, is to pursue one of the standard strategies for getting out of trackless woods:

walk carefully in a straight line by sighting along trees, or go consistently downhill. Some such strategy is rational, even though I am confident it will not take me along the route I would travel with full information. What is rational, then, is not what an agent would do with full information. It is not even what he would do with all the information he should have obtained: my being lost in the woods without a map or compass is likely the result of previous irrationality, but rationality now consists in coping without the information I ought earlier to have secured. If I unexpectedly meet someone who knows the woods, then what I shall want is advice. I shall not want to know what it is rational for me to do; I already know that the rational thing is to ask for directions. The expert can then tell me what is advisable: he can tell me the shortest way out of the woods. In his advice, he draws on full information. Of course, once I have his advice, it then becomes rational for me to do what he says—but only then. Rationality, we may conclude, is related to advisability, but the connection is this: in the special case in which I know all that bears on my choice, what it is rational for me to do is what it is advisable for me to do. Otherwise the two may differ, and full information pertains to advisability.[21]

Perhaps rationality in action is best construed, in the spirit of Brandt's proposal, as acting in full and vivid awareness of whatever information one has. Whether or not that is the best way to fix things up, the definition as he gives it seems best taken as an analysis of advisability, or rationality in light of full information. How does it fare if so taken? Brandt himself offers the proposal not as an analysis of our actual usage but as a reform. Nevertheless, we may ask whether the proposed reform misses anything worth preserving in our unreformed use of the term.

Now we ordinarily suppose that there is more to rationality than Brandt's proposal captures—as his own examples show. Whether an intrinsic desire is rational, on Brandt's account, is a matter of whether it would be extinguished in cognitive psychotherapy. In consequence, Brandt points out, any intrinsic desire that is so deeply ingrained in early childhood as to be inextinguishable by cognitive psychotherapy will count as rational on his definition (113). Suppose, for instance, a

---

21. Harman makes this point (1982, 127). Brandt does speak of "subjective" and "objective" rationality (1979, 72–73); my question is whether "objective rationality" is rationality at all. Brandt's "objective rationality" differs somewhat from what I am calling "advisability": it is rationality not in light of all the facts, known and unknown, but in light of everything currently known by experts.

person neurotically wants to keep his hands as germ-free as possible, and so washes his hands a number of times each hour. The desire, to be sure, might extinguish with vivid and repeated awareness of certain facts: that keeping his hands perfectly germ-free will not promote health, that incessant washing may indeed threaten his health, that the hand-washing interferes with all the other activities that he finds of value, and that if he did not care about germs so much, he would find nothing missing in his life on that account. Suppose, though, he has confronted all these facts, repeatedly and vividly, and he nevertheless says "I realize all that. But I just don't want those creepy-crawly things on my hands—and least of all do I want to be a person who would be willing to tolerate them on his hands." Then the person is rational in his preferences, on Brandt's account.

Brandt, I take it, does not regard this conclusion as a virtue of his account. It is an unsought consequence, which Brandt accepts only because, in his opinion, any account that yields the opposite answer will have defects far worse. What he claims, then, is not that his account does everything we should want, but that no alternative will do better on the whole. What I have said is thus no refutation of Brandt: it simply shows a respect in which we might hope to do better.

What we should note, though, is that the funny cases—the cases where Brandt's account labels crazy acts rational—have a systematic import. The word 'rational', in the sense we are after, has an automatically recommending force. Brandt indeed spends a whole chapter trying to show that his account preserves this recommending force (chap. 8). Rationality in Brandt's sense, however, need not be a recommendation. Suppose, for instance, I think that full and vivid realization of all the relevant facts would evoke a debilitating neurosis—a neurosis I have kept from controlling my life only by avoiding vivid confrontation with certain facts. Perhaps with a more vivid realization of what peoples' innards are like, I would want to stay away from dinner parties and do all my eating alone—although then I would feel lonely and isolated. Suppose on that ground I accept the claim "If you were fully rational in Brandt's sense, you would not ever eat with other people." Would that have recommending force?

A civil servant who firmly rejects all offers of bribes might fear that if he dwelt vividly on all that he is forgoing, he would yield to temptation. That, roughly, is to fear that his determination not to take bribes is irrational in Brandt's sense. Cognitive psychotherapy, to be sure, would involve vivid awareness of the social consequences of bribery and its personal dangers. If the personal danger is minimal, though, the civil servant may well suspect that vivid realization of the social consequences of bribery would little avail against vivid realization of the pleasures accepting bribes would open to him. Moreover, once temptations had done their work, he might well be glad they had. Suppose all this is so. Is he being irrational when out of moral conviction he avoids contemplating the temptations of his position? Is it irrational for him to refuse a bribe? On Brandt's account, his moral compunctions against losing his moral compunctions do not count if they would not survive cognitive psychotherapy. Does that recommend dwelling on the temptations? Does that recommend bribery? The honest civil servant might well think not.

The same kind of story might be told for an egoist. Suppose an egoist achieves happiness by keeping his mind off the joys and sorrows of others, but he thinks that if he fully realized what suffering he could alleviate and what joy he could spread by a life of self-sacrifice in the service of others, he would sadly forsake his life of self-centered enjoyment, and take on an irksome burden of service to humanity. Must he find that a recommendation for self-sacrifice? Why is it not instead a reason to shield himself from the facts? Can he not say without linguistic error, "It's crazy to dwell on the effects one can have on the lives of others. For if you do, then next thing you know, you will be making all sorts of sacrifices for others at the expense of your own enjoyment. Why deliberately take a path that leads to sorrow?" Now perhaps human psychology is not as I have described it, and a life of service to others is more personally rewarding than a life of ignorant, selfish enjoyments. That, however, is not the situation this egoist thinks he faces. He is convinced that the life he would want to lead if he fully realized what was at stake for others is painful in comparison to the life he will lead with his egoism fostered by ignorance. If, thinking that, he is also convinced that the altruistic life is the one he would choose with full knowledge, why should that commend the altruistic life to him?

These examples have a common structure. Often we suppose that we are reliable formers of rational desires, if only we get the facts straight and have them clearly and vividly in view. The examples I have given are cases in which a person thinks himself an unreliable transformer of vivid realizations into rational desires, and so avoids dwelling on the facts he thinks would lead him astray. On a full-information account like Brandt's, this talk of reliability has no substance: that we are reliable transformers of vivid realizations into rational desires is analytic—true just in virtue of what 'rational' means. Brandt himself does not claim this for any ordinary sense of 'rational', for he thinks in ordinary use the term has no clear meaning (6–7). In all the examples, though, there is a common element that an account like 'Brandt's misses: the protagonist endorses a system of ends he thinks would not survive a vivid, repeated confrontation with the facts. In that sense, he thinks his desires would no longer be rational if he underwent such a confrontation. In the argument that follows I pursue the element of endorsement that full-information accounts leave out. In that element, if I am right, lies the specially normative aspect of the term.

2 · Nature and Judgment

If we try to paint normative life as a part of nature, crucial parts keep looking off shape. Reasons in the picture look not quite like genuine reasons. Meanings are hardly recognizable. For reasons and for meanings both, naturalistic depiction seems wrong, or if somehow it can be got to work, artistry is needed. We have reason to do various things, or so we think, but if we try to brush that fact into a picture of nature, we risk a botched likeness; bald descriptions do not straight off yield reasons. The normative things we say have meaning, but how can we include these meanings, and others too, in a picture of nature? The job may not be impossible, but it will require invention.

The task is to put in one picture apparent facts of three kinds:

1. Naturalistic facts: us as a part of nature, our acts and thoughts and feelings as they might be understood in a natural science
2. Normative facts: what it is rational to do and to think and to feel, what it *makes sense* to do or think or feel
3. Facts of meaning: what our words mean in general, and in particular what our normative claims mean—what it means to say it is rational to do or think or feel such-and-such

In my own picture, all strict facts will be naturalistic. Facts of meaning will come out as genuine facts, and so as naturalistic. Apparent normative facts will come out, strictly, as no real facts at all; instead there will be facts of what we are doing when we make normative judgments. It does make sense to do some things and not others, but that will not be part of a systematic picture of nature. Our thinking about these things will.

In this chapter, I talk about the kind of naturalistic picture I shall be painting, and then I go on to talk about meanings. To do what I plan to do, I need an empirical psychology. In the first place, there is no good reason to think that normative theory itself can be done apart from psychology. Whether it can or not, though, a theory of normative meanings will require a psychology. My own psychology must be speculative, and it will draw on thoughts of how human normative capacities might have evolved. Evolution has tended toward giving a person capacities that would best advance his own reproductive prospects. Humanity evolved in groups, and anyone's reproductive prospects depended on bonds with others and on dealings with them. Here is a place to look for a story of human normative capacities, and the shapes they might take. Here also we should find stories of morally significant emotions. Evolutionary stories have their pitfalls, and at the outset I wave my hand across some of them, and think how to proceed. I glance at controversies. The psychology itself comes in later chapters (esp. 4, 7, and 8).

Then to meanings: We are part of nature, our thought and talk included. Or so I want to depict us, and a major part of my project is to explore how to fill in this naturalistic picture. Meaning analysis, though, goes most easily into a picture of magic, with facts of meaning placed in a special, enchanted realm. I talk here about how I intend my own analyses to be taken, since they are certainly not meant as claims of what things mean by magic. I talk about how we can do without thoughts of magic and still judge analyses as good or bad. Norms infuse facts, and I talk about whether nevertheless the two can be distinguished. Again, the discussion here is preliminary; more of a theory of meaning comes in Chapter 6.

Normative Psychology

Our normative life is a part of nature—perhaps so, but does that bear on anything philosophical? Philosophers often put empirical questions aside. They divorce normative studies from psychology and biology, and even studies of meaning they may try to divorce from the empirical. They limit their inquiries to what can be said *a priori*. Kant spoke of a metaphysics of morals and a metaphysics of nature, and wrote, "These prior sciences must be carefully purified of everything empirical so that we can know how much pure reason can accomplish in each case and from what sources it creates its *a priori* teaching" (1785, 388–389). Kant's division has endured.

Rationales for these separations give way once they are pressed. Take, first, ethics. No one has been able to show how the foundations of ethics can be laid *a priori*. This claim is controversial, since some think they have done so, but it is widely shared and widely argued.[1] Indeed it would make no sense for a reader to proceed with me if he thought any such *a priori* formulation to be firm. Accept, then, tentatively, that no such foundations are to be had. We still need to think about how to live, and since we cannot say *a priori* how to proceed, we should harken to such clues as we can find.

A prime replacement philosophers offer for *a priori* ethics is "reflective equilibrium".[2] Nothing in the theory of reflective equilibrium bans psychology from ethical theory, or biology either. *Reflective equilibrium* is an ideal state we might reach if we had considered everything fully and achieved entirely consistent judgments. Now, I do not accept this fully as a characterization of the moral theorist's goal (see Chapter 9). Still, if it is even on the right track, then there is no such thing as a consideration that is ruled out from the start.

In particular, then, in advance of inquiry we have no reason for supposing our moral natures irrelevant to ethics. Indeed antecedently this claim of irrelevance would be quite implausible, unless some argument clinched it. Human nature, it seems, must be one of the things we should ponder in any search for broad reflective equilibrium in ethics.[3]

I myself need to look at human psychology for another reason: an expressivistic analysis like mine requires it. The analysis reduces the

1. Among prime attempts at *a priori* ethics have been Kant (1785), Sidgwick (1907), Moore (1903), and Ross (1930). For recent attempts see, for example, Gewirth (1978), Donagan (1977), and Gauthier (1986). Such systems have been subject to far more attacks than it would make sense to try to list; see, for instance, Brandt (1959, chaps. 2, 8) and Williams (1985, chap. 4).

2. The term stems from Rawls (1971, 46–53); I convey what he means by it quickly and roughly. Brandt, in a like spirit, develops a "qualified attitude method" of justifying moral judgments and a "quasi-naturalist definition" of moral terms (1959, chap. 10).

3. See Murphy (1982) for an extensive discussion of how biology might bear on moral theory. Nagel (1978) denies any significant bearing. If ethics, he says, "is a theoretical inquiry that can be approached by rational methods and that has internal standards of justification and criticism, the attempt to understand it from outside by means of biology will be much less valuable." (Much less, that is, than if ethics is "just a certain type of behavioral pattern or habit, accompanied by some emotional responses.") "This is true for the same reason that the search for a biological explanation of mathematical or physical theories, or biological theories for that matter, would be relatively futile" (196). "Biology may tell us about perceptual and motivational starting points, but in its present state it has little bearing on the thinking process by which these starting points are transcended" (204).

meanings of normative terms to psychology. Not that to call something rational is to make a psychological claim; but we are to understand the term 'rational' by understanding what it is for a person to think something rational—by understanding what it is to make a normative judgment. Normative judgments are to be explained psychologically, and so I need a psychology.

Having said all this, I must confess that I shall not be drawing chiefly on the literature of experimental psychology. Experiments tell us much about human normative faculties, but not yet nearly enough. The problem is not empirical intractability in principle; it is the difficulty of the subject. Experimentalists may not entirely know what to look for, nor do the rest of us. We need more thought, perhaps, before experimental investigation can look in enough right places.

How, then, are we to understand our normative life as part of nature? The key must be that human beings live socially; we are, in effect, designed for social life. Our normative capacities are part of the design. This may be a truism, but it should also be puzzling. The initial puzzle is in what sense we are designed at all. Darwin and his successors found the answer: we result not from design literally, but from that remarkable surrogate for design, genetic variation and natural selection. The deeper puzzle is what we could expect humans to be like on the basis of Darwinian considerations. The best Darwinian picture must be familiar in many ways—after all, we know a lot about our species apart from evolutionary thinking. There may be patterns, though, that had not been recognized.

The key to human moral nature, I suggest, lies in *coordination* broadly conceived. The need for complex coordination stands behind much of the way language works in our thoughts, in our feelings, and in social life. It figures centrally in our emotional dispositions, especially for such morally significant emotions as outrage, guilt, shame, respect, moral admiration, and moral inspiration. Matters of coordination, in the picture I shall sketch, stand squarely behind the psychology of norms, and hence behind what is involved in thinking something rational or irrational. Primitive human life is intensely social. In the conditions under which we evolved, anyone's prospects for survival and reproduction depended crucially on the beneficial human bonds he could cultivate. Human cooperation, and coordination more broadly, has always rested on a refined network of kinds of human rapport, supported by emotion and thought. A person sustains and develops this network, draws advantages from it, and on occasion keeps his distance from aspects of it. He does these things only in virtue of a refined configuration of emotional and cognitive dispositions. It is this picture of human biology that might represent us, however crudely, still as recognizably human.

Biological pictures of humanity need not be simplistic. They need not depict us as rough, bestial creatures, stripped of what makes us most delightfully and inspiringly human. Much of behavioral human biology may do so, but that cannot be adequate biology. We are evolved animals, and so biological evolution must account for our potentialities. If a theory misses some of them, it is in that regard a defective biological theory. Inevitably, of course, any theory will be too crude; but we should work for as richly successful theories as we can get—theories that combine biological rigor with a humanistic eye for the complexities of the human psyche. We should draw on the anthropologist's sense of the scope of cultural variation and the typical patterns of human life, and on analytical tools from the social sciences. All this should be our ideal, even if every time we try we must settle for something less.

Good evolutionary treatments of human life will be indirect. Not much genetic change, it is generally thought, has occurred in the couple of hundred generations since our ancestors turned to agriculture. We are genetically adapted to hunting and gathering (see Symons 1979, 35–36). Our hunting-gathering ancestors had genetic makeups typical of us, and the interplay of those genotypes with their environments resulted in those dispositions in virtue of which our ancestors' genes were passed on, and later formed us. Our genes gave us the propensities we had at conception—propensities to have certain characteristics in various hunting-gathering environments. That tells us nothing directly about what we are like in fact, in our own environments.

The hope for explanation must lie in tractably simple patterns. A characteristic that enhances survival and reproduction among hunting-gathering societies may stem from a genotype that produces it in a wide range of environments. Hunter-gatherers talk, joke, and chide, and so do we (see Marshall 1976). What I shall be suggesting is broad propensities to accept norms, engage in normative discussion, and to act, believe, and feel in ways that are somewhat guided by the norms one has accepted. I shall be exploring the shape of broad emotional propensities concerning such things as resentment, guilt, shame, and moral inspiration. The ways these propensities manifest themselves may differ sharply across different kinds of societies, but common elements may be discernible.

Biological Pitfalls

Even tractable evolutionary pictures need not show us as rigid and acultural. We evolved as culture emerged through our evolving. We evolved to have flexible genetic propensities—propensities to be affected profoundly in response to culture. We evolved to interact with others, in response to culture, in ways that themselves constitute having a culture. We acquired not a shapeless capacity for culture, but perhaps a whole configuration of adaptations to the kinds of cultures humans form and sustain. In early human environments, successful acculturation must have been crucial to one's prospects. The evolutionary twist to explanation is to look for complex, more or less flexible propensities we may have, and see how they might contribute to an individual's prospects for reproduction in a variety of primitive cultural, social, and natural settings.

In such explanations, it is crucial to distinguish human goals from the Darwinian surrogate of purpose in the "design" of human beings. Darwin's achievement was to show how the appearance of purpose and intricate design in living things, which suggested marvelous divine workmanship, could be explained without supposing purposeful design. The Darwinian evolutionary surrogate for divine purpose is now seen to be the reproduction of one's genes.[4] That has not, as far as I know, been anyone's goal, but the biological world looks as if someone quite resourceful had designed each living thing for that purpose. Let me then call this surrogate purpose, the reproduction of an organism's genes, its evolutionary *telos*. A person's evolutionary *telos* explains his having the propensities in virtue of which he develops the goals he does, but his own goals are distinct from this surrogate purpose.[5]

---

4. This includes the reproduction of one's genes by kin. Biologists speak of *inclusive fitness*, which includes characteristics that promote the reproduction of close kin. The theory of kin selection was modeled by Hamilton (1964); for one of many accessible presentations, see Dawkins (1976, chap. 6).

5. I choose the Greek term *telos* as one with few connotations for speakers of English. For readers immersed in Aristotelian tradition, however, the term will have strong connotations and the wrong ones. Here it means no more than the Darwinian surrogate for a purpose shaping our design.

My evolutionary *telos*, the reproduction of my genes, has no straight-forward bearing on what it makes sense for me to want or to act to attain. Specifically, that something would fulfill my *telos* is neither a reason for wanting it to come about nor a reason for wanting it not to. A like conclusion would hold if I knew that I was created by a deity for some purpose of his: his goal need not be mine. If, fantastically, I knew that I had been created by a perverse deity so that he could laugh at my discomfitures, that would give me no reason to seek discomfi-tures, though perhaps reason to expect them. Likewise, if I know that my evolutionary *telos* is to reproduce my genes, that in itself gives me no reason for wanting many descendants, nephews, and nieces, or for caring specially for my kin because they share my genes—nor, of course, a reason to the contrary. Any link between evolutionary con-siderations and what it makes sense to want will be subtle and indirect.

Evolutionary thought about humanity has been controversial.[6] Some of the controversy stems from the kinds of simplistic pictures I have been denouncing, and some of it stems from grave defects in actual examples of evolutionary theorizing—defects I claim can be avoided. Some of the controversy I regard as specious, but some is serious. It is specious to think that evolutionary thinking must be racist or sexist. Racists and sexists may try claiming support from biology, but there is no reason to leave the field to them. Evolution should not make us attribute a greater worth to some human groups than to others. Its workings depend, to be sure, on genetic differences, differences on which natural selection can operate, and these differences have accu-mulated to give us a worth other animals lack. The end result, though, might easily be for groups all to be the same, genetically, in the ways that matter for human worth. Like selection pressures can make for like outcomes.

It is specious also to assume that evolutionary thinking must be unduly conservative. Human ways of life vary immensely, and new ones are worth seeking. We do have to be careful, since utopian exper-iments and millenarian programs can fail tragically. New social arrangements rarely work as anyone expects, nor do old arrangements in new conditions. More understanding of human propensities might tell us more about why. There is no reason, though, to suppose that

6. Much of the controversy stems from Wilson (1975). For examples of attacks, see pieces in Caplan (1978) and Lewontin, Rose, and Kamin (1984). Among philosophers of science, Kitcher (1985) attacks what he calls "pop sociobiology", and Ruse (1985) takes on a number of claims against sociobiology.

evolutionary thinking must assign humanity fewer potentialities than we have.

The serious charge is that evolutionary thinking about humans is premature. Darwinian theory provides too few constraints. Any specific hypothesis becomes a "just so story", with no more credibility than scores of alternatives. Now I agree that anything we say at this point must be speculative, but we have some ways of assessing speculations as promising or unpromising, and we need to speculate to know where to look next. As for the speculation of my own that follows, I am skeptical of it in detail, but I think that enough coheres in common observation, ethnographic reports, scattered findings of experimental psychology, and evolutionary considerations regarding complex coordination in human life to make this speculation well worth developing.

In short, then: The philosophical program I develop in this book rests on a human psychology. My theory of the meaning of moral terms rests on a psychology of norms. Fundamental normative principles may, for all I can establish, be accepted or rejected on the basis of psychological considerations. These may be, in Mill's words, among the considerations "capable of determining the intellect." The relevant psychology is not sitting neatly arranged on library shelves, and I am forced to be speculative. That, to be sure, gives the philosophy an uncertain empirical base—but I do not think either that we can develop good fundamental theory independently of empirical considerations, or that the empirical findings we need are firmly established. We need to go by our best guesses.

The general line I take can, no doubt, be developed independently of the detailed psychological speculation in which I embed it. It would be difficult, though, to work out exactly how empirically robust each part of the theory is. What I say, then, should be read as having a conditional form: If the psychological facts are roughly as I speculate, here is what might be said philosophically.

Analysis

In popular lore and philosophic tradition, meanings are given by definitions—by analyses, as philosophers came to say. Non-cognitivists like Ayer, Stevenson, and Hare broadened the tradition: an analysis need not say the same thing in other words. It can describe a use, saying directly what the person who uses a term is doing with it. Still, the tradition now seems dated. The problem is not just fashion; major developments in the philosophy of language seem to discredit analysis. Where do meanings and analyses fit in the best picture of thought and talk?

The naive reason for starting with analyses is, of course, to clarify what we are asking. We want to know what makes acts right or wrong, sensible or foolish. If we want good answers, it seems, we ought first to know what we are asking. When questions seem deeply problematical, part of the problem may lie in confusion over terms. We resolve the confusion if we say clearly what our questions mean, and meanings seem to call for definitions.

Recent philosophy of language throws this rationale into doubt. When a term is central to our conceptions, the lesson seems to be, a search for definitions is misguided. To expect analyses to do serious philosophical work is to succumb to a myth of meaning.

The myth may take the form of accepting a sharp analytic-synthetic distinction—a divide between truth in virtue of logic and meaning alone, and truth in virtue of the ways things substantively are. Quine challenged the myth in this form. He despaired of tying meanings straight to empirical tests, and suggested "It is nonsense, and the root of much nonsense, to speak of a linguistic component and a factual component in the truth of any individual statement. Science has its double dependence on language and experience; but this duality is not significantly traceable into the statements of science taken one by one" (1951, 39). Now, without a linguistic component, how can there be clear sense in asking what a term means? And if we cannot ask about the meanings of terms, one by one, how is there any room for non-cognitivism? Non-cognitivists think there is something special about normative language that makes it peculiarly resist straightforward definition. Language, they think, can be divided into expressions that are descriptive and expressions that are not—and normative language falls on the non-descriptive side. If Quine is right, though, and all philosophically interesting notions resist definition, then normative terms call for no special remedy.

Other writers attack a fact-value distinction by insisting that facts themselves are infused with values. The same would presumably go for a fact-norm distinction. Putnam writes, "The practices of scientific inquiry upon which we rely to decide what is and what is not a fact, presuppose values" (1981, 128). The terms that ground our conception of rational acceptability—'coherent', 'simple', 'justified', and the like—"are often used as terms of *praise*," and they "have too many characteristics in common with the paradigmatic value terms" for us to deny that that is what they are (136).

Is there still, then, any important place for analysis in normative theory? In particular, if we treat thought and talk naturalistically, if we reject meanings as magic, can we still proceed by analysis? I cannot respond fully, especially at the outset. At this point, though, I should say a little.

An analysis must be judged by its fruits: How much does it explain? How much thought does it make intelligible, and how little would it have us dismiss as unintelligible? How good an explanation emerges of the role of a kind of language in human life? How, by these tests, do the alternatives compare? I claim that much of ordinary thought comes out as intelligible on the analyses I shall be giving. Important parts of human life are explained.

An analysis can be offered not as a bald statement of fact about what people mean, but as a proposal. Where a term is problematical, a new and clearer sense may serve its purposes—or some of them. No unique analysis need be correct; rather, we can expect some analyses to work better than others. There may be an analysis that is clearly best for certain purposes, and there may not. Even if not, trying out top candidates is bound to reveal something about the term.[7]

Any philosophical analysis strains its concept. We can learn about a concept by seeing what choice of strains it offers. When an analysis keeps us from saying things we want to say, then we have to think how important it is to go on saying them, and we have to think about costs. Analyses let us compare the strains of alternatives.

Of course, once our conception of analysis is loosened in this way, simple tests cannot settle matters. Descriptivistic analyses strain the concepts they analyze, but so, in all likelihood, will any analysis. What I shall be arguing is this: For an important range of purposes—the purposes of fundamental inquiry into how to live—the norm-expressivistic analysis of 'rational' strains the concept less than do the alternatives.

7. Quine (1960) gives an account much like this of what may properly be done, and calls such an analysis a "paraphrase". Stevenson (1944, 34–36) speaks of ordinary language as vague, and provides what he calls "working models". "They provide a meaning that can be *assigned* to the ethical terms, and which is well suited to certain contexts" (36).

The analysis allows questions other analyses preclude, the questions that lie most deeply embedded in the inquiry. More broadly, the analysis can transform our view of what we are doing when we ponder fundamental normative questions, and allow us to proceed more effectively in our normative thinking because we now have a clear account of what we are doing. No sharp analytic-synthetic distinction, no myth of meaning is needed for claims like these.

What, though, of the special element that makes normative thought and language normative? There is such an element, I am claiming, and it involves a kind of endorsement—an endorsement that any descriptivistic analysis treats inadequately. The problem is not merely that every time one loophole in the analysis is closed, others remain. It is that a single loophole remains unpluggable by descriptivistic analysis.

In a community of stable, widely accepted norms, this element of endorsement might be carried by properties—the properties that, in everyone's mind, qualify a thing for this kind of endorsement. We might imagine a community where everyone condemns as wrong, say, whatever violates the Ten Commandments, and only that. Their use of this standard is confident, and their interpretations of the commandments are clear and agreed upon. Then there might be no fact of the matter whether 'wrong' means "violates the Ten Commandments" or something expressive.

This quiescent community, though, would not have language suited for philosophical inquiry. Philosophy is a child of leisure, but of leisure conjoined with turmoil and clashes of ways of life. If different ways of thinking seem open to us, we need a language in which to put the alternatives. We need to be able to ask whether it is ever right to violate one of the Ten Commandments. Norm-expressivism, I claim, describes a coherent language for doing so.

A philosopher might hope to find an account of normative terms that transformed discussion, and thereby put us into the position of this quiescent community. Perhaps some property of the things it makes sense to do, to think, and to feel is so compelling, so obviously what matters once we see matters clearly, that the only thing left to discuss is what things have that property. In that case we can indifferently either use that property to define 'rational' or stick to an expressivistic analysis. We will be confident beyond all need for discussion that just those things that have that property are rational in the expressivistic sense.

No one, though, has found such a property, and so we still need a language fit for fundamental normative inquiry.[8] Moreover, suppose someone did. We might still want to examine our bases for the ways of thinking we now found undoubtedly right, and we would need a language that let us do so. We might want to explain what had happened since our days of basic puzzlement. What we now realize, we could say, is that something is rational precisely if it has property *P*—or at least that is what we could say if we still gave 'rational' an expressivistic sense.

Examples will not shatter an analysis. What examples can show is a kind of strain we might hope to avoid, a purpose the analysis serves inadequately. The examples of the last chapter showed that for normative terms, prime descriptivistic analyses rule out a use we need. They strain their concepts in ways we cannot afford for some purposes—for purposes of basic inquiry into how to live. They do this because they narrow too far the endorsement these terms carry. For other ends these may be the best analyses, but the examples identify ways we might hope to do better.

What, then, of Putnam's claim that norms infuse facts? With this I fully agree: the beliefs I am calling factual depend on epistemic norms—on norms for belief. That we continue to hold the beliefs we do depends on our thinking it makes sense to do so. It would be incoherent, then, to dismiss all normative judgments as merely subjective, while accepting some factual beliefs as firmly and objectively grounded. From the point of view of their justification, they are on a par; factual beliefs and normative judgments stand or fall together.

None of this means that epistemic norms themselves are facts, or that factual judgments themselves are normative. The justification of factual beliefs is a normative matter, but that does not turn factual beliefs into normative judgments. There remains the challenge to say what the difference is. I have suggested a simple linguistic test: a notion is normative if we can paraphrase it in terms of what it *makes*

8. "Moral realists" treat goodness and the like as properties, but as some recent moral realists conceive properties, telling which property a term picks out will not give its meaning. 'Hot' and 'of high mean kinetic energy' will pick out the same property, but no claim is made that the two have the same meaning. See Sturgeon (1985a, 28–30), Railton (1986a, 1986b), and Boyd (1988). Such a theory of denotation will need a theory of meaning as well—a theory of what gives terms the references they have, and how we can reason about properties. Current moral realists, as I read them, are suspicious of the forms theories of meaning traditionally take, and are working to develop other forms.

sense to do, to think, or to feel. Later I try for a more systematic account of the correspondence a factual judgment can have to fact, and the place of this correspondence in nature (see Chapter 6). I do this by developing a theory of natural and artificial representation.

The charge that norms infuse facts can be pushed further: Norms infuse meaning itself, it is widely held. Statements imputing meaning are normative; they invoke standards of *correctness*; they say what *commitments* accepting a statement brings. If nature contains no normative facts, it follows it contains no facts of meaning. Talk of meaning works on different "constitutive principles" from talk of nature, and so even though we can speak of ourselves as a part of nature, thoughts and meanings are no part of that talk. Naturalistic theorizing and imputations of meaning are both legitimate, but they are two different kinds of discourse that cannot be fused.[9]

I think, on the contrary, that we need something very much like meanings in an adequate naturalistic theory of talk and what lies behind it—and so in an adequate naturalistic theory of human interactions. Naturalistically conceived, we are immensely complex products of Darwinian selection. A naturalistic treatment of animals, *homo sapiens* included, requires stratagems: the patterns are not just in the details of the neurons, but in the shaping of brain mechanisms to promote inclusive fitness in a world of complex and subtle interactions among organisms. Try to understand how all this might work, I suggest, and we are led to patterns in nature that fit, roughly, the things we already believed about meanings.

This, of course, is far from the only way of trying to understand the place of meaning in nature, and other philosophers are at work on alternatives. We are part of nature, some agree, and yet our meanings are not; they then try to explain. My aim is not to assess these competing programs. I allude to them only occasionally, and then only to particular aspects of particular attempts. My goal, rather (or one of them), is to try out a way of conceiving meaning and normative life as a part of nature, and to see how much that might explain.

9. Davidson (1980, 223) speaks of "the constitutive ideal of rationality" as controlling the evolution of a scheme of translation. Kripke (1982, 37) says, "The relation of meaning and intention to future action is *normative*, not *descriptive*." McDowell (1984, 336) quotes this approvingly, and talks of "the normativeness of meaning".

3 · Analyses Broached

What Is Appraised as Rational or Not

We appraise a wide variety of human attributes as rational or irrational. Not only can a person act rationally or irrationally, but he can believe rationally or irrationally, and he can be angry or grateful or envious rationally or irrationally. It is irrational, say, to be angry at the messenger who brings bad tidings, but rational to be angry at the miscreant who deliberately wrongs one. At least this is what we tend to think in the normal course of life. If the word 'rational' seems overly learned here, substitutes come with a more homely flavor: It "doesn't make sense" to be angry at the person who brings bad news he had no part in making. The anger "isn't warranted". You "shouldn't be grateful" to someone who benefited you only inadvertently in seeking his own gain.

It is this family of appraisals that I want to interpret. Do they make genuine sense, and if so, how are they to be understood? If the term 'rational' applies intelligibly to acts and beliefs and feelings, does it have the same meaning in all these uses?

It might be thought that for something to be rational is for it to be desirable or advantageous. Such a crude pragmatism, though, would leave ordinary thought about rationality mysterious: it may fit actions, but it fails with beliefs and attitudes.[1] Take the stock example of the man who has evidence his wife is unfaithful. Whether it is still rational for him to believe her faithful—whether such a belief would be war-

1. What I am calling "crude pragmatism" about belief is not the pragmatism of Peirce, James, or Dewey. James came closest: he thought that there are cases when we should believe whatever it is most beneficial to believe. The cases, though, are well circumscribed. The option to believe must be, in his terms, forced, living, and momentous, and one "that cannot be decided on intellectual grounds" (1897, 3–11).

ranted—depends on his evidence, and on his evidence alone. Whether it is desirable for him to believe her faithful, and whether his believing her faithful is good for him, depend as well on how his beliefs would affect his feelings toward her. The rationality of a belief and its desirability, then, are different, if ordinary thought is to be trusted. Likewise, it might be disadvantageous for one of Cleopatra's courtiers to be angry at her, even if she ordered an execution unjustly and it thus "made sense" to be angry at her. For the courtier might want to ingratiate himself with her, and he might rightly fear that anger would cloud his countenance and spoil his charm. In that case, he would have every reason to want not to be angry, and still, we seem to think, it would make sense for him to be angry. It did not, in contrast, make sense for Cleopatra to be angry at the bearer of bad tidings, however therapeutic or palliative her anger might have been. It would make sense for the courtier to be angry, and so for anger to make sense is not for it to be advantageous.

The point is not chiefly about how we use words. Perhaps we can call anger "irrational" for the courtier, just because of the bad consequences he knows it must bring. Perhaps we can say "it makes no sense" for him to be angry, because anger would be disastrous. That, however, is a different judgment from the one I want to pursue. The judgments I want us to consider are ones of warrant. It makes no sense, we judge, for Cleopatra to be angry at the messenger, in that her anger is ill founded. It would be rational for the courtier to be angry, in that his anger is well founded or warranted, because Cleopatra has acted outrageously and without excuse. I reserve 'rational' and 'make sense' for these uses.

If we understood the word 'rational' in this sense, we could put the distinction as follows. In the case of the courtier and the queen, even though it is *rational* for him *to be angry* with her for ordering an execution unjustly, it may also be *rational* for him *to want* to ingratiate himself with her, for his own good or for that of others. If anger would prevent that, then it may be rational for him *to want* not to be angry with her. In such a case it is rational *to be angry*, but also rational *to want not to be angry*. This pattern applies not only to emotion but also to belief. Take again the case of the deceived husband: his evidence may make it rational for him *to believe* his wife unfaithful, but the way the belief would affect his feelings toward her may make it rational for him *to want to believe* her faithful. Rationally *feeling* or *believing* something is distinct from rationally *wanting* to feel or believe it.

We must also distinguish saying that it makes sense *for* a person *to be* angry from saying that it makes sense *that* the person *is* angry. If I have had a bad day and now face a new disappointment, it "makes sense that I am angry"—we can expect me to be angry in the circumstances, for reasons we understand—even if it doesn't "make sense for me to be angry" because the new disappointment is no one's fault. Likewise, it makes sense *that* Cleopatra *was* angry at the messenger, but it made no sense *for* her *to be* angry at him. Misdirected anger in the circumstances was to be expected, but the bad news was not the messenger's fault.

Talk of emotions as "rational" or "irrational" will strike many as dubious. True, we may say the kinds of things I have been claiming we say: that it "makes sense to be angry" in certain cases and it "makes no sense to be angry" in others. It may still be asked, though, whether these judgments can bear scrutiny. It may well seem that we can appraise as rational or irrational only what is under a person's voluntary control. Emotions fail this test, since they are not under a person's direct voluntary control. True, they can be nurtured or repressed, but a person cannot simply be angry at will, or grateful at will. Nor can a person refrain from any of these things simply at will. What can be appraised as rational or irrational is not an emotion itself, but taking measures to nurture or repress it.

Now I accept, of course, that emotions cannot be had or cast off at will. What I deny is the dictum "Only the voluntary can be appraised as rational or irrational." Beliefs seem prime examples of what we can appraise as rational or irrational, but beliefs, like emotions, cannot be had or cast off at will. We may be able to "make believe" at will, but that is not the same as really believing at will.

It is common enough, then, for states of mind to be appraised as rational or irrational, even though they cannot be had or cast off at will. Indeed I think that something stronger can be said: even in the case of actions, what is primarily appraised as rational or irrational is not the directly voluntary. What, after all, makes an action voluntary? It is presumably at least in part that the action is tied to wanting, in a certain familiar way. When an action is voluntary, wanting or preference has led in a familiar way to intention, and the intention has been carried out. What, then, makes a voluntary action rational? It is the rationality of the intention that stands behind the action—and that is a matter of whether the intention is suited to satisfying a rational set of preferences. To appraise a voluntary action as rational, then, is to appraise the preferences that stand behind it as rational, and to appraise the intention it carries out as rational as a means to satisfying those preferences. Whether a voluntary action is rational, then, is a matter of the rationality of preferences and intentions.

Now preferences and intentions are not themselves voluntary. In the case of preferences, that is clear enough. I might, for instance, be convinced that I will be happy if and only if I cease to want to be happy, but I cannot on that account stop wanting to be happy, simply at will. There may be things I can do to cultivate an indifference to happiness, but that is not the same as being indifferent at will. In the case of intentions, matters are less clear than with preferences, but to ask whether the forming of intentions is voluntary seems puzzling. The question appears misdirected; it smacks of a category mistake.[2] Whether or not, then, we should call intentions "involuntary", we can at least deny that they are, in the most straightforward sense, "voluntary". Thus even in the case of actions, appraisals of rationality depend at base on appraisals of things that are not straightforwardly voluntary.

It is widely accepted that beliefs can be appraised as rational or irrational, even though they are not voluntary. Emotions are more controversial: it is sometimes maintained that an emotion can be rational or irrational only inasmuch as a belief involved in it is rational or irrational.[3] If it didn't make sense for Cleopatra to be angry at the messenger, that must be because her anger involved thinking the slave had wronged her, and that belief was irrational.

It would be hard, though, to identify what the irrational belief involved is supposed to be. Most of us have experienced being angry and yet thinking that no wrong has been done, so that the anger is unjustified. In such cases, one *feels* as if a wrong had been done, but *thinks* that no wrong has been done. Where is the irrational belief? True, if the anger is indeed irrational, as one thinks, then there is a belief it *would* be irrational to have. It would be irrational to believe a wrong has been done. That, however, is precisely what one doesn't

<hr>

2. A "category mistake", Ryle says (1949, 6–7), is the sort of mistake a child makes who, having come to the parade to see the division march by, sees the battalions, batteries, and squadrons, and asks when the division is coming.

3. Hume (1740, bk. 2, part 3, sec. 3) gives the classic defense of this position. See also Solomon (1976, 185), and Sabini and Silver (1982, 171). Others think an emotion involves an evaluation or appraisal, and that these can be assessed as rational or irrational. I discuss both beliefs and appraisals in Chapter 7.

believe; that is why one considers one's own anger irrational in such cases.

Perhaps the belief is subconscious: one believes subconsciously that a wrong has been done, in the face of a conscious realization to the contrary. Why, though, might we think one really has this subconscious belief? Chiefly because one is angry: to be angry is for it to be as if one thought a wrong had been done, even if one consciously thinks otherwise. Does thinking subconsciously that a wrong has been done, then, consist in anything independent of being angry? If we try to reduce talk of irrational anger to talk of irrational subconscious beliefs about wrongs, the beliefs are beliefs of a special kind. They are so parasitical on emotions that little has been gained by the reduction.

In short, then, we appraise as rational or irrational things that are clearly involuntary, like beliefs and attitudes—and there is no special reason to think we are mistaken. Even in the case of action, appraisals of rationality apply primarily to states of mind that are not straightforwardly voluntary. In itself, then, the fact that emotions are involuntary gives us no reason to think that they cannot be appraised as rational or not. When we do appraise the rationality of an emotion, moreover, it seems hard to make out that we are really appraising a belief. No independently identifiable kind of belief is always involved in a given kind of emotion.

None of this is to say that when we call something "rational"—an act, belief, or emotion—we are saying anything intelligible. That remains to be seen. I am saying that we talk and think as if such appraisals are intelligible. It may be worthwhile, then, to see if we can interpret them as intelligible.

Rationality and Morality

It would be good to know what the term 'rational' means, as applied to acts, beliefs, and emotions. Before hunting down an account of its meaning, though, I turn to morality and its tie to rationality. Suppose naively, for now, that we know what 'rational' means.

In the history of moral philosophy, there seem to be at least two sharply different conceptions of what morality is. On the broadest of conceptions, morality is simply practical rationality in the fullest sense: to say that an act is morally right is to say that it is rational. Sidgwick is a prime exponent of this broad conception, and perhaps Kant is; it is shared by many current writers.[4] On this conception, it makes no sense to ask "Is it always rational to do what is morally right?" for "the morally right" simply means "the rational". On a narrow conception of morality, in contrast, moral considerations are just some of the considerations that bear on what it makes sense to do. Non-moral considerations matter too. On the narrow conception it is normally wrong, say, to injure others, to steal, or break one's word. It would normally not be morally wrong, though, to fritter away a day for which one had planned an enjoyable hike—however irrational that might be. On the broad conception of morality, morally right action simply is action that is truly rational, whereas on the narrow conception, an act may be truly irrational without being morally wrong. (Perhaps too an action can be morally wrong without being truly irrational.)

In chapter 5 of *Utilitarianism*, John Stuart Mill uses the term 'morality' in this narrow sense, and offers an account of what is distinctive about morality so taken. "Morality", he says, "pertains to what is wrong or not wrong, and to say that an act is wrong is to say that there ought to be a sanction against it, a sanction of law, of public opinion, or of conscience." The 'ought' here, Mill proposes, should be judged by the standards of the greatest happiness principle—but that is part of the normative theory Mill is giving, not a part of his analysis of the term 'morally wrong'. What I propose to do is to take over Mill's analysis of what morality is in the narrow sense, with various interpretations and modifications.[5]

When Mill says there "ought" to be a sanction, let us read him as saying that a sanction is rational—or, perhaps, rationally required. Let us also drop talk of legal sanctions. Suppose we think that people who overpark at parking meters ought to be fined, but that they ought not to feel guilty, and ought not to be resented by others for overparking. In that case, it seems to me, we do not think overparking morally wrong; we merely think that a price should be charged. That leaves sanctions of conscience and of public opinion: sanctions of guilt and

4. Sidgwick (1907, esp. bk. 1, chap. 3, sec. 1). Kant (1785) is more difficult: he takes morality to be the realm of the "categorical imperative", which expresses the demands of pure practical reason. In addition, though, he recognizes non-moral "hypothetical imperatives", which express what is needed for one's own happiness. If we read him as taking hypothetical imperatives as demands of rationality, then we must not attribute the broad conception of morality to him.

5. Mill's theory was brought to recent philosophical attention by Lyons in a series of articles; see especially Lyons (1976).

remorse on the one hand, and of blame, resentment, and moral outrage on the other. Thus, as the proposal now stands, what a person does is *morally wrong* if and only if it is rational for him to feel guilty for doing it, and for others to resent him for doing it.[6]

'Resent' here is in some ways the wrong term. It suggests a sense of personal injury, injury to oneself, whereas blame may well be impartial. Resentment, outrage, condemnation, indignation, blame—all these get roughly at the sentiment I want. Now all these terms suggest anger, perhaps along with a sense of justification. The sense of justification goes with my talk of rationality, and so what is left is anger of various kinds. Try this formulation, then: what a person does is *morally wrong* if and only if it is rational for him to feel guilty for having done it, and for others to be angry at him for having done it.

As the formulation stands, it is more plausible for 'blameworthy' than for 'morally wrong'. What is it, then, for an act to be morally wrong? The term 'wrong' is often said to have two distinct moral senses, the *objective* and the *subjective*. The difference between the two is displayed through stories like this: Yesterday, I had the brakes of my car checked. Today, I drive a friend to the supermarket, but on the way, my brakes fail and I kill a pedestrian. Driving my car, then, has turned out to be wrong in the objective sense, but not in the subjective sense—since I had every reason to think my brakes reliable, and my friend needed to get to the store. Thus an act is wrong in the objective sense if it is wrong in light of all the facts, knowable and unknowable, whereas it is wrong in the subjective sense if it is wrong in light of what the agent had good reason to believe. More precisely, an act is wrong in the subjective sense if it is wrong in light of the degrees of plausibility (or "subjective probabilities") the agent has reason to ascribe to relevant propositions.

Now the analysis I have proposed will clearly not work for 'wrong' in the objective sense. In the story, my driving my car turns out to be

6. This is roughly the analysis Ewing proposed for one sense of 'ought' (1939, 14). 'Ought' in another sense, he suggests, is simple and unanalyzable; this simple *ought* seems to correspond to my term 'rational'. Brandt (1946) develops this pattern of analysis for such terms as 'detestable' and 'meritorious'. He speaks of the emotions it is "fitting" to have toward an action, and a fitting emotion seems to be what I am calling a rational emotion. He is neutral on what fitting means, or whether it has any real meaning. Brentano (1889) offers a similar analysis for 'good': a thing is good if "love relating to it is correct" (*richtig*), if it is "worthy of love" (18). In some cases, he thinks, love is "experienced as being correct" (22), and that constitutes "insight—the clarity and evidence of certain judgments that is inseparable from their truth" (79). See the discussion by Carson (1984, 1–4 and elsewhere).

wrong in the objective sense, but it would not make sense for me to feel guilty over it, or for others to resent me for it. Thus an act may be wrong in the objective sense without being wrong on the proposed analysis. That in itself is no defect, for, as I shall argue, the objective sense is not the useful one. It will turn out, though, that even for the subjective sense, the analysis does not work as it stands.

It is clear enough why we should want a theory of what kinds of acts are right in the subjective sense. Such a theory offers moral guidance: even when we know we are ignorant of the relevant facts, we can use the theory, together with what we think we do know, to decide what acts to avoid on moral grounds. Why, though, should we want a theory of what kinds of acts are right in the objective sense? Such a theory offers no guidance when we know we are ignorant of relevant facts; in that case we need rules for acting without full information. To be sure, if I could place myself under the guidance of a reliable sooth-sayer, I would want him to tell me which of the things I might do is right in the objective rather than the subjective sense—but reliable soothsayers are hard to find. It might seem that a theory for the objective sense would at least be useful in those rare cases when I take myself to know all the relevant facts. Even then, however, the theory is superfluous if we have criteria for rightness in the subjective sense, for in the case of full knowledge, the subjective and the objective senses of 'wrong' coincide; thus to determine what is right in the objective sense, the agent with full knowledge need only determine what is right in the subjective sense. In short, then, for an agent who knows he is ignorant, standards for objective rightness are useless; what he needs is standards for subjective rightness; whereas for the agent with full knowledge, standards for objective rightness are superfluous so long as he has standards for rightness in the subjective sense. I see no need, then, for an account of what it means to call an act wrong in the objective sense. If no such account could be given, there would be no practical loss, since what we need for moral guidance is criteria for what kinds of acts are wrong in the subjective sense.[7] Henceforth, when I use the words 'right' and 'wrong', I intend the subjective sense.

7. I argue this in Gibbard (1978, 95–96). It might be thought that we need objective rightness as an aim. Often, though, we should not do what we think most probably right in the objective sense; often to do so would be to run unconscionable risks. It may be thought that we need an objective sense to encourage people to get needed information. Information, though, is sometimes worth acquiring and sometimes not, and a subjective treatment can tell us when it is. For a decision-theoretic treatment of paying for information, see Raiffa (1968, 105–107 and chap. 7).

Might the analysis I have proposed work as it stands, then, for 'wrong' in the subjective sense? Might an act be wrong in the subjective sense if and only if it fits the analysis—if and only if it is rational for the agent to feel guilty over the act and for others to resent him for it? The proposal seems most apt, as I have said, as an analysis of 'blameworthiness', and wrongness in the subjective sense is not the same as blameworthiness. To see the difference, imagine that in a paroxysm of grief I speak rudely to a friend who offers condolences, and so hurt his feelings. My rudeness is unprovoked, but understandable in the circumstances. I have thus acted wrongly, but because of my agitated state, it may not make sense to blame me. If it does not, then my act is wrong in the subjective sense, but not blameworthy.[8]

How, then, can the proposal be modified to serve as an analysis of 'wrong' in the subjective sense? We might first ask why we should need a distinct concept of wrong in the subjective sense, as opposed to blameworthy. The answer seems to be that the concepts of right and wrong are forward-looking in a way that the concept of blameworthiness is not. The morally conscientious agent is one who asks himself which of the acts open to him are right and which are wrong, and then rules out any act he judges wrong. That means, among other things, that the rightness or wrongness of an alternative does not depend on the agent's motives. Rather, conscientious motivation consists in trying to confine one's actions to what is right. Blame, in contrast, attaches to the agent in retrospect; the agent is blamed for acting with insufficient morally desirable motivation. Rightness is prospective; blame is retrospective.

How can we exploit this difference? Mill's proposal, as I have said, applies most plausibly to blame. Let us tentatively accept it, then, as an account of blameworthiness, so that to call an action *morally reprehensible* (or to say that an agent is *blameworthy* or *to be blamed* on account of that action) is to say this: it would be rational for the agent to feel guilt over having performed the action, and for others to feel angry at him for having performed it.

What, then, might it mean to call an act wrong? Roughly, we might say, the standards of right and wrong are the standards we demand an agent use to rule out certain alternatives. In assessing blame, we apply two kinds of tests. First, we ask whether the agent's level of

8. Brandt (1959, 458) makes this distinction, and argues that 'reprehensible' cannot be defined in terms of 'moral obligation'. He then offers a definition of 'reprehensible' that is quite close, in some respects, to the one I am offering.

morally desirable motivation was satisfactory. If not, we ask whether there are extenuating circumstances that render the agent not fully responsible. Standards of right and wrong pertain to the first part: an agent's motives are morally acceptable if he is sufficiently motivated to avoid wrong acts. Standards for wrongness, then, are the standards such that an agent is *prima facie* blameworthy if he does not use them to rule out acts that violate them. The reason the blameworthiness is only *prima facie* is that facts about the person's motivational state may be extenuating. Blame thus depends both on standards for wrongness in the subjective sense, and on standards for responsibility. Formally put, then, the definitions I propose are these: An act is *wrong* if and only if it violates standards for ruling out actions, such that if an agent in a normal frame of mind violated those standards because he was not substantially motivated to conform to them, he would be to blame. To say that he would *be to blame* is to say that it would be rational for him to feel guilty and for others to resent him.

An act can be seriously wrong or trivially wrong, and we can say something about this with the framework I have sketched. When a person violates a standard, how seriously wrong that is is a matter of the degree of motivation a person must normally have to abide by that standard, if he is not to be blamed for lack of sufficient motivation. Alternatively, we might say, it is the degree to which an agent is normally to be blamed if he lacks all motivation to abide by that standard. (These two characterizations are logically distinct, but I cannot think of circumstances in which judgments on the two characterizations would significantly diverge.) Call what we have characterized the agent's *prima facie degree of blameworthiness*. A person has diminished responsibility, then, to the extent that his degree of blameworthiness for an action falls short of his degree of *prima facie* blameworthiness for it.

What I have done in this section is to suppose that we know what 'rational' means, and to propose a way of interpreting the relation between rationality and concepts that are "moral" in the narrow sense. In the next section, I propose in rough terms an analysis of 'rational', and plug it into the analyses I have given these moral concepts.

The Norm-Expressivistic Analysis

What does it mean to call something "rational"? One way of tackling such a question is to psychologize it. What, we may ask, is the psychological state of *regarding* something as rational, of *taking* it to be rational, of *believing* it rational? Put roughly and cryptically, my hypothesis is that to think something rational is to accept norms that permit it. Much of the book will consist of elucidation, refinement, and assessment of this rough hypothesis. I begin with some preliminary explanation.

By a *norm* here, I mean a possible norm: a possible rule or prescription, expressible by an imperative. The prescription need not actually be made by anyone, or accepted by anyone, to count as a "norm" as I am using the term. The main thing to be explained is not what a norm is, but what "accepting a norm" is—or, more precisely, what it is for something to be permitted or required by the norms a person "accepts". I mean these latter notions to be psychological: they are meant to figure in an explanatory theory of human experience and action.

Take next some schematic illustrations. Delilah, suppose, is pondering whether various of Samson's acts, beliefs, and feelings are rational. What is it for her to come to an opinion? It is to come to accept norms. When Samson destroys the Philistine temple, Delilah considers that rational if and only if she accepts norms that permit, for Samson's situation as she takes it to be, destroying the temple. Perhaps she accepts the norm "When in the hands of one's enemies with no hope of escape, kill as many of them as possible, even if you must kill yourself in the process." Then if she believes that Samson is in the hands of his enemies with no hope of escape, and that destroying the temple will kill as many as possible, she thinks his action rational. Earlier Samson believed Delilah loyal. Delilah thinks this belief to have been rational if and only if she accepts the right sorts of norms for belief. She must accept norms that, for Samson's situation at the time as she now conceives it, permit believing one's woman loyal. Samson hates the Philistines, and Delilah considers his hatred rational if and only if she accepts norms that, for his situation, permit such hatred.

Nothing I have said here, I stress, speaks to whether Samson's acts, beliefs, and emotions really *were* rational. I might have tried an analysis of quite a different form: that an act, belief, or attitude of a person *is* rational if someone—be it I, or he, or a commentator—accepts norms that prescribe it for that person's circumstances. My own analysis, though, is not directly a hypothesis about what it *is* for something to be rational at all. It is a hypothesis about what it is to *think* or *believe* something rational, to *regard* it as rational, to *consider* it rational. An observer *believes* an action, belief, or attitude *A* of mine to be rational if and only if he accepts norms that permit *A* for my circumstances. It follows that if we want to decide what really *is* rational, we shall have to settle what norms to accept ourselves—for that is what it is to form an opinion as to the rationality of something.

Return now to norms of morality. In analyzing the narrowly moral notions "blameworthy" and "wrong", I took the term 'rational' as understood. If we now combine these analyses with our rough analysis of 'rational', we can derive an account of the distinction between moral norms and norms of rationality. All norms, in a sense, are norms of rationality, but moral norms in particular are norms for the rationality of guilt and resentment. Consider first what it is for an action to be "blameworthy". The analyses given so far tell us this: First, an observer thinks an act *blameworthy*, or *morally reprehensible*, if and only if he thinks it rational for the agent to feel guilty over the act, and for others to resent the agent for it. Second, to think something 'rational' is to accept norms that prescribe it. Therefore, we may conclude, to think an act *morally reprehensible* is to accept norms that prescribe, for such a situation, guilt on the part of the agent and resentment on the part of others.[9]

Next consider the term 'morally wrong' (in the subjective sense). The standards for whether an act is wrong, we have said, are the standards such that guilt and resentment are *prima facie* rational if the agent is not disposed to rule out alternatives that violate them. Thus to think an act wrong is to accept norms for guilt and resentment that, *prima facie*, would sanction guilt and resentment if the act were performed. '*Prima facie*' here means before questions of the psychological peculiarities of the agent are raised—the psychological peculiarities, that is, that bear on whether the agent is to be considered fully responsible. Norms for wrongness are thus explained in terms of norms for guilt and resentment.

This proposal as it stands requires an independent account of responsibility. Now the psychic makeup of the agent has some bearing not only on whether the agent is responsible, but on what acts open

9. Adam Smith (1790) holds something like this. Morality, he argues, concerns the propriety of moral sentiments. "The love of praise is the desire of obtaining the favorable sentiments of our brethren. The love of praise-worthiness is the desire of rendering ourselves the proper objects of those sentiments . . . The like affinity and resemblance take place between the dread of blame and that of blameworthiness" (III.2.25; see all of III.2). Smith, though, unlike me, thinks that to call an emotion proper is to say that it is what a detached observer in fact would feel. See my discussion in Chapter 15.

to him are wrong. How do we separate the two? Suppose, for instance, that an act is the only one that is eligible, in the sense that all alternatives to it would leave the agent desperately unhappy. That fact may, in our opinion, tend to justify the act morally: it might be that even though the act would otherwise be wrong, this consideration turns it right. That, in any case, is what we might well think, and an analysis should allow for the possibility. In what ways, then, might psychological peculiarities of an agent bear on his degree of moral responsibility by itself, without bearing on the rightness and wrongness of the acts open to him?

Standards for responsibility, I might say, are standards for when an agent is to blame for acting on *prima facie* blameworthy motivations, and *prima facie* blameworthy motivations are motives for which an agent is to blame if he is fully responsible. If I say this, however, then even though the term 'blameworthy' itself has been defined independently, the terms '*prima facie* blameworthy' and 'responsible' will be defined only in terms of each other.

This circularity can be eliminated as follows. Consider an agent who has various psychological peculiarities, and an act for which I would consider the agent to blame if I thought him normal. Our problem is to untangle whether, because of his psychological peculiarities, I regard the act as right, or whether instead I consider the act to be wrong but the agent not to blame. The test I propose is this: Take an agent with psychological peculiarities, and imagine him for the moment rendered normal, but expecting to reacquire his psychological peculiarities once he had decided how to act on this occasion. He thus must take these psychological peculiarities into account in deciding what to do, though he is rid of them for the moment, apart from his belief that he has them. Whether I consider the act to be wrong, then, is a matter of whether I accept norms that would sanction guilt and anger if the agent, while temporarily rendered normal, were to perform that act.

Second Thoughts

'Rational' is in some ways the wrong word for my purposes. I treat calling something "rational" as a flat recommendation, but it has a special flavor—a flavor some do not like. Some people are irrationalists: they think rationality overrated; they prefer passion and spontaneity. The lover of reason disagrees. On the account I am giving, though, it seems both must mistake what is at issue. The irrationalist cannot be what he thinks himself to be, for whatever he endorses he thereby thinks rational. If that is implausible, perhaps that shows the term 'rational' does not mean what I say it does.

My real claim is not for the word 'rational', but for a meaning I want to exploit. Perhaps the word 'rational' rarely has this meaning, but when it does, then what it is rational to do settles what to do. Likewise, what it is rational to believe settles what to believe, and what it is rational to feel about something settles how to feel about it. Not that a person will always do what he thinks it rational to do, but settling what it is rational to do at least ends discussion. The person who agrees and then acts otherwise has not been effectively governed by what he himself has conceded. For this sense of 'rational', there is no such thing as a considered determination to do what one thinks irrational.

Other phrases may capture this notion better. I have freely substituted talk of what it "makes sense" to do, to think, and to feel about things; that might be my best canonical phrase. Alternatively, we might talk of what one "ought" to do, think, or feel, and explain that the 'ought' is not the moral one. With feelings and beliefs, we can talk of what states of mind are "warranted", "well grounded", or "apt"; with acts we can talk of the "best thing to do". We might talk simply of "the thing to do" or "the thing to feel" about something. If a flavorless recommendation on balance can be found in any of these terms, then that is what 'rational' shall mean in this book. My claim is that some phrase or other can be used in this sense, and that a wide range of important concepts can be paraphrased in terms of this one.

Still, what is the irrationalist rejecting as "rational", and what is the lover of reason embracing? The word 'rational' is connected with reasoning. Reasoning is a natural, psychological phenomenon, something we do at times and avoid at times. It involves thinking through the possibilities, drawing inferences, and the like. Now a person can reason and act on the basis of his reasoning, or he can act spontaneously without reasoning. He can act on his reasoning, or he can act from whim or unreasoned passion. In one sense, the word 'rational' just means "pertaining to reasoning". The irrationalist is against being guided in one's actions by reasoning, or by reasoning pressed too far. Reasoning is to be explained naturalistically, and one can intelligibly be against it.

In another sense, a person is rational only if he tends to be guided by reasoning that is good. This sense is normative, and so, I would claim, not straightforwardly naturalistic. A rational person in this sense is not only guided by reasoning; he reasons in ways it makes sense to reason—in ways it is "rational" in my own chief sense to reason. Can rationality in this normative sense be suspect?

One question is whether to reason well or badly, but another is how much to reason at all. We can ask how much to be guided even by our best reasoning. Being guided by good reasoning has advantages, but it has drawbacks too. It can detract from spontaneity; it can work against the free flow of feelings. Acting from feelings is part of what gives life its flavor, and reasoning can stifle that. The irrationalist does not favor being guided by reasoning he thinks bad; he is against being guided by reasoning of any kind. That is intelligible, and even when the wild irrationalist goes overboard, we can see what drove him. We too can appreciate the drawbacks of reasoned action. We can see being guided by good reasoning as competing with other goods, and in that sense, we think rationality simply one good that competes with others.

All this is to talk of rational people: a person is rational if he guides himself by good reasoning. I have been talking about rational acts, beliefs, and feelings, and not directly about rational people. Can one reject acts one thinks rational? It does seem so: "That would be the rational thing to do" can be said in a sour tone of voice.

A lover might say such a thing, when his prospects look bleak and we urge him to turn elsewhere. Perhaps his opinions are simply at odds with his feelings, and he speaks from his feelings. He might, though, want to praise his feelings, and have a rationale. He might agree that it makes sense to turn elsewhere, but think, nevertheless, it makes sense to want to be the sort of person who will not. One whose loves are too much guided by reasoning, he may think—even the best of reasoning—will never truly kiss. It makes sense to give up, he agrees, but it makes sense to want to be someone who would not.

Alternatively, the rational act may not be the best one given what one knows, but the one good reasoning would select. The two might differ, for perhaps in some realms even the best of reasoning is not the best guide. The best reasoning is best for the things reasoning can promote, but perhaps that leaves out some aspects of life. In some realms, perhaps, faith does better, though good reasoning will not endorse it. The thing to do, then, is what faith picks out, and not what reasoning would pick out—even the best of reasoning.

That is what someone might mean by 'rational', but it is not what I mean. When we settle the thing to do, then in my sense we have thereby made up our minds that it is the rational thing to do.

So much for the irrationalist. What now of the moralist with special views, the moralist who rejects guilt and anger? The morality of guilt and anger alone is morality very narrowly understood. Guilt and anger are bleakly negative, and even morality tightly construed seems to take in positive feelings of moral approbation. Then too, other cultures may lack guilt altogether, or may give it no great play in their norms of social control. Could there not be shame moralities, or fear moralities?

The question is really one of stipulation. The term 'moral' has no sharp boundaries in normal thought, and I am proposing one reading among others. Morality, construed narrowly in this way, concerns what is blameworthy and what is innocent, what is morally wrong and what is morally permissible. More broadly conceived, it could easily take in what is morally admirable and what is morally indifferent. We could even throw in what is shameful and what is dangerous.[10]

The important thing is the pattern of analysis, and it can apply in all these realms. An action is morally admirable, we can say, if on the part both of the agent and of others it makes sense to feel moral approbation toward the agent for having done it. An action is shameful if it makes sense for the agent to feel ashamed for having done it, and for others to disdain him for having done it. An act is dangerous if it makes sense for the agent to feel afraid on account of having done it. All these notions concern the ways it makes sense to feel about things people do, the feelings that are warranted.

All norms, we might say, are primarily norms of rationality. The various different kinds of norms governing a thing—moral norms, aes-

---

10. Two recent works that mark off "morality" in a narrow sense are Brandt (1979, chaps. 9–10) and Williams (1985, esp. chap. 10). Brandt characterizes the "moral code" of a society as involving intrinsic motivation, guilt feelings and disapproval, believed importance, admiration or esteem, special terminology, and believed justification (164–176). Williams picks out morality as using a special notion of obligation and giving obligations a special significance (174). He does not try to define this special notion, but he does give some of its characteristics, and he contrasts obligations as they figure in the "morality system" with obligations "when they are rightly seen as merely one kind of consideration among others" (182). "Blame is the characteristic reaction of the morality system. The remorse or self-reproach or guilt I have already mentioned is the characteristic first-personal reaction within the system, and if an agent never felt such sentiments, he would not belong to the morality system or be a full moral agent in its terms" (177). Morality, he complains, turns everything into obligations; deliberation issues in oughts and mays (180, 175). In terms, then, of the narrow and broad conceptions of morality with which I started, we might read Williams's complaint as this: Morality takes narrowly moral notions, with their tie to blame, and invests them with the significance of moral notions in the broad sense. It treats them as figuring alone in the reasonable outcome of deliberation.

thetic norms, norms of propriety—are each norms for the rationality of some one kind of attitude one can have toward it. Just as moral norms are norms for the rationality of guilt and resentment, so aesthetic norms are norms for the rationality of kinds of aesthetic appreciation. Norms of propriety are norms for the rationality of shock, so that something is improper if it makes sense to be shocked by it.[11]

Return, though, to the opponent of guilt or anger. He might think, say, that guilt is always irrational because it is self-destructive, or that anger is rational whenever it makes us feel good. Those opinions, though, would not concern whether it is rational to feel guilty or angry, but whether it is rational to *want* ever to feel guilty or angry. When it makes sense to *want* to feel guilty is not, in my narrow sense, a moral question, whereas whether it makes sense to feel guilty is.

Suppose, though, he thinks that guilt itself is always irrational—say because it would only be rational if we had free will, which we don't. In that case, I am maintaining, he does deny that anything is ever morally reprehensible. Thus, in my narrow sense of the term, he denies that acts are ever morally wrong. He can still very well think that acts are bad in various other ways, and that some acts are much to be avoided. In some senses, then, he does think that acts can be morally wrong, and that many are. In my sense, though, he does not—and drawing the boundary where I do marks off a region in our moral thought that is worth exploring. Some of the moral questions that puzzle us may be questions of what norms to accept as governing guilt and resentment, and hence what acts to avoid as fit objects of guilt and resentment.[12]

Structural Problems

The analysis lets us reformulate questions about the structure of morality, and about what morality has to do with rationality. Is it always rational to be moral? On the broadest construal of morality, the

11. Brandt elaborates a proposal like this (1946). See also Adam Smith: "An amiable action, a respectable action, an horrid action, are all of them actions which naturally excite for the person who performs them, the love, the respect, or the horror of the spectator" (1790, III.4.10).

12. Scanlon proposes another characterization of morality. "An act is wrong if its performance . . . would be disallowed by any system of rules . . . which no one could reasonably reject as a basis for informed, unforced general agreement" (1982, 110). He proposes this as a substantive claim about morality, not as a theory of meaning (107). His proposal, then, is not a direct alternative to mine, but we can ask whether the two

problem is trivial: to be moral is simply to be, in the deepest sense, rational. On the narrow construal, in contrast, the question makes good sense. Does rationality ever require a person to do something morality forbids?[13] Diminished responsibility aside, this becomes, in my terms, two closely related questions. First, does it ever make sense to feel guilty over something it would not have made sense to omit? Second, does it ever make sense to resent something that it would not have made sense for the agent to omit?

The question, then, is how our norms for guilt and resentment are to tie in with our norms for action. Deciding whether rationality ever countermands morality is deciding whether to accept norms that can both permit an act and prescribe guilt and blame for it.

Turn next to moral dilemmas. Does the moral *ought* imply *can*, so that no matter how appalling the alternatives, at least one of them must be morally permissible? Or are there cases where anything one can do would be wrong?[14] Here again, the norm-expressivistic analysis provides an interpretation of the dispute. Diminished responsibility aside, the issue concerns the structure of well-founded guilt and anger. Are there situations in which, no matter what the agent does, it will make sense for him to feel guilty for having done it, and for others to be angry at him for having done it? Guilt here must be more than mere compunction, and part of the problem may be whether a distinction between compunction and full-fledged guilt can be drawn.

Is morality of value? It is sometimes held more of a burden than a blessing: we would all be better off, some claim, if morality were not part of our lives. Can we make enough sense of this claim to assess it? The question, I take it, is not whether it would be a good thing if there were more killing, cruelty, and other heinous deeds in the world,

---

fit naturally together. Much in Scanlon's proposal remains to be worked out: we need to know about the term 'reasonable', about the conditions that will count as those of unforced agreement, and about the parties' motivations. Suppose all that is worked out, though; would morality, on Scanlon's characterization, depend by its nature on sentiments of guilt and blame? If parties expected compliance by magic, they could reasonably decide what to accept or not without regard to these sentiments. Morality might help explain the sentiments, but not the reverse. Perhaps, though, the force the parties expect their agreement to have is moral: they will have some special motivation to keep the agreement. Must that motivation involve guilt and blame? This raises deep questions about whether guilt and blame have anything special to do with such things as agreements—questions I look to in Chapter 7.

13. Brandt formulates this question in terms of his own analyses of rationality and morality (1979, chap. 17).

14. This issue is discussed by van Fraassen (1973) and by Marcus (1980).

but whether, in light of its costs, morality is the best shield against such deeds. When people claim, then, that we would be better off without morality, how do they conceive "morality"? No doubt different people mean different things, but the norm-expressivistic analysis provides one possible interpretation—an interpretation on which the issue seems well worth pondering. Is it a good thing, we may ask, for norms for guilt and resentment to play a big role in our lives? Or might other kinds of motivation—good will, wide sympathies, pride, a sense of shame, or some combination of these and others—bring many of the same benefits without the same costs?[15]

How much choice do we have? Are there cultures that get along without morality? Here again, much hinges on what is meant by the term. Some brand morality a peculiarly Western phenomenon, with its roots in the Judeo-Christian tradition; others think morality a cultural universal. I do not claim to know what in general is at issue in these claims, but the norm-expressivistic analysis does direct us to a significant question: are norms for guilt and resentment universal? The question is not about norms in general, or about practices of criticism in general: it is not whether all cultures have norms or practices of criticism. The question is rather whether the emotions I have been calling "specifically moral" are culturally universal, and whether the existence of norms for these emotions is a cultural universal.

I have been reformulating old puzzles, not trying to solve them. The point is to see what Mill's proposal does. Once morality is delimited as he suggests, familiar problems can be put in new form, as questions about the structure of well-founded sentiments.

15. Nietzsche attacks *ressentiment* (1887, Essay I) and bad conscience (Essay II), and so he is attacking morality in the sense I am considering. "The bad conscience is an illness . . . but an illness as pregnancy is an illness" (II, sec. 19). It is needed in history "to breed an animal with the right to make promises" (II, sec. 1). His attack may be still broader, though, than the kind of attack I am contemplating: He seems willing to do without the protections I have assumed the antimoralist still wants; the self-torturing repression of natural inclinations that these protections exact will not be worth its cost when Zarathustra comes. "The attainment of this goal would require a *different* kind of spirit from that likely to appear in this present age: spirits strengthened by war and victory, for whom conquest, adventure, danger, and even pain have become needs; it would require habituation to the keen air of the heights, to winter journeys, to ice and mountains in every sense; it would require even a kind of sublime wickedness, an ultimate, supremely self-confident mischievousness in knowledge that goes with great health; it would require, in brief and alas, precisely this *great health*" (II, sec. 24). He does favor protection when it is mutual among those of roughly equal power. That is the origin of justice, he insists (1878, sec. 92).

4 · Normative Psychology

The analyses of the last chapter were incomplete. In that chapter, I analyzed two concepts central to ethical theory: a person's being *to blame* for an act, and an act's being *wrong* in the subjective sense. I put these analyses, though, in terms of another notion that I left unexplained—in terms of "accepting norms". Not that I was entirely silent on the nature of norms; I did, after all, broach various claims. All norms, I suggested, are primarily norms of rationality: norms for what it "makes sense" to do, to believe, to feel, and the like. What it means to call something "rational" is to be understood in terms of what it is to *think* or *believe* it rational, and to think something rational is to accept norms that permit it. Missing, though, was any real attempt to explain what it means for a person to *accept norms*.

How can the "acceptance of norms" be explained? The straightest course would be further analysis: we might look for a straightforward definition of what it means to say that a person accepts such-and-such a norm. I doubt, though, that such an analysis is possible. Philosophers are familiar with crucial terms that stymie analysis. I suspect that were all philosophers to turn to analyzing the "acceptance of norms", all would fail.

How, then, if not by analysis, might I hope to explain the acceptance of norms? What I shall do, in effect, is to engage in incipient psychological theorizing. "Accepting a norm", I want to suggest, is a significant kind of psychological state that we are far from entirely understanding. We can hope not to define this state precisely, but to point to it. There is a centrally important psychological state, I suggest, that roughly fits the ordinary notion of a person's "accepting a norm". I shall say what I can about this putative state, adducing various shreds of evidence and lines of reasoning that I think lend plausibility to the claim that there is such a state. The shreds of evidence consist in part of commonsense belief and vocabulary, and in part of observation, both systematic and casual. I shall then announce that I am interested in whatever theoretically significant psychological state, if any, roughly fits what I have said.

My goal, then, is not just to elucidate ordinary concepts and beliefs, but to use them as a guide. They can guide us in speculating about what an adequate scientific psychology might be like. The vague hypothesis I shall be developing is that in a scientifically adequate psychology, there would figure a state that roughly fits the commonsense notion of "accepting a norm". This state would figure centrally in the story of human thinking and motivation.

Competing Systems of Control

Start by considering cases of "weakness of will" and the struggle for "self-control". Suppose I can't get myself to stop eating nuts at a party. What is happening? One commonsense description is this: I think it makes sense to stop eating the nuts—indeed that it doesn't make sense to go on eating them—but I nevertheless go on eating them. In this case, it seems, I accept a norm that prescribes eating no more nuts, but go on eating them even so.

In this commonsense account, it is assumed that the acceptance of a norm is motivating, at least to a degree: believing I ought to stop tends to make me stop. On this occasion, though, the motivation that stems from my accepting a norm is "overpowered" by motivation of another kind: my craving or appetite for nuts. The craving is not itself a matter of my accepting norms; indeed such cravings are sometimes referred to as "animal": we think that they are motivations of a kind we share with beasts.

This is a picture of two motivational systems in conflict. One system is of a kind we think peculiar to human beings; it works through a person's accepting norms. We might call this kind of motivation *normative* motivation, and the putative psychological faculty involved the *normative control system*. The other putative system we might call the *animal control system*, since it, we think, is the part of our motivational system that we share with the beasts. Let us treat this picture as a vague psychological hypothesis about what is going on in typical cases of "weakness of will".

How plausible is this hypothesis? It draws some support from common sense, and so has some claim to fit the motley array of observations that have shaped our ordinary views of the world. This plausibility alone, though, is weak: common sense, after all, may cling to a picture that fits only a part of everyday observation. In any case, it is untouched by the further observations that can be made in the course of a systematic psychological investigation. Common sense may be a good starting point for psychological theorizing, but it is no place to stop.

Some plausibility is added to the hypothesis by considerations of human evolution. Why did language evolve in the genus *Homo?* Why might linguistic ability have been fitness-enhancing in proto-humans? A significant part of the story must of course be that language allows the straightforward communication of beliefs. The story must also involve, though, the kinds of planned, coordinated activities that language makes possible. Humans plan together; they make agreements; they exhort. Their language facilitates both complex coordination among individuals and complex individual plans—and if words lacked all power to move us, none of these things would be possible. Words, then, must motivate. What does this have to do with norms? In many cases a norm is stated in language, or thought in words. A norm, we might say, is a linguistically encoded precept. Perhaps, then, we should think of the motivation I have been calling "normative" as motivation of a particular, linguistically infused kind—a kind of motivation that evolved because of the advantages of coordination and planning through language.

If language figures centrally in human motivation, then we should expect conflicts between motivation of different kinds: the peculiarly human, linguistically infused kind of motivation on the one hand, and evolutionarily prior kinds of motivation on the other. Biology, after all, offers numerous examples of duplicate systems sharing the same function, with one system evolutionarily more recent than the other. The normative control system and the animal control system might be a case in point.

To understand norms, we need to ask how language motivates. A special, linguistically infused motivational system might well have arisen as part of the evolution of human linguistic abilities; and if it did, we could introduce talk of "accepting a norm" by pointing to that system, and saying that *accepting a norm* is whatever that system does.

We cannot, I think, rest content with this proposal, but it makes a good start.

Conflicts with Social Motivations

"Weakness of will" involves conflict, and so far in my discussion, the conflict has been between the norms a person accepts and an appetite. Many apparent cases of "weakness of will" are not of this kind. Often what we experience is a conflict between our "better judgment" and powerful social motivations. We are paralyzed by embarrassment, or a desire to ingratiate, or some other motivation that is peculiarly social. Examples abound: I may be unable to get myself to walk out of a lecture, even though it is important for me to be somewhere else. I may find myself unable to say something I know will be painful to my listener, even though I think it needs to be said. My discussion of "normative control" seems not to have addressed cases like these.

An especially powerful demonstration of this kind of conflict is Milgram's series of experiments on obedience.[1] Subjects of his experiments were told to administer electric shocks—shocks that were increasingly painful, and might eventually even be lethal—to another subject. Or that is what they thought; in fact the other subject was not being shocked, but was acting as a confederate of the experimenter. Roughly two-thirds of the subjects eventually did all they were ordered to do, although they were upset and protested vigorously. Even when subjects balked, once the experimenter said such things as "The experiment requires that you continue," a majority complied.[2]

Now when we read about these experiments, we are shocked by what the subjects did. Their actions violate norms that we accept. The near uniformity with which the subjects substantially acquiesced, however, should suggest to each of us, "Had I been a subject in one of these experiments before I first read or heard of them, I too would have cooperated with the experimenter—perhaps fully, and almost certainly

---

1. Milgram (1974). A fascinating discussion of these experiments and their implications is to be found in Sabini and Silver (1982, esp. chaps. 3–5 and 9–11).

2. See Milgram (1974, 35) for a table of his main experimental results. In a variant of the experiment, the subject was placed in the same room with the victim a few feet away from him; then only a minority of the subjects complied to the end—but still a large minority (40 percent).

more than I would like to acknowledge. I would have felt immensely disturbed about the situation in which I found myself, and I would have protested vigorously and regarded the experimenter as a madman. Nevertheless, I probably would have complied."[3]

A typical subject in one of these experiments clearly experiences conflict of some sort; that is shown by his protests and his extreme agitation.[4] The conflict, though, is not between a norm he accepts and a bodily appetite. It seems rather to be a conflict between one norm and another. The subject accepts the norm against intentional harm—the norm in terms of which we ourselves condemn his behavior. That is shown by the vigor of his protests. Nevertheless, he obeys an experimenter who tells him to violate that norm. He does so, it would appear, from a complex of motivations: he comes to the experiment all set to be polite and cooperative, to do his job in the experiment, to follow the directions of the man in charge. The conflict, we might therefore say, is between opposing norms: a norm of non-harm on the one hand and norms of following directions, cooperating, doing one's job on the other.

What are we to make of this conflict? Much of what I have been saying about the subject applies as well to us, as we read about the experiment. We, like the subject, accept norms of politeness, cooperativeness, and doing one's job—the norms that determine the subject's behavior. Like him, we accept norms against inflicting pain and endangering others. What, then, distinguishes us from the subject? The difference seems to be that we, the readers, take these norms of politeness and cooperation to be decisively overridden by the norms against inflicting pain and endangering people, whereas the subject is moved, in the end, by norms of politeness and cooperativeness despite his acceptance of these other norms. The difference is not one of character, but one of circumstance—of the context in which we think, judge, and act. The subject, had he been a reader instead, would have reacted

---

3. This is not what people in fact predict about themselves, or indeed about others. See Milgram (1974, chap. 3). Some of the explanations Milgram quotes (p. 28) suggest that in thinking about the situation, people are not separating the question of what *to do* from the question of what in fact *they would do*. Rather, they think out what to do in the situation—they make a hypothetical decision—and then assume that what they have decided to do is what they would really do if they were in the situation.

4. Different subjects responded in quite different ways. For sample descriptions, see Milgram (1974, chaps. 5, 7). The reactions he describes range from agitation and protest to quiet defiance, to resignation, to giggles, to quiet obedience.

very much as we do. Had we been subjects, the evidence is, we too might well have done as they did.[5]

What is the role of norms in all this? The conflict is between one set of norms and another, true enough, but that suggests a symmetry that is specious. For Milgram's setup, the two sets of norms play different psychological roles. The norm of non-infliction of harm prevails in the judgments of detached observers, whereas the norms of cooperativeness, taking directions, doing one's job control the agent in the heat of social encounter. From our detached perspective, norms against the infliction of pain and danger are, in their application to this situation, plainly overriding. For the subject, the norms of cooperativeness prevail.

Ordinary language has devices that come close to labeling this contrast. We, as judges, *accept* a norm against infliction of harm, and *accept* that this norm, in the situation of Milgram's subjects, overrides norms of cooperativeness and doing one's job—norms that we also accept. The subjects, on the other hand, do not genuinely *accept* that in their situation, norms of cooperativeness and the like override all other norms. Rather, we might say, they are *in the grip* of these norms. In common language, then, the contrast is between *accepting* a norm (or more precisely, *accepting* that one set of norms outweighs another in a given situation) and *being in the grip of* a norm.

If there is a distinction of this kind to be drawn, how is it tied to ascriptions of rationality? To call something rational, I proposed in the last chapter, is to express one's acceptance of norms that, on balance, permit it. Once "accepting" a norm has been distinguished from "being in its grip", we need to ask which of the two belongs in the norm-expressivistic analysis of 'rational'. In the examples I used to display the distinction, the answer seems clear: It is accepting norms that matters here, not being in their grip. What, after all, does a subject in one of Milgram's obedience experiments think it rational to do? If his plight is genuinely one of "weakness of will", that is presumably because he thinks that it makes no sense to cooperate, but finds himself cooperating nevertheless. In other words, he does what he thinks irrational. Now what he actually does, in this case, is a matter of the norms that have him in their grip—norms of politeness and coopera-

---

5. Sabini and Silver (1982, chap. 4) use Milgram's experiment to show how people who initially were decent and ordinary could, in circumstances the Nazis designed, turn unimaginably brutal. Normal decency, they argue, depends on social circumstances in which people can keep their moral bearings.

tiveness. What he thinks it rational to do, on the other hand, is what is required by norms against inflicting pain and danger—and these are the norms he accepts as having most weight in his situation. In this case, then, his thinking it irrational to cooperate apparently consists of his *accepting*, as having most weight in his circumstances, norms that turn out to prohibit cooperation. Thinking something rational or irrational thus seems to be a matter not of being in the grip of norms, but of accepting them.

Biological Adaptation

So far I have illustrated the distinction between accepting a norm and being in its grip, but I have offered no theory of the difference. What I can suggest will have to be quite speculative, but the speculation, I hope, may prompt more solid investigation. It may lend some plausibility to the central claim I am making: that something like the ordinary notion of "accepting a norm" must figure in an adequate human psychology.

First I set out some background. I want to understand acceptance of norms as a natural, biological phenomenon. I do not mean by this that we should fit the acceptance of norms to a crude preconception of what could be biological; human life demands a biology adequate to its subject. I do mean that I shall be drawing on biological theory to help us understand the phenomena I have been displaying.

If there is such a thing as governance by norms, there must be psychic mechanisms that accomplish it, and we can ask about their biological function. That function, I want to suggest, is to *coordinate*. Accepting a norm and being in its grip manifest two different systems of coordination. Of these, the capacity to accept norms is peculiarly human and depends on language.

Start with biological function in general. Biological stories are stories of function. How, say, could we understand the heart, except as a pump? To understand the psychic mechanisms that underlie accepting norms and being in their grip, we should likewise try to understand their function.

This talk of function should be glossed in Darwinian terms.[6] The results of natural selection mimic intentional design, and biological function is the Darwinistic analog of purpose in design. What grand

6. Among the many accessible treatments of evolution and animal behavior are Maynard Smith (1978), Dawkins (1976), and Wilson (1975).

purpose, then, can we discern in the design of organisms? Nature displays competing purposes in the design of competing organisms. The lioness is strong, cunning, and camouflaged so as to kill antelopes; the antelope is sharp of sense and fleet of foot so as to evade lionesses. As a result of natural selection, each organism looks as if it were designed for a separate purpose, and these separate purposes may conflict.

Darwinian theory explains away this talk of nature's purpose. The appearance of design in organisms, the theory says, results from an accumulation of mutations and genetic recombinations that have favored reproduction. Certain characteristics of organisms are heritable. Parents pass genes to their offspring, determining the offspring's *genotype*, and genotype and environment together determine what the organism is like—the organism's *phenotype*. The genes occasionally mutate, and so new phenotypical characteristics arise, often as slight variants of the old ones. In the long run, those characteristics that have led to greater reproductive success come to predominate, and in the even longer run, these reproduction-enhancing mutations accumulate. That explains the appearance of design in nature: each organism that results will look as if it had been designed for the purpose of reproducing itself.

Biologists speak of "reproductive success", "selection pressures", and "adaptation". An organism's reproductive success is roughly the number of descendants it has in the distant future. It is enhanced by whatever enhances survival, the begetting of offspring, and fostering these offspring so that they too may survive, beget, and foster their own offspring.[7] An organism's *fitness* is its expected degree of reproductive success, given its characteristics and its environment. Fitness-enhancing mutations are thus the ones that tend to be perpetuated, and in the course of time they accumulate. What is fitness-enhancing, then, is what tends toward survival, mating, and the fostering of reproductive success in offspring and other close relatives.

Conditions that render certain characteristics of an organism fitness-enhancing are called *selection pressures*. A feature of an organism that

7. One's genes are also reproduced when close kin reproduce; hence fitness may be enhanced by things that help kin to survive and reproduce. Fitness, then, should be understood as inclusive fitness; it includes the bases of kin-selection: an organism's effects on the reproduction of its genetic material by close relatives. Hamilton (1964) first modeled kin-selection rigorously; earlier Fisher and Haldane had proposed it informally. In my own discussion, though, I shall be relying not on kin-selection but on considerations of reciprocity.

results from a history of selection pressures favoring that feature is called an *adaptation*. An adaptation is thus a feature that comes to predominate in a population because it has contributed to reproductive success in historical environments. We can speak of *systems* in an organism that do various things, and something is a *biological function* of that system if the system's doing that thing constitutes an adaptation—if the system is adapted to doing that thing.

Not every characteristic of an organism is an adaptation, and not every useful thing an organ does constitutes a biological function of that organ. Noses are not adapted to holding eyeglasses—it is no part of their biological function to do so. There were, after all, no eyeglasses in the environments in which human noses evolved, and so there were no selection pressures for ability to support eyeglasses. The valves of the heart, on the other hand, do constitute adaptations, for what they are like results from a history of selection pressures favoring blocking the flow of blood in one direction but not the other. This unidirectional blocking of the flow of blood is their biological function. In being adapted to block the back-flow of blood, they mimic the design of valves in a man-made pump.[8]

Inherited genotype, it should be stressed, need not translate in a simple, direct way into the phenotype we observe. Genotype and environment interact to yield phenotype, and the same genotype in different environments can yield quite different phenotypes. If historical environments have varied, then the organisms may be adapted to respond differentially, in fitness-enhancing ways, to different kinds of environments in the ancestral history. In novel or unusual environments organisms are prone to do things that do not enhance their fitness, since evolution works systematically to adapt organisms only to the environments of their ancestors. If organisms are adapted to respond differently to different ancestral environments, then in novel environments they may well respond to cues that, in some way, resemble cues in their ancestral environments. Their responses to these cues may enhance their fitness or may detract from it.

This applies especially to human beings, who are adapted to live in circumstances of many kinds, to respond flexibly to a vast diversity of cues their cultures might offer—and who, because of culture and its ramified effects, live throughout the world in evolutionarily novel cir-

8. Symons (1979) has a careful discussion of what an adaptation is and what kind of evidence can support the conclusion that a given feature of an organism constitutes an adaptation.

cumstances. In applying Darwinian theory to the human psyche, we should look not for rigid patterns of behavior, but for capacities to respond differently to different environments. We should look, in effect, for nature's contingency plans for human thought, emotion, and motivation. Tendencies to respond differently to different kinds of situations may in some cases constitute adaptations. Whether they do is roughly a matter of whether, in early human environments, these patterns would have tended on balance to promote individuals' reproduction.[9]

The Biology of Coordination

With this sketch of biological adaptation on the table, I turn to coordination. Systems of normative control in human beings, I am suggesting, are adapted to achieve interpersonal coordination. What might this mean? To answer this, I sketch work of Thomas Schelling on rational coordination in pursuit of human goals, and John Maynard Smith's evolutionary analog of Schelling's theory.[10]

Turn first to coordination in the pursuit of human goals. Meeting a person provides one of Schelling's paradigms. Suppose it will further the purposes of both of us if we meet successfully in Chicago, and it matters relatively little to each of us where or when. If you are in front of the Art Institute at 12:30, I do best myself to be in front of the Art Institute at 12:30. If instead you are behind the Picasso statue at City Hall at noon, I do best to be behind the statue at noon. The same goes for you with respect to me. We coordinate if we succeed in being at the same place at the same time. If we are, then each of us has done best for himself, given what the other does.

Here coordinated expectations could coordinate behavior. If I expect you to be in front of the Art Institute at 12:30, then I will find it advantageous to be there too. If we each expect the other, then each will find it advantageous to do what in fact fulfills the other's expectations.

9. In recent years a vast literature has appeared speculating and presenting evidence about the evolutionary bases of human nature. Wilson (1975, 1978) and Alexander (1979) are prime examples. I find some of this literature highly valuable, some puzzling, and some unpromising. See Ruse (1985), Kitcher (1985), and Symons (1987) for discussion and critiques.

10. Schelling (1960, chap. 2) has the classic discussion of coordination and bargaining. Maynard Smith (1976, 1982) pioneered the application of game theory to the evolution of behavior; see the earlier work for an accessible presentation and the later for a more thorough development.

In this case, there is a near-coincidence of interests, but coordinated expectations matter even when interests are substantially opposed. Take price haggling, for instance. The buyer wants to buy cheap, the seller to sell dear; but there may be a range of prices for which each prefers a sale at that price to no sale at all. Within this range, the buyer holds out for the lowest price he thinks he can get; the seller for the highest. There will be a sale if expectations are suitably coordinated— if the lowest price the buyer thinks he can get is no lower than the highest price the seller thinks he can get. Here again, coordinated expectations make for mutual benefit.

Indeed coordinated expectations matter even in systems of threats: In many circumstances, a threat will be carried out only if it has not been believed—only if the person threatened did not expect the threat to be carried out if he did what he did. Even with hostility, coordinated expectations can make for mutual restraint.

Cooperation requires coordinated expectations in at least two ways. There must, of course, be coordinated expectations of how each shall contribute to the project, or the project fails. In addition, though, there must be coordinated expectations of how the fruits of cooperation shall be shared. Hunting, for example, often requires cooperation, and there are various ways the kill can be divided. Hunters in effect trade benefits, and they must coordinate their expectations of the terms of trade. A system of cooperation may be mutually advantageous in the sense that everyone does better with the system than he would with no cooperation at all, and yet it may well be that for each person, there is an alternative mutually advantageous system of cooperation that would benefit him more.

Game theorists call situations of the kinds I have been discussing "bargaining problems". More specifically, a *bargaining problem* has these features: There are alternative systems of cooperation or mutual restraint, each of which is mutually beneficial in the sense that its implementation would make everyone involved better off than he would be with no cooperation or restraint. There is a conflict of interest, though, over which of these alternative mutually beneficial systems to implement: For each such system, there is another which makes someone better off.[11]

Return now to natural selection. In discussing coordination and bargaining, I have spoken of "interests", "benefit", and "advantage", and

11. See Luce and Raiffa (1957, 124–137). The bargaining problem was formulated, as such, by Nash (1951).

this talk was to be understood in terms of human goals and preferences—in terms of "preference satisfaction", let me say. We could, though, substitute "biological fitness" or "reproductive success" for "preference satisfaction", and consider situations that have the same formal structure as human bargaining problems. An *evolutionary bargaining situation* is a recurrent kind of interaction among organisms in which the following conditions hold. First, there are mutual benefits to be gained, with benefits now to be glossed in terms of fitness. That is to say, as compared to some combination of behaviors of the organisms involved, called their *threatened combination*, some other combinations result in greater fitness for all. Call any such combination a *mutual fitness-enhancing combination*. Second, there is a conflict of interest over how these benefits are to be divided. That is, for any mutual fitness-enhancing combination, there is an individual whose fitness is more enhanced by some other mutual fitness-enhancing combination.[12]

Evolutionary bargaining situations are recurrent in the annals of natural selection. From the point of view of fitness, having exclusive access to a territory without a fight beats ceding all access without a fight, but that in turn beats getting into a deadly fight. Various combinations of behavior, then, are mutually fitness-enhancing compared with the threatened combination, fighting—namely, that A enjoys the territory and B keeps out, that A and B share the territory, or that B enjoys the territory and A keeps out. Between any two of these combinations, though, the one that is more fitness-enhancing for A is less so for B.

---

12. Various evolutionary bargaining situations are analyzed in Maynard Smith (1982, 151–161). Trivers (1971) started discussion of biological reciprocity. The cases he treats are like evolutionary bargaining situations in that there exists a mutual fitness-enhancing combination of behaviors. They are unlike evolutionary bargaining situations in that there is only one mutual fitness-enhancing combination. In effect, there is no problem of settling the terms of trade. Axelrod and Hamilton (1981) apply the theory of biological reciprocity to a wide range of biological phenomena.

A prisoner's dilemma repeated an indefinite number of times does constitute a bargaining situation. There are gains to be had from cooperation, and there are different ways of producing and allocating the gains. One party may cooperate less than the other, and still leave both with more than if they did not cooperate at all. So long as his partner does not retaliate, he gets slightly more than he would get if he were fully cooperative. His partner gets much less than if both cooperated fully, but still more than if neither cooperated. Still, in this case, bargaining should be unproblematic. Full cooperation is simple and symmetric, and it produces by far the largest joint gains. Axelrod has studied repeated prisoner's dilemmas extensively (1984). My interest here will be with evolutionary bargaining situations in which terms of trade are problematical, in which, that is to say, there is a genuine problem of how to divide the gains of cooperation.

What can we expect to happen in an evolutionary bargaining situation? Let *P* be a mutual fitness-enhancing combination of behaviors, and suppose each animal is genetically disposed to the following behavioral strategy: play its part in *P* if the others do, and otherwise carry out its threatened behavior. Then each animal's strategy will be what Maynard Smith calls an *evolutionarily stable strategy*—roughly, a strategy such that if all adopt it, then for each individual that strategy is at least as fitness-enhancing as would be any other strategy easily accessible by mutation.[13]

Consider now human beings evolving in hunting-gathering societies. We could expect them to face an abundance of human bargaining situations, involving mutual aid, personal property, mates, territory, use of housing, and the like. Human bargaining situations tend to be evolutionary bargaining situations. Human goals tend toward biological fitness, toward reproduction. The point is not, of course, that a person's sole goal is to maximize his reproduction; few if any people have that as a goal at all. Rather, the point concerns propensities to develop goals. Those propensities that conferred greatest fitness were selected; hence in a hunting-gathering society, people tended to want the various things it was fitness-enhancing for them to want. Conditions of primitive human life must have required intricate coordination—both of the simple cooperative kinds involved, say, in meeting a person, and of the kind required for bargaining problems to yield mutually beneficial outcomes. Propensities well coordinated with the propensities of others would have been fitness-enhancing, and so we may view a vast array of human propensities as coordinating devices. Our emotional propensities, I suggest, are largely the results of these selection pressures, and so are our normative capacities.

Consider emotions. So far I have spoken chiefly of coordinated expectations and actions, but coordinated emotions will figure too in the story. Take guilt and resentment: if one person resents an action of another and the other does not feel a corresponding guilt, we may expect trouble. Guilt makes possible the acknowledgment of wrong, and such modes of reconciliation as restitution, compensation, apology, and forgiveness.[14] One's chances of damaging conflict are

---

13. The notion of an evolutionarily stable strategy has proved extremely important. It was first used in Maynard Smith and Price (1973). The best introduction may be Maynard Smith (1976). Maynard Smith (1982) gives an extended theoretical treatment of the notion. In the precise definition of an evolutionarily stable strategy, a clause must be included about resistance to invasion by a mutation.

14. Murphy (1982) has a fine discussion of resentment and the feelings that can mesh with it.

reduced, then, if one feels guilty when guilt and its normal accompaniments are demanded by others, and if one demands guilt and its normal accompaniments only when others are prepared to feel guilty. Hence it tends to be advantageous for an individual to coordinate his guilt with the resentment of others and his resentment with the guilt of others. That, of course, will not be the only tendency governing these emotions, but it is a tendency that may well explain many aspects of the significant and complex coordinating mechanisms of a complex social animal.

Similar things can be said for other emotions. Take gratitude: if one is not grateful when one is expected to be, and hence cannot be expected to reciprocate on terms others regard as fair, one may destroy one's chances of continuing to benefit from the actions of others. Informal exchange underlies much of human life, and it works through coordinated expectations of gratitude and the goodwill that normally stems from gratitude.

Now human beings have a capacity to be guided by words, in their actions and emotions. This capacity is central to our psychic makeup, and it must have much to do with the selection pressures that led to the evolution of linguistic ability in human beings. Being guided by language could enhance a proto-human's biological fitness, both by enabling him to develop complex plans for action, and by leading him to coordinate his emotions and actions with those of his fellows. It is in the role of language in coordinating behavior and expectations, I shall be suggesting, that we can discern what is special about accepting norms.

Internalizing Norms

What is it to be in the grip of a norm as opposed to accepting it? Presumably, whatever happens when I am in the grip of a norm that I do not accept happens also, much of the time, when I do accept a norm. Take again our ordinary norms of politeness and cooperativeness. In my usual dealings with people, I not only accept these norms as having some weight; I accept them as having enough weight to override any conflicting norms that apply to my situation. I normally give people directions when asked, even if I am in a slight hurry, and this I do not out of weakness of will, but because I accept that it makes sense to help people who need it when the cost is small. In these cases, we would not say that I am "in the grip" of the norms of politeness and cooperativeness that guide my conduct, since I accept them as reasonably controlling in the situation. It may well be, though, that these norms would control my behavior even if I did not accept them, or did not accept them as having greatest weight in my situation. In this respect, my psychological state is like the state of being in the grip of a norm.

We need, then, some term for what is common to situations in which I am in the grip of a norm and situations of the more usual kind: situations in which I accept no opposing norm, but would still tend to be in the grip of this norm even if on balance I did accept opposing norms. I propose the colorless, somewhat technical term *internalizing* a norm.[15]

How are we to understand internalizing a norm? The capacity to do so is one we share with other mammals, especially those who live in groups. Consider dogs: a dog will mark off its territory and bark at other dogs who encroach; two dogs meeting on neutral ground will engage in elaborate rituals. My anthropomorphic language suggests that something akin to our own internalizing norms may be in play. As in the human case, these animal interactions follow certain regular patterns, and the patterns seem, in a way, to have a rationale. They constitute adaptations, we may presume; that is to say, they are the result of natural selection favoring these patterns. The selection pressures are in large part a matter of coordinating the behavior of the animals as they interact, and so the patterns of behavior constitute evolutionarily stable strategies. It is as if these patterns of behavior were designed into the lives of social beasts, and in this special sense the beasts "follow rules" for social interaction.

They have not, of course, decided to conduct themselves by these rules, and they do not criticize each other for deviations. In these respects, their behavior differs from some of the human behavior we call norm-governed. Human life as well, though, has its share of such behaviors. Many patterns of human behavior are not explicitly formulated and demanded, but serve nonetheless to coordinate our lives in various ways. Think of conversational distance: most people have no opinions about proper conversational distance, and yet conversa-

---

15. Perhaps the term is not colorless enough. Psychologists use the term to mark off a different contrast: between obeying a norm or tending to out of heed to what others will think or do, and tending to obey it independently of the reactions of others. The things I call internalizing a norm and accepting one both would count for psychologists as internalizing.

tional distance in a sense "signals" varying degrees of familiarity and intimacy. There is a strong cultural element to conversational distance: Though in any given culture closer means more intimate, cultures differ on the distance that is appropriate for a given kind of relationship. That will sometimes become obvious when people from two cultures stand and talk, and one keeps advancing as the other retreats. A culture has norms of conversational distance, then, in some sense of the term 'norm', even though members of the culture are not explicitly aware of them and do not explicitly avow them. The signals by which people avoid bumping into each other on a crowded sidewalk make for another case in point. These cases seem in many respects like cases in which we may speak of "norms" and "rituals" in the lives of beasts, and the behaviors involved may well rest on like psychic mechanisms. As with animal ritual, we have here behavioral patterns without explicit rules. To the extent that the behaviors result from inborn mechanisms, it is as if their designer had hit on a useful rule. To the extent that they result as well from social training, the story is more complex, but still, even though there is no explicit awareness of a rule, what goes on is much like following a rule. Children are not normally given explicit instructions concerning conversational distance, but they may be primed genetically to take closeness as a sign of intimacy, and to pick up the practices with which they grow up. The end result is the following of complex rules without explicit awareness of them.

In the same limited sense, then, in which various beasts have norms, we do too. In one respect the rules are in the eye of the beholder: neither the beast nor the human can state them, but they can be formulated—with considerable ingenuity and effort—by a sophisticated observer. In another respect, the rules are really in the actor: if they were not somehow represented internally, it would be mysterious how these patterns of behavior could be maintained.

What, then, might we mean here by a "norm"? By the norm itself, I suggest, we should mean simply a prescription or imperative that gives the rule a sophisticated observer could formulate. The imperative is a formulation of a pattern which, in effect, controls the organism's behavior.

If a norm is simply an imperative, the real psychological question is what it is to internalize it. A norm prescribes a pattern of behavior, and to internalize a norm, I want to say, is to have a motivational tendency of a particular kind to act on that pattern. The particular kind of motivational tendency is the one I have tried to pick out—partly by example, and partly by giving a theory of what unites the examples. The examples are united by a purpose of coordination. Tendencies to act on the pattern (or propensities to acquire these tendencies when growing up exposed to the pattern) constitute biological adaptations for coordination. I hope that in saying this, I have picked out a natural kind of motivational tendency. If I have, then I can say that where norm N prescribes a certain behavioral pattern B, an organism *internalizes* N if and only if it has a motivational tendency, of the kind I have picked out, to act on pattern B.

I have been speaking here of action, but like things could be said of emotion. Socially significant emotions tend to be coordinated. Emotions coordinate action, and so natural selection will work to coordinate emotions. Here again, then, the sophisticated observer can formulate patterns—patterns to which various emotional tendencies are adapted to conform. When a person's emotions tend to follow a pattern in this way, we can say the person *internalizes* the norm that prescribes this pattern.

Internalizing a norm involves tendencies toward action and emotion, tendencies that are coordinated with the tendencies of others in ways that constitute matched adaptations, or are the results of matched adaptations. We share the capacity to internalize norms with other animals, although the greater complexity of human social life may well mean that our capacities to internalize norms are more refined than those of any other animal.

Accepting Norms

Earlier I contrasted *internalizing* a norm with *accepting* one, but so far I have speculated only about internalization. Acceptance is what chiefly interests me. In the Milgram experiment, recall, the subject accepts norms against inflicting pain and danger, and accepts them as outweighing all other norms in the circumstance. These norms prevail in what he would say and think away from the scene. The norms he most strongly internalizes, though, say to do one's job, and so those are the ones that prevail in the heat of social encounter.

What is it, then, to accept a norm? To understand acceptance we should look to language. Think of what language has to do with motivation, apart from simply making us aware of the states of affairs we confront. Although the most obvious function of language is to convey information, much of language is more than merely informative. Language is used to exhort, to criticize, and to summon up emotions; narrative has a fascination that does not disappear if the tale is thought to be fiction.

One way language influences actions and emotions is by letting people think together on absent situations. With language, people share not only their immediate situation, but past, future, and hypothetical situations as well. Various kinds of reactions can then be expressed, in various ways: emotional responses can be shared simply by evincing them. Special language can be used to express hypothetical decisions—decisions on what to do in the place of someone in the situation under discussion. Emotionally laden words can be used to label actions and characters. Explicit precepts can be formulated. In a rich number of ways, language allows for shared evaluation of absent situations.

That opens great new scope for coordination, and so a capacity for shared evaluation would be fitness-enhancing in a species with a complex social life. Those who can work out together reactions to an absent situation—what to do and what to feel—are ready for like situations. They are better prepared than they would otherwise be to do what is advantageous in a new situation, and they can rely on complex schemes of interpersonal coordination. On general evolutionary grounds, then, we might expect shared evaluation to figure centrally in a complex social life—and in human life it does. Much of our speech fosters shared reactions to absent circumstances. Think of the familiar human fascination with stories. Think of how much of overheard conversation on sidewalks, buses, and the like consists in recounting problematic events such as personal confrontations, apparently to elicit reactions. Think of gossip.[16] Shared evaluation is central to human life, I suggest, because it serves biological functions of rehearsal and coordination.

Working out in community what to do, what to think, and how to feel in absent situations, if it has these biological functions, must presumably influence what we do, think, and feel when faced with like situations. I shall call this influence *normative governance*. It is in this governance of action, belief, and emotion that we might find a place for phenomena that constitute acceptance of norms, as opposed merely to internalizing them. When we work out at a distance, in community, what to do or think or feel in a situation we are discussing,

16. See Sabini and Silver (1982), chap. 5, "A Plea for Gossip".

we come to accept norms for the situation. This is the hypothesis I want to develop, and I shall call the discussion involved *normative discussion.*

Here, then, in brief, is the proposal. Normative discussion might coordinate acts and feelings if two things hold. First, normative discussion tends toward consensus. The mechanisms here, I shall propose, are two: mutual influence, and a responsiveness to demands for consistency. Second, the consensus must move people to do or feel accordingly. That is where normative governance comes in.

We evaluate in community, but part of what goes on is individual. Groups often reach consensus, but sometimes they do not. Even when they do, the consensus may emerge from individuals' taking their separate positions and then, to some degree, persuading each other. Acceptance of norms is tied not only to a consensus that emerges from normative discussion, but to individuals' taking positions.

This taking of normative positions I shall call *normative avowal.* By "avowal" here, I mean to include a wide range of expressions we might count as taking a position in normative discussion—in the discussion of absent states of affairs. The simplest kind might be evincing an emotion toward the absent situation. Other kinds of avowal are more explicit: we may express a hypothetical decision in words, or label an action in words that are emotively charged. To understand acceptance of norms, we need to look to such avowal—the kind of avowal from which consensus can emerge, and which may persist even when there is no approach to consensus.

What is the connection of avowal to acceptance? As a first approximation, we might say that to accept a norm is to be prepared to avow it in normative discussion. This, however, cannot be entirely right. To be prepared to avow something is not always to accept it: people sometimes avow norms insincerely. We need, then, to develop an account of accepting norms that ties acceptance to avowal in normative discussion, but allows for insincere avowal as well.

On our normal way of thinking, we would have to speak of acceptance in order to explain sincerity. To avow sincerely is simply to avow what one genuinely accepts—and if this explains sincerity, then sincerity cannot be used to explain acceptance. This order of explanation, though, should be suspect. Sincerity itself is problematical. True, we do distinguish sharply between honest avowal and dishonest feigning of a convenient opinion; we celebrate martyrs who have proclaimed their convictions when they had much to lose by so doing. Often, though, a person will not know what his "true opinion" is, and yet avow something anyway. If we knew what acceptance is, we could explain sincerity as avowing what one accepts, but both sincerity and acceptance are problematical.

Can we, then, explain acceptance by tying it to avowal? Perhaps so, if we distinguish two kinds of sincerity. One kind is deliberately holding oneself to standards of honest avowal; the other is a childlike openness or spontaneity—speaking without the psychic complications of self-censorship. Perhaps we should begin with this sincerity as spontaneity, and explain acceptance as a disposition to avow spontaneously.[17]

That spontaneous avowal does have psychological primacy is suggested by the sense of liberation a person may feel when he has been deprived of contexts in which he can relax and speak openly, and then newly finds himself in such a context. This may stem from the human need to work through normative commitments in community. Always having to think secretly is felt as a strain; the person who must do so will soon feel that he is losing his normative moorings. Constant secrecy deprives him of a community within which to think. We seek, then, contexts in which we can relax the psychological mechanisms of self-censorship.

Acceptance, though, involves more than spontaneous avowal, or being disposed to avow in unconstrained contexts. It involves a response to demands for consistency. Normative discussion consists of taking positions; even a conversational groan stakes out a position. Consensus may then be reached partly by a mechanism that is incipiently Socratic. Discussants hold each other to consistency in their positions, and thus force each other to shift positions by exposing inconsistency. A person, then, must take positions in order to engage in normative discussion responsibly, and in doing so, he exposes himself to pressures toward consistency. To accept a norm, we might say, is in part to be disposed to avow it in unconstrained normative discussion, as a result of the workings of demands for consistency in the positions one takes in normative discussion.

To prepare oneself to meet demands for consistency may require a strong imaginative life. A person will engage in imaginative rehearsal for actual normative discussion; he practices by holding himself to consistency. The pressure for consistency need not be so strong as it is in

17. Ryle talks somewhat in this vein, with refinements (1949, 181–185).

good philosophical discussion, but it will be there, and it may be significant. From this imaginative rehearsal, then, a kind of imaginative persona may emerge, an "I" who develops a consistent position to take in normative discussion. It is then that we can speak most clearly of what the person accepts; he then has a worked out normative position to take in unconstrained contexts.

Why expose oneself to these demands for consistency? We do so naturally, but what selection pressures might have shaped us to do so? The answer should be clear from what I have said. The demands for consistency are reciprocal, and the system of mutual demands is part of a coordinating device. It is partly because of these mutual demands that there is any hope of reaching consensus in normative discussion. A person who refuses these demands must therefore be a poor candidate for cooperation of any kind—and in human life, cooperation is vital. It is fitness-enhancing, then, to stand ready to engage in normative discussion, and so to accept the demands for consistency that are part of the package.

The state of accepting a norm, in short, is identified by its place in a syndrome of tendencies toward action and avowal—a syndrome produced by the language-infused system of coordination peculiar to human beings. The system works through discussion of absent situations, and it allows for the delicate adjustments of coordination that human social life requires. The syndrome that manifests accepting a norm takes in normative discussion and normative governance. In this normative discussion, in unrestrained contexts, one tends to avow the norm. One tends to be influenced by the avowals of others, and to be responsive to their demands for consistency. Normative governance by the norm is a tendency to conform to it. *Accepting* a norm is whatever psychic state, if any, gives rise to this syndrome of avowal of the norm and governance by it.

What, then, of the distinction between accepting a norm and internalizing it? Accepting a norm is something that we do primarily in the context of normative discussion, actual and imaginary. We take positions, and thereby expose ourselves to demands for consistency. Normative discussion of a situation influences action and emotion in like situations. It is then that we can speak of norms as governing action and emotion, and it is through this governance that normative discussion serves to coordinate. Internalizing a norm is likewise a matter of coordinating propensities, but the propensities are of a different kind: they work independently of normative discussion.

Acceptance, Action, Persuasion

The chief biological function of normative discussion is to coordinate. Normative discussion allows for common enterprises and adjusts terms of reciprocity—both the friendly give-and-take of cooperative schemes and hostile standoffs with their threats and mutual restraint. For such a mechanism to work, two things are needed: tendencies toward consensus, and normative governance. Normative discussion must tend toward all accepting the same norms, and acceptance of norms must tend to guide action. Selection pressures could develop and maintain these tendencies only if, in the context of others' having them, having these tendencies oneself enhanced one's fitness. The tendencies, in other words, would have to constitute an evolutionarily stable strategy.[18]

Why might they? Turn first to normative governance. The ties that link avowal to action will be complex: anthropologists warn us against uncritically taking the norms people avow to describe their behavior, and common sense supports this caution. Still, there must be some tie of avowal to action, or the entire coordinative story I have been telling would have no basis.[19] I need, then, to sketch a picture that will allow for the variety to be found in human life, with both its genuine normative motivation and its hypocrisy and self-serving argument.[20]

Selection pressures shaped our propensities both to abide by norms and to violate them, and these pressures must have been diverse. On the one hand, as I have stressed, there are great gains to be had from

18. I argue from evolutionary theory and the general human condition, but psychologists have built a vast experimental corpus that should bear on the subject. The subject is attitude theory; see, for instance, much of Newcomb, Turner, and Converse (1965). (Since the subject has not been central to recent social psychology, older surveys say more.) As developed by Newcomb et al., attitude theory sweeps over some of the distinctions I am supposing crucial. In particular, internalizing a norm (in my sense of the term) is not distinguished from accepting it (46–48). They do talk of "rules" in somewhat the way I talk of "norms". The term 'norm' itself they use quite differently from me, and since their use or something like it is widespread, readers should be warned of the difference. As I gloss Newcomb et al., a "norm" is a rule whose acceptance is shared by a group: the rule is widely accepted, and it is widely known that the rule is widely accepted. (Again, "acceptance" in Newcomb et al. takes in what I call internalization. See 233–235; the explicit definition of 'norm' on p. 229 is different.)

19. Attitude theory includes studies of relations between attitudes and overt behavior; see Newcomb et al. (1965, 67–73).

20. Schank (1932) studied a Methodist community whose members publicly opposed cardplaying, tobacco, and liquor. A number of them secretly smoked, drank, or played cards, Schank discovered, each believing himself the only one who would think of doing so.

coordinating one's actions and expectations with those of others. This coordination is fostered if one accepts the norms accepted by others, and acts on those norms. Opposing pressures, though, would stem from the gains to be had from avowing one thing and doing another. In an animal whose reproduction depends on a complex social life, these opposing pressures might well have shaped subtle and intricate psychic mechanisms—mechanisms as subtle and intricate as the ones we observe. We could expect, then, some tendency for the norms a person accepts to control his actions, but a mitigated tendency.[21]

Normative governance, then, is like political governance. Governments do not always prevail: what a government commands, people do not invariably do. On the other hand, what a government commands has some influence on what people do, or it is no government. Likewise normative governance will not always prevail, but it has some influence on what people do and feel.

So far I have assumed consensus, and asked how there might be selection pressures toward normative governance. Now I ask the reverse: given normative governance, what could give rise to consensus? My broad question is whether the tendencies I am hypothesizing could exist in evolutionary equilibrium: would each of these tendencies be maintained in the presence of the others? Suppose now that action tends to match avowal. Would some set of dispositions tending toward consensus be evolutionarily stable? Are there consensus-producing dispositions that would enhance an individual's fitness, if those he deals with have those same dispositions?

To reap gains from normative discussion takes both a certain firmness and a certain persuadability. Without persuadability, there can be no consensus. A person who is wholly unpersuadable would get few benefits from normative discussion—unless he were surrounded by people who were themselves completely persuadable. He would be a poor candidate for cooperative social life; he would risk ostracism. It would also be costly, though, to be a pushover in discussion. To evince compliance to any demands whatsoever, so long as they were made

---

21. These questions need further study. In recent years there has been a large economic literature on schemes that will elicit sincere revelation of preferences from instrumentally rational agents. The question parallels my question of whether normative avowal will reveal genuine and strong normative motivation. "Bluffing", the misrevelation of intentions, is discussed by Maynard Smith and Parker (1976). Maynard Smith (1982, chap. 12, 147–166) treats biological analogs of honesty, bargaining, and commitment. Honest signaling of motivations is problematical in a way that honest signaling of resources is not (148). Some models of animal interactions allow for honest signaling of intention; others do not (155–158, 161–166).

in the name of putative norms, would open a person to manipulation. What might be advantageous, then, is some tendency to gravitate toward the norms of those around one, together with some firmness in sticking to the norms one has hitherto accepted.[22]

This balance of firmness and persuadability must not be the only force shaping norms. If it were, there would be nothing to make the norms that emerged from discussion at all responsive to anyone's needs. The gains of sociability might be outweighed by the price of accepting debilitating norms. We should expect a person, then, not only to respond to the advantages of having his norms well coordinated with norms around him, but to respond as well to other ways norms pay or cost.

The rewards and costs of avowal are many, and complex propensities toward normative discussion might evolve in response to these pressures. Avowal influences what the audience accepts, and it influences what others expect one to do and their attitudes toward one. Because one's avowals influence what others accept, self-serving arguments will sometimes pay, at least when they have a chance of being convincing. On the other hand, arguments that are too blatantly self-serving may discredit one as a partner in cooperative life—though not so thoroughly as would a proclaimed indifference to all norms. A person may often do best, from the standpoints that shape human nature, to profess his devotion to norms that can attract others, while bending the norms a little in his own favor. Still, self-serving arguments would be in vain if no one ever tended to accept normative conclusions that went against some of his interests. The importance of coordination explains why we often do genuinely accept norms.[23]

22. Vast experimental work has been done on influence and persuasion; see Newcomb et al. (1965, 94–110, 242–286). Even perceptions and beliefs can be influenced. Sherif (1935) used a perceptual illusion and found subjects highly influenceable. A spot of light in a dark room appears to move a few centimeters; when subjects think the movement real, how far it seems to move is highly influenced by the judgments others express. Asch found that a minority of subjects would disbelieve their judgments of length—judgments they otherwise made accurately—when seven planted subjects had agreed on something different. The effect was greatly reduced if one stooge gave the correct answer, even though all the others agreed on a wrong answer. On attitude change, see Newcomb et al. (1965, chap. 4). Laboratory changes tend to be weak but changes in mores can be strong (110–114). Much more change in behavior comes from peer discussion than from a lecture; see Lewin (1947).

23. Gulliver (1973) reports a case of negotiation among the Arusha of Tanzania, and discusses the role of self-serving normative appeals. "At a minimum, human beings appear to feel the need to justify, and to explain or explain away, their actions" (681). "It is as important to avoid the Scylla that all is controlled by norms and rules, as it is to eschew the Charybdis that they are unimportant, and that might is right" (684). See also Nash (1970) for a fascinating transcript of a traditional Maya court proceeding.

To say all this is of course to caricature important aspects of human life, but the caricature is familiar, and even in the caricature we can see how central normative talk is to human life. The forms of life the caricature depicts would be impossible without an involved interplay of action, feeling, and avowal in normative discussion.

I have been hypothesizing psychic mechanisms that were shaped in the course of human evolution by pressures of reproductive advantage. The mechanisms themselves, though, are by no means fully egoistic. We care intrinsically about norms and their validity, and about whether we and others accept these norms and conform to them. Self-interested calculation, to be sure, could in principle serve the various functions I have pictured. It would probably not be as reliable, though, as our simpler general tendencies and intrinsic concerns, or if enough reliability could be had, it might not be cheap; reliable calculation might require too much brain circuitry. I am not suggesting that a person's own motives for action or avowal must lie chiefly in the kinds of gains and losses I have been listing. In many cases a simple integrity, say, may better foster reproduction than a finely calculated honesty as best policy. Rather, the gains and losses I cite might be sources of pressures that shaped the human psyche in the course of evolution—and led to simple integrity in some cases and self-deception or unprincipled cunning in others. In these selection pressures, we may find clues to psychic mechanisms that yield the diversity of characters we see.

The questions I have been discussing might best be tackled through careful mathematical modeling. A good model would allow us to see what conditions would have to have been met for a recognizably human complex of normative tendencies to evolve. What I have been doing, in effect, is to speculate about what some of the elements of a good model would be.[24]

The story to be modeled is one of psychic mechanisms shaped by complex pressures. These mechanisms will be shaped to respond, in a rough way, to clues about the kinds of strategies that pay in various different kinds of circumstances—pay reproductively. Now a crucial

24. It would be especially important to understand actual cases of normative change in a society in the way I am proposing, as a result of the interaction of individual normative propensities. Some extant studies more or less fit this framework. Brandt (1954) discusses normative change among the Hopi, and his story is fairly straightforwardly one of individual adaptive mechanisms. Rappaport (1979, 233–234) discusses sanctification as a way of certifying commitments, and desanctification as an adaptive response to oppression. His treatment suggests to me an interaction of individual adaptations, although the story he tells does not explicitly take that form.

element in many of these strategies will be coordination, and one way to get coordination is through normative discussion. That requires two things: normative governance and normative consensus. Each of these will often pay if the other is present; they can make for an evolutionary equilibrium. We might expect, then, a mitigated tendency to do what the norms one accepts say to do. That is what I label "normative governance". We might expect also mechanisms that tend toward consensus in normative discussion. I propose, first, a delicate combination of firmness and persuadability, and second, some responsiveness to demands for consistency. Still, these cannot be the only pressures shaping our normative natures. We will respond to the different gains and costs that different norms hold out. We will respond to the payoffs of hypocrisy as well as the wages of fidelity. We might expect psychic switches that flip to cues indicating that one strategy or the other holds out better reproductive prospects. These psychic mechanisms, then, are shaped by reproductive advantage, but they are by no means fully egoistic. Given some cues, an intrinsic concern with normative matters has been evolution's cheapest, most reliable way to promote the reproduction of a person's genes.

Normative Discussion and Philosophy

The picture I have been sketching is familiar in some respects: it is a picture of mental faculties that may conflict. True, the psychic states and processes I have depicted—the acceptance of norms, and normative control of action and emotion—do not fit neatly into the traditional psychologists' categories of cognition, affect, and conation. The capacities involved, though, do fit a traditional conception of the faculty of reason. They involve the use of language, demands for consistency, and a limited governance of action and emotion. This last, indeed, may be what psychologists sometimes call "rational control". Now, since there is such an affinity between traditional talk of "reason" and "rational control" and my talk of normative capacities and normative control, I should stress why I could not myself call the faculty of normative control "reason", or use the word 'rational' to mean "dictated by the faculty of normative control". I have avoided these terms because they are normative as well as descriptive. If I were to speak of "rational control", I would be hard put to avoid the suggestion that what is done under "rational control" is rational in the normative sense—that it is something that it really makes sense to do.

Likewise, though I might speak of a faculty of "reason", it would be hard to do so without seeming to endorse whatever that faculty does as reasonable. The term 'rational', as I am using it, expresses endorsement. There is no human faculty whose deliverances I want always to endorse, and so I do not consider the deliverances of any human faculty—even this faculty of normative governance—always to be rational. A person may accept norms that are misguided or even crazy. If he acts on those norms, against all other motivations, then normative governance has prevailed, but he is not being rational.[25]

Although it would be misleading to call the normative control system the faculty of reason, the system might aptly be called the faculty of "putative reason". If there is such a faculty, and if a person's accepting a norm is to be understood as the norm's playing a particular kind of role in the workings of this faculty, then on the analysis I have proposed, the connection between rationality and the deliverances of putative reason is this. For a person's faculty of putative reason to permit something is for the person to *believe* that thing to be rational. Take Samson's suicidal destruction of the Philistine temple. If Samson's faculty of putative reason dictates destroying the temple, then Samson himself thinks his act to be rationally required. That does not settle whether the act truly is rationally required, and indeed nothing I have said here settles that substantive issue. Delilah may, without contradicting anything I have said, believe both that Samson's faculty of putative reason dictates his destruction of the temple, and that Samson's destroying the temple is irrational. Her believing it irrational consists in what her own faculty of putative reason does: it commands not destroying the temple in Samson's circumstance.

In trying to decide what is rational, we are engaging our normative capacities to try to decide what norms to accept. We do this in normative discussion, actual and imaginative, as we take positions, subject ourselves to demands for consistency, and undergo mutual influence. Saying this should tell us something about the nature of philosophy. Philosophical discussion is continuous with ordinary dis-

---

25. Kant, we might say freely, takes rationality to consist in the deliverances of a special mental faculty, but a faculty that cannot be studied empirically. He endorses all deliverances of the faculty and treats them as supremely authoritative. In effect, though, he identifies the deliverances of this faculty by settling on what, ultimately, to endorse. Hume, on the other hand, identifies reason as the mental faculty that works on certain principles, by perceiving relations of ideas. He does not always treat this faculty as alone having special authority. For example, he regards causal beliefs as acceptable even though, he insists, they do not proceed from reason.

cussion, and often with ordinary normative discussion—the kind of normative discussion that is a part of all human life. Philosophical ethics is normative inquiry into conduct, and we may think of various other branches of philosophy as fundamental inquiry into norms of other kinds. Epistemology, for instance, is inquiry into norms for belief. Philosophical inquiry, to be sure, is single-minded in a way that most normative discussion is not. Normative discussion will be quite unphilosophical when there is little confrontation among competing normative systems.[26] Philosophy is normative discussion, but normative discussion pursued to extraordinary depths.

26. Horton (1970) discusses this as he contrasts traditional African thought and scientific thought. Traditional cultures are "closed", he suggests, in that there is "no developed awareness of alternatives to the established body of theoretical tenets; whereas in scientifically oriented cultures, such an awareness is highly developed" (153). Hence in traditional societies, "any challenge to established tenets is a threat of chaos, of the cosmic abyss, and therefore evokes intense anxiety" (154). This should apply to traditional normative thought as well, in contrast to philosophical normative thought in which alternatives to established tenets are sought out and tested. Think again of Socrates.

5 · Normative Logic

I use the term "logic" in this chapter broadly. My aims are to state the norm-expressivistic analysis more explicitly and to correct some of its defects. In its first, rough formulation, the analysis was this: to call an act, belief, or emotion rational is to express one's acceptance of a system of norms that permits it. Much more needs to be said. In the last chapter I argued for the psychological reality of the state of mind *accepting a system of norms*. So far, though, I have said little about what a "system of norms" is supposed to be. Many questions are left. How can we talk about systems of norms and their properties? What is it to express one's acceptance of a system of norms, and what is it for a system of norms to permit or require something? What can be said about the structure of systems of norms? What it is for one norm to override another, or outweigh it? Then too, how can we cope with problems of information? In virtually any context, there are things the subject does not know and things the observer does not know. How does the analysis handle this ignorance?

Finally, in one crucial respect at least, the analysis as it stands is simply inadequate. It says what it is directly to call something rational, but not what it is to say more complex things about rationality—to say, for instance, that Cleopatra often does irrational things. What does the term 'rational' mean in such embedded contexts?

Issues like these could fill a highly technical book. In this chapter, I try to keep technicalities to a minimum, and so what I say must be sketchy. I do, however, try to say enough to make it clear how the technical account could be filled in, and all but the first section might best be skipped by readers who are not consumed by these doubts.

Expressing a State of Mind

What is it to express one's acceptance of a system of norms? It is not, I have stressed, to *say that* one accepts the system. The contrast is the same here as it is with the expression of straightforwardly factual beliefs. Let Cleopatra say

> Antony's fleet outnumbers the enemy's.

She thereby expresses her belief that Antony's fleet outnumbers the enemy's, but she does not *say that* she has this belief. She is talking about the opposing fleets, not about her beliefs. Likewise, suppose she says

> It makes sense for Antony to give battle.

Here again, she is expressing a state of mind, but she is not *saying that* she is in it. Specifically, she is expressing her acceptance of a system of norms, but not saying that she accepts it. When one says one is in a certain state of mind, then actually being in that state of mind constitutes speaking truly. When one expresses a state of mind, on the other hand, being in that state of mind constitutes not speaking truly but being sincere.

An expressivistic analysis of 'rational' takes this special form: what 'rational' means is explained by saying what it is to call something "rational", and to call something "rational", the analysis says, is to express a state of mind. We might call this state of mind the "judgment" that the thing is rational. The analysis, then, consists of two parts: an account of what it is to *judge* that such-and-such is rational, and an account of what it is in general to *express* a state of mind. Just as a straightforwardly factual assertion expresses a straightforwardly factual belief, so an assertion that such-and-such is rational expresses a normative judgment. To judge something rational is to accept a system of norms that on balance permits it.

That words express judgments will, of course, be accepted by almost anyone. The controversial elements of the norm-expressivistic analysis are these: first, its account of what it is to make a normative judgment, and second, its claim that the meaning of normative terms is to be given by saying what judgments normative statements express—what states of mind they express.

What is it, then, to express a state of mind, and how could expressing a state of mind make for communication? Take first straightforwardly factual beliefs. Suppose Caesar tells Cleopatra, "I was captured by pirates in my youth." Why might he do this? Assume he is simply informing her about his youth; the story, then, will be something like this. He wants her to know about his capture by pirates. He thinks she lacks true belief on the subject, but he believes that she thinks him sincere and that she thinks him an authority on events of his youth. Here to be sincere is to express only beliefs one actually has, and to be an authority on something is to be quite unlikely to be mistaken about it. Caesar thus intends to get Cleopatra to believe that he was captured by pirates in his youth, and to do so in the following manner. He utters words that conventionally purport to express, on the part of any speaker, a belief that he was captured by pirates in his youth. He intends her to come to accept that he has that belief, and to do so in virtue of her recognition of this intention.[1] Since she takes him to be sincere, she has reason to accept, upon hearing his words, that he does believe that he was captured by pirates in his youth. Since she thinks him an authority on his youth, she concludes from his believing it that he indeed was captured by pirates in his youth.

All this is not to say, of course, that speaker and hearer go through these calculations each time anyone tells anybody anything. The point is rather that this is the kind of reasoning that would give sense to what speakers and hearers do. It is the rationale that would guide them if, by common knowledge, they were carefully and cogently checking whether all they were doing made sense. Ordinarily, as we converse we have no need to spell out our rationales even to ourselves, but if we did, and were it common knowledge we were doing so, our rationales would go like this.

Can a similar rationale, then, be given for calling something rational or irrational, for saying what it makes sense to do, to think, or to feel? Suppose Caesar tells Cleopatra, "It makes best sense to divide the command of your army." He is thereby expressing a state of mind, his judgment that it makes best sense for Cleopatra to divide the command of her army. For him to make this judgment is for him to accept a system of norms that all told, as applied to Cleopatra's circumstances, tells her to divide the command of her army. In what, then, does his expressing this state of mind consist? As with straightforward belief, it consists in uttering words conventionally intended to get her to think that he is in this state of mind, by means of her recognition of this

---

1. This is drawn roughly from Grice (1957), with a revision from Grice (1969, 171).

intention. His words, that is to say, are conventionally intended to get her to think he judges that dividing the command of her army makes best sense. If, then, she takes him to be sincere—if she thinks he genuinely holds the judgment his words express—she thereupon comes to believe that he is in this state of mind: that he does accept that it makes best sense to divide the command of her army. She believes, that is to say, that he accepts norms which, as applied to her situation as he thinks it to be, say to divide the command of her army.

So far, the parallel with straightforward communication of belief is exact—but can it be extended? Once Cleopatra comes to think that Caesar accepts norms which, applied to her circumstances as he thinks them to be, say to divide the command of her army, will that give her reason to divide the command?

In at least one kind of case, it will. Suppose Cleopatra thinks that Caesar accepts the basic norms that she accepts—say, that the over-riding goal in organizing an army is to minimize the chance of a coup. Suppose also that she takes him to be an excellent judge of what will minimize the chance of a coup. She may then think he knows how to apply this norm to her circumstances better than she does herself. She can therefore take his normative judgment as proxy for her own. Hence, just as she could regard him as a factual authority if he said "Dividing the command of your army will reduce the chance of a coup," so she can regard him as a normative authority when he says "It makes best sense to divide the command of your army".

Authority of this kind I shall be calling "contextual"; it arises from a context in which basic norms are shared. Is all normative authority likewise contextual? That difficult question is taken up in later chapters.

Systems of Norms

The norm-expressivistic analysis speaks of a "system of norms", and not simply of norms. A person's normative judgments all told on a given matter will typically depend on his acceptance of more than one norm, and the norms he accepts may weigh in opposing directions. In the Milgram obedience experiments, we as observers accept the norms of cooperativeness and good faith on which the subjects act, but we think the subjects irrational. For although we accept these norms, we think them outweighed or overridden by norms against the infliction of suffering. Our normative judgments thus depend not on a single norm, but on a plurality of norms that we accept as having some force, and on the ways we take some of these norms to outweigh or override others.

The system of norms we accept is a matter both of the norms we accept as having some force and of the ways we cope with normative conflicts. How can all this be represented? What is it for one norm to override another, or for one set of norms to outweigh another in a given circumstance? We might respond by trying to develop careful definitions of such terms as 'norm', 'weight', 'priority', and the like, or by developing a system of axioms that defines these terms implicitly. My purposes, though, will be served by a simpler course: describe the end result of all these weights and priorities of individual norms, and so consider a system of norms as a system of permissions and requirements, applicable to a wide range of actual and hypothetical circumstances.

What matters about a system of norms is what it requires and what it permits in various conceivable circumstances.[2] We can characterize any system *N* of norms by a family of basic predicates '*N*-forbidden', '*N*-optional', and '*N*-required'. Here '*N*-forbidden' simply means "forbidden by system of norms *N*", and likewise for its siblings. Other predicates can be constructed from these basic ones; in particular '*N*-permitted' will mean "either *N*-optional or *N*-required".

These predicates are descriptive rather than normative: whether a thing, say, is *N*-permitted will be a matter of fact. It might be *N*-permitted without being rational, for the system *N* might have little to recommend it. People who agree on the facts will agree on what is *N*-permitted and what is not, even if they disagree normatively—even if, for instance, one accepts *N* and the other does not.

A system of norms will apply to alternatives of some kind: a system of norms for action, for instance, will apply to alternative courses of action, and a system of norms for anger, say, will apply to alternative degrees of anger one might have at someone for doing something. Now when a system *N* of norms applies in a definite way to an alternative, that results in the alternative's having exactly one of the three

---

2. We might want to think instead of a gradation from highest ranked to lowest ranked. That, however, would be less a system of norms than a system of value. Presumably many of the things we can say about normative judgments—judgments of what it makes sense to do, think, and feel and what it doesn't—we could say also about judgments of value. In this study, though, I avoid scales from best to worst, and stick with normative judgments proper.

basic properties, being N-forbidden, N-optional, or N-required. We can call a system *complete* if these predicates trichotomize the possibilities: if on every occasion, actual or hypothetical, each alternative is either N-forbidden, N-optional, or N-required. (So long as N is consistent, nothing will be more than one of these things.)[3]

Ordinarily, a person will accept only a system of norms that is *incomplete*. He may be undecided whether to accept or reject certain norms, or he may be unsettled on the relative weights of the various norms he accepts—so that when those norms conflict, he is unsettled as to which one prevails. These kinds of normative uncertainty are different from factual uncertainty: even an observer who knew all the facts of a case might still be ambivalent in his normative judgments. Ordinarily, normative uncertainty is combined with some degree of factual uncertainty, but factual certainty, even if achieved, might not resolve all normative uncertainty.

A person who accepts only an incomplete system of norms is, in effect, undecided among complete systems of norms that are compatible with it. He is undecided on how to extend or sharpen his incomplete system of norms to make it complete. We might, then, represent an incomplete system of norms by the ways it could be sharpened without change of mind. Speak, then, of the various possible *completions* of the incomplete system of norms an observer accepts. A *completion* of an incomplete system N of norms will be a complete system of norms that preserves everything which N definitely settles. With this terminology, we can say things like this: let N be an incomplete system of norms and let X be an act or attitude. Then X is N-permitted if and only if for every completion N^* of N, X is N^*-permitted. A like relation will hold for any other term in the family: for 'N-forbidden', 'N-required', and the like.

A system of norms will apply to a wide variety of circumstances, actual and hypothetical. In each fully specific set of circumstances, there will be a set of alternatives open to the subject. In each specific circumstance, a complete system of norms trichotomizes the alterna-

3. These classifications might be generated from the dichotomy of permitted and forbidden. An alternative is *required* if it is permitted and all its alternatives are forbidden. It is *optional* if it is permitted and at least one of its alternatives is permitted. That will place some new structural constraints on the system, for instance that an alternative cannot be optional if all its alternatives are forbidden. We might add a requirement that on each occasion at least one alternative is permitted. That might be controversial; see van Fraassen (1973) and Marcus (1980).

tives: each is forbidden, optional, or required. An incomplete system of norms is characterized by the set of its completions—the set of complete systems of norms governing its subject matter with which it is compatible. Much more might be said about the structure of systems of norms, but this will be enough for my purposes.

Ignorance

No one is omniscient; we act, believe, feel, and judge without all relevant information—at least some of the time, and perhaps always. Consider an *observer* who judges what it makes sense for a *subject* to do; observer and subject may be the same person or different people. Both the observer's and the subject's information may be limited. A satisfactory analysis must handle both kinds of limitations.

Take first a subject whose actions are being judged. His information may be limited, and rationality will involve coping well with this limited information. In Chapter 1, I distinguished what it makes sense *objectively* to do and what it makes sense *subjectively* to do—what it makes sense to do in light of all the facts, and what it makes sense to do in light of information available to the agent at the time. The *rational* course of action is what it makes sense to do subjectively, in light of one's limited information. What it makes sense to do objectively, in light of all the facts, I called *advisable*. Because subjects may lack information, we needed to distinguish rationality from advisability.

The analysis copes with this distinction straightforwardly enough. To think it made sense for Cleopatra to flee, I have said, is to accept a system of norms that permits flight in Cleopatra's exact circumstances. Now we can distinguish her objective circumstances from her subjective circumstances. Her objective circumstances consist of all the facts that bear on what she does, whether or not she has any way of knowing them. Her subjective circumstances consist of what she knows, what she has reason to believe, and the degrees of plausibility she should ascribe to various eventualities given her information. Now a system of norms might apply either to a person's objective circumstances or to his subjective circumstances—or as I shall say, "objectively" or "subjectively". To think an act *rational* is to accept a system of subjectively applicable norms that permit the act in question when applied to the subject's exact subjective circumstances. The term 'rational' is permissive rather than obliging, and the corresponding permissive predicate in the 'advisable' family is 'not inadvisable'. Accordingly, to think an act *not inadvisable* is to accept a system of objectively applicable norms that permit the act when applied to the subject's objective circumstances. To think an act *advisable* is also to accept a system of objectively applicable norms, but in this case a system that, as applied to the subject's objective circumstances, requires the act. The significant difference here is between "rational" and "not inadvisable"—the difference between applying norms in a way that is not at all limited by the information available to the subject, and applying those norms in the only way the subject himself could: in light of the information available to him.

Suppose N is a set of norms that, as applied to driving, puts slight weight on speed and great weight on getting there without accident. N will have objective and subjective variants. Consider Lepidus approaching a blind intersection in his chariot, and suppose that unbeknownst to him, no cross-traffic is coming. Then driving through without slowing down to check for cross-traffic is N-required objectively, but N-forbidden subjectively. For, in fact, speeding through would save time without causing an accident, and so it is objectively N-required. In light of what Lepidus knows, on the other hand, speeding through without stopping to look runs a substantial risk of an accident for a small savings in time, and so it is subjectively N-forbidden. Hence a knowledgeable observer who accepts both variants of N will consider driving through without looking to be advisable but irrational. As an advisor with a clear view of the crossroad, he would wave the driver through. With no well-placed advisor in the offing, our observer would reject driving on through as a way of coping with the driver's limited information.

So much for limited subject and omniscient observer. Turn now to the harder problem: limitations on the observer's information. An observer will often not think he knows all the facts that bear on whether a given act is rational or advisable. Take a courtier observing Cleopatra. To make judgments of advisability, he needs to know about her objective circumstances, and to make judgments about rationality, he needs to know about her subjective circumstances—what she has reason to think she knows, and the probabilities she has reason to ascribe to various eventualities on which she is uncertain. Even if he accepts a complete system of general norms, he might still have no idea how it applies to the case, because he knows he lacks some of the facts.

As a second approximation to an analysis, we might treat limitations on observers' knowledge as follows: An observer, we assume, accepts at least an incomplete system of general norms; call that system N. He then thinks an alternative rational if and only if he thinks it N-permitted—that is to say, rational according to N. For any particular system N of norms, recall, whether an alternative is N-permitted is a matter of fact, and so a belief that the alternative is N-permitted is a factual belief. Thinking X rational, then, is a combination of a normative state and a state of factual belief. It is accepting a system N of norms such that one believes the subject to be in circumstances for which N permits X.

Suppose, for example, the system of norms Octavia accepts consists solely of one norm, "Maximize your expected length of life." Lepidus is again approaching a blind intersection. Octavia then thinks driving through without looking to be irrational if and only if she thinks that doing so, given what Lepidus knows, fails to maximize his expected length of life.

The normative belief is only partly factual. To think that driving through without looking fails to maximize length of life is not in itself to think that driving through without looking is irrational. We can see this by considering another observer, Claudia, who accepts an alternative sparse system of norms. Let system M consist of the single norm "Always maximize immediate excitement," and let Claudia accept system M. Then Claudia, if she knows the facts, will accept the descriptive statement "Given what Lepidus knows, driving through without looking fails to maximize expected length of life." She will reject, however, the claim that driving through without looking is irrational. For given the general norms she accepts, she would accept this normative conclusion only if she thought that driving on through without looking failed to maximize immediate excitement—a strange thing to think.

An observer, of course, will often fail to have an opinion on a given normative question. He may fail to have an opinion even when he himself is the subject. The observer may be agnostic for either of two reasons or for a combination of them. First, he may think himself ignorant of relevant facts. Second, he may accept only an incomplete system of norms, and so be undecided about aspects of his normative system that bear on the situation he is considering.

That completes the second approximation of what it is for a person to think an alternative rational or irrational, advisable or inadvisable.

The observer thinks an alternative rational if he accepts some system of norms, complete or incomplete, and thinks the subject to be in circumstances for which that system permits that alternative.

Three Remaining Problems

The second approximation is still an approximation; it fails with at least three kinds of problems. One is the problem of embedding: The analysis applies to simple contexts, in which it is simply asserted or denied that such-and-such is rational. It says nothing about more complex normative assertions. A second problem concerns communication: the analysis leaves it mysterious how a normative opinion can be communicated from speaker to hearer. The third concerns normative naivete. The analysis requires that all one's normative opinions be coherently grounded on general normative principles that one accepts. What are we to say of the naif who accepts normative conclusions without accepting a full set of grounds for them?

Handling these problems will require a substantial transformation of the analysis, but a single transformation solves them all. Here are the problems, starting with embedding.

Suppose we have an adequate account of the state of mind expressed by such simple statements as "It makes sense for Antony to give battle." What are we to say of more complex contexts, like "Whenever Antony does anything it doesn't make sense to do, he clings to his purpose stubbornly." Sentences of indefinite complexity can be built recursively from simpler elements, and these get their meanings from the meanings of their elements, in systematic ways. For sentences that express truths or falsehoods, we have a rich legacy of accounts that tell us how this happens: Tarski and his successors tell us how the truth conditions of a sentence depend on the truth conditions of its components. Can we do anything of the sort with an expressivistic theory? A normative sentence, the expressivist says, expresses a state of mind; its meaning is explained not by giving its truth conditions but by telling what state of mind it expresses. When a normative term appears in a complex context, can we still say what state of mind is being expressed? Can we give a systematic account of how the state of mind a complex normative sentence expresses depends on the states of mind that would be expressed by its components alone?[4]

4. Geach (1958, p. 54) makes this criticism in a brief footnote. The point is developed by Searle (1962; 1969, pp. 136–141) and by Geach (1965), who attributes the point to Frege.

Take next the problem of communication. When a person calls something rational, as the proposal now stands, he expresses his acceptance of a system of norms, possibly incomplete, that he thinks permits that thing. The speaker, though, need not evince which specific system of norms he accepts. When Cleopatra says "It made sense for Antony to give battle," we the audience do not know whether she puts safety first and thinks giving battle the safest course, or thinks giving battle dangerous but puts honor first—or what. She herself accepts a specific system of norms, however incomplete, and draws normative conclusions jointly from the system and her factual beliefs. What she expresses, though, is a property of the combination. She expresses her acceptance of a system N of norms and a set B of factual beliefs with this joint property: that B includes the belief that N, as applied to Antony's circumstances, permits giving battle. If she is sincere, the analysis says, she has some specific combination of factual beliefs and normative commitments that has this property. We listeners, though, learn much less; we learn only the joint property. What, then, do we understand from Cleopatra's normative assertion? What do we entertain when we understand what she has said? A joint property of beliefs and norms? What is it to entertain that?

That leads to a further problem, which we might call the problem of *normative naivete*. Suppose we not only entertain but accept what Cleopatra says, and do so on her authority. What state of mind constitutes this acceptance? Even if we listeners are fully prepared to believe what she says—to accept it, once she has said it—we cannot then come to share the specific state of mind she is in. No matter how willing to believe her we may be, no matter how willing to share her state of mind whatever it is, we cannot do so; we lack the necessary information. What could it be, then, to accept a normative conclusion—to accept, in effect, a property of a combined normative system and set of beliefs—and yet to fail to accept any specific normative system that, together with our beliefs, has that property? People do sometimes seem to be in such a state; the analysis should explain its nature.

The problem can extend to the speaker as well: Cleopatra might have little idea what system of norms properly applies to Antony's situation; she might, say, simply follow her advisors' lead in politics, even when they do not explain their grounds to her. She might, then, be quite convinced that it made sense for Antony to give battle, and assert that it did, even though she was unsure what general normative principles applied. In that case, there is no general system of norms that she accepts. She expresses a normative opinion without expressing her acceptance of any particular system of norms. How can an expressivistic analysis allow for this?

Indeed for most speakers the state the analysis depicts seems too complex. Normative beliefs seem plain enough, and the people who have them may be incapable of dealing with the logical constructions I have been presenting—or at least of dealing with them at a speed that would sustain conversation. What, then, can we say is going on?

Content: The Formalism

In its second approximation, the analysis ran into three problems: embedding, communication, and normative naivete. Repair will proceed in two stages. In this section I develop a formal representation of the "normative content" expressed by normative statements. Roughly the normative content of a statement is the set of fully opinionated states one could be in and still accept the statement. Here I say almost nothing about what the representation might have to do with meaning, with what the person who accepts the statement has in mind. In the next section I go on to the second stage: saying how the representation helps in a theory of meaning. What is the psychological reality behind meaning? In crucial part, it is the logical relations people attribute to statements. People take some things to follow from others; they take some things to be consistent with each other and some things not. The formal representation provides a way of talking about logical relations among normative statements.

Normative statements are of many kinds. In the first place there are the general normative principles that combine to form systems of norms—such principles as "Whenever the chance arises, give battle" or "Never give battle unless cornered." In the second place, there are normative conclusions for particular situations. "It makes sense for Antony to give battle." This could follow from a set of general normative principles combined with a description of the circumstances. Finally, there are the various complex constructions that include normative terms. "Unless Antony finds his fleet outnumbered, it will make sense for him to give battle." Our problem is to give a uniform representation to normative statements of all these different kinds.

The idea will be to construct the set of fully opinionated ways a person could accept a normative statement—putting off, for the moment, all question of what this might have to do with meaning, with what people have in mind. Begin as before with complete systems of norms. A system of norms, recall, is the end result of the ways the various general normative principles a person accepts combine, weigh against each other, and override one another. If it is complete, then for every conceivable fully described occasion governed by norms, the system classifies each alternative as required, optional, or forbidden.

The next notion we require is that of a completely opinionated credal-normative state. Imagine a goddess Hera who is entirely coherent and completely opinionated both normatively and factually. She suffers no factual uncertainty; there is a completely determinate way w she thinks the world to be.[5] She likewise lacks all normative uncertainty; there is a complete system n of general norms that she accepts. She is consistent in her factual and normative beliefs, and accepts everything descriptive and normative that follows from the things she accepts. Together, w and n constitute a completely opinionated credal-normative state, a *factual-normative world* $\langle w, n \rangle$.[6]

Together, w and n entail a normative judgment for every occasion. They entail, for instance, whether or not it is rational for Antony to give battle. Hera is not at all uncertain what Antony's subjective circumstances are, and she is not at all undecided what norms to apply or how to weigh them against each other. She applies the norms she accepts to Antony's subjective circumstances as she thinks them to be, and comes to one of three definite conclusions: that for Antony, giving battle is rationally required, that it is rationally optional, or that it is irrational. Any particular normative judgment *holds* or not, as a matter of logic, *in* the factual-normative world $\langle w, n \rangle$.

Now return to Cleopatra, who is no goddess. She is uncertain both factually and normatively; she thinks that giving battle is rational, but she is uncertain of her grounds. She accepts, we might say, the piece of "normative content" that it is rational for Antony to give battle, but she accepts no single version of what Antony's subjective circumstances are, nor any one system of general norms from which the normative content she accepts follows. How can we represent what she accepts?

---

5. This characterization of possible worlds is from Stalnaker (1976). For an attack on characterizations like this, see Lewis (1986, chap. 3).

6. Those who distrust possible worlds might prefer to keep strictly to talk of completely opinionated credal-normative states of mind. I myself see nothing worse in positing completely determinate ways the world might be than in positing possible states of opinion a person might be in, and so I shall use the two ways of talking interchangeably.

The piece of normative content she accepts is in effect a disjunction of all the complete factual-plus-normative opinions that might have yielded it. Formally, we might speak in terms of sets: the piece of normative content she accepts—that it is rational for Antony to give battle—can be represented by the set of maximally opinionated ways in which she might accept it. Where the statement is S, call this set O_S. S can be represented, that is to say, by the set of all factual-normative worlds $\langle w, n \rangle$ for which it holds. This, recall, is the set of all pairs $\langle w, n \rangle$, where w is a possible world and n is a complete system of norms, with this joint property: that system n, as applied to Antony's subjective circumstances in world w, permits giving battle.

We now have a formal representation of the piece of normative content Cleopatra accepts. We have not said how this formal representation explains the meaning of what she says. As a first try, we might say this: When she thinks S—say, that it makes sense for Antony to give battle—she rules out every possibility outside the set O_S. She rules out every pair of a way things might be and a normative system, that together have the following property: that the normative system, applied to that way things might be, says not to give battle.

Let me postpone meaning, though, and consider embedding again. Formally, our new representation solves not only the problem of communication but the problem of embedding as well. No matter how complex a normative statement is, we can still represent its content by a set of factual-normative worlds—by the set of all factual-normative worlds for which the statement holds. To do this, we have to say when, in general, a normative statement holds for a given factual-normative world. Let S be a statement with normative terms in it, and let $\langle w, n \rangle$ be a factual-normative world. What is it for S to hold in $\langle w, n \rangle$?

Earlier I spoke of the descriptive predicate that, for a given system of norms N, *N-corresponds* to a normative predicate. Take the normative predicate 'rational', for instance; its N-corresponding descriptive predicate is 'rational according to N', or 'N-permitted'. Now to settle whether normative statement S holds in factual-normative world $\langle w, n \rangle$, we do the following. Replace each normative predicate in S with its n-corresponding descriptive predicate. That yields a purely descriptive statement S_n. Then normative statement S holds in $\langle w, n \rangle$ if and only if S_n holds in w.

Take, for example, Cleopatra's claim,

> Whenever Antony does anything irrational, he sticks to his purpose stubbornly.

It holds in a factual-normative world $\langle w, n \rangle$ if and only if

> Whenever Antony does anything forbidden by n, he
> clings to his purposes stubbornly

holds in w.

This new representation of normative content yields answers to all three problems that beset the second approximation. Embedded contexts now pose no special problem: so long as we have an account of what it is for a descriptive statement to hold in a possible world w— for a maximally specific way the world might be—we can now say what it is for any normative statement to hold for a factual-normative world $\langle w, n \rangle$. Having said that, we need only add the dictum "The content of a normative statement is the set of factual-normative worlds for which the statement holds." This lets us represent what is communicated by a normative statement—even when the speaker expresses acceptance of no one general system of norms. What is communicated is the normative content of the statement he makes. It is a set of factual-normative worlds. The representation also lets us say what the naif accepts—the naif who accepts a normative statement but cannot derive it from any facts and general normative principles that he accepts. He accepts the normative content of the statement.

The analysis has been rebuilt partway: we now have a unified formal solution to the problem of embedding, the problem of communication, and the problem of normative naivete. We can say what set of factual-normative worlds represents any normative statement. We still need to connect this set to the states of mind people are in when they understand normative statements and when they accept them.

Ruling Things Out

Talk of a set of factual-normative worlds seems psychologically far-fetched. How could that be what anyone has in mind when he thinks normatively? As a first step toward something more plausible, we could speak again of what is ruled out by a normative claim. Where we represent a statement S by its set O_S of factual-normative worlds, S rules out every possibility outside O_S. It rules out various factual-normative worlds, but that is not the most important thing. It also rules out various ordinary kinds of possibilities—possibilities that are not whole determinate worlds, but leave many things unsettled.

Let us work with an example: Cleopatra entertains the disjunction

> *A:* Antony finds himself outnumbered or it makes
> sense for him to give battle.

This rules out many combinations of descriptions and normative principles. It precludes, for example, this combination:

> *P:* Antony finds he slightly outnumbers the enemy.
> *N:* Never give battle unless you find you vastly outnumber the enemy.

When Cleopatra entertains *S*, we might say, she entertains the following state of mind: ruling out every combination of descriptions with normative principles that is inconsistent with what she is saying. The pair *P* and *N* is one of the combinations she rules out.

How does the formal representation O_S bear on this? What it does is to give us a systematic way of talking about consistency, and about other logical relations as well. It therefore lets us talk about what rules out what: normative statements rule each other out if their representations have no factual-normative world in common.[7]

With statement *S*, I have been saying, Cleopatra rules out the combination of *P* with *N*. There is no pair $\langle w, n \rangle$, consisting of a completely determinate way w that *P* might hold and a completion n of *N*, such that the pair $\langle w, n \rangle$ is in O_S. We can see this, if you like, by working tediously through what the representations are. (Otherwise skip this paragraph and the next.) *S* is that Antony finds himself outnumbered or it makes sense for him to give battle. Its representation O_S consists of every world in which Antony finds himself outnumbered, plus every world whose norms, as applied to its facts, allow giving battle. It thus rules out every world in which Antony does not find himself outnumbered, but whose norms even so, as applied to its facts, say not to give battle.

That rules out all worlds in which both *N* and *P* obtain. For *N* says never to give battle unless you find you vastly outnumber the enemy. O_N thus rules out every world in which one does not find one vastly outnumbers the enemy, but whose norms, as applied to its facts, permit giving battle. O_P includes only worlds in which one does not

---

7. Possible-world semantics is a standard way of representing logical structures, though whether it is the best way is a matter of controversy. I use factual-normative worlds as a way of latching on to standard devices that use factual possible worlds. See, for example, Carnap (1947).

find one vastly outnumbers the enemy. Thus for any world in both O_N and O_P, the norms of that world applied to its facts say not to give battle. O_N and O_P together, then, consist only of worlds in which (1) P obtains—one finds one slightly outnumbers the enemy—and (2) the norms of the world as applied to its facts say not to give battle. Call these the NP worlds. In Antony's case, those worlds are all ruled out by O_S. For what O_S does, we saw, is to rule out every world in which Antony does not find himself outnumbered, but whose norms applied to its facts say not to give battle. That includes all NP worlds, and so S rules out the combination of N and P.

In short, then, as a first way of saying what a normative statement means, we can try this: its meaning is what it rules out. That goes for simple normative statements, and also for complex statements with normative components—statements like "Unless Octavian has done something irrational, it makes no sense for Antony to attack." A normative statement rules out various combinations of factual possibilities with normative principles, and its meaning, we now say, lies in the set of combinations it rules out. The formal representation lets us talk systematically about what rules out what. It is a way of capturing the logical relations that hold among normative statements, and those include mutual inconsistency.

The norm-expressivistic analysis as revised now runs as follows. As before, when a speaker makes a normative statement, he expresses a state of mind. Now, though, the state of mind he expresses consists in his ruling out various combinations of normative systems with factual possibilities. Which combinations those are is given canonically by the formal representation of the last section.

Normative States of Mind

Meaning lies in what is ruled out. There is some plausibility in saying this, and so it is not utterly wild to claim that when a person says something normative, he is ruling out various combinations of fact with norm. Still, what is all this supposed to mean? Does it give what the person has in mind when he thinks some normative thought? He could not have in mind consciously everything he rules out. Indeed the set of things he rules out is infinite, and so how could they all be in his finite mind at all? His logical powers are limited, and so with many things, even if he thought about whether he was ruling them out, he could not say.

These are versions of wider questions of what logic has to do with meaning, and what meaning has to do with things that go on in the mind. Here I venture a few words on normative meaning in particular, and what it has to do with psychic reality. I draw on extant theories of meaning that give no special heed to norms.

As we experience them, beliefs simply are what they are; they have a gestalt-like quality we can say little about. What we can hope is to give a logical-philosophical account of their structure. That is not to display their intrinsic psychological nature; it is to see how they fit into a system.

What does our formal representation, then, have to do with meaning? It tells us nothing direct: psychologically, normative beliefs are much like any other beliefs. The fact-norm distinction is not between two quite disparate kinds of psychological states but between the kinds of content that can reasonably be ascribed to them.

To display the objects of belief as a system, we need to show two main things: the inferential relations among them and their connection to the world. Inferential relations are a matter of logic. For normative statements, they come with the formal representation: the representation tells us systematically what follows from what. As for a connection to the world, for straightforwardly factual propositions, it runs through sense experience. We need some parallel for normative statements.

Normative content too connects to the world through sense experience, but not only through sense experience. It connects as well by normative governance. That is the theory I shall be proposing. Normative governance is the special kind of motivation that stems from making a normative judgment that applies to oneself right now. Cleopatra may have thought it made sense for Antony to give battle, but that judgment could govern no action of hers. If Antony, though, thought it made sense to give battle at that very moment, his opinion could very well govern his actions. Whereas purely descriptive propositions are tied to the world through sense experience alone, pieces of normative content are tied to the world not only through sense experience but also through normative governance of actions.[8]

8. Normative judgments may govern action indirectly too, by governing planning. If Antony thinks that later it will make sense to give battle, or that it will later make sense to do so if certain eventualities arise, he will tend to plan accordingly. That makes for an additional tie of normative language to the world. The independent motivational role of planning is explored by Bratman (1983; 1984; 1987, chap. 5).

Just as few descriptive propositions describe present sense experience, so few pieces of normative content directly govern present action. Propositions and normative content are tied to the world through a web of inference. It is here that the formal representation I have given plays its part. Given the representation, we can treat entailment in the usual way: content P entails content Q if and only if Q holds in all the factual-normative worlds in which P holds. When we apply our formalism to interpret a person's normative thoughts, the psychic facts our formalism must match are the inferences the person takes as immediate and unproblematical. These inferences must be interpretable as recognitions of entailment: where the person confidently infers statement Q from statement P, we must represent Q as being entailed by P and the other content we interpret him as accepting. That is a prime constraint on our attribution of content.[9]

Our problem is thus one of radical interpretation of a person's thoughts. We match normative content to his thoughts under at least two constraints. First, the inferences he makes with confidence are to be explained by relations of entailment among the pieces of normative content we attribute to him. Second, his propensities toward normative governance are to match the content we attribute to his normative judgments. When the normative judgments we interpret a person as making at a time apply to that person himself at that very time, he must be normatively motivated. Conversely, when he is normatively motivated, we must attribute to him a normative judgment that applies to himself at that time. It is these constraints on interpretation that turn the formal representation I have given into an account of the meaning of normative language.

These constraints do not do all the work by themselves; other strong desiderata guide interpretation. The normative beliefs one attributes should be intelligible: they should be generated from considerations familiar in our own lore, combined in ways that have familiar parallels. To accommodate this desideratum, the translator will have to move back to a richer conception of normative systems, a conception that makes it explicit what the considerations are that enter into normative judgment and how they weigh against each other or override one another.[10] The more bizarre normative thought comes out on an inter-

9. The extensive philosophical literature on radical interpretation stems from Quine (1960, 26–79). See especially Davidson (1984, essays 1, 2, 9–11, 13).

10. The need for this line of thought or something like it was pressed on me by Richard Burian. Davidson (1986) discusses joint constraints on the interpretation of beliefs and desires.

pretation, the more our appraisal of the interpretive scheme must suffer. Some bizarreness, though, must surely be allowed; the normative thought of headhunters must not be made out to match that of Quakers. Desiderata of intelligibility work within the rough constraints I have been depicting: that inferences seem as obvious really do follow from things accepted, and normative motivation stems from normative beliefs. The job of our formal representation of normative content is to allow us to formulate these constraints.

What, then, is a person doing when he voices a complicated normative thought? He is doing nothing that could be put in a better mouthful, and for the rest of the book I shall keep reverting to my old, sloppy ways: I shall still say the speaker expresses his acceptance of a system of norms. Cryptically but accurately, I could say instead that he expresses a set of factual-normative worlds. Better, I could say he expresses his ruling out certain combinations of factual possibilities with norms. Best, though, I can say this: he expresses a thought that gets its meaning from its logical ties to other statements, and through them not only to sense experience, but also to normative governance. The formalism represents these logical ties.

II · PSYCHE IN NATURE

6 · Natural Representation

Part II of this book copes with two pieces of neglected business. The first is meanings; the second is emotions. Both emotions and meaningful thoughts are topics in psychology, and so both fit under one rubric: how to conceive aspects of the human psyche as parts of nature. In both discussions, nature is Darwinian. Beyond that, do not look for great thematic connections. First, then, to meaning, and start with a quick review.

Normative judgments are not pure judgments of fact. If Antony thinks it makes most sense for Cleopatra to flee, he does not attribute a special property to her fleeing—the property of being the thing it makes most sense for her to do. He does something else: roughly, he accepts a system of norms that tells her to flee. More precisely, he accepts a piece of normative content. His judgment gets its content through inferential ties: through the combinations of norm and fact it rules out, and through its ties both to experience and to normative governance. In any case, when Antony makes a normative judgment, he does not simply judge a fact to obtain, or accept a proposition, or ascribe a property.

So I have been claiming, but a bald fact-norm distinction is problematical. We can speak of facts and properties, to be sure, and such talk makes good loose sense, but are these notions sharp enough to do systematic work? On the account as I am now giving it, after all, normative terms act much like other terms. What are we denying if we claim that normative judgments are not strictly factual?

Perhaps such a claim betrays the grip of a myth, the myth of the bare unadorned fact—the myth that facts are presented to us by experience, or at least tied straightforwardly to the experiences that would verify them. Really, though, experience is never independent of the things we already accept, and there is no specifiable tie of belief to experience that renders beliefs factual, alone and always. Beliefs and norms color experience, experience presses on our beliefs and norms without forcing them—and so, in the end, nothing in their tie to experience sharply marks off norms from beliefs.[1]

Or perhaps the myth is of a mind that encompasses the outside world by a kind of magic. There are facts in the world, and the mind reaches out to grasp them or to entertain the possibilities. It makes sense, then, to ask what kinds of facts are out there in the world for the grasping, however difficult the question is to answer. So goes the myth, but as philosophers we should not let talk of minds and their contents bewitch us. Such talk plays a central part in our lives, but there is no organ with the magical powers we seem to ascribe to minds. There is only nature and human life within nature. If we are to take facts seriously, along with minds that grasp the facts, all this talk will need to be vindicated. We cannot rest content with magic, and the simple picture of facts and minds that grasp them is magical. Naked claims about what is factual and what is not take this magical picture as background.

It might be reasonable to ignore these challenges for now, if we find that norm-expressivism explains enough. We might find that norm-expressivism captures a pattern in our thought and language, whether or not we can yet integrate it into a broader philosophy of thought and language. In this chapter, though, I take up the broader issues. I have no quarrel with a broadly pragmatistic account of how we must start out in our most comprehensive thinking. We ride Neurath's boat, in normative matters and in everything else.[2] I claim, though, that in our thinking about our own nature and our place in the world, talk of "representation" has a job. We can ask what in the world, if anything, our judgments represent. There is a sense in which some thoughts are cor-

1. Broad movements in recent theories of meaning and knowledge take up these themes. Logical positivists tried to single out a class of genuinely empirical statements, tied to the facts of experience in a special way. Precise attempts to delineate this class of factual statements collapsed (see Ayer 1946, 11–13; Church 1949, 53). In the wake of gestalt psychology and Wittgenstein (1953, part 2), moreover, the idea of a pure experience conveying facts was attacked by such writers as Hanson (1958) and Kuhn (1962). That left the notion of fact in some disrepute, and a sharp fact-norm or fact-value distinction falls with it. Among recent attacks on a fact-value distinction are McDowell (1978) and Putnam (1981, chap. 6). See also Rorty (1982, chap. 11).

2. "We are like sailors who have to rebuild their ship in the open sea, without being able to take it apart in a drydock and build it up from best components" Neurath (1932, 206, my translation). Quine (1960) uses this as his motto.

rect only if they represent features of the world, whereas normative thoughts need not represent features of the world.

Representation

Are there normative facts? Are some judgments normative and others not, and if so, is that because some of them are judgments of normative facts and others of other kinds of facts? That is the position of a normative objectivist. A non-cognitivist agrees that some judgments are distinctly normative, but not, he says, because they are judgments of normative fact. They are not judgments of fact at all, and there are no peculiarly normative facts.

The speculative evolutionary account I sketched may help make sense of this dispute. If the account is on the right track, then our normative capacities can be explained without supposing that there is a special kind of normative fact to which they typically respond.[3]

That contrasts with the upshot of various other accounts of our normative capacities. Ethical intuitionists like Sidgwick and Moore seemed to think of normative judgment as a power to apprehend facts of a special kind, much as the senses involve a power to apprehend the layout of surrounding objects.[4] We might have had the normative capacities we do because they respond to facts of a special, normative kind, just as we have sense organs and capacities to make perceptual judgments because they respond to certain kinds of facts about our surroundings. Instead, I have speculated that we have these capacities because they coordinate our actions in mutually beneficial ways. Other philosophers think that normative facts are natural facts, open to empirical investigation—but natural facts of a particular kind.[5] In my evolutionary speculation there were purported natural facts in abundance, but none singled out as peculiarly normative. Norms attached to whatever facts the dynamics of consensus formation selected, and that could vary from group to group.

We can take this speculation as a hypothesis and see where it leads. That way, perhaps, we can illustrate how biology could settle whether

3. This way of contrasting normative judgments with judgments of other kinds is proposed, more or less, by Harman (1977, 6–7), Blackburn (1981, 164–165, 185–186), Gibbard (1982, 40–43), Blackburn (1984, 182, 247), and Williams (1985, 132–155).
4. Sidgwick (1907, part 1, chaps. 3, 8), Moore (1903, 74–77). A prime attack on the view was Strawson's (1949).
5. Sturgeon (1985b, esp. p. 56) suggests something like this for moral properties, and Railton (1986b) develops an account of good as a natural property.

there are normative facts. If the hypothesis holds good, we do not need normative facts to explain our making the normative judgments we do. Our making them is to be explained by the rewards of coordination. To suppose there are normative facts is gratuitous.

The argument, though, has gone too fast. In the first place, judgments of fact can themselves coordinate. Take two people who manage to move a piano from one room to another. They succeed partly because their internal representations correspond to the facts of their situation. They correctly apprehend the position, shape, and weight of the piano, the positions of various obstacles, and each others' last and next moves. That is what enables them to coordinate. Thus even if we have the normative capacities we do because they coordinate, the coordination might work through judgments of fact.

We need, then, to think further about what sort of story would certify a kind of judgment as factual. In what sense can something represent things the way they are?[6] Consider a stylized case: Marks in a teacher's roll book represent pupils' attendance in class. The teacher makes it so: he deliberately puts the fact of whether a particular place in the roll book is marked in correspondence with the fact of whether a particular pupil is present. The teacher, then, maintains a somewhat arbitrary system of correspondence between attendance and marks in the book. With computerization, the system might be maintained automatically; it would then be a function of the computer to maintain the system of correspondence. The computer is an artifact, and so we may call the marks it makes *artificial representations* of the pupils' attendance. Now the sense in which the computer constitutes a *system of artificial representation* seems to be this: *it is a function of the computer to adjust one feature of the world* (whether certain spaces are marked in the roll book) *to correspond, in a somewhat arbitrary way, to another feature of the world* (which pupils are present on which days). We may call the adjusted feature the *representation*, and the feature to which the representation is supposed to correspond the *subject matter*.

Can we then think of beliefs, perceptual images, and so on as features of the brain that likewise represent features of the world without resembling them? In what sense is the adjustment of a representing feature to a subject matter a "function" of a system of representation?

6. The theory of natural representation that follows is drawn from Gibbard (1982, 40–43). Stampe (1977) proposes explaining representation by appeal to a function; he does not treat biological function as I do. See also Enç (1982), Millikan (1984), and Dretske (1986), who give accounts very much like the one given here.

With artificial representation, function is a matter of designer's intention; a system is designed to adjust representation to correspond to subject matter. This straightforward kind of function we can call *artificial function* or *function by design*. Now Darwin's achievement, as I keep saying, was to explain how nature could mimic design where in fact there was no intentional design. Let us therefore draw on Darwinian theory and speak of natural function, the Darwinian analog of artificial function. Natural function, on Darwinian theory, is to be explained in terms of natural selection. It is a *natural function* of a system to do F in an organism, let us say, if and only if the system has some of the features it has in that organism because of natural selection to do F: because, that is, a genetic propensity toward the system's having those features was selected for in the organism's ancestors because systems that had those features did F.[7]

We may now characterize *natural representation* by analogy with artificial representation. A *system of natural representation* for a feature S of the world is a system one of whose natural functions is to adjust some feature R of the world to correspond to S—again by a scheme of correspondence that is somewhat arbitrary. R can then be called a *natural representation* of *subject matter S.*

Natural representation is more than correspondence. "Correspondence" here is a weak notion: A corresponds to B if A tends to vary systematically in response to B. Representation is correspondence by design, or by the Darwinian surrogate for design.

Ordinary, prosaic beliefs about our surroundings are prime cases of natural representations. Clearly we do have a system that adjusts features of our descriptive beliefs to correspond to features of the world: the system includes our observational capacities and many of our cognitive ones. The correspondence is somewhat arbitrary—this claim is vague, but it will come out true on any reasonable way of making it precise. It seems clear enough what the evolutionary explanation of this capacity must be. A genetic propensity toward having the capacity must have been selected for, among our ancestors, because it adjusted features of their descriptive beliefs to correspond to features of the world, and the propensity contributed to our ancestors' survival in obvious ways. Now, if all this is so, the system that adjusts those beliefs is a system of natural representation, by the definition I have given, and so our prosaic beliefs about our surroundings are natural representations of them.

7. This account owes much to Wright (1973). See Symons (1979, 10–14).

Not all natural representations are beliefs. Take circadian rhythms: they presumably depend on one or more "biological clocks", mechanisms that naturally represent time of day. Think too of homeostatic systems: they may involve natural representations of the states they regulate. The system that regulates body temperature in a mammal, for instance, might well involve a natural representation of its body temperature. The theory of natural representation, then, is not meant to capture something peculiar to belief or judgment. We pick out judgments in other ways: by the role they play in explaining actions, by their ready accessibility to being expressed in language, and by their susceptibility to normative governance. Our question is not which such things are judgments, but which judgments naturally represent and which do not.

Two Questions

Suppose the speculative evolutionary account I have sketched is at least roughly correct. Do our normative judgments, then, naturally represent a special, normative kind of subject matter? We might try arguing as follows. The biological function of the mechanisms underlying our normative capacities is to coordinate. Hence the psychic mechanisms that produce normative judgments are not systems of natural representation, they are coordinating systems. Their biological function is not to put something in the head in correspondence with their subject matter; it is to coordinate what is in one person's head with what is in another's. Therefore the judgments are not natural representations but something else. We might call them "natural conations", for their biological function is to govern our actions, beliefs, and emotions.

Again, though, judgments of fact can coordinate. We still need to ask whether, when normative judgments coordinate, they do so in virtue of being natural representations of some special kind of subject matter. I have explained the biological function of normative judgments without mentioning correspondence. Perhaps, though, when we ascribe biological functions, there is more than one way to put the same set of facts. Perhaps we can still find some feature of the world that our normative capacities are adapted to make our normative judgments match.

Indeed in simple systems we can well imagine states that act both as natural representations and as natural conations. Think of a housefly at rest. It flies off at the slightest sudden movement in its vicinity. That might well be due to single state that both responds to sudden movement and elicits immediate flight. We could describe it as a natural conation to fly away: a mechanism that has the biological function of producing flight when the state is activated. It is also, though, a natural representation of sudden movement in the vicinity: the mechanism that produces it has the biological function of making activation of the state correspond with sudden movement in the vicinity.

What, then, of human normative judgments? Can we describe them as naturally representing a subject matter? Two general kinds of candidates need to be explored—roughly, objective and subjective. Think of an observer who makes normative judgments and a subject whom the judgments concern. We as observers might form judgments, say, about tribal headhunters as subjects. Alternatively, observer and subject may be the same, or at least from the same culture. Now, some facts are substantive: they are facts about the scene observed and judged, facts that have nothing to do with who the observer is. That headhunting involves killing is a substantive fact about what headhunters do, and that headhunting is approved in the headhunter's own community is also a substantive fact. Other facts concern the observer as well: that the observer disapproves of headhunting, say, or that people in the observer's society disapprove. We can divide our search for a subject matter for normative judgments into two parts. First, do normative judgments naturally represent substantive facts alone—substantive facts about the scene observed? Second, if not, do they naturally represent facts that involve the observer as well as the scene observed?

When subject and observer are the same or they are related, the distinction may seem hard to draw. The observer is part of the scene. The question, though, is always this: why does the judgment naturally represent what it does? Is it solely because of what the fact has to do with the subject, regardless of who is observing? Or is it also because of who is observing? If the properties of the observer matter, is that at least partly *because* he is the observer? Suppose I judge something I have done, and the judgment naturally represents, say, my feeling repugnance at the deed. Why, then, my own repugnance?—That is the question. Is it because it is I who did the deed? Or is it because it is I who am making the judgment? In the first case my judgment naturally represents a substantive fact; in the second, an observer fact.

Substantive Facts

Do normative judgments naturally represent some special kind of substantive fact about the situation judged? It seems the answer must be no. On the speculative account I have sketched, normative judgments will depend not only on features of the situation judged, but on discussion in the observer's own community and the consensus that emerges from that discussion. Normative discussion, as I have pictured it, will lead to the consensus it does in virtue of various pressures on the discussants; different pressures on them will lead to different consensus judgments. This is a matter of what the psychic mechanisms that underlie normative judgment are adapted to do. There is no special kind of fact about the situations judged to which these mechanisms are adapted to produce a correspondence.

This argument, though, relies on too narrow a conception of how a mechanism could be adapted to produce a correspondence. Think what happens when we recognize a wheel as a wheel. Human mental powers presumably evolved before there were wheels, and so we are not adapted specifically to recognize wheels. We are adapted, rather, to form useful classifications or take them from our culture, and then match things with those classifications. This is part of the workings of a system that makes what is in the head correspond, in a refined and flexible way, with what is outside it.

Could a culture not, then, tie the judgment that it makes most sense to do such-and-such to a determinate kind of action, just as the judgment that such-and-such is a wheel is tied to a determinate kind of artifact? That would immediately raise the question of what entitles us to identify the judgment as one of what it makes most sense to do; the answer would presumably be its tie to normative governance. Might there be a judgment, then, that was tied in two directions: to a special kind of action—in the same, culturally influenced way as the judgment that something is a wheel is tied to a special kind of artifact—and also to normative governance? If so, would that not be a normative judgment that naturally represents the act's being of that special kind?

I know of nothing to rule this out, and indeed something of the sort seems to happen with "thick" concepts. Take a judgment that I have *committed myself* to doing something. It is closely tied to my circumstances: I judge that I have committed myself to something if, in an appropriate context, I have said I would do it. The judgment is also closely tied to normative governance: if I judge that I have committed myself, then I am motivated, in a special way that is responsive to normative discussion, toward doing it.[8] Like things can be said of concepts we ourselves rightly abhor. In the old American South, whites called black people who did not strongly abase themselves before whites "uppity". The term was tied closely to circumstances; certain kinds of assertive behavior counted as uppity. It was also tied closely with there being reason for certain kinds of feelings and actions: reason to take offense and to act repressively. We might call these *thick judgments*; they are tied closely both to circumstance of a particular kind and to normative governance.

Thick judgments, let me agree, are normative, and they also naturally represent substantive facts of the circumstance judged. The judgment that Caesar had committed himself to obey the Senate naturally represents the fact that he said he would do it. Miss Watson's judgment that Jim is getting uppity naturally represents the fact that he is no longer humbling himself before whites.

Still, there are no substantive *normative* facts that these normative judgments naturally represent. Moreover, even if some normative judgments naturally represent aspects of the world, it is not in virtue of what they naturally represent that these judgments are normative. In these two senses, there are no normative facts: there is no class of facts which makes judgments normative. There is no class of facts such that a judgment is normative if and only if it naturally represents a fact in that class.

Miss Watson thinks that Jim is getting uppity. If this thought of hers naturally represents a substantive fact, it is the fact that he is no longer abasing himself before whites. "Jim is getting uppity" and "Jim is no longer abasing himself before whites", then, naturally represent the same fact. Now this bare fact itself is in no way normative; a person can accept it without making a normative judgment. An outsider can group together the circumstances in which Miss Watson would call a black man 'uppity' without himself being normatively governed to take

8. In general, then, we can say, thick concepts are concepts that, by rules of meaning or something of the kind, both apply to things of a certain kind and provide certain kinds of reasons. Foot (1958, 507–509) discusses the term 'rude'. It is condemnatory, she says, but one cannot consistently admit that an action causes offense by showing lack of respect and deny that the action is rude. One can admit the description and not assent to calling it rude, but only by refusing to use the term at all, rejecting the whole practice in which it is embedded. McDowell (1978) pictures the virtuous man as one who, in effect, conceives his circumstances in terms of such concepts. His "conception of the situation, properly understood, suffices to show us the favorable light in which his action appeared to him". See also Williams (1985, 140–152).

offense or act repressively. His judgment and hers naturally represent the same fact, but her judgment is normative and his is not. It is not a special subject matter, naturally represented, that makes normative judgments normative.

Alternative treatments are possible of this tie to normative governance. Perhaps what is normative about Miss Watson's judgment lies not in its content but in its presuppositions. Unless a black man abases himself before whites, she judges, it makes sense for whites to take offense and to act repressively. That, however, is not really part of her judgment that Jim is getting uppity; it is presupposed by it. On this treatment too, though, the difference between "Jim is getting uppity" and "Jim is no longer abasing himself before whites" is a normative one—this time in the normative presuppositions. There is still no fact this difference represents.[9]

Likewise, someone—a con man, say—could group together the kinds of circumstances in which I judge that a person has committed himself, but not at all be normatively governed to act accordingly when he himself is in those circumstances. His judgment would naturally represent the same factual circumstances as mine, but his judgment would not have the connection to normative governance that makes it normative.

In general, then, the claim is this: where normative judgment naturally represents something, a plainly non-normative judgment could naturally represent the same thing. A judgment could be made by someone who classifies things in the same way but is not normatively governed in the same way. This is not to claim that when a person makes a normative judgment, he himself must be capable of making a plainly non-normative judgment that naturally represents the same state of affairs. If the tie of the classification to normative governance is automatic for him, he will not be able to do so.[10] Neither is it to claim

9. See Blackburn (1984, 149–150) for a treatment of similar terms. What we must not say is that by rules of meaning, 'Jim is getting uppity' is both entailed by the facts of the situation, and entails that it makes sense to resent him and repress him. This last does not follow from the facts of the situation, and so to attribute these meaning rules to people who use the term 'uppity' is, in effect, to accuse them of a fallacy—a fallacy of overdefinition, we might say. We do not need to do this; the treatments I discuss here attribute not semantic confusion but substantively objectionable normative views. This is preferable, since among other things, innocent terms like 'to commit oneself' have a similar logic, and we should allow ourselves to use them without having to accuse ourselves of fallacy. Searle (1964) seems to commit such a fallacy of overdefinition for our term 'promise'; see Hare (1964).

10. Indeed, in this case, observers too may lack any test for settling whether the tie to normative governance is part of the meaning of the judgment itself, or just something inferred without question from the judgment. Again see Blackburn (1984, 149–150).

that an outside observer free of the subject's normative commitments must always be able to form a representationally equivalent, plainly non-normative judgment. Perhaps he can, and perhaps he cannot. All I need to claim is that we can say what it would be for him to make such a judgment. It is, first, for the judgment to correspond to the same situations, actual and possible, while second, for him not to be normatively governed in a certain way on forming the judgment. In this sense, thick judgments do not naturally represent specially normative states of affairs: a thick judgment naturally represents a state of affairs, true enough, but we can understand what it would be for the judgment naturally to represent that same state of affairs and be non-normative.[11]

There is a second sense in which normative judgments are not judgments of substantive normative fact: not all normative judgments naturally represent anything substantive at all. Take judgments of what it makes most sense to do, pondered in circumstances in which no consensus is in the offing as to what to do. Consider the person uncertain of what it makes most sense to do and uncertain of what standards to apply. The question he is asking himself is not meaningless. It is clear what will constitute coming to a conclusion: it is to be disposed to avow that conclusion and be governed by it—as well as being set to draw inferences to other judgments which are tied to the world in various ways. The question can be discussed, perhaps as cogently as a controversial scientific question, or a murder case with circumstantial evidence some find conclusive and some do not. Here, though, we cannot draw a parallel with the way judgments about wheels invoke a certain loose set of properties. If the speculative picture I sketched

11. McDowell (1981, 144) rejects a related claim as implausible: that for every value concept a community has, an outside observer could always form a concept that sorts things the same way, without even comprehending the point the community finds in that way of sorting. The claim McDowell rejects is stronger than the one I am making, since I allow the observer to understand the normative point of the concepts he matches. Still, this perhaps gives us a way of distinguishing some properties as normative: a property is normative, we might say, if it could not be recognized by anyone who had missed its normative point. The property that makes racists consider a way of acting "uppity" would be normative, in this sense, if we outsiders could pick it out only by thinking what ways of acting a racist would think fit to resent and repress. Nevertheless our own concept of this property would be non-normative in the primary sense: our judgments in terms of it would not involve thinking it makes sense to resent and repress people who act that way; it would not normatively govern us to resent and repress them. Judgments, then, would still not be normative in virtue of picking out properties of a special kind. McDowell himself may accept this; he does not want to treat values as primary qualities but on a parallel to secondary qualities. I take up this possibility later (Chapter 9). Blackburn (1981), in a reply to McDowell, treats 'comic' as a term we apply to a class of things we could not pick out apart from our own reaction to them.

is right, then we can explain the biological function of such judgments: it is one of coordination. In this case, though, we cannot tell a story of coordination through natural representation of some features of the world. Not all intelligible normative judgments naturally represent anything, and so in this sense too there are no special substantive states of affairs that normative judgments naturally represent.

The argument here works uncertainly by exhaustion. Even if I am right that normative judgments have coordination as their biological function, that does not by itself show that there is no kind of fact these judgments naturally represent. It does not by itself show that there is no general kind of fact to which these judgments are adapted to correspond. One might imagine a program of "normative realism" that proposes a kind of fact to do the job.[12] If such a program is developed and a candidate is proposed, we shall have to examine it. I myself, though, have found no kind of fact that works: no substantive kind of fact, correspondence to which might plausibly, among our ancestors, have done the coordinating job of normative judgments.[13]

In this section I have asked whether normative judgments naturally represent substantive states of affairs, the states of affairs that would make the judgments true. In the case of "thick" judgments—like the judgment that someone has committed himself or the judgment that someone is being uppity—it seems they might. These judgments are tied in two directions: to factual states of affairs and to normative governance. Conceding that thick judgments naturally represent factual

---

12. Compare the recent "moral realism" of Sturgeon (1985b) and Railton (1986b, 1986a). Neither puts things in terms of the theory of natural representation I am using, and so neither addresses quite the question I myself am asking. They do, however, propose candidates for normative properties. For the most part they fix not on rationality but on good and right and wrong; Sturgeon does make a proposal for 'rational' as well, and a full argument of the kind I am sketching would have to examine his proposal. See Sturgeon (1985a, 29) and Gibbard (1985).

13. There may be no determinate fact of the matter whether a given judgment naturally represents a determinate state of affairs. Millikan (1986) and Dretske (1986) both discuss indeterminacy in how the function of a representing system is to be described. To what kind of fact is it the function of the system to produce a correspondence? Does the frog's visual system have as its function detecting flies or detecting small dark specks—which in its normal environment are almost always flies? If the frog snaps up a piece of buckshot, has the visual system misrepresented the buckshot as a fly, or has the executive system taken a gamble on what was correctly represented as a dark speck. There seems no fact of the matter. My plight here, though, is that I can find no property that *rational* (or its making the most sense to) might naturally represent. Indeterminacy of function might have made matters ambiguous, but so far in this discussion, it does not.

states of affairs, we can still say two things. First, the states of affairs they represent are non-normative. A logically weaker, non-normative judgment might naturally represent the same state of affairs, and so in that sense, the state of affairs naturally represented is non-normative. Second, even with thick judgments, it is not what the judgment naturally represents that makes it normative. Then too, we can add, not all normative judgments are thick in this sense, and so not all normative judgments naturally represent anything at all.

Representing Content

Normative judgments coordinate. It is adaptive, for the most part, to fall in with the normative consensus around one—while nudging matters in one's own favor. Suppose now we filled this rough story out. We are adapted, the story would now say, to make normative judgments of such-and-such a kind, judgments that bear a certain complex relation to the circumstances judged. Call this relation, whatever exactly it is, *adaptively fitting* the scene observed and judged. Roughly, we can say, *adaptively fitting* a scene is fitting it as directed by our consensus. It is fitting the scene in the way prescribed by whatever consensus is in the offing in one's own group. We are adapted, we can say in this new jargon, to make normative judgments that adaptively fit the circumstances we are judging.

That suggests another kind of fact that normative judgments might naturally represent. We are designed by nature, as it were, to make normative judgments that adaptively fit the scene we are judging. Could this adaptive fitting be what a normative judgment naturally represents? We could try saying this: *A normative judgment about a circumstance naturally represents the fact that it itself adaptively fits the circumstance judged.*

This would be an observer fact. How adaptive normative judgments were for an ancestor depended on the workings of his own community. It need not have enhanced an observer's fitness to follow the consensus of the group he was observing, unless that were because it was his own community. If I observe headhunters from afar, my judgments coordinate my actions with those of people around me only if they fit the consensus of my own community. The headhunters' consensus will have no direct bearing on how my judgments coordinate my actions with actions of others. I need to coordinate at home, not with headhunters—even when headhunters are the topic of discussion. The same went for our ancestors as observers: it was matching the consensus within their own communities that led to coordination and thus enhanced their fitness.

Suppose we had an account of what it is for normative judgments "adaptively to fit" a scene. We would then have identified a special kind of fact that normative judgments naturally represent. In that sense there would be normative facts, and these facts would be observer facts.

We need, though, a tighter characterization of normative facts. We wanted to capture the sense in which judgments of our manifest surroundings represent them. An important feature of these judgments is this: My judgment that I am sitting in a chair naturally represents the fact that I am sitting in a chair. The judgment, then, naturally represents its content, where content is understood in traditional ways. In contrast, even if a normative judgment does naturally represent the fact that it adaptively fits the circumstances judged, it does not naturally represent its content.

Tests with a Moorean flavor show this (Moore 1903, 10–21, esp. 10–12). Suppose a man rejects sheer jealousy: he thinks that so long as one's lover's attentions to oneself are not threatened, it can never really make sense to feel jealous of her attentions to others. He might, with full consistency and intelligibility, hold this view and yet admit that there is no consensus in the offing for it. He might realize that his judgment does not adaptively fit its subject matter, and still hold to his judgment without confusion. He may know what kinds of normative judgments would have been adaptive in the ancestral population, and know that his own judgment is not of that kind. That will in no way refute his view.[14] He could still hold that it never really makes sense to be jealous on the mere grounds that one's lover's love is for others as well as for oneself.

His belief that sheer jealousy makes no sense, then, may naturally represent an observer fact—that it adaptively fits the nature of jealousy—but that is no part of its content. A person can accept that sheer jealousy makes no sense, and yet reject the observer fact it naturally represents. What it naturally represents, then, is no part of its content.

---

14. Indeed evolutionary considerations suggest why it would not. A crucial part of normative discussion is that people take positions and influence each other. The mechanism works because people are both influenceable and stubborn. Anyone who was ready at the drop of a hat to think whatever others think would have little influence himself.

In this, normative judgments contrast with judgments about our manifest surroundings. The latter naturally represent their content. Normative judgments may naturally represent something, but if there is any class of fact that they naturally represent in virtue of being normative, it is a complex kind of fact about the observer and his community. These facts, though, are never the content of a normative judgment. There is no class of facts, then, that bear a relation to normative judgments parallel to the relation the facts of our manifest surroundings bear to our judgments about them. In this sense, there are no normative facts.

Here we might add a further claim. Return to thick judgments and substantive facts. Does Miss Watson's belief that Jim is getting uppity naturally represent its content? That Jim is getting "uppity" says more than that he is no longer abasing himself before whites. Thinking he is getting uppity commits her, in effect, to thinking he is no longer abasing himself—whether or not she herself has the concepts to express this neutral thought. If, on the other hand, we ourselves agree he is no longer abasing himself, that does not commit us to thinking that he is getting uppity. What her thought naturally represents, if anything, is just that he is no longer abasing himself before whites. That, we are saying, is not the entire content of her thought. It is the content of a weaker thought that her own thought entails. The judgment that Jim is getting uppity does not naturally represent its whole content; it naturally represents only a part, the part that is non-normative. Again, then, normative judgments do not naturally represent their content.

Normative judgments coordinate. If that is their biological function, that suggests one kind of fact our normative judgments might naturally represent—an observer fact. It suggests a kind of fact that it is the biological function of our normative capacities to put normative judgments in correspondence with. The function of the psychic mechanisms involved in the acceptance of norms is to fit one's judgments to the ones everyone else will tend toward. If we can find the relation between observer and scene that settles which way normative discussion will tend, that will give us something for normative judgments naturally to represent. It will give something for the judgments to get in correspondence with in order to coordinate. I labeled this relation "adaptively fitting". We can thus consider facts of this kind—a judgment's adaptively fitting the scene that is judged—to be peculiarly normative facts. The search for a special kind of fact that normative judgments naturally represent may not be in vain. Still, though, a contrast remains between normative judgments and manifest judgments— judgments of manifest objects around us. Whereas the latter naturally represent their content, normative judgments do not. The tests that show this are Moore-like: a person can without contradiction make a normative judgment and deny that it adaptively fits the circumstances.

Theoretical Beliefs

Beliefs about our manifest surroundings pick out facts of a special class: *manifest facts*, we might call them. Beliefs concerning these facts naturally represent their content. In no like way do normative beliefs pick out a class of specially normative facts. This distinguishes norms from facts of a most prosaic kind. Perhaps the contrast points to what could be made precise in a fact-norm distinction in general.

It was not, though, with facts like these that the distinction seemed problematical in the first place. The puzzle lay in other realms: with abstruse theoretical talk, and with talk of human affairs. Is normative talk less factual than physics? Can we separate, in any sharp way, describing a person from judging him, or describing a social practice from praising it or condemning it?

Take first atomic physics. Understanding it is no biological function of the human mind. Whatever selection pressures led to minds that could understand atoms, they did not directly involve any such understanding; none of our remote ancestors had an inkling of quantum theory. The abilities involved in grasping it may be adaptations, but if they are, they must have functions other than enabling us to grasp atomic physics.

Physicists' beliefs do represent their content, I shall still maintain, but artificially. Natural representation is no help for these beliefs, for they do not represent their content naturally. Rather, physicists invent elaborate schemes of representation. Their beliefs correspond to nature not by any Darwinian surrogate for design, but by design itself.

Does this make for a genuine contrast with norms? We have to take atomic physics at face value, after all, if we are to think that the beliefs involved correspond to a realm of facts. Suppose we proceeded likewise with norms. Take normative facts at face value; can we not then claim that our normative beliefs correspond to normative facts, and do so by design?

We cannot. Even supposing there are normative facts, we can explain why we have the normative beliefs we do without citing any normative facts. To explain, in contrast, why atomic physicists have the beliefs they do, we have to talk about atoms. Normative beliefs do not represent any special realm of content naturally; so I argued already. Now we can add something more: even if there were a special realm of normative facts, it would be gratuitous to think that normative beliefs represent facts in this realm, even artificially. If the speculative evolutionary story I have told is correct, then we have another explanation of these beliefs.

Why do physicists believe in electrons? Part of the story is this: in 1911, Millikan put tiny oil droplets in an electric field. Sometimes he would find a droplet that rose in this field. By turning the field on and off, he could repeatedly make the droplet rise and then let it fall. He observed how fast the charge rose in the field, and he found that every so often, the speed would change. For a given droplet, moreover, the change in speed was always the same, or at least always an integral multiple of a set minimal difference in speed. Most often the speed changed by that minimal amount, and sometimes it changed by twice that amount. Millikan concluded that the droplet, every so often, captured or lost one or more chunks of electric charge, and—crucially— *that these chunks were always the same size.* (He had calculated that the same difference of charge would always make the same difference to the speed.) Physicists accepted his explanation, and called a single minimal chunk of electric charge an "electron" (Millikan 1917, 66–72).

Electrons figure in this explanation. Millikan observed what he did because, every so often, the moving droplet captured or lost an integral number of electrons. That made the droplet speed up or slow down in the field by a fixed amount. (The amount depended on the droplet's size, and hence on the amount of air resistance.) We explain Millikan's conclusion in part by telling what he observed, and we explain why he observed what he did—why the phenomenon was there to be observed—by citing electrons. No explanation without electrons will be complete and credible.

In contrast, I speculated about how we come to have the normative beliefs we do, and in that speculation I cited nothing normative. I did start out with firm normative convictions. I accepted such truisms as that it is wrong to torture children for fun, and that the fact that one would find something painful speaks against doing it. Not that I expressed these judgments, for I did not need to; they did not figure in my explanation of why we accept such things. In explaining why we make the normative judgments we do, I found normative facts superfluous.[15]

In the end, to be sure, I do deny that there are normative facts—but only in the end. Normative facts, if there were any, would be the facts of the special kind represented, naturally or artificially, by normative judgments. That is what would pick them out as normative. As it turns out, I claimed, our making these judgments can be explained without supposing they represent facts of any special kind. Thus at the end of the argument we can conclude that, at least in this sense, there are no normative facts.

My explanations were of course guided by norms—epistemic norms. Why, say, did no basic tendency toward perfection figure in the explanations I gave? No such thing should be posited, I assumed, when observed patterns can be explained just as well without it. This is a normative judgment, and it and others like it guided me. Norms are fundamental to thought: we cannot think systematically and self-consciously without accepting norms, and we cannot think at all without some implicit guidance by norms—without at least internalizing epistemic norms. The norms that guide explanation, though, are not themselves parts of the explanation. I did not suggest that we developed our normative capacities *because* basic tendencies to perfection should not be posited gratuitously. Epistemic norms tell us what constitutes a good explanation, but that does not make them part of the explanation.

There is a realm of atomic facts, and the beliefs of atomic physicists artificially represent facts in this realm. We cannot fully explain why atomic physicists have the beliefs they do without citing facts about atoms. No corresponding realm of normative facts need appear in a full explanation of why we have the normative beliefs we do.

Psychic and Social Facts

Are there facts about people and societies? The staunchest upholders of a fact-norm distinction agree that in normal thought we blur the

15. Harman (1977, 6–7) makes a similar contrast. Sturgeon (1985b) and Railton (1986b) accept this as the crux of the issue between "moral realists" and their opponents, but suggest that moral properties are natural properties of a special kind, which figure in the best explanations of our making the moral judgments we do. My difference with these writers may well be empirical: I doubt that any sufficiently determinate natural property guides people's moral judgments in the ways these writers picture.

distinction.[16] We make thick judgments. We have few terms for labeling a person's character without evaluating it. We can hardly describe a lazy person without censure, much less a person who is cruel.

This much I have accepted, but still I argued that in an important sense there is no special realm of normative facts. The question for us now is whether by the same test there are psychic and social facts. Do we make psychic and social judgments that naturally represent their content?

Perhaps in the normal course of life we do not, or do so rarely. Perhaps without thick concepts, ordinary thoughts about people and society would be impoverished—impoverished not only normatively but explanatorily. The account I gave of our normative capacities, though, was meant to explain in a special way. The goal was to understand ourselves fundamentally as a part of nature, to include an account of ourselves in what we might call the Galilean core. The Galilean core is our story of nature; it is our rough story of how, ultimately, a wide range of things are matters of fundamental physics. The story includes chemistry, molecular biology, and the theory of natural selection. Human life is not well integrated into this core, at least yet. Now, as we begin to expand the Galilean core to include a view of human life, we must develop concepts that are non-normative. We must invent means of psychological and sociological explanation. We treat these broadly Galilean explanations as special; they explain in a specially fundamental way. The speculative evolutionary story I told of our normative capacities aspired to this status.

Do these explanations represent facts, at least artificially? Again the question is how we explain our accepting these explanations. Can we do so without citing the kinds of facts that figure in them? Perhaps we might, but if we did, we would have debunked these explanations. We must explain our Galilean judgments as responsive to the kinds of facts that figure in them, or we lose our grounds for making the judgments.

Take our view that humanity evolved by natural selection, and suppose we came to think, say, that our accepting this view could be

16. Stevenson, for example, offers two broad patterns of analysis that remove the vagueness of ethical terms in different, somewhat arbitrary ways. The first pattern limits the descriptive reference of ethical terms to the speaker's own attitudes, taking everything else conveyed as merely suggested. The second pattern treats ethical terms as having substantive descriptions built into their meanings (1944, esp. 89). Hare (1952, chap. 7, 111–126) treats 'good' as having not only evaluative meaning but various kinds of factual meaning: "descriptive", "conventional", and "inverted commas" meanings.

explained entirely by the social status it gives to scientists. Scientists dimly realized that if Darwinian explanations were accepted, they would attain the cultural role of priests. They were motivated by this prospect, and they had the cultural influence to get the theory accepted. The fossil record, the logic of natural selection, the nature of observed adaptations had nothing to do with it. If we came to think all this, we would have lost all basis for thinking that humanity had evolved by natural selection. We would have explained our belief away. It is because we think that biologists were responsive to evidence of evolution that we can accept what they tell us about it.

We are beginning to accept broadly Galilean explanations of people and social phenomena. That involves thinking that our acceptance of these explanations stems from their being correct. Our acceptance can be explained, we think, only by citing the kinds of facts that figure in the explanations. In an important sense, then, we are committed to thinking there are psychic and social facts: we cannot seriously explain our making the judgments we do without appealing to such facts. We also accept normative claims: clearly, for example (and to say the least), it is wrong to torture people for fun. If the story I told was right, though, we can explain how we come to think this without citing, in our explanation, the wrongness of torturing people for fun.

Still, what about everyday judgments of people, the ones we use to steer ourselves around in our social world? In them, everyone agrees, fact and norm do not come neatly apart. The question, though, is the adequacy of a language, a way of thinking, that does separate fact and norm. I am proposing such a language. It uses the terms of the Galilean core plus one explicitly normative term, 'it makes sense to'. What we can ask about everyday personal judgments, then, is whether we could interpret their claims in this normative-Galilean language—a language that does make a neat fact-norm distinction.[17] If we can, that will not mean we should ditch our everyday ways of thinking. It will mean that no great mystery remains about the place of personal facts among norms and Galilean facts. To remove the mystery, we do not need a single, determinate gloss for each everyday thought. The noncognitivist tradition admits great indeterminacy in the interpretation of

17. 'Interpret' here will not mean translate. Galilean psychological concepts, if we achieve them, will not be our old folk concepts—any more than the concept of a massive electric discharge is the same as our old folk concept of lightning. The question will be whether the Galilean concepts are adequate substitutes for the folk concepts in contexts where the validity of the science is presupposed. In Chapter 5, in contrast, 'interpret' did mean translate; the question was how to attribute concepts.

everyday thoughts. We understand these thoughts even if we think them indeterminate—in ways that don't matter for immediate purposes. I make no claim, of course, that we could do this now. The Galilean project is far from explanatorily complete for human beings. Even apart from that, there are lots of questions about whether the things we need to say about each other for social purposes could be interpreted in this austere new language once it was developed. In part, then, a claim for a fact-norm distinction is a bet that the interpretation can be made to work.

Start out, then, taking both Galilean explanations and normative claims seriously. We end up still taking both seriously, but denying there are normative facts. We could not have denied that there are psychic and social facts and still have gone on taking seriously our Galilean explanations of psychic and social happenings.

7 · Moral Emotions

Resentment and Guilt

In my analysis of moral judgments, I spoke of guilt and resentment: a person is to blame for something if it would make sense for him to feel guilty for having done it and for others to resent him for having done it. 'Resent', though, is not the right word: it suggests feeling harmed or offended, whereas the moral feeling can be impartial. 'Indignation', 'outrage', or 'moral condemnation' might name the feeling, but they suggest full-fledged moral judgment. We need an emotion that can be felt even by a person who thinks it makes no sense to feel that way.

Resentment, indignation and the like seem to be kinds of anger. Perhaps, then, we should stick to talk of anger: a person is to blame for something he has done if it makes sense both for him to feel guilty for having done it and for others to be angry with him for having done it. Moral convictions, we are then saying, consist in norms for anger and for that first-person counterpart of anger, guilt.

Not all norms for anger, though, will be moral. Morality is impartial, whereas with anger we may demand partiality. If my camel is stolen I will be outraged, and we may all agree it makes sense for me to be outraged. If, though, I were outraged at the theft of a stranger's camel far away, that would be strange. It doesn't make sense, you might tell me, to fume over a camel theft far away—there are so many worse things happening in the world. How angry it makes sense for me to be depends on what the theft has to do with me. How much the thief is to blame does not.

An account of what moral terms mean must allow for these views; it should not rule them out as nonsensical. What, then, do we think anger has to do with culpability? How greatly the thief is to blame is not straightforwardly a matter of how angry at him it makes sense to be. Even when the theft of a faraway camel is truly outrageous, my own outrage may be excessive. My problem is not that I take theft too seriously altogether; we admit that theft is serious if we think it makes sense for me to be outraged when I discover my own camel stolen. My problem might be that my feelings are unreasonably engaged.

It does make sense to be upset and angered when faraway deeds are specially heinous. It even makes sense to engage one's feelings in fictions from time to time. It makes no sense, though, to go through life with utterly impartial feelings; each of us needs feelings specially engaged in himself and in special other people. Only small portions of human life can claim our fullest emotions.

How fully to engage one's feelings in a situation, then, is a separate question from how to feel if one's feelings are fully engaged. We can accept norms for both. The norms we accept for engagement may let proximity, love, and acquaintance matter, and they may also make way for flows of sentiment and eddies of fascination. Moral norms, on the other hand, set aside the question of how fully engaged one's feelings are to be; they are norms for how to feel given full, impartial engagement. Full engagement is vivid awareness of everything generic that would affect one's feelings toward a situation. It requires, moreover, an undistracted contemplative leisure, for in responding to an emergency I might be vividly aware of all that was involved but have no time for feelings.

Moral norms tell how to feel only given a special standpoint—one it does not always make sense to take. For anger the standpoint is one of full, impartial engagement; for guilt it is full engagement in an aspect of one's own place in the world. Moral norms coordinate the anger and the guilt it makes sense to feel from these special standpoints, and in turn these standpoints will have something to do with the feelings it makes sense to have in the flux of life. A person's feelings will not often be impartial and fully engaged, but they do need to be coordinated to some degree with the feelings of others. The ways he feels about himself, about his qualities and his actions, will need to be coordinated to some degree with the ways others feel about him, or his feelings may prompt him to act to his detriment. This coordination may be fostered by a common judgment of how it would make sense to feel from a standpoint of full and impartial engagement.

Problems for Emotion

We have norms not only for conduct and belief but for emotions. That explains moral judgment: morality, on a narrow reading, concerns the moral emotions it makes sense to have from a standpoint of full and impartial engagement. It concerns the things it makes sense to feel guilty for having done and the things it makes sense to be angry with others for having done.

Now on some accounts of emotion this gets things backward. Anger and guilt themselves include moral judgments, it is said: to be angry with a person is in part to judge that he has acted wrongly, and to feel guilty is in part to judge that one has acted wrongly oneself. We cannot explain moral judgments in terms of guilt and anger, for we must explain guilt and anger in terms of moral judgments.

I need enough of an account of emotions to cope with this objection—and I need an account of emotions for other reasons too. Different kinds of normative judgments, I proposed, concern different ways a person could feel toward something. A thing is shameful if it makes sense to be ashamed of it and for others to disdain one for it. It is admirable if it makes sense for others to admire one for it, and for one to feel self-approbation because of it. Different cultures stress different emotions for broadly ethical purposes: we stress guilt, whereas others stress shame or fear. Hence we can intelligibly ask whether a given culture really has a morality in this narrow sense, and that amounts to asking whether they have norms for guilt and for anger. We can even ponder whether it is a good thing that we ourselves have a morality, when alternative kinds of norms could serve many of the same purposes.

Now all this seems to presuppose that terms like 'guilt', 'shame', and 'fear' name distinct emotions, and that we can speak meaningfully of these different emotions both in ourselves and in peoples whose norms are far different from ours. A group will stress and refine some emotions and leave others to operate on the fringes of discursive life. Still, they have emotions that we ourselves can name and distinguish.

Cross-cultural attributions of emotions, though, can be challenged. The very terms in which different cultures express emotions resist translation. If others speak of emotions in ways that are incomprehensible to us, then it is hard to see why our own ways of thinking should get things right. Exotic peoples may be wildly unscientific in their talk of emotions, but then so are we. When we talk of guilt, shame, approbation, and the like, we are not drawing on a special scientific vocabulary, systematically refined by observation and experiment. We are speaking in folk terms, and what our folk psychology might have to do with a well-founded scientific psychology is a point of lively controversy in current philosophy of mind (see Stich 1983). Now if the folk psychologies of different peoples are wildly incompatible, perhaps that settles the issue: If we are right, then the rest are off track, and yet we have no reason to think our own tradition specially reliable. The only reasonable course is to distrust all traditional psychology, ours included.

These challenges need more response than I can give. No theory of human emotions is currently well established, and so I must offer more speculation. If moral language works at all as I am sketching, then the theory of moral judgments includes the theory of moral emotions, for moral judgments consist in the acceptance of norms to govern moral emotions. I need, then, to say something about emotions, however tentative and speculative. Hints and evidence to fuel speculation are available from many sources: common experience and literary observation, experimental psychology and physiology, sociology and ethnography, and Darwinian theory. Little of what I can speculate will be new with me, but thinking about the normative control of emotions and its coordinating function may let us give new twists to existing theories.

Judgmental Theories of Emotion

A prime view in recent philosophical work on emotion is *judgmentalism*. Solomon writes, "A change in my beliefs (for example, the refutation of my belief that John stole my car) entails (not causes) a change in my emotion (my being angry that John stole my car). I cannot be angry if I do not believe that someone has wronged or offended me. Accordingly, we might say that anger involves a *moral* judgment as well, an appeal to moral standards and not merely personal evaluations."[1]

1. Solomon (1976, 185). This kind of view is also sometimes called "emotional cognitivism"—perhaps inappropriately, since the judgments of Solomon might not be strictly cognitive, and if they are it is not clear what that amounts to; 'cognitive' is not a word that carries its meaning on its face. In any case, emotional cognitivism is not to be confused with metaethical cognitivism, with cognitivism in the theory of the meaning of normative terms. Emotional cognitivism is the thesis that emotions are cognitive judgments, whereas metaethical cognitivism is a thesis about ethical judgments. Emotional cognitivism might come in strong and weak versions: on a strong version emotions con-

What, then, are the judgments in emotions supposed to be? Solomon says that anger requires believing "that someone has wronged or offended me," but a person can be angry over a wrong to someone else, and be so without thinking himself personally offended. Perhaps the judgment that anger requires is just that someone has been wronged or offended, or more broadly that a moral transgression has occurred (see Sabini and Silver 1982, 171). That, however, would be unsatisfactory in two ways. In the first place, it is of course controversial what moral judgments are, whether they are factual beliefs of some kind or something else. Anyone who claims that anger includes a judgment of moral transgression needs to explain the judgment. In the second place, it is not even true that anger requires a judgment of wrong—at least in any informative sense. I can feel angry at you and yet think it makes no sense to do so; I can think that really you have acted as you should. Perhaps I judge you wrong subconsciously, or emotionally, or in my heart but not in my mind. What do any of these things mean, though, but that I am angry at you for something you did?

The judgments involved in emotion are often said to be "assessments" or "evaluations".[2] Again, though, we need to know what these things are. Lyons speaks of placement on a rating scale (Lyons 1980). Can we understand different kinds of rating independently of the emo-

---

sist entirely of cognitive judgments, whereas on a weak version emotions consist of cognitive judgments at least in part. Now emotional cognitivism logically allows for metaethical non-cognitivism: emotions might be cognitive and normative judgments not. In its usual versions, though, emotional cognitivism does seem to require metaethical cognitivism. Solomon's treatment of anger is a case in point: Suppose we read him as a cognitivist. If anger is cognitive, on his view, that must be because anger consists, at least in part, of the judgment that someone has wronged or offended me. The judgment must therefore be cognitive, or else the fact that anger includes the judgment would not make anger cognitive. Specific versions of emotional cognitivism, then, will often require a metaethical cognitivism.

2. Arnold has been prominent among psychologists for insisting that emotions require appraisals. "To arouse an emotion, the object must be appraised as affecting me in some way, affecting me personally as an individual with my particular experience and my particular aims" (1960, vol. 1, 171). What counts as affecting me is fairly loose; it can be that a fellow vertebrate is about to come to harm (172). Among philosophers, see, for example, Pitcher (1965, 339–340). Lyons (1980) develops a "cognitive-evaluation" philosophical theory of emotions, but he remarks that the evaluations are not epistemologically cognitive—not matters of knowledge, perception, or acquaintance (59). Roberts (1988) speaks of "construals". Provis (1981), on the other hand, thinks that emotions can be reasonable or unreasonable apart from the beliefs and evaluations involved. He develops a coherence theory to account for this.

tions to which they pertain? What would make one scale pertinent, say, to fear and another to anger? When evaluations are put in words, we understand them; if you say "That's terrible!" I shall understand, and I shall agree that you have expressed an evaluation. That does not mean, though, that emotions can safely be explained in terms of evaluations. Perhaps we understand evaluations only because we have the relevant emotions, and evaluations must be explained in terms of emotions—as I am proposing.

Perhaps we should explain evaluation as an emotion minus physiological arousal. There is much to emotion besides physiological arousal, after all. Our problem, though, is to say what that is. Physiological arousal plays little part in emotion as I need to treat it; norms for guilt and anger will not primarily govern physiological arousal. In these terms my own puzzle is not what an emotion is besides an evaluation, but what an evaluation is.

The bald question of whether emotions include judgments seems to me the wrong one to ask—especially if we speak of "cognitive" judgments. We have no sharp notion of cognitive judgment to apply. At one extreme, mental arithmetic is clearly a matter of cognitive judgment, and at another extreme, a tired feeling is clearly non-cognitive and seems fairly non-judgmental. Emotions, though, are not much like either; they have some of the features of cognitive judgments in their clearest instances and lack others.[3]

Solomon writes, "An emotion is a *judgment* (or a set of judgments), something we *do*. An emotion is a (set of) judgment(s) which constitute our world, our surreality, and its 'intentional objects.' An emotion is a basic judgment about our Selves and our place in our world, the projection of the values and ideals, structures and mythologies, according to which we live and through which we experience our lives" (1976, 185). An emotion, we can say, involves a special way of experiencing one's world, a way that will be difficult to express and perhaps can only be whistled. Nothing I have been saying rules out calling this kind of state a judgment, but if that is what we call it, we must remember that we are using the term for a kind of mental operation we little understand. To explain what judgments of this kind are may be most of the work of explaining what an emotion is.

3. Zajonc (1980) argues that emotional reactions come faster than cognitive judgments, and so cannot require them. This contention has sparked lively debate; perhaps a feeling does require a cognitive evaluation, but a very quick one. Much in the debate must hinge on just what "cognitive" is supposed to mean.

Emotions are cognitive in some clear respects: When I am angry I am normally angry *at* someone *for* something he has done. Normal anger is directed in a way that warm glows and tickles are not. Abnormal anger may be undirected; but normal, directed anger is not a mere sum of this undirected anger and a belief. A theory of emotions, then, must explain how guilt and anger can be about something.

In what follows I explore two pictures of human emotions. Each explains how emotions can be about something, and each allows for normative governance of emotions. On the first an emotion is a biologically *adaptive syndrome;* its symptoms are typical expressions and tendencies to action, and it typically responds to a special class of circumstances. On the alternative picture, a person's own classification of his feelings or his situation, his *self-attribution,* plays a crucial part in the workings of an emotion, and we can distinguish emotions only by the different ways people conceive of themselves and their situations. Both pictures have some plausibility, and norm-expressivism can accommodate either.

Animal Emotions as Adaptive Syndromes

To understand human emotions, start with the beasts; that postpones complications. Think of a dog whose territory is approached by another dog. The dog stands up, it takes a special kind of stance or it runs back and forth, it barks, and it is primed to attack if the other dog keeps approaching. This story combines features of various kinds: a cause (territorial intrusion), expressive behavior (barking and taking threatening stances), and other behavioral tendencies (the dog is primed to attack).

Where in all this is the emotion? We don't suppose the pattern arises by chance or by magic; the dog is specially constructed so as to respond in these ways to intrusion. There is a state of the dog—presumably a state of its neurons and endocrine system—that tends to be incited by certain kinds of events, of which territorial intrusion is a prime example. This state leads to special kinds of overt expression (barking and the like) and primes the dog toward special kinds of action (attack). The combination of these constitutes a syndrome, and the emotion is whatever state of the organism stands behind the syndrome. It is whatever state has these typical causes, is typically expressed in these ways, and tends toward these kinds of actions.[4]

4. There have been many evolutionary treatments of emotion, beginning with Darwin (1872). See, for example, Plutchik (1980) and Panksepp (1982).

The syndrome, moreover, has a rationale: creationists can see in it the handiwork of God, and Darwinists can see in it the result of natural selection. The angry dog drives off or destroys those who threaten it or its resources. The state is triggered by special kinds of circumstances, each of which typically has a special cluster of properties: another animal threatens the dog or its resources; the threat will be averted if the other animal is cowed, driven off, or incapacitated; and our dog has a fair chance of being able to do at least one of these things. The state leads the dog to do things that tend to achieve the goal of cowing, incapacitating, or driving off the threatening animal. Doing these things in similar circumstances normally enhances the dog's prospects for survival and reproduction.[5]

Some of the things it does are expressive. The natural expression of emotions can be understood by analogy to explicit conventions of communication. Barks and growls would accomplish nothing were their addressee not disposed to be cowed by them. Likewise, being cowed by barking and growling profits an animal only if barks and growls are good indications of danger of attack. If the dog who barks and growls at me is likely to attack, it is adaptive for me to back down, and if I am likely to back down when confronted with barking or growling, it is adaptive for the dog to bark or to growl at me. These are matched adaptations: neither would be adaptive without the other, and each is adaptive in the presence of the other. These matched adaptations are evolutionary analogs of a communicative convention (see Schelling 1960, chap. 2; Maynard Smith 1974, 1976, 1982).

Of course, any inference from a syndrome to a physiological state will have its pitfalls. Organisms are complex. We hypothesize an internal state that accounts for a syndrome, but even if we are right, the connection of internal state to syndrome will be rough. The causes are only typical, not invariable, and the manifestations will likewise be only typical. It may turn out, moreover, that more than one mechanism stands behind a syndrome, normally working together. In that case there may be no fact of the matter which of these constitutes the emotion: when all work together the animal has the emotion; when all

---

5. In central ways my account follows Kenny (1963). "The concept of each emotion," Kenny writes, "is linked with non-emotional concepts in three ways. The concept, for example, of *fear* stands on three struts: (a) fearful circumstances; (b) symptoms of fear; (c) action taken to avoid what is feared." Kenny, though, for the most part treats these things directly as criteria for attributing a given emotion in a particular instance. I am suggesting rather that we use these criteria to point to an emotional mechanism. The animal counts as being afraid if the mechanism is operating, whether or not there are fearful circumstances, symptoms of fear, and evasive actions in that particular instance.

are absent it lacks it—and otherwise there is no clear fact of the matter. In an abnormal case with some of the mechanisms at work and some not, the animal neither clearly has the emotion nor clearly lacks it.

Psychic mechanisms will be only roughly adaptive. They may turn out to consist of layer upon layer of activators and inhibitors. These will often be responsive to the complex demands of life, and they may work as well, on average over many generations, as would any slight variant. They will look, though, less like divine handiwork than the outcome of ingenious tinkering, with no fresh starts but many small modifications to cope with new problems (see Jacob 1977, esp. 1163–66). There may be no clear single mechanism that serves a given function; in an organism shaped by natural selection, patterns of function may be more striking than patterns of mechanism. What unites the various specific physiological states that constitute anger may not be a similarity that would strike a physiologist who had put all thought of function aside, but a similarity of biological function.

Despite all this, we may tentatively suppose that syndromes that appear strongly adaptive do manifest special adaptive mechanisms. In advance of physiological knowledge, we can try to pick out the states in a number of ways, each of which will only tend to coincide with the others. We pick out animal emotions provisionally as syndromes of tendencies to action, expressive tendencies, and tendencies to be caused in certain special ways, where the entire pattern seems to be adaptive.

Of course we know more about the physiology of emotion than all this suggests.[6] At the outset, though, we need to explore what can be said about emotions in advance of such knowledge. Otherwise we cannot say what sorts of physiological findings tell us about emotions as opposed to something else. Physiologists, we can now say, discover the nature of emotional states when they discover how physiological mechanisms account for syndromes of the kinds I have been sketching.

Even animal emotions, on this kind of account, have more structure than bare tingles, palpitations, and feelings of nausea.[7] The angry dog

6. Buck (1985) gives a fine review and interpretation of psychological and neurological findings on emotion. He presents some of the material more fully in his textbook (1976).

7. Pitcher (1965) and others strongly attack the view that emotions are undirected sensations, like pains, tickles, and itches. Hume is said to be an advocate of this view, as is James (1884). On my own reading, Hume and James do both think that emotions are internal sensations, but each ascribes much more structure to these sensations than we ordinarily think of itches and tickles as having. Both think an emotion is *about* something, and felt *toward* something. Hume (1739) classifies emotions as "reflective impres-

is not simply angry, he is angry at an intruder. He gives every sign of focusing his attention on the intruder, his barking and growling are directed toward the intruder, and he is primed not just to attack but specifically to attack the intruder. The anger is directed: its expressions are to an audience, and it tends toward actions with a goal. In these terms we can speak of the *focus* of the anger: we can say at whom the dog is angry and about what.

Human Emotions

Humans differ sharply from beasts, but it is puzzling which differences are crucial. Language makes us special, and so does the complex social life that language makes possible. In addition, humans seem to have a specially wide range of emotional states; we do not readily attribute amusement, guilt, reverence, envy, pity, embarrassment, or admiration to beasts. That is not surprising if, as I have been suggesting, a prime biological function of emotions is to coordinate actions and expectations, for in human social life there is much to coordinate.

In part no doubt our special emotional complexity stems from language: we report emotions and label them in our thoughts, and the ways we conceive an emotion affect what that emotion is like.[8] Language, though, is unlikely to be the whole story. The human brain differs from the other mammalian brains most strikingly in its large neocortex. The left and right halves of the cerebrum do different things; although linguistic abilities are seated predominantly in the left

---

sions" (bk. 2, part 2, chap. 1, para. 1), which are, in effect, sensations caused by other sensations or by ideas. A passion like pride is a "simple and uniform impression", recognizable by its feel (bk. 2, part 2, chap. 2, para. 1). It has, though, a "subject" (the thing one is proud of) and an object (the self). These are explained as causal relations, innate ("original") or developed, not as part of the feeling itself. One is proud of a house in that a thought about the house—that I designed it and it is beautiful—causes the feeling. I myself am the object of my pride in that the feeling causes thoughts about myself. James proclaims the "priority of bodily symptoms to the felt emotion" (1884, 199). His thesis is "that the bodily changes follow directly the PERCEPTION of the exciting fact, and that our feeling of the same changes as they occur IS the emotion" (190). These bodily accompaniments, though, are "much more far-reaching and complicated than we ordinarily suppose"; they include such things as impulses to action (194).

8. When, for example, subjects are told they will get mild electric shocks, those who are told that they will experience certain symptoms as the result of a pill they have taken tolerate the shocks better than those who are not. Those who are told nothing about what causes their symptoms presumably attribute them, correctly, to fear. See Buck (1976, 354–356) for a review.

hemisphere, the right hemisphere is roughly as big, and it too is mostly new with human beings (Buck 1976, 77). The right hemisphere is specially important, among other things, for emotionality, and seems capable by itself of emotions that are peculiarly human—amusement for instance.[9] The things that go on in the mute right hemisphere may have much to do with the special complexity of human emotional life.

If so, then human emotionality may consist of more than mere variations on animal emotion with language tacked on. The old emotions operate at least partly in the limbic system we share with all mammals; these include rage, fear, and sexually tinged excitement (Buck 1976, 79–92). Whatever goes on in most of the right neocortex, though, is special to humans, at least anatomically. The pattern of explanation stays the same: we can still look for syndromes of typical causes, typical expressions, and typical action tendencies, and call these emotions. The syndromes, though, may be special to humans.

Since humans can speak, we as observers can say more about emotions in humans than about emotions in beasts. There is more to be said with humans about the focus of an emotion, because we can ask the one who is feeling it what it is about. Emotions involve patterns of salience: if I am angry at you I dwell on special features of what you have done; if what you did instead had made me afraid then I would have dwelt on different features.[10] With beasts we could talk of an emotion's focus only by looking at its causes, its expression, and its action tendencies. All these things would bear on the radical translation of emotional reports, but so will analogies to our own experiences and connections with the rest of language.

Can we find plausible candidates for specially human syndromes? Consider guilt and shame. They seem peculiarly human, and they are emotions that specially concern ethics. Can we depict them as distinct syndromes, with typical causes, typical expressions, and typical action tendencies? Can we find distinct biological functions for them?

Guilt and shame differ, it is often said, in that guilt is internalized and shame is not: whereas I can feel guilty about things I alone know

9. See Buck (1985, 394–396) and Tucker (1981) for reviews of the evidence for right hemisphere specialization in emotion. Studies of brain damage and its effects show that right brain damage makes people less expressive of emotion in their faces and voices, and less able to judge emotion in voices. There is some indication that the left, linguistic hemisphere acts to inhibit emotions; see Tucker (1981) and Buck and Duffy (1980). Evidence for what the mute right hemisphere can do by itself comes from studies of patients whose cerebral hemispheres were separated; see Sperry, Zaidel, and Zaidel (1979).

10. I owe this to Adam Morton.

I have done, I can feel ashamed only of things that expose me to the judgment of others. Guilt can be over a secret, but shame must always be about things that are public. Now that seems wrong. Some emotions close to shame must be over public matters—humiliation and embarrassment seem like that—but shame need not. A teenaged boy could boast convincingly to other boys of sexual conquests he had never made, and yet feel ashamed of his virginity. He might feel guilty about lying, but he would not feel guilty about his virginity. To be sure, his shame might intensify if he were found out and mocked, but the like holds of guilt: if he had fulfilled his sexual fantasies he might then feel guilty, and the guilt might intensify if his parents learned of what he had done and scolded him. Guilt and shame are both possible in secret, and they may each be intensified by exposure (see Singer 1953, chap. 2).

Guilt, we might say, normally involves a consciousness of having done wrong, and shame a consciousness of some personal inadequacy. Any such explanation would have to deal with guilt and shame that are free-floating, and with guilt and shame a person thinks it makes no sense to feel but feels none the less. We should be puzzled, though, by something else: what shames one person leaves another untouched. One person might be ashamed of his shabby clothes, while for me, say, shabby clothes matter not at all. Must we have different beliefs about clothes? We may, of course, but it is hard to identify any belief that utterly must distinguish us. Each of us might well know his clothes are shabby, and each of us might have like beliefs about what sorts of people have shabby clothes and who will disdain us for it and who will not. Our difference seems to be just that he finds shabby clothes shameful and I do not—and it is not clear what that amounts to apart from the fact that he feels ashamed of it and I do not.[11] If what is special about shame is its subject matter, that subject matter needs to be explained.

Now much would fall into place if guilt and shame were distinct adaptive syndromes, with different typical causes, different natural expressions, and different tendencies to action. We know that different kinds of circumstances typically produce guilt or produce shame, but it is hard to characterize the differences without at least a covert reference to the emotions themselves—guilt, in effect, is produced by

11. There will be more of a story, no doubt, but it will not change the point. Clothes perhaps are a badge of allegiance, and he is a gentleman: he adheres to a well-dressed tribe, and prizes the things that matter to it. I do not. Even if the story is this or something more complex, nothing in it need require that we have clearly distinct beliefs.

guilty acts and shame by things that are shameful. In any case the classes of typical causes differ from person to person, and they differ strikingly from culture to culture. Can we tell an adaptive story that would explain why different sorts of things would make people feel guilty or feel ashamed? Can we tell it and still avoid the conclusion that all must feel guilty about the same things and ashamed of the same things?

Guilt and Shame as Adaptive Syndromes

Human emotions are above all social. A person invariably depends on intricate systems of cooperation and reciprocity if he is to have any decent chance of survival, reproduction, and the fostering of his children. Negative human emotions respond preeminently to threats to one's place in cooperative schemes—or so we should expect.[12] Many things could threaten one's candidacy for inclusion in cooperative schemes, but we could place them into two main classes, lack of resources and lack of good motivations. On the one hand, a person may lack the ability to contribute to cooperative schemes. That may be a matter of personal skills and abilities, or it may be a matter of his power to elicit support from others: he may lack useful family connections; he may be blemished in ways that make others shy away. On the other hand a person may have all the abilities and social connections needed for a cooperative scheme, but be a poor cooperator because of insufficient motivation to play his part and reciprocate benefits.

Here, then, is a rough division of the typical causes of shame and those of guilt. Shame stems from things that indicate a lack of the abilities, powers, or resources one needs if one is to be valued for one's cooperation and reciprocity. Guilt stems from things that indicate insufficient motivation.

None of this means that the person who feels guilty or ashamed thinks in any such terms. None of this means that I have specified the properties a circumstance must have if a person is to feel guilty over

12. Many scientific studies of emotion have focused on emotions humans share with the beasts. Plutchik (1980) suggests that all emotions are mixtures of "a small number of basic, primary, or prototype emotions" (129), and that we should expect these to function everywhere in the evolutionary scale (138) and to be tied to needs all animals share. I am suggesting instead that human life differs radically from the life of most animals, and requires such complex social dispositions that new emotions might have evolved.

it or ashamed over it. Specific sorts of things will make a person feel guilty, and specific sorts of things will make him feel ashamed. What biological speculation suggests is a reason why these particular types of things should be lumped together when they are otherwise so varied.

Why, though, should there be distinct syndromes activated by these particular two rough classes of circumstances? Emotions, in evolutionary terms, cash out in action: in the actions to which they lead and in the actions they elicit in others. It is through actions that reproductive prospects are enhanced or diminished. Guilt and shame, on the story I have been telling, are both induced by things that typically portend bad treatment from others. The kinds of bad treatment will differ, though, and so will the remedies. Bad motivations elicit anger and other inadequacies elicit disdain. These tend toward different kinds of action. Anger is punitive, whereas disdain leads chiefly to indifference and neglect. That is as we should expect: where a desired motivation is lacking, punishment can provide it; where other powers are lacking, nothing can be done but to cut one's losses with the person. Guilt, then, responds to circumstances that typically portend punishment, and shame to circumstances that typically portend neglect. Now, anger and neglect have different remedies. To cope with the anger of others, we need to placate them through apology, restitution, and open contrition. To cope with disdain that leads to neglect, on the other hand, we need either to withdraw or to display our powers—to show that we can contribute importantly to cooperative schemes. Guilt tends toward amends; shame toward withdrawal or the development of one's powers.[13]

Guilt and shame, then, are first-person counterparts to anger and disdain. Not that guilt is self-directed anger; feeling guilty is different from feeling you could kick yourself. Rather, guilt is coordinated with anger in a special way: it aims to placate anger, and it is governed by the same norms as govern anger. Anger need not be met with guilt,

13. See extensive discussions by Rawls (1971, secs. 67, 70–75, and esp. pp. 445, 484). See also Piers (1953): "Guilt anxiety accompanies transgression; shame, failure" (24). This requires some independent characterization of transgression and failure; Piers rests the distinction on talk of the "superego" and the "ego ideal". "The unconscious, irrational threat implied in shame anxiety is abandonment, and not mutilation (castration) as in guilt" (24). I myself stress related but realistic threats: disdain and anger and their consequences. Not that the feelings must necessarily involve thoughts of such threats, but these threats are the frequent accompaniments of situations that call forth shame and guilt—and not by accident.

to be sure; it may be met with anger in turn or with fear. When anger is met by anger, though, trouble brews. When anger breeds fear, trouble may be averted, but not through an emotion specially adapted to placate anger. Guilt meshes with anger in a special way, and shame meshes with disdain.

Folk Psychologies

The adaptive syndrome picture of guilt and shame needs to be tied to evidence, and some of the evidence from exotic cultures seems to weigh against it. Shame or something like it appears everywhere, and so does anger, but guilt seems culturally special. Many languages have no word for guilt, and so if the people who speak those languages do feel guilt they cannot say so. Yet if guilt and shame are distinct biological adaptations to the human condition, then they were widely present as human nature evolved, and they should appear distinctly in a wide range of present cultures.

Other cultures speak of emotions in ways that will strike us as bizarre. Gleanings from two recent articles give some of the flavor. Jean Smith tells us of the Maori of a century ago (Smith 1981). For fear they had two words: *hauhauaitu*, which meant languid, cold, or trembling, and *hae*, which meant to be torn, and was also used for jealousy and hatred. *Aroha* was yearning love, but also seemed at times to be grief. The *ngakau* was a mind located in the guts; it could feel well, laugh, feel pain, be weak, or be dark. It could lose clarity; it could desire, remember, know, or execute a plan. It could be strong or be foolishly obstinate. The *manawa* was in the chest and connected with breathing; to have quivering *manawa* was to be happily moved, fidgety, or anxious, and to have closed *manawa* was to dislike or to be depressed. Both *manawa* and *ngakau* could experience yearning or anger. Shame alone was not located in an organ and it was not subject to kinds of ritual manipulation that could control other emotions; it was abolished only by revenge.

Charlotte Hardman reports on the Lohorung Rai of eastern Nepal (Hardman 1981). They distinguish three psychophysical substances which can be in various states. *Saya*, the ancestral substance or ancestral pride, gives strength, courage, and vitality. Normally it is located in the head, but it can fall, leaving one depressed and vulnerable to enemies. It is highest in chiefs. *Lawa* is the essence of life and the essence of timidity. A person's *lawa* can be lost or stolen, and if it is not replaced within two or three weeks, death comes. Male and female *lawa* differ; male *lawa* is crafty, skillful, intelligent and tricky. One's *lawa* wanders in dreams to warn or to visit old haunts, and it can be frightened away, or drawn away by an ancestral spirit, leaving one insane.

Niwa, roughly mind or good sense, may be in the stomach or in the head. If it is deep inside, then one knows how to keep silent, whereas if it is in the head one speaks too freely. *Niwa* involves knowing the correct feelings for people and when they may be expressed; it must remember and keep a watchful eye on duties, on respectful behavior, and on posture. A person has *niwa* for persons in each of various roles: for spouse, for guests, and so forth. *Niwa* comes in types: it may be big or little (generous or stingy); it may be soft (compassionate); it may be crafty, shy, hard-working, brave, boastful, jealous, clever, undecided, or self-important. It develops slowly in children, and begins to die in old age. A child's anger in the stomach shows lack of *niwa*, but by the age of ten he should have developed a controlled, adult anger in his heart, a desire to fight. A man angry at his wife, say, might express his anger by doing a piece of women's work. Childish fear develops into adult respect and shame. One's own personal *niwa*, in contrast, is something like one's fancy; it is allowed full scope in informal situations, where individual personality is expressed without inhibition.

Could we have used Maori or Lohorung Rai folk terms instead of our own and explained what emotions norms of morality govern? It looks as though we could not. Now that does not in itself refute a norm-expressivistic analysis of moral terms. We ourselves experience guilt and shame, anger and disdain as distinct emotions, and morality in the narrow sense is ours. It consists, we can still say, in norms governing emotions that we ourselves experience and name. If others lack concepts of guilt and anger, that simply means they lack morality on this narrow construal.

If, though, emotional conceptions differ as much as these reports suggest, that seems to spoil the view of guilt and shame as distinct biological adaptations. The explanation of what these emotions are cannot be the one I have sketched.

Attributional Theories

The diversity of folk concepts of emotions suggests a picture quite different from the adaptive syndrome picture. It suggests that the distinct emotions a person can have are chiefly a matter of his own conceptions—conceptions which will vary sharply from culture to culture. Perhaps a few crude differentiations can be made interculturally: a person may be greatly aroused or slightly, and his feelings toward something may be pro or con. Finer differentiations, though, will be culturally idiosyncratic. A person is angry if he is strongly aroused in a negative way and thinks of himself as angry. Likewise he is afraid if he is strongly aroused in a negative way and thinks of himself as afraid. The states of arousal differ only in the interpretations put on them by the person who is in the state, and he interprets himself through the conceptions of his own culture. Hence a specific emotion, like guilt or anger, will exist only in a culture that has the corresponding concepts.

Rodney Needham attacks all claims that familiar emotional states are universal. A traveler or ethnographer will find that he can label many emotions with confidence, and he will be able to confirm these identifications in various ways. He may see a man scowling and call him angry. This procedure, though, "begs the important questions, for he does not yet know the conventional significance of grimaces in this society, and he cannot know by simple observation that the inner state of the man under observation is identical with anything that he would recognize in himself as anger" (Needham 1981, 70). To understand the inner state of the scowling man, "He will need to find out, just as he does in his own society, . . . what are the particular circumstances that justify attributing precisely this inner state, rather than some other, to the man who he infers is angry. To do this calls for a comprehensive knowledge of the values, collective representations, modes of organization and so on which comprise the society" (70).

As I read Needham, the story is something like this. Kwasi scowls, and it is correct in his Akan culture to call his state *abufuw*. His state is one of anger only if *abufuw* means anger. However, *abufuw* does not mean anger, because the Akan rules for applying the term *abufuw* do not match our rules for applying 'anger'. "This means that 'anger' in another civilization is not equivalent to anger in our own" (72).

There are two steps here, and both need examination. First, Kwasi is in a state of anger only if *abufuw* means anger. Why should this be, though? If we ask whether Kwasi is angry, the question is whether we ourselves are correct in calling him angry. It is not, at least directly, whether Kwasi's term *abufuw* means anger. Perhaps we are right to think him in a state of anger, and the Akans are right to think him in a state of *abufuw*—even though 'anger' is not a correct translation of *abufuw*. Think of other classifications: the Nuer of the Sudan have an intricate vocabulary for kinds of cattle, and it meshes terribly with ours (see Needham 1972, 19–20). That does not mean that either they or we get things wrong; they are right and we are right (or our experts are), though we classify cattle by different characteristics. Grant, then, that the Akan term *abufuw* does not really mean anger, and that they are right to think him in a state of *abufuw*. Why should that show *us* wrong in thinking Kwasi angry?

Perhaps the point is that anger is guided by self-attribution. Seeing oneself as angry plays a role in producing the syndrome we label anger—so crucial a role that a person cannot be angry unless he can think himself angry. This is a psychological claim about the workings of those states we pick out as anger. If this claim held, that would secure one step of Needham's argument. It would explain why Kwasi cannot be angry unless he can think of himself as angry.

Can Kwasi think himself angry? Needham's second premise, on my reading, was that if two terms have different rules for their application they mean different things. Now if these rules gave truth conditions, that would clearly be right. The rules Needham invokes, though, are criterial: they give "the particular circumstances that justify attributing precisely this inner state, rather than some other, to the man who he infers is angry" (70). Now the criterial account of meaning could be challenged, but the theory of meaning in general is not our concern here; what matters for us is the way this theory of meaning combines with a self-attribution theory of emotion. In combination, the thesis is this: If Kwasi lacks any term with the criteria of our term 'angry' then he cannot be angry. For to be angry one must be able to think of oneself as angry, and that now means that one must be able to apply a term to oneself that carries the same criteria as our term 'angry'. Anger depends on self-attribution, and what is crucial to the self-attribution is that it have the same criteria as anger as we conceive it.

This self-attribution view could be combined with the judgmentalism I discussed earlier to give a broader attributional theory of emotion. The workings of anger, we might claim, are guided not only by a view of oneself as angry, but by a view of one's situation as somehow calling for anger. Both the ways one can see oneself and the ways one can see one's circumstances are largely set by one's culture, and so in both these ways anger will be peculiar to a culture or a range of cultures. Let me call any such theory of emotion *attributional*. On such a theory, the workings of emotions are crucially guided by attributions of some kind—to oneself, to circumstances, or to both. The terms of these attributions will be more or less peculiar to a culture, and the workings of an emotion will depend so intimately on the peculiarities of these attributions that cross-cultural labels for emotions will simply mislead. Needham's conclusions would hold not only on a strictly self-attributional theory of the workings of emotion, but on a more broadly attributional view.

In either case, the argument rests ultimately on a claim as to what is distinctive about anger—what allows us to speak of a person as angry and to do so fruitfully and systematically. The claim is that anger is distinguished by the criteria of the terms the angry person could correctly apply to himself and his circumstances. Now this claim will be plausible only if the alternatives are independently discredited. If there existed in human beings the kind of syndrome I sketched as anger, with special adaptive mechanisms behind it, then there would be no reason to demand that a person have a term that means 'angry' before we count him as angry.

At this point, then, we simply have two hypotheses about the nature of distinctive emotions such as anger. On the adaptive syndrome picture, anger is a biologically adaptive state with certain typical causes, typical expressions, and typical action tendencies. On an attributional picture, nothing sharply distinguishes the states we count as anger from a continuum of other states of negative arousal, except for the attributions involved in these states and the consequences of these attributions. The concepts of specific emotional states in different cultures do not form neat clusters; others will have concepts more or less like our concept of anger, but the likenesses and differences will be matters of degree. Likewise different cultures will see a set of circumstances in different ways. Hence there will be states that are like our anger in some ways and different in some ways, and all we can do is be specific about these likenesses and differences. The emotional states of disparate peoples do not cluster into natural kinds, and using our own terms will make us think exotic peoples too much like ourselves.[14]

14. Heelas (1984) discusses what in effect is the issue between an adaptive syndrome picture and an attributional picture. He takes up a group (the Chewong of Malaya) who suppress emotions strongly, and finds the best account of their emotional life in a combination of "innate motor scripts" and "cultural models", drawn respectively from Leventhal (1980) and Schachter (1971). See Howell (1981) for a description of Chewong folk psychology.

Evidence and Attributional Theories

Part of the evidence for the attributional picture of emotion lies simply in the disparate terminology we observe for emotions from culture to culture. If there were the kinds of distinct syndromes I have hypothesized, would different cultures have failed to have noticed them? Perhaps they would; even intuitive physics can be refuted by simple observation—but if they have, then why expect our own folk psychology to have got things right?

Even with the old mammalian emotions of fear and anger, it is controversial whether the difference is in some way attributional, but the case for non-attributional differences seems fairly strong.[15] Among humans in far cultures, distinct words can usually be found that seem best translated as 'afraid' and as 'angry'. The translations may be rough, and the peoples they study may conceive of fear and anger in ways we find bizarre, but fear and anger do seem to be recognizable as distinct in a variety of cultures.[16]

The same cannot be said for the ethically significant emotions I need to distinguish. It is common for ethnographers to speak of shame and find words for shame, but guilt is rarely reported. The word 'shame' may be used loosely in these accounts, sometimes suggesting diffidence, sometimes humiliation, sometimes embarrassment. Perhaps the term is sometimes applied to guilt. In any case separate terms for

15. See Buck (1976, 351) for criticism of the claim that distinct emotions are alike apart from attributions. Some evidence suggests that of two related hormones, epinephrine and norepinephrine (adrenaline and noradrenaline), a higher level of epinephrine is present with fear, and of norepinephrine with anger (35–36). Electrical stimulation of a part of the limbic system can produce unmotivated rage; see Buck (1976, 83–85). The interpretation of this evidence, though, is still in controversy.

Schachter and Singer (1962) showed that attribution can have something to do with emotion. Injections of epinephrine (adrenaline) by themselves produced symptoms of emotional arousal but no emotion. Some of the subjects were told that the injections would produce these symptoms and some were not. Left with a playful stooge, informed subjects felt less euphoric than uninformed ones, and left with an angry stooge informed subjects felt less angry than uninformed ones. That does not tell us whether the differences between fear and euphoria are chiefly attributional, although Schachter himself supports such a theory. See Schachter (1971, esp. 44–55).

16. See, for instance, Howell (1981) for the Chewong of Malaya, and Needham (1972) for the Nuer. Smith (1981, 149) writes: "The Maori did not consider the emotion of fear to be caused by what we would see as a fear-causing event such as a forthcoming battle, but rather believed it to be inflicted upon a man by a hostile *atua* [god] angered by some violation of a *tapu* rule. If a man felt fear before battle it was considered to be a bad omen and sufficient reason for him not to fight."

guilt and shame are not often reported. Can emotions in this region be distinguished when the culture is not our own?[17]

Guilt is a first-person counterpart to anger; it meshes with anger. Anger appears to be universal, and we need to know much more about how people in other cultures respond to anger. Anger can prompt anger in return, it can induce plain fear—and in some cultures at least it can be met with feelings of guilt. Now guilt, as we know it, motivates in special ways. Psychiatrists are interested in its devious workings, but we need to think of the motivations that might make guilt adaptive. The person who feels guilty is moved to placate anger by shows of repentance and by making amends. How widespread and uniform are such tendencies? In what other ways do people cope when others are angry with them? Do these ways fall into syndromes, as fear and anger seem to in spite of the different ways cultures elaborate them? Or do they vary smoothly and indefinitely?

Perhaps conciliatory emotional responses to anger are more uniform than many emotional lexicons suggest. Perhaps on the other hand they are much less uniform than is anger itself. Anger is continuous with an emotion of the beasts, and beasts cope with anger in ways available to humans, with fear, with anger in return, or with submission. In humans the possibilities are wider, and we still need to ask whether some of these new possibilities constitute specific biological adaptations to the needs of social life.

On the attribution picture, guilt is not a specific biological adaptation; it shows the workings of a more general set of mechanisms in a special set of cultural circumstances. Universally, being the object of someone's anger will evoke some kind of negative agitation. One's culture will give one a repertory for coping with the situation, and for labeling and expressing one's agitation. What gives identity to the agitation will be the label drawn from this cultural repertory. The responses will still form a syndrome of typical expressions and tendencies to action, typically caused by having done something it would make one angry for someone else to have done. The syndrome, though, will not constitute a specific biological adaptation. Biological adaptations will of course stand behind it, but they will consist of gen-

17. See Singer (1953) for one important discussion of this question. Levy (1974) looks at Tahiti, and argues that in traditional, steady-state societies, shame/embarrassment is adequate as a response to immediate visibility. In changing societies, "one must be rebellious, one must do harm in relation to some traditional system aspects. Now guilt comes to the fore, and the question becomes the authority of feelings of guilt"—that is, in effect, whether they are warranted (300).

eral tendencies—tendencies to label and guide emotional agitation with items drawn from one's cultural repertory.

Normative Control and Moral Judgments

Much experimental study of emotion has taken up emotions we share with the beasts. We needed to ask how to treat emotions that seem peculiarly human. What gives a specific human emotion like guilt its identity? I have sketched two broad kinds of theories, particularly for guilt and shame. We can ask how norm-expressivism would stand with each.

Take first the adaptive syndrome view. Here things are straightforward. Major specifically human emotions like guilt and shame are distinct biological adaptations; we pick them out by their different typical causes, the different kinds of action they prompt, and often by different typical expressions. Moral norms are norms governing guilt and anger, whereas norms of shamefulness govern shame and disdain.

Whence the temptation, then, to see these emotions as full-fledged judgments, or as including such judgments? When someone is angry with me for something I have done, his anger seems to include a judgment that I was to blame for it. That must be wrong, since he can be angry with me for something I did and yet think that I was in the right. He can be angry but think it makes no sense to be angry. Still there is some connection between anger and judgments of blame, and the temptation to fuse them needs to be explained.

The temptation stems in part from anger's having its typical causes and typical foci. The causes are typically insults, injuries, and other moral outrages, and it is on such things that anger is prone to focus. Norm-expressivism tells why this should be so: We judge a deed blameworthy if we accept norms that prescribe guilt and anger for such a deed. The norms we accept for guilt and for anger mesh, and they ordinarily endorse our chief tendencies in feeling angry—while smoothing things out and correcting for partiality. Hence we normally think angering things blameful.

Anger is assimilated to moral judgments for a further reason, we can now say. Not only do we tend not to be angered by what we think morally innocent, but the norms we accept tell us not to be. If I do something and you judge that there was nothing morally wrong with it, you will think it makes no sense to be angry with me. When you are angry and you do think it makes sense to be, you then judge that

I have done something morally objectionable. So long as normative governance prevails, you will be angry only when you think it makes sense to be so, and so you will be angry at me only when you judge my deeds blameworthy.

Turn, then, to attributional pictures. Do they allow for normative governance of emotions? Do they let us explain particular emotions like anger without invoking normative concepts like being to blame? Unless they do, the norm-expressivistic account of moral judgments is circular: it invokes anger and guilt to characterize moral judgments, but we must understand moral judgments already if we are to characterize guilt and anger.

On an attributional picture, to understand the nature of an emotion, we need to understand the various possible views a person can take of his circumstances and his feelings. This is judgmentalism with a twist: that the range of judgments a person can make is set by his culture, and so will differ from culture to culture. To feel guilty I must have guilt in my cultural repertory of feelings and see myself as feeling guilty, or I must have being at fault in my cultural repertory and see myself as at fault.

On self-attributional versions, the judgments that form an emotion are judgments of one's own state. The ways a person thinks of himself shape his emotions: feeling guilty is a matter of seeing oneself as such. When I think of myself as guilty, I see myself as being in a state that I conceive as follows: it is typically caused by my own acts of certain kinds, it is expressed by a guilty mien, and it typically moves me toward apology and amends. These thoughts guide what I do; thinking myself to feel guilty tends to give me a guilty mien and moves me to apology and amends.

Does this make for problems for norm-expressivism? It would if, according to my cultural repertory, I can feel guilty only if I am at fault, or if I think myself at fault. In that case, we as observers could explain feelings of guilt only if we could already attribute the concept of fault. We would need to understand thinking oneself at fault before we could explain feeling guilty. If all that were so, then on pain of circularity we could not invoke feelings of guilt to explain thinking oneself at fault— whereas that is what norm-expressivism tries to do.

In fact, though, no such thing obtains. It is not part of guilt, as it appears in my cultural repertory, that I can feel it only if I am at fault or think myself so. For it is allowed by the concept that I can feel guilt inappropriately: I can feel it without being at fault and without thinking myself at fault. That is what happens when I realize I feel guilty senselessly.

Still, perhaps as they appear in my cultural repertory, guilt feelings come *normally* with thinking oneself at fault. Perhaps that is one of the cluster of normal circumstances that shapes guilt in my culture. At first glance that looks plausible enough: to feel guilty is to feel as if one were at fault. Nothing, though, forces the observer to characterize guilt in this way. He need not invoke a notion of fault itself. Instead, he can appeal directly to the central kinds of circumstances in which, in my culture, one is thought to be at fault. Those circumstances will be part of the cluster the observer uses to define guilt; other parts will be the expressive and action tendencies that come with guilt. The observer can then go on to use this characterization of guilt to say what it is to think a person at fault.

Perhaps, though, the circumstances in which one is thought to be at fault themselves define fault. Then no detour would be needed through the acceptance of norms: the normative concept *fault* would already have been defined. In fact, however, fault cannot be defined by examples, and this for two reasons at least: In the first place, one example or another could be denied without contradiction—perhaps not the most central ones, but there are many things we normally think faults but on which we could change our minds.[18] More important, knowing examples, even central ones, does not tell us how to go on to new or uncertain cases. How a particular person in the culture goes on is a matter of the norms he accepts. Imagine a culture, say, that is uncertain about sex without commitment. If the norms a person accepts say not to resent casual sex and not to feel guilty about it, then the person thinks casual sex morally all right. He thinks so without logical or linguistic error. Whether casual sex is correctly judged all right cannot just be extrapolated from the cases on which everyone firmly agrees.

We might want to say that the central examples define a protoconcept of fault. The full concept, though, gets its shape from a connection with norms. The protoconcept at most helps define feelings of guilt. Feelings of guilt can then be invoked, with no circularity, to define a full concept of fault.

This is how norm-expressivism might work with self-attributional

---

18. Foot (1959) insists that some bizarre moral judgments are ruled out by rules of meaning. I am not clear whether Foot thinks rules of meaning settle less extreme cases. I myself am claiming that any such conclusion would be implausible.

theories of guilt and anger. The concept of guilt is given by a cluster of circumstances in which it will normally be felt, by a set of normal expressions, and by tendencies to action it normally stirs. In a culture with the concept in its repertory, people will see themselves from time to time as feeling guilty, and will tend accordingly to fit themselves to the concept. The same goes for anger. In a culture with concepts of guilt and anger, people may accept norms as governing these emotions. To hold a person to blame for an action will then be to accept norms that tell him to feel guilty for having done it, and tell others to be angry with him for having done it. Other cultures will have no such concepts in their repertory, and then we cannot interpret any of their talk as narrowly moral. Still other cultures might have emotional concepts somewhat like ours and somewhat different. If they accept norms as governing the emotions they recognize and experience, they can then entertain questions that are somewhat like our own narrowly moral questions.

III · NORMATIVE OBJECTIVITY

8 · Objectivity: First Steps

To call something rational, I said at the start, is to express one's acceptance of a system of norms that permits it. That was cryptic and incomplete, and I spent later chapters trying to work the analysis into better shape. Still I have skipped past a chief ground for doubt: that any expressivistic theory must have an air of "subjectivism".

When a person calls something rational, he seems to be doing more than simply expressing his own acceptance of a system of norms—or even expressing the complicated state of mind I described in Chapter 5. He claims to speak with authority; he claims to recognize and report something that is true independently of what he himself happens to accept or reject. He claims the backing of considerations that, in some sense, "compel acceptance" of what he is saying. Perhaps he is wrong, but that is the claim he is making. Any account of his language that ignores this claim must be defective. It may capture all that the speaker could claim without illusion, but it will not capture all that he in fact is claiming. It will not be a genuine analysis of the concepts involved, but a way of defanging a claim that originally had bite.

If the accusation were strictly one of subjectivism, it would misfire. In the strict sense, no expressivistic analysis is "subjectivistic". To be subjectivistic, the analysis would have to say that when a person calls something rational, he is reporting a state of mind: he is saying that someone—be it he, or his group, or perhaps the agent or the agent's group—is in some particular state of mind with respect to that thing. It is easy to confuse expressivistic analyses with subjectivistic ones; norm-expressivism itself is easily confused with the subjectivistic theory that 'X is rational' means "I accept a system of norms that permits X." Clearly, though, the analysis says no such thing. It says not that the speaker *states that he accepts* a system of norms that permits X, but that the speaker *expresses his acceptance* of a system of norms that permits X. To express a state of mind is not to say that one is in it.

All this is true enough, but it misses the chief concerns that prompt the charge of subjectivism. True, the analysis is not subjectivistic; neither, though, is it objectivistic—as it would have to be, the objector may think, to capture what is being claimed when a person calls something rational. If the person claims objective backing and the analysis misses the claim, then the analysis is defective whether it is "subjectivistic" or not.

What is to be said, then, about claims to normative objectivity? Does norm-expressivism miss something in ordinary normative talk? Normative language does involve claims to objectivity in some sense—that seems clear enough. That in itself, though, is no objection, for some claims to objectivity are well explained by norm-expressivism. That is what I try to show in this long part of the book. Even so, the analysis may still end up missing something in our ordinary claims to objectivity. Here I think matters indeterminate.

It might be thought that ordinary conceptions of rationality are Platonistic or intuitionistic. On the Platonistic picture, among the facts of the world are facts of what is rational and what is not. A person of normal mental powers can discern these facts. Judgments of rationality are thus straightforward apprehensions of fact, not through sense perception but through a mental faculty analogous to sense perception. When a person claims authority to pronounce on what is rational, he must base his claim on this power of apprehension.[1]

If this is what anyone seriously believes, then I simply want to debunk it. Nothing in a plausible, naturalistic picture of our place in the universe requires these non-natural facts and these powers of nonsensory apprehension. The Platonistic strain, though, is not strong in ordinary thought. To the naive ear, the claims of Platonism sound fantastic; their appeal comes chiefly from a lack of anything to put in their place.

Norm-expressivism is meant to capture whatever there is to ordinary notions of rationality if Platonism is excluded. Even with Platonism excluded, our ordinary thought about rationality involves strong claims to a kind of objectivity, and it is these non-Platonistic claims

---

1. Sidgwick (1907, bk. 1, chap. 3) is explicitly intuitionistic about our knowledge of what is rational, and Ewing (1939) is intuitionistic about an 'ought' that I read as the ought of rationality.

that I want to elucidate. My hope, then, is to save what is clear in ordinary thought about rationality, and to find our reflective thinking about rationality reasonably clear and fully rectifiable, with one exception: our wavering penchant for Platonism.

What is at issue with objectivity? In one form, as I have said, the question is simply whether a Platonistic account is correct. Other important questions, though, may be confused with this one. Platonism has its allure, and this allure no doubt stems from features of ordinary thought; questions about these features are in effect versions of the question of objectivity. I find at least three broad questions of this kind. First, anyone who takes a norm to constitute a requirement of rationality takes that norm to apply independently of his own accepting it. He thinks that even if he rejected the norm, that norm would still be valid. The first question is what this could mean. Second, we seem to distinguish between accepting something as a demand of rationality and making an idiosyncratic existential commitment to it. Is there any sense to be made of this distinction? Finally, when a speaker pronounces something rational or irrational, he seems to be claiming some authority. He is not merely exposing his opinion to public scrutiny; he is claiming to be right. He claims that his opinion is interpersonally valid. What is the nature of this claim to authority? These are the questions I want to explore.

How, then, can we explain the objective pretensions in our normative talk? We might try radical interpretation: perhaps the strict demands of rationality are the ones we must take people to satisfy if we are to find them intelligible. Alternatively we might try weighing reasons: it is rational to do something when doing it is supported by the preponderance of reasons—and so if we could say what reasons are, we could then characterize what it is for an act, belief, or emotion to be rational. Neither of these proposals gets us far, I argue, and so I turn to lines of thought that do. First, a person who thinks something rational thinks that it would still be rational even if he thought it were not. Validity, he thinks, is independent of acceptance. An expressivistic analysis renders this nicely. Second, some norms govern the acceptance of other norms, and the structure of these higher order norms can distinguish between a person's accepting something as a demand of rationality and his treating it as an existential commitment. As for questions of normative authority, I defer them to subsequent chapters: they turn out to have deep ramifications, and they require one last revision of the norm-expressivistic analysis.

Coherence and Interpretation

Man is a rational animal, we are told. Perhaps the strict demands of rationality are simply those a being must meet to count as human; to be rational is for one's thoughts and actions to be intelligible as thoughts and actions, and so as manifestations of the capacities that make us human.

Rationality, this line of thought may continue, is somewhat in the eye of the beholder. To count a being as rational is ourselves to find his thoughts and acts intelligible, and doing so requires interpretation: we do not know what his thoughts are until we have interpreted them. Interpretation, moreover, is no mere recognition of what is going on in the other's head; it involves matching his thoughts and words with our own. Meanings are not discovered; they are ascribed—under tight constraints, to be sure, but constraints that allow some slack. Whether a being is rational is a matter of what mental properties we ascribe to him: we regard him as rational if we succeed without undue strain in ascribing him the right mental properties.

In order to assess a being as rational or irrational, then, we must try to make sense of his words and thoughts, and of the reasons he has for his actions. To do that we have to suppose him rational in a wide variety of ways—or at least rational for the most part. Otherwise we could find anyone crazy on a wealth of gerrymandered interpretive schemes, and we would have no more grounds for accepting one scheme than for accepting the next. We try to interpret a person under the constraint that he must come out for the most part as rational. If we succeed, we then do regard him as rational.[2]

Might the requirements of rationality, then, simply be the things needed for interpretability? Might they be the requirements we must suppose a person meets, for the most part, if we are to treat him as an intelligible human being? Are his existential commitments, in contrast, just whatever commitments he might not have and still be intelligible?

The demands of rationality, on this proposal, will in part be ones of coherence. One constraint on interpretation, after all, will be that we

2. Quine (1960, chap. 2) develops a theory of radical interpretation. Davidson too draws extensive philosophical consequences from considerations of radical interpretation (1984, essays 1, 2, 9–11, 13).

must interpret a person as coherent. Coherence as I am using the term is a matter of formal, internal consistency in one's beliefs and normative judgments. An ideally coherent person could accept the logical consequences of everything he accepts without falling into logical contradiction. Coherence is thus a weaker requirement than full rationality; a person might be ideally coherent and yet be crazy. Rationality is a matter of what it really makes sense to do, to believe, and to feel; coherence is simply consistency, whether one's judgments be well- or ill-founded.

Coherence is a matter of logic. How do we attribute coherence or incoherence to a person? The story might go something like this: We the community of interpreters begin by noticing patterns in our own inferences, the inferences we confidently accept. We then formulate rules to accept as governing inferences. We demand of ourselves and each other that our inferences follow those rules. Rules that address all thought independently of its subject matter we count as rules of logic. Once we accept these rules, we apply them not only to ourselves but to others. When we try to interpret others, one of our goals is to find them logically coherent, at least for the most part. We do not, then, discover the logic that implicitly guides their thought. What we discover is whether they can be interpreted as being guided by logic as we already know it.

Now to interpret a being, we must assume him not only logically coherent but many other things as well. We must suppose him to have a somewhat normal stock of beliefs given his evidence. We must attribute to him a fairly normal stock of desires and a somewhat familiar emotional makeup. We must see him as engaging in familiar kinds of probable reasoning and practical reasoning. It would count heavily against an interpretation if on that interpretation the beliefs and norms that guided a being came out utterly bizarre. We must attribute to him, in short, an important core of substantive rationality—of rationality going beyond mere coherence (see Davidson 1984, essays 10, 11; 1980, essay 12).

The chief puzzle of rationality is not what constitutes coherence, but what rationality requires beyond mere formal coherence. Does the theory of interpretation offer a solution? Substantive rationality, we might say, consists of those things beyond mere formal coherence that we must attribute to a being—at least for the most part—if we are to find him thinking intelligibly.

I think this solution fails, at least for our purposes. In asking what it makes sense to do, to think, and to feel, we are asking for more than bare intelligibility. A minimal rationality may well be required for intelligibility, but explaining this minimal rationality will not explain the rationality that goes beyond the minimum. Does it really make sense to value anything beyond one's own enjoyment? Does it ever make sense to feel guilty for what one has done, or to condemn someone else in one's heart and in one's talk for what he has done? These are not questions about intelligibility in some minimal sense. If we come to accept answers to these questions, we will not add those answers to our stock of commonplaces—to our stock of things a person must be seen as accepting, for the most part, if he is to be seen as thinking with any intelligibility. Perhaps we must attribute a minimal rationality to anyone we regard as thinking intelligibly, and the minimal rationality we must attribute may turn out to be quite rich in its content. Still, the deepest questions of what it makes sense to do, to think, and to feel are ones on which a person could be wrong without prejudice to his interpretability.

What we need for interpretation, moreover, is not precisely rationality, but extensive parallels with our own lore.[3] Domestic lore contains much that is rational, and so to demand extensive parallels is indeed to demand that much be interpretable as rational. Still, believing in ghosts is intelligible enough. It is intelligible to invest more in a project because one has already invested so much. It is all too intelligible to lock the barn after the horse has been stolen, or to take comfort in the plight of others. Whether any of these things is rational is open to doubt, but we need not assess the rationality of these things simply to find them intelligible.

Indeed ascribing too much rationality might count against an interpretation. We should not interpret people as avoiding the most common fallacies; attributions of hyperrationality are less plausible than attributions of rationality to a normal degree. We label a piece of reasoning a fallacy when we decide what norms to accept and see that the piece of reasoning violates those norms. The norms we come to accept may perfectly well go against the most common ways of thinking about a matter. In those cases, we should interpret people as being

3. Grandy (1973) criticizes the principle of charity, and proposes instead a "principle of humanity": that the imputed pattern of relations among beliefs, desires and the world be as similar to our own as possible. See Lewis (1974) and Lukes (1982, 262–271). Anthropologists Horton (1970) and Sperber (1982) have fine discussions of the attribution of irrational beliefs.

normally rational, not as being perfectly rational by our lights. Perfect rationality is not just minimal rationality smoothed over.[4]

In many ways, furthermore, people in a radically different culture simply are not intelligible—or at least, they are not intelligible until one has been acculturated. Acculturation is not simply a matter of accumulating evidence to test interpretive hypotheses; it is a matter of the kinds of influences that make human beings somewhat like those around them, and make human beings react to the familiar as intelligible. Anyone lives in a sharply limited range of cultures, and so if we have any anthropological sophistication, we must expect that there is much in human life that is not only unknown to us, but unintelligible in our own terms.

That raises a further doubt concerning rationality as intelligibility. Must I regard as irrational all I would find unintelligible in terms of my current stock of concepts? True, the most direct way to judge something rational is to interpret it and inspect it—but the same goes for judging something irrational. Much that is intelligible is irrational, and much that is rational may be unintelligible to me. We do not need faraway cultures to make this point; uniform gauge theories in physics provide fine examples. As one comes to find a realm of human life intelligible, one comes to internalize standards for judging that realm of life. It is when one accepts or rejects those standards that one makes direct judgments of the rationality, as opposed to the mere intelligibility, of those ways of life.[5]

Interpretation matters: we can directly assess another person's judgment as rational or irrational only under an interpretation, and the assessments we make can always be challenged on the grounds that we have misunderstood. Interpretation requires parallels with our own lore, and so interpreting a person requires ascribing important strains of rationality to him. What is needed, though, falls well short of full rationality. Coherence itself might be a smoothed out version of the minimal coherence required for interpretation. Substantive rationality is no such thing. True, we succeed in attributing a minimal substantive rationality to a person or we fail to interpret him. Once having interpreted him, though, we assess what it really makes sense for him to

4. Nisbett and Ross (1980) argue that human beings employ a large number of heuristics that, in certain circumstances, fall short of ideal rationality. Thagard and Nisbett (1983) draw on psychological evidence to criticize versions of the principle of charity that say we should never interpret people as irrational, or that we should interpret them as irrational only given overwhelming evidence.

5. Davidson may disagree (1984, essay 13).

do, to think, and to feel in much the way we do for ourselves. My puzzle is what we are doing then.

Reasons

What it makes sense to do is what we have most reason to do. The rational alternative is the one supported by a preponderance of reasons. If we could say what constitutes the force of reasons, that might tell us what a person is claiming when he calls something rational or irrational.

One common account of reasons is a broadly Humean one: that reasons are settled by desires or preferences. If it is going to rain, taking an umbrella will keep one dry, and that is a reason for taking one. More precisely, the Humean says, it is a reason for anyone who prefers keeping dry to getting wet. What makes it a reason is that taking an umbrella would satisfy a preference—in this case, a preference for keeping dry. A fact constitutes a reason for a person if and only if it bears the right relation to his own intrinsic preferences.

Various emendations could be made: First, it might be the norm-sanctioned preferences of a person that are relevant, not all of his preferences. Second, we might want to speak of the preferences a person would have on full reflection, not his unreflective preferences. Finally, it might be best to put the account in terms of expected utility cashed out in terms of preferences. Let me skip over all this, though, and start with the unrefined version.

There is something wrong with this kind of analysis in general, I want to suggest. It fits not an expressivistic analysis of rationality but a full information analysis. It is therefore open to the same kinds of objections as full information analyses of 'rational'.

Suppose Pompey has harmed me, and harmed me deliberately. If I harm him, that will even the score of harms. Is that any reason in itself for me to harm him? Some people would say no. True, harming him would deter others, and that might be a reason. The sheer fact that harming him would even the score, though, is no reason in itself to harm him.

Let Octavia make this last statement. What is she claiming? Perhaps she thinks that I myself want to harm Pompey only for the sake of deterrence. She thinks I want to harm him only because I want to reduce total harm in the future. She thinks that sheer revenge gives no reason for me to harm him because she thinks it is not my own reason for wanting to harm him.

That, however, is nothing she need think. She might be perfectly clear that I treat revenge for its own sake as a reason, that sheer revenge is my own reason for wanting to harm Pompey. Yet she might deny that it is *a* reason—a *good* reason. Sheer revenge, the sheer fact that it would even the score, is no reason in itself for inflicting harm on the person.

What is she insisting? She admits that I want sheer revenge. She is not denying that I have desires that would be satisfied by inflicting harm on Pompey. She thinks that those desires are at base unreasonable, that they won't bear real scrutiny. What does that mean?[6]

There is a close connection, I have been saying, between what it is rational to do and reasons for actions, between the ways it is rational to feel and reasons for feelings. To say it is rational to do something is to say that doing it is supported by the preponderance of reasons. Call this the *weighting principle*. Given analyses of the two terms 'rational' and 'a reason', we can ask whether they fit together— whether they make this weighting principle come out true. It is in this sense that the Humean analysis of 'a reason' *fits* a full information account of 'rational', but not an expressivistic analysis.

We need at the outset to clarify the weighting principle. In one sense of the term 'reason', a fact may constitute a reason for a person to do something, even though the person has no way of knowing that fact. If in fact rain is coming, the fact that an umbrella would keep me dry is a reason, in this sense, for me to take one—even if I have no inkling it might rain. In this sense, it is not what is *rational* that is supported by the preponderance of "reasons", since what is rational depends on what one knows. We might say that reasons of this kind bear on what is "advisable". If it is going to rain, it is advisable to take an umbrella, even though you may have no way of telling it may rain. I am inter-

---

6. Some writers speak of "reasons" in a non-Humean way, and indeed try to ground ethical theory on a non-Humean concept of reasons. See especially Grice (1967), Nagel (1970), and Bond (1983). These writers, I take it, all mean to allow the kind of thing Octavia is saying. None of them, so far as I can discover, explains what he is using the term 'reason' to mean.

Kurt Baier (1958, 1978), if I understand him, holds that reasons are general guidelines, socially accepted in most cases, that are *sound*, in the sense that "their use in settling particular issues usually yields desired results" (1978, 718). I am unclear whether this is meant as an account of what the term 'reason' means, but if it were it would face problems. A person might admit, say, that revenge is a result people desire, but deny that effective guidelines for getting it make for good reasons. Moreover, talk of what "usually yields" results of a given kind skips past controversies about what constitutes instrumental rationality—questions on which people can disagree without linguistic or conceptual confusion. See the discussion in Chapter 1 of Russian roulette and the prisoner's dilemma.

ested here in reasons not in this sense, but in a sense in which a person cannot have a reason and be ignorant of it. In this sense, I have no reason to carry an umbrella unless I have some indication it may rain. We might call this an *available reason*, and the former kind a *potential reason*. Advisability, then, is supported by the preponderance of potential reasons, and rationality by the preponderance of available reasons. "Reasons" in the weighting principle are available reasons.

Even available reasons need to be distinguished from merely putative reasons: what a person takes to be available reasons. When a person does something we think ill considered, we distinguish "his reasons" for doing it from "a reason" to do it. If he throws bad money after good, his reason may be that he has already spent so much. We can still refuse to regard that as "a reason". Likewise, we might say that "a reason" to go to college is to acquire a broad perspective on the nature of humanity and its place in the universe, and yet deny that anything like that is the typical undergraduate's reason, or even one of his reasons. To say that something is a person's reason, or one of his reasons for doing what he does, is to say that he took it to be "a reason", and acted on it. Call this kind of reason a *motivating reason*. To say that it is "a reason" is to say, in some sense, that it provides grounds. Reasons in the weighting principle are grounding reasons, whether or not they are motivating reasons. An act, belief, or emotion is rational if and only if it is supported by the preponderance of available grounding reasons.[7]

To call an act "rational", my proposal was, is to express one's acceptance of a system of norms that permits that act. The rational act is supported by the preponderance of reasons—by the preponderance of available grounding reasons. That is the weighting principle, and we can use it to say what it means to call something a "reason". We can use it to develop an analysis of available good reasons that fits the norm-expressivistic analysis.

What is Octavia saying, if she denies that sheer revenge is a reason for harming Pompey? She is denying that sheer revenge counts toward harming him. She admits that if I harmed him, that would even the

---

7. The terms "motivating reasons" and "grounding reasons" I take from Bond (1983, chap. 2), but his use is somewhat different from mine. A "grounding reason" as he uses the term is what I am calling a potential reason: it must be something true, whether or not the person has any way of knowing it. My own use of the terms lets me speak too of "available grounding reasons". Audi (1986, 513) distinguishes "a reason for S to A" from "a reason S has for A-ing".

score, but that, she says, in no way tends to make harming him the rational thing to do.

A system of norms for action can work by assigning weight to considerations. It can say what sorts of things to weigh in favor of an action or against it, and how much. Octavia accepts such a system of norms. She thinks something a reason only when the norms she accepts say to give it weight. Harming Pompey would even the score, but the norms she accepts say not to weigh that in favor of harming him.

That gives us an expressivistic theory of what it means to call something a reason for doing something. When a person calls something— call it R—a reason for doing X, he expresses his acceptance of norms that say to treat R as weighing in favor of doing X. Calpurnia tells Caesar, "If you cross the Rubicon, you will be top man in Rome, and that is a weighty reason for crossing." She thereby expresses her acceptance of a system of norms that tells him to treat this fact—the fact that crossing the Rubicon will make him top man in Rome—as weighing heavily in favor of crossing.

This analysis of 'a reason' fits the norm-expressivistic analysis of 'rational': the two analyses satisfy the weighting principle. To say that an act is rational is to say that it is supported by the preponderance of reasons. For to say either one of these things is to express one's acceptance of a system of norms for weighing considerations that, as things come out, supports doing that act.

The Humean analysis of 'a reason', on the other hand, fits a full information analysis of 'rational'. Or at least it does if the Humean analysis is refined to speak of the desires the agent would have with full information. Say that I am fully informed. A Humean reason for me to do something will be a way in which doing it would satisfy one of my intrinsic desires.[8] I want to even the score with Pompey, and I want it intrinsically, not for the sake of anything else. It is this desire, the Humean says, that makes the fact—the fact that harming Pompey would even the score—a reason to harm him. That fits a full information analysis of 'rational': that an act is rational if it most satisfies my intrinsic desires—the intrinsic desires I have being fully informed. The weights of Humean reasons for an action add up to the degree to which the action would satisfy my desires. Each Humean reason,

---

8. This needs to be modified to take uncertainty into account, but here I attempt no careful formulation.

after all, is a way in which the act would satisfy one of my intrinsic desires. Add these ways up, and we get the degree to which the act would satisfy my intrinsic desires altogether. Let these desires be the ones I would have if informed, and this yields the equivalence of the two analyses: the refined Humean analysis of 'a reason' and the full information analysis of 'rational'.

Discussing reasons, then, has left us where we started on objectivity. The rational thing to do is what we have most reason to do. If we had said what makes something a reason, that might have told us what is at stake in calling something rational. There is indeed a standard account of what makes something a reason, the Humean one—but it fails, at least as an account of meaning. That analysis, suitably refined, fits a full information analysis of what it means to call something 'rational'. Given the weighting principle, the two analyses are equivalent. The Humean account of 'reasons', then, shares the defects of full information analyses of 'rational'.

We can explain what it is to call something a reason. Start with the norm-expressivistic analysis of 'rational' and apply the weighting principle. That yields an analysis of what it means to call something a reason. From this we learn something new about talk of reasons, but nothing fresh about talk of rationality.

To call something *rational*, and to say that such-and-such is *a reason* for it, are alike to express one's acceptance of a system of norms with a certain property. That leaves the old puzzles of objectivity, now put in terms of reasons. First, a person who thinks something a reason thinks it would still be a reason even if he thought it were not. What does that mean? Second, existential commitments give rise to reasons of their own: a person existentially committed to honor treats matters of honor as reasons. How does that differ from treating them as matters of rationality? Finally (and perhaps equivalently), when a speaker puts something forth as a reason, he may seem to be insisting that it must weigh with someone else. What authority is he claiming?

Neither interpretation nor reasons have proved the key to rationality. The three puzzles of objectivity remain. I now turn to them one by one and propose solutions.

How is Validity Independent of Acceptance?

A person who thinks an act, belief, or emotion rational thinks that it would be so even if he thought not. In that sense among others, he takes his normative judgments to be objective. Is there any way to interpret this opinion on an expressivistic analysis?

If rationality were just a matter of taste, he could think no such thing; thus one way to put the question is to ask, "In what sense is rationality not a matter of taste?" We think "matters of taste" to be non-objective in at least this sense: if a person thinks something a matter of taste, then he does not think "This taste would be valid even if I lacked it." In matters of rationality, in contrast, we do think "This norm would be valid even if I did not accept it." In this respect we think rationality not just a matter of taste.[9]

What is the difference, then, between a "taste" and the sort of thing a commitment to rationality is? Let me illustrate the distinction with a stylized example, putting matters substantively: I shall be expressing judgments that many of us share. Suppose a woman were to starve herself to death for the sake of a trim figure.[10] She acts irrationally, I would say. Perhaps some of us treat a preference for life over starvation as just matter of taste, but I shall speak for those of us who do not. We maintain that this preference is not just a matter of taste: it is irrational to starve oneself to death for the sake of a trim figure; it is irrational to prefer death to life with a figure plump enough to sustain it—and even given such a preference, it is irrational to act on it. Indeed even if one is convinced that starvation is rationally required, one thinks so irrationally, and it is irrational to act on the conviction.

What does this mean? Our so thinking consists in accepting a norm that says without qualification, "Do not starve yourself to death for the sake of a trim figure." That implies, among other things, such injunctions as "Do not starve yourself to death for the sake of a trim figure, even if you prefer to do so" and "Do not starve yourself to death for the sake of a trim figure even if you are convinced that doing so is rationally required." It is in senses like these that we regard the woman who starves for the sake of a trim figure to be acting irrationally. She is not, we think, simply acting rationally in the light of tastes we happen not to share. We think her to be acting irrationally even if she genuinely prefers death by starvation to a figure plump enough to sustain life. We think her to be acting irrationally even if she accepts

---

9. Blackburn (1985, 11) discusses objectivity in roughly this sense.

10. I appeal to a well-known syndrome, but in a way that is fanciful. Real anorexia nervosa does not consist in acting on coherent preferences. More realistic examples of irrational preference, though, would likely be more complex and less clear-cut. With qualms I stay with the simple, dramatic fancy.

norms that prescribe what she is doing. We do not take a preference for life over starvation in these circumstances to be a matter of taste.

None of this is to say that she should be forced to eat. Whether her course is rational and whether she should be forced off it are two separate questions. Likewise, it is not to say that she thinks herself irrational. Consider an idealized anorexic—one who is acting not against her reflective preferences, but on them. She prefers, for her situation, starvation to life with a figure plump enough to sustain life. This preference, let us suppose, accords with the system of norms that she accepts. She, then, considers what she is doing to be rational, if my analysis is right. The point here is, the rest of us do not. We think it irrational to starve oneself to death for the sake of a trim figure, and in this we disagree with her. We disagree with her, even if we do not think that she should be coerced into eating. We do not think that what she is doing is irrational simply in virtue of our own tastes or preferences in the matter. Nor do we think that it is irrational in virtue of the norms we accept. The norms we accept prohibit starving for a trim figure, regardless of what one prefers or what norms one accepts. For a hypothetical case in which we ourselves are ideally coherent anorexics, these norms prohibit us too from starving. It is in this sense that we think that the prohibition against starving for a trim figure is valid independently of our own acceptance of it. If I say, "It makes no sense for her to starve herself," I am claiming objectivity in this sense at least (see Blackburn 1985, 11).

Existential Commitment

People hold ideals for themselves that they do not regard as matters of rationality. In our culture, we are familiar with the ideal of having a free and inquiring mind, with the ideal of physical vigor and the cultivation of athletic skills, with ideals of manliness for men and femininity and ladylikeness for women, and with ideals of humility, piety, and humanity. It is notorious that these ideals are highly valued by some and little by others. Most of us, I suppose, are ambivalent about some of the conflicting ideals that our varied culture holds out to us, and ambivalent about how strongly to hold to ideals we accept when their pursuit is painful, burdensome, or in conflict with other ideals we accept. On the other hand, it is often the ideals we hold strongly that give a sense of meaning to our lives (see Strawson 1961, esp. 1–4).

It is partly because of the importance of our ideals to us, and our ambivalence and our disagreements over them, that questions of rationality are crucial. "To what extent and in what ways," a person wants to know, "will reason resolve my ambivalence over ideals, if only I am rational? To what extent and in what ways will reason resolve my disputes with others if only we are all rational? What is left to be settled when reason has had its full say?"

It might seem that on an expressivistic analysis, all personal ideals are matters of rationality, and all incompatibilities of personal ideals are disagreements on the demands of rationality. Ideals differ from tastes: I dislike spinach but think it a matter of taste; that means in part that although I dislike spinach, I am willing to eat it if I like it. The norms I accept endorse eating it if I like it and not otherwise. I oppose cruelty unconditionally: I want myself not to be cruel even if, hypothetically, I should want to be; the norms I accept forbid being cruel even if one wants to be. Commitment to anything one thinks a fundamental requirement of rationality is likewise unconditional. What, then, is the difference, if any, between thinking something a requirement of rationality, and being committed to it as an ideal?

The ideal of not being cruel is moral, but not all personal ideals are. I might have a personal ideal of being a winner—an ideal that seems non-moral and is manifestly not universalizable. To have a strong personal ideal of being a winner, as opposed to a taste for winning, amounts to something like this: I not only care strongly about winning, I want myself to care strongly about winning, and to win whether or not I care, even if it be at considerable cost. Now on an expressivistic analysis, it might be argued, if I have a strong personal ideal of being a winner, then I hold that rationality requires anyone to win who can, even at great cost. Suppose, for example, you can win only by cheating, and suppose you oppose cheating and care little about winning. Suppose I have a strong personal ideal of being a winner, and no opposing ideal either of honesty or of authenticity—in the sense of living up to my standards whatever they may be. Does that not amount to accepting norms that, as applied to your situation, require cheating to win despite one's opposition? On the norm-expressivistic analysis, to do this constitutes thinking it irrational for you not to cheat to win.

On ordinary ways of thinking, in contrast, it seems consistent for a person to have a strong or even overriding personal ideal of being a winner, and yet not to think it a demand of rationality. True, a person *might* think trying to win at any cost to be a demand of rationality, but he need not. "I want to be a winner," he might say, "from now until I die, come what may, however I later feel about it. Others may not. I don't esteem them, but neither do I think they are irrational." Such a commitment we may call *existential:* it is a choice of what kind of person to be, in a fundamental way, come what might, which the chooser does not take to be dictated by considerations of rationality. He chooses freely and for all of humanity, in the sense that he is not choosing out of obedience to the dictates of reason as he takes them to be, and he chooses what to do no matter who he is or what he is like.[11] On our ordinary way of thinking, it seems possible for a commitment to be existential in this sense.

Higher Order Norms

Some norms govern the acceptance of norms. These include norms of coherence, and they include norms that go beyond sheer coherence. Suppose I think something like this: a person should accept a norm only when he has considered it in a calm frame of mind, and thought vividly about everything that might move him toward accepting it or not. To think this is to accept a norm, a norm that says "Accept norms only when . . ." The norm tells when to accept other norms, and it requires more than coherence. A person might, after all, be coherent but agitated, or coherent but dull in his imaginings. Or suppose I muse that anyone's thoughts are bound to be influenced by other people, and hold that a person should always correct what he accepts to counteract the influence of others. To think this too is to accept a norm that demands more than sheer coherence: I might be coherent but welcome influence. Think also of normative philosophy of science: in part it too consists of norms governing the acceptance of norms—in this case, of norms governing the acceptance of norms of scientific methodology.

Call norms that govern the acceptance of other norms *higher order norms.* Perhaps it is to them we should look to distinguish rationality and personal ideals. Norms may be mandatory or permissive, and the higher order norms one accepts might be permissive without being mandatory. That is to say, they might permit accepting any one of various incompatible systems of lower order norms. Perhaps it is then

11. See Sartre (1946). According to existentialism as Sartre presents it, "man is condemned to be free," and in making any choice, one is "choosing for all mankind as well as himself." Hence my appropriation of the term 'existential'.

that existential commitments arise. To accept a norm as a requirement of rationality, we might say, is to accept it along with higher order norms that require its acceptance. To treat it as an existential commitment is to accept it along with higher order norms that permit it, but that permit accepting at least one incompatible alternative.[12]

These are not the only ways a norm might be accepted. One might be a kind of relativist, and think norms valid in a way that depends on the circumstances of the thinker. The analogy is with norms for action. They, after all, demand different things in different circumstances: it makes sense to flee from a lion but not from a chameleon. Might higher order norms likewise prescribe different things in different circumstances—in this case, the acceptance of different, incompatible norms? Should the lower order norms I accept depend on features of my situation?

This is a substantive question of a higher order: a question of what kinds of higher order norms to accept. Now the normative opinions it makes sense to accept do depend in some ways on circumstance—that seems clear enough. Information varies, and what it makes sense to accept may depend on one's information. This concession to normative diversity, though, is limited. It applies most clearly not to basic norms but to norms that are contingent. I deplore cruelty anywhere, but then whether I deplore fishing, say, will depend on whether I think fish suffer. Moreover, the differences the concession allows are resolvable by more information.

Unproblematically too, the same norm can prescribe different things for different circumstances. A norm against rudeness will prescribe belching for some cultural surroundings and forbid it for others. This is not a case of incompatible norms, but of the same norm—a norm forbidding rudeness—applying differently to different cases.

The puzzling question, then, is whether different people should ever accept genuinely incompatible norms when they have like information. Familiar systems of higher order norms say yes. Take the theory of reflective equilibrium. We might think of it as a system of higher order norms: norms that say to accept whatever norms one would

12. Michael Bratman and Adrian Piper first urged me to think about higher order norms as providing a possible solution to this problem. Nicholas Smith later pressed the point, and provided the immediate impetus for further thought along these lines. Frankfurt (1971) speaks of "second order desires", wanting to be different in one's preferences and purposes. Since my own speculative psychology includes norms as well as desires, some of what Frankfurt wants second order desires to do, I would have first order norms doing. The work would be done by first order norms that govern desires.

accept if one were in reflective equilibrium. To be in reflective equilibrium is roughly to have considered vividly all relevant facts and philosophical arguments, and to have achieved consistent judgments. Now notoriously we have no guarantee that reflective equilibrium will be the same for everyone—especially with people from sharply different cultures. Two people may achieve opposing reflective equilibria. If so, then reflective equilibrium theory will tell them to accept opposing norms.

Suppose then I accept reflective equilibrium theory. Suppose also that both you and I are in reflective equilibrium and we accept incompatible norms. We each recognize the other as logically coherent, and we know we are each in reflective equilibrium. How am I to regard our disagreement? I take the judgments I make to be rationally required of me, and the judgments you make to be rationally required of you—but our judgments conflict. Do I think you rational but wrong?

Instead, we can say, I do not regard the norms I accept as norms of rationality. I regard them as having only a *standpoint dependent validity*. Not that I think my accepting them a case of existential commitment. I accept no higher order norms that leave me slack at the lower level. I could not have thought otherwise, being who I was and where I was, and still be rational—so I myself believe. Neither, though, do I treat these norms as themselves constituting demands of rationality. I think that there are ways I must look at the world but you must not. Here, then, is another way to treat one's norms as something other than demands of rationality.

Such a position leaves notorious puzzles—puzzles I take up later (see Chapter 11). What of the very highest order norms I accept, norms governed by no further norms? Might they declare themselves valid for me but not for you? Would that be coherent? In the meantime, we may celebrate that higher order norms have led us to two further distinctions. We have two further ways a person might treat norms as less than full demands of rationality. He might accept higher order norms that are permissive. Then he treats his lower order norms as existential commitments: the higher order norms he accepts permit him alternatives. Or he might accept higher order norms that leave no slack to anyone, but tell different people to accept incompatible things. He then regards the norms he accepts not as demands of rationality, but as requirements valid from one's own standpoint.

9 · Normative Authority

The ideally coherent anorexic accepts norms that prescribe death by starvation, if the alternative is a figure plump enough to sustain life. She proceeds to starve herself to death, and I, along with many others, think her course of action irrational. Now suppose I tell her so. Why should she give heed? All analysis aside, I seem to be claiming that she must. I seem to be claiming that, in some important sense, I am right and she is wrong. Perhaps I am indeed expressing my acceptance of norms that forbid her starving, and perhaps I do accept higher order norms that tell everyone else to do so. I seem, though, to be doing something more as well. I am demanding, with purported right, that she change her view of the situation.

When I tell her it doesn't make sense to starve, what am I doing? On the analysis as it now stands, I am expressing features of my state of mind: (1) that the norms I accept, as applied to her subjective situation, say not to starve; (2) that those norms tell her not to starve even if she herself accepts norms that demand starvation; (3) that the higher order norms I accept require not only me but everyone to accept norms that forbid starvation in her circumstances. Why, though, should all that matter to her? She herself is coherent, I am supposing: the norms she accepts tell her to starve, and the higher order norms she accepts tell her to accept those lower order norms. What is it to her if I accept a coherent normative system that says otherwise?

Something is missing from the analysis, and what is missing, it would seem, is the authority I am claiming for the norms I accept. This claim to authority, to be sure, must be treated with caution. Alas, not every time I call something irrational do my listeners cede the point. Sometimes they accept what I say, and sometimes they do not. The norm-expressivistic analysis does have the advantage of allowing for both possibilities: for my audience to accept what I say is for it to share the state of mind that I express, and for it not to accept what I say is for it not to share that state of mind. The analysis fails to guarantee that my audience will always accept what I say, and that fits life. Still, a person who calls something rational or irrational does seem to be claiming authority of some kind, and we need to identify this claim.

Conversational Demands

What is it, then, to claim authority for a judgment? It is more than just to evince my acceptance of higher order norms. That would have little impact on the coherent anorexic. She, after all, does not accept these norms, and there is nothing inconsistent in the norms she does accept. I do more than simply evince the norms I accept; what I do is to exert a conversational pressure. In effect I demand acceptance of what I am saying.

Conversation is full of implicit demands and pressures. Suppose I confidently expound astrology, and you give no credence. The result will be discomfort: in effect I demand that what I say be accepted, and you will not accede. The discussion is no longer cooperative; it is strained; it threatens to become a quarrel.

We have stratagems for restoring cooperation; they chiefly involve changing the subject. We can limit our discussion to questions of who believes what on astrology, for on that topic each of us may be willing to accept what the other says. You can accept my statement "I believe that the stars form a person's character," even though you yourself reject the influence of the stars. My new, more limited conversational demands will be acceptable, though my old ones were not.

This demand, I propose, is part of what has been missing in the analysis. Before, I said roughly that when a person calls something 'rational', he is expressing his acceptance of norms that permit it. Moreover, I added, he expresses his acceptance of higher order norms that tell everyone to accept these lowest order norms. Now I say he is doing more: he is making a conversational demand. He is demanding that the audience accept what he says, that it share the state of mind he expresses.

Like many demands, this one is revocable: the audience may respond in a way that convinces the speaker to withdraw it. As with many demands, this one may be resisted without rupturing all further relations between speaker and hearer. Life goes on, even though the demand has been neither met nor withdrawn. Still, a conversational pressure is there, and it needs to be included in the analysis.

Stevenson said that when a person calls something "good", he is saying something like this: "I like it; do so as well."[1] I am now, in effect, adding Stevenson's "Do so as well" to my own analysis. My own analysis is unlike Stevenson's in other respects: The states of mind involved in normative judgments, I say, are not mere likings, but the acceptance of norms. In making a normative statement, I do not report my state of mind, I express it—I speak my mind. Still, my analysis includes a crucial Stevensonian element: the conversational demand.

Claims to authority I locate, then, in conversational demands. Left at that, the move explains little. We need to ask how conversational demands can work in normative life, what role they play in normative discussion. Central to normative discussion, as I pictured it earlier, is mutual influence. Conversational demands amount to demands for influence. To claim authority is to demand influence, and influence is part of what leads normative discussion to consensus. I say, implicitly, "Accept these norms!" and if you accept them because I have made the demand, I have influenced you. If we influence each other, that moves us toward consensus in the norms we accept.

Now we need to ask about all this from two standpoints: the standpoint of the speaker and the standpoint of the audience. Take first the audience. I the speaker implicitly make conversational demands. I seek to exercise a conversational influence. Should my audience comply, and if so, why? Take next the speaker. I as a speaker do not simply demand; I claim to have a basis for my demands. I might browbeat, I might issue demands for which I myself think I have no basis—but that is not the ordinary case. Speakers distinguish browbeating demands from reasonable demands, and in normal conversation a speaker confines himself to demands he thinks reasonable. That is part of what it is to speak sincerely. What is it, then, for a speaker to think his conversational demands reasonable? What is it for him to issue his implicit demands with sincerity?

I turn first, then, to the side of the audience, to taking things on authority. In the next chapter I turn to the speaker's side, to what it

---

1. Stevenson (1937, 25). He goes on to say, "But this is certainly not accurate. For the imperative makes an appeal to the conscious efforts of the hearer. Of course he can't like something just by trying. He must be led to like it through suggestion. Hence an ethical sentence differs from an imperative in that it enables one to make changes in a much more subtle, less fully conscious way." See also Stevenson (1944, 21–22).

is to ascribe authority to oneself, to claim authority sincerely. A speaker, I am saying, issues conversational demands, and these demands amount to claims to authority. If he thinks something a demand of rationality, he is prepared to claim authority, and to do so sincerely. We need to know why such a claim might be accepted, and what could make such a claim sincere.

The Puzzle of Authority in Judgment

What is it to accept something on authority? I take it on authority that the atomic number of oxygen is eight. That means that my reason for believing this fact is that chemists believe it. When we say that a person accepts something *on authority*, we mean that he takes someone else's acceptance of it as his own reason for accepting it.

What about normative judgments? Might I take someone else's accepting something normative as my own reason for accepting it? In some cases I might well. Suppose you tell me it made no sense for Cleopatra to be angry at the messenger. I am ignorant of history, perhaps, and confident that you know your history, and that you and I share the same basic norms for anger. In that case, I can take your normative reasoning as proxy for my own. I think that you are reasoning just as I would if I knew the facts. I can let you draw normative conclusions for me, and so I take the fact that you draw a normative conclusion as reason for accepting it myself. I accept what you say on your authority.

Let me call authority of this kind *contextual*, because it presupposes a context of shared norms. Authority is contextual, then, if it stems from a presupposition that the speaker is guided by norms the audience shares, so that the audience can use the speaker's reasoning as proxy for its own.

At other times, hearers come to accept what a speaker says even without according him authority. The speaker may prod hearers to think along certain lines and come to their own conclusions. Call this *Socratic influence*; it is the kind of influence that Socrates exercises on the slave boy in the *Meno*. One way to exert Socratic influence is just to say the thing one wants the hearers to conclude. Hearers may accept what a speaker says not because the speaker accepts it, but on the basis of things they were prone to accept anyway if they thought along certain lines. Lectures in mathematics can proceed this way. Socratic influence, then, can work by assertion, so long as the assertions produce conviction solely by prodding listeners to work things out for themselves, on the basis of what they already accept. Socratic influence, in short, is influence that could be exercised simply by asking appropriate questions.

When a person calls something rational or irrational, then, he may be claiming contextual authority, or he may be trying to exert Socratic influence. In either case, he makes no problematic claim to authority. Whatever authority he claims parallels a kind of authority he might claim for an assertion of fact.

What am I doing, though, when I tell the coherent anorexic it makes no sense to starve herself to death? I am not trying to exert Socratic influence; that would make sense only if I thought her incoherent. Her problem, as I see it, is not that she fails to draw the right conclusions from premises she accepts, but that her premises are crazy. By the same token I cannot be claiming contextual authority: the premises from which I reason are not ones she accepts. If, then, I were asking her to take my reasoning as proxy for her own, and doing so on the grounds that my premises are ones she accepts, I would be a charlatan.

I claim rather to be "seeing" something that she doesn't: that the fundamental norms she accepts just don't make sense. I am claiming a kind of fundamental authority, an authority that does not stem from any common acceptance of more fundamental norms. I am claiming that her norms are crazy, so that my own are, in a fundamental way, more to be trusted than hers.

I may not make this claim dogmatically and inflexibly: I find her state of mind bizarre and inexplicable, and I am therefore quite prepared to learn more and to be surprised by what I learn. I do not rule out the possibility that were I to understand better, I would change my mind about whether she is being rational, and change it justifiably. What I would be doing, in that case, is refining the norms that I accept as they apply to her psychologically bizarre situation so that, for her situation, they came to prescribe the course of action she is taking. I expect, though, that that is not what I would do if I learned more. I expect that if I understood more deeply, I would continue to accept norms that prescribed, for her situation, eating enough to sustain life and vigor.

Authority in judgment need not be one-sided, and it need not be all or nothing. With fundamental authority especially, if we accord it at all we will likely accord it mutually, and in limited degrees. I may trust your judgment, but not entirely. I will trust my own judgment too, and I will expect you to trust it to some degree.

Still, even if it is limited and mutual, fundamental authority is puzzling. It is reasonable enough, in many cases, to accord a person contextual authority. I can perfectly well take your reasoning as proxy for my own when you reason as I would. Should anyone, though, ever accord someone else an authority that is fundamental? Should I ever take your acceptance of norms as reason for accepting them, when I do not independently accept norms from which they follow? Should the ideally coherent anorexic give any heed to my judgment, when it shares no grounds with judgments of her own?

The puzzle is not just one for expressivists, to be sure. A Platonist must ask, "Why suppose that the speaker can see things *a priori* to be true? How do we tell someone veridically apprehending an *a priori* truth from someone who only thinks he is? How, indeed, can I tell if I myself, when I seem clearly and distinctly to 'see' something to be the case, really do?"[2]

Seen apart from Platonism, the puzzle is this: A person may find a norm credible, fully or to some degree, independently of other norms that support it. Or if a norm itself lacks independent credibility, then its credibility, if any, traces to other norms that are independently credible. Now suppose someone else finds a norm independently credible. The puzzle is, should that fact make me too accept the norm, or in any way tend toward accepting it? Should it make me tend to accept the conclusions he draws from it? If so, why?[3]

Self-Trust

Ptolemy's friends find it apparent that revenge, just for the sake of revenge, is in no way worth having. Should that move him toward thinking so too?

2. Strawson (1949) vexes intuitionists with questions like these.

3. Epistemological debates rage between "foundationalists" and "coherentists". Foundationalists, as their name suggests, think that some judgments are foundational: these judgments have an independent credibility amounting to certainty, and other judgments draw all their credibility from these foundational judgments. Coherentists think that the various things a person accepts lend each other support. Here and in what follows, I am trying to speak in a way compatible with both kinds of accounts. I may slip into foundationalistic talk at points, but I hope that even then what I am saying can be put in terms of a coherence theory as well. Coherence theories we can think of as saying that judgments each with their own, limited independent credibility lend each other support.

People are influenced in fact by the judgments of others, even without contextual justification. That strikes me as undeniable. The puzzle of fundamental authority is not whether there is such influence, but whether such influence is ever reasonable. The ideally coherent anorexic may be influenced by me. There is nothing in her ideal coherence, after all, to keep her from changing her mind, and what changes her mind may be my exhortation. Still, can this influence be rational?

Perhaps all fundamental authority is bogus. Clearly it is non-rational in one sense in which philosophers commonly use the term: it does not proceed by the straightforward contextual mechanisms I have laid out; it is not entirely a matter of contextual authority. In a more important sense, though, it is deeply puzzling whether this kind of influence is ever rational. Does it ever make sense to be influenced in this fundamental way?

We may have little choice in the matter; we simply *are* influenced in a fundamental way by what those around us think. Mutual influence, I have been claiming, is part of what accounts for the very existence of normative discussion. What, then, are we doing when we try to decide whether it *makes sense* to be so influenced? We are, I suggest, trying to decide what norms to accept as governing our thought. We are trying to decide what norms to accept for letting one's judgments depend on what others think. We are thus trying to settle on norms for the acceptance of norms. The issue, then, is a substantive one of what higher order norms to accept.

Now we might adopt a Protestant-like independence of mind. A rational person, we might say, will resist any tendency to be influenced by the judgments of others. He can accord them contextual authority, but apart from that, he will use the opinions of others only as suggestions.

Can there be any stopping here, though? We need to ask next, Why trust oneself? If I am to accord no fundamental authority to the judgments of others, why accord any to my own?

One class of judgments raises no such problem: one's own present fundamental judgments. To accept a norm as fundamental, to "see it as self-evidently valid," is simply this: to accept it without being prompted, even on challenge, to doubt it, or to appeal to something else in its support. The fact that I would enjoy something speaks in favor of doing it. I find that self-evident. I accept it, and if asked why, I find the question needs no answer. I am not shaken, and I am not moved to find some further basis. The fact that I find the thing self-evident is not my grounds for accepting it; my finding it self-evident *consists* in accepting it this way.[4]

Self-evidence, then, is not rooted in self-trust—but many other things are. Take multi-step reasoning: Reasoning normally depends on trusting one's past conclusions. One must normally trust past conclusions without reviewing all one's grounds. In effect, then, one accords authority to one's past self. The same goes for the conclusions one would accept in hypothetical circumstances. I may take it as a reason for accepting a judgment that I would accept it if I had known certain relevant facts and thought about them in certain ways. Here again I am trusting my own authority—in this case, the authority of a hypothetical self. Indeed even setting out to ponder or investigate an issue requires reliance on one's own authority. Why should I bother to think about an issue when I do not yet have a firm opinion? I might inquire just for fun or to pass the time, but normally if I inquire, it is because I place some value on accepting the conclusions I may reach. In that sense, I rely again on my own authority: I accord probable validity to the conclusion I would accept if I investigated.

Indeed contextual authority itself rests in the end on a kind of fundamental authority. Contextual authority is a matter of trusting someone else to reason as I myself would from his observations. Suppose, though, I have no reason to trust myself, or even to put faith in the ways I would reason if I knew more. Then I have no reason to trust others on the grounds that they reason as I would. Even contextual authority traces back to a basic self-trust.

To reject all fundamental authority, then, is to settle for a kind of hyperskepticism. This hyperskeptic does find some things self-evident. He accepts a thing as self-evident, though, only at the moment of finding it so. Apart from that he doubts, and he sees no point in inquiry that might resolve his doubts. He accords no authority to the judgments he would make if he inquired.

Why, then, take one's own fundamental judgments, past, future, or hypothetical, as proxy for one's present ones? In asking this, I am trying to decide what norms to accept as governing the acceptance of things on my own authority. At this point, I have not much more to say. The basic considerations to determine the intellect are these. First, we do accept that our past, future, and hypothetical judgments have some legitimate authority. Second, we could not avoid taking things

4. A line of thought something like this may figure importantly in Descartes; see Frankfurt (1965, esp. sec. 1).

on our own authority, even if we resolved not to. Third, as I have been arguing, if we did accept norms forbidding all reliance on one's own fundamental authority, we would be committed to the hyperskepticism I have described. Hence, when I consider the bleak alternatives, I come at least to a weak conclusion. I conclude that one's judgments, even in fundamental matters, do carry some authority. It is reasonable to take one's own past, future, and hypothetical judgments as proxies for one's own present judgment. In so speaking, I express the state of mind I reach after pondering the considerations that I have been laying out. I express my acceptance of a higher-order norm that accords authority to my own normative judgments.

Trusting Others

I have arrived at some degree of self-trust; what, then, of the judgments of others? If I trust myself, why not others too? Is there anything special about me as a judge—or at least is there anything that should be special about me to myself? Each person should trust himself, I said, because we cannot help it, and we already think ourselves justified in doing so, and the alternative is hyperskepticism. Do these reasons apply to others?

Each of us is influenced by others in fact. The influence of others has pervaded our thinking since before we could talk. Suppose, then, I reject all fundamental influence from others. Then I have much to correct: my current thought has been shaped in ways I judge distorting. Before I can reasonably think my judgment good, I have to rid it of this distortion. Now if the influence of others on my thought runs deep enough, I shall have to correct my thinking beyond all recognition. Indeed I shall have no idea how to correct it. If I could reject wholesale the past fundamental influence of others, it would carry a prohibitive cost.

Could I accept past influence, then, and still reject all further influence? Inevitably I shall be influenced further; that seems hard to doubt. Shall I therefore distrust myself as I shall be as a result? Shall I consider myself at this instant to be at the peak of my judgmental powers? Suppose I do: I trust my present judgment, but think that all further influence would deprave it. Can I do this without a story of why that is? What is so special about my judgment right now? I have no story of what is special about it, and any story I might cook up would strike me as ridiculous.

Suppose, then, I accept some influence from others, both past and future. I treat the ways I will think after further influence as improvements—at least for some kinds of influence. Then, it follows, I must accord some fundamental authority to others. Suppose you find some normative matter apparent—again, say, that revenge just for the sake of revenge is in no way worth having. Should the fact that you find this apparent weigh in my own judgment? We can now see it must, if circumstances are right. I think that past influences have gone toward making me a good normative judge, and that further influences, of certain kinds, would improve my judgments. If we discuss the matter I will be influenced, and be the better judge for it—so I now think. Against this background, even before we discuss it, the fact that you see the matter as you do weighs toward my seeing it that way too. I accord authority to myself as I would be as a result of your influence. I take the fact that I would accept something then as reason for accepting it now. I know that what I then accepted would tend toward whatever you accept. I thus have some reason, by my lights, for accepting what you accept.

I must accord some fundamental authority to others. The authority I accord will be partial and discriminate, no doubt, but I cannot deny it wholesale. The argument that got us here has three main steps:

1. I must accord legitimacy to past influences from others. My present normative views stem pervasively from their influence. The norms I accept must not tell me, on that account, to throw out all my present judgments—for if they do, I am left a bleak skeptic. To some past influences, then, I must accord legitimacy.
2. That means that I must accord legitimacy as well to future influences—not to all of them, but to ones that meet certain standards. I have no plausible story of why past influences were all right but future ones will not be. There is nothing special about now as now.
3. In a discriminate way, then, I must accord others some fundamental authority.

When conditions are right and someone else finds a norm independently credible, I must take that as favoring my own accepting the norm. For take such a norm: if we discussed it, I would be influenced toward accepting it, and I think the influence would improve my judgment. If I would accept the norm with my judgment improved, that supports the norm. In short, suppose under good conditions for judgment that others find a norm independently credible. Then that must favor the norm in my own eyes. I must accept norms that say to treat that fact as weighing with me in favor of accepting the norm.

The argument does not say what constitutes good conditions. It appeals, rather, to epistemological consistency, to consistency in norms for the acceptance of norms. These norms, we can say, make up an epistemology of norm acceptance, an epistemic story. They say when accepting a norm is warranted. Take a lowest order normative claim *R:* say, that revenge for its own sake is not worth having. Suppose I accept a system *H* of higher order norms, and *H* says to accept *R*. *H*, suppose, says to accept what I would accept in a cool hour—and I think that in a cool hour, I would accept *R*. Then I think it is rational to accept *R:* I think it makes sense to accept that revenge for its own sake is not worth having. Accepting *H*, and thinking *H* endorses *R*, add together to constitute thinking it is rational to accept *R*; that is the thesis of norm-expressivism. The system *H* of higher order norms, then, amounts to a story of when it is rational to accept norms and when it is not. The norms in *H* we might call epistemic norms.

The argument I have been giving constrains epistemic stories. The epistemic story I accept will say what constitutes good conditions for normative judgment. Suppose the story calls a set of conditions good and in those conditions you accept *R*. Then, the argument concludes, the story must treat the fact that you accept *R* in those conditions as tending to warrant *R*.

Judge-Centered Appeals

The argument went quickly, and much of the rest of the book explores paths of escape. To see what the argument does, we might start with another, quicker one.

What is it to treat one's normative judgments as objective? I have proposed a number of answers, but another goes like this. To treat judgments as objective is to treat them as knowledge—as objective knowledge. That means supposing their contents can be known, and can be known by anyone—in principle at least. A person who treats his normative judgments as objective has an epistemic story, and the story cannot center on him; it cannot treat him specially, just as himself and for no further reason. Or, more likely, the person acts as if there were such a story, even if he cannot find it. An eligible story will say what constitutes good conditions for judgment, and anyone in those conditions it will count as a good judge. If people are in equally good positions to judge on a matter, then the judgment of each must weigh equally. None may give special weight to his own judgment simply as his own. That, we might say, is what it is for the story to treat a realm as objective.

A person could, of course, accept norms that say to treat one's own lights as special. His epistemic norms might say to trust one's own judgment specially just because it is one's own. To accept such norms, though, is to deny objectivity to one's judgments. Imagine that I accept the epistemic norm, "Accept those norms you would find independently credible in a cool hour." This epistemic norm tells me to accept what I myself would find credible, and tells you to accept what you would find credible. If that is the epistemic norm I accept, then I ascribe no objectivity to normative judgments. My standards of warrant center on the person making the judgment. They give each judge a special place in the warrant for his own judgments.

Alternatively, though, my standards of warrant might be universalistic. I might accept the norm, "Give equal weight to what each person, in a cool hour, would find independently credible." In that case, I do ascribe objectivity to normative judgments.

Now why not just say this and stop? We can simply classify judgments as ones that claim objectivity and ones that do not. Judgments claim objectivity if all warrant centered on the judge is ruled out. If judge-centered warrant is allowed, objectivity is renounced. If a person has not worked out whether or not to allow judge-centered warrant for his judgments, then he has not decided whether his judgments are to be objective or subjective.

The question all this leaves open is why objectivity matters. Why might anyone treat his normative judgments as objective? It is here that the main argument of this chapter comes to bear. A nearly inescapable stance towards oneself, I have been arguing, brings with it a pressure toward objectivity. I might instead simply treat my normative judgments as whims of the present moment. Then I shall see no reason to investigate normative questions further, and I shall accord fundamental authority to others only minimally—in that I shall not treat their influence on my present judgments as blanket reason to renounce those judgments.

Suppose, though, I think that further normative investigation might be worthwhile. I treat my normative judgments as scrutinizable over time. I treat the present moment as having no special bearing on warrant just by being the present moment. Then, I have been saying, I must accord some fundamental authority to the judgments of others. I have not rejected all past influence, and I ascribe no special status to the present. Therefore I cannot, in a blanket way, reject all future influence. I must regard some possible future influences as improving. Therefore I must give some weight to the judgments that would influence me. Objectivity across time brings with it some objectivity across persons. One must give weight to the judgment of anyone whose influence, one admits, would improve one's own judgment.

This falls short of an argument for full objectivity, for fully equal weighing of the judgments of equally qualified observers. It does show that—unpalatable alternatives aside—a person must stand ready to accord some weight to the judgments of others. Eve, suppose, finds it independently credible that knowledge is worth having. On Adam's epistemic story, moreover, there is nothing she lacks as a normative judge. Adam, in that case, must take the fact that Eve sees things as she does as weighing in support of the claim she sees as true, the claim that knowledge is worth having for its own sake. He must accord her some degree of fundamental authority.

Postscript: Secondary Qualities

We experience objects as colored; we experience food as tasty and storms as noisy. Likewise we experience people as fair-minded, generous, lazy, courageous. We experience institutions as oppressive or liberating, and acts as right or wrong, admirable or despicable. These judgments are normative or verge on it. Now we already have accounts of secondary qualities like color, taste, and sound. A thing is red if under favorable conditions a normal observer experiences it as red.[5] Might normative judgments fit like accounts?

At the start of the book I attacked full information analyses of 'rational'. We might think of those analyses as secondary quality analyses; they treat 'rational' as a second quality term. An analysis of 'red' will specify two things: first, what constitutes favorable conditions for vision, and second, a response—being "appeared to redly", say—that amounts to experiencing something as red. A thing is red, then, if it evokes that response under the specified conditions. Just so, a full

5. There is much debate about exactly how this should go, but I skip over it. See Locke (1690a, bk. 2, chap. 8) and Kripke (1972, 323–327) for quite different versions of the kind of account I have in mind.

information analysis specifies what constitutes ideally favorable conditions for a normative response. The ideally favorable conditions are conditions of full information. As for the response, it varies from analysis to analysis. In Brandt's analysis of rational intrinsic desires, the response is intrinsic desire itself. To desire something intrinsically, we might say, is to experience it as intrinsically desirable. The thing really is intrinsically desirable, Brandt proposes in effect, if one would so experience it under ideally favorable conditions—conditions of full information confronted vividly and repeatedly.

This is also the pattern of reflective equilibrium analyses, on one plausible reading (see Chapter 2). Rawls describes his grand project as giving "an account of our considered judgments in reflective equilibrium" (Rawls 1971, 51). *Considered judgments* are judgments made under certain specified conditions that are "favorable for deliberation and judgment in general." *Reflective equilibrium* is the hypothetical state reached "after a person has weighed various proposed conceptions and has either revised his judgments to accord with one of them or held fast to his initial convictions" (48). In the course of this weighing, one is presented "with all possible descriptions to which one might plausibly conform one's judgments together with all relevant philosophical arguments for them" (49). We might try saying, then, that a desire is rational if in reflective equilibrium we would find it rational. Fill out this sketch and we would have a *reflective equilibrium analysis* of the term 'rational' applied to desires. Again, then, the secondary quality pattern holds. Ideally favorable conditions for judgment are conditions of reflective equilibrium (where this notion is made suitably precise). The response is finding a desire rational. (Some independent characterization must be given of this psychic state; I myself could say it consists in accepting norms.[6]) Again, a thing is rational if it would evoke the response under the specified conditions. It is rational, that is, if it would be found rational under conditions of reflective equilibrium.[7]

---

6. Even this requirement of independence is controversial: Wiggins (1987, Essay 5) tries to explain secondary quality concepts without this requirement. That seems, he recognizes, to threaten a circularity: Specifying the quality in terms of the response and the response in terms of the quality. He grapples with the threat and tries to show it benign.

7. Ideal observer definitions of moral language too share the pattern. See especially Firth (1952). Much may hinge on whose response is in question: everyone's, or just the speaker's, or everyone's in the speaker's community. I struggle with like questions for my own analyses, but ignore them for secondary quality analyses.

Now equipped at this point with thoughts on authority, we can go back and see both why secondary quality analyses come close to working, and why counterexamples can be devised.

Are normative judgments like color judgments? Too straight a parallel would soon go askew. Think of the abolitionist in a world of slaveholders. He admits that almost everyone experiences slavery as right, and yet he insists that slavery is wrong. He is not talking nonsense; he is disagreeing cogently with those around him. No like story goes for color: Suppose I experience as yellow what everyone else experiences as red. At the outset we might ask how I or anyone else could know I do so—and it is significant that there seems to be no like puzzle of how we could know that the abolitionist finds slavery wrong. Still, we can imagine I see alike things others find yellow and things others find red. Even then, I am in no serious disagreement with people around me. If I insist on calling red things yellow, I am being perverse. I am ignoring the nature of color, or using terms idiosyncratically.

Secondary quality analyses correct for much of this. Just as colors are picked out by normal people in normal light, so normative properties are picked out in the most favorable conditions for judgment. This, as I said, is the pattern of a full information analysis of 'rational' such as the one I drew from Brandt.[8] Perhaps, then, what the abolitionist is claiming is that others have failed to achieve certain conditions most favorable for normative judgment—and that if they succeeded, they too would find slavery wrong.

Full information analyses of 'rational' almost work. The attitudes I think it makes sense to have will normally be the ones I think I would have on full confrontation with full information. My normal stance toward myself is to regard my authority as limited chiefly by lack of information or lack of thought.

Take even the simplest investigations. Suppose I don't know the outdoor temperature, and I want to know. I look at an outdoor thermometer that I think to be accurate. Prior to looking at the thermometer, I regard myself as I would be right afterward as an authority on the outdoor temperature. I thus look at the thermometer to make myself into an authority, by my lights, on the temperature. Authority is at work here, not meaning: I do not think that the very meaning of 'the outdoor temperature' is "what I would regard as the outdoor temperature were I to look at the thermometer". I simply think myself a

---

8. Brandt (1979), discussed above in Chapter 1. Again, Brandt himself offers the analysis not as an account of our present meaning but as a reform. See also Hare (1979).

trustworthy reader of thermometers. In this case as in most, I think my authority limited by ignorance alone.

In some cases, though, I will distrust my hypothetical authority on gaining more information. The cases in Chapter 1 were of this kind. Take the civil servant who is honest, but thinks that vivid dwelling on the rewards of corruption would change his preferences and the norms he accepts. He does not treat his hypothetical self—himself as he would be if he had dwelt on those temptations—as a normative authority. That is how he differs from most people most of the time, who expect to improve their authoritativeness by investigation. The same goes for the egoist who thinks that vivid realization of the plights of others would cause him to develop an irrational concern for them. Ordinarily a person thinks of himself better informed—of himself as he would be after dwelling on such things as the plight of others—as a normative authority. This egoist does not. That is to say, he is not willing to let the norms he accepts depend on the norms he would hypothetically accept once he had dwelt on the plight of others. It is in cases like these that a person rejects full information as the sole standard for rationality: cases when he is not willing to treat his hypothetical self, himself as he would be if he were maximally informed, as a normative authority.

The point holds for the whole family of analyses that treat normative judgments as judgments of a secondary quality. What conditions are ideally favorable for judgment is itself a normative question. It is a question of when it makes sense to accord authority to normative judgments. Fix an account of what conditions for judgment are ideally favorable, and select a response. Call the conditions C and the response R. The analysis says that normative judgment J is correct if and only if a person in conditions C would have response R. We can imagine someone, though, who admits that response R was evoked in conditions C, but who disagrees with judgment J and disagrees coherently. He makes no mistake of language or logic. Rather, he has a different account of what conditions for normative judgment are ideally favorable.

Dispositional analyses work for secondary qualities and fail with norms. Normative judgments nevertheless parallel secondary quality judgments in important ways. If I see something as blue, I normally suppose that I do so because the thing really is blue. Likewise if an action angers me, I normally suppose that it does because it really is outrageous. I see my experience as responsive to the way things are.

The stories I can tell myself of why this is, though, will differ for colors and norms. For colors, I come to see, responsiveness is simply a matter of normal vision. I accord my senses a *prima facie* authority, and when I ponder my basis I come up with a simple story: with vision, correctness is normality. All I seriously claim when I go from "It looks blue" to "It is blue" is that my color vision is normal and conditions are normal.

In the case of responses governed by norms, correctness is not sheer normality. Weird haircuts, I might think, make people angry, regularly and normally. Still, they are not morally outrageous. Our anger is mistaken.

True, my judgments of what is outrageous are guided by feelings. Ordinarily when I am angry at someone, I think what he has done outrageous: I think it makes sense to feel angry. Sometimes, of course, I may treat my anger as registering an illusion: I sometimes feel angry, but think it makes no sense to do so. Ordinarily, though, my judgments will fit the feelings, and I will treat the feelings as registering the content of the judgment. I feel angry, I think, because what he did was outrageous. I feel angry because what he did merits anger. I accord authority, in effect, to my feelings: I accord authority to myself as I am when I both have those feelings and make normative judgments accordingly.[9]

Still, the contrast between judgments of the two kinds is crucial. The story of how our feelings track the world is not one of sheer normality. I cannot explain trust in my normal feelings by a straight appeal to

9. McDowell (1985) stresses an analogy between normative judgments and judgments of secondary qualities, but agrees there is also a disanalogy. To judge something blue is to think it *will normally cause* blue color experiences, and to think it outrageous is to think it *merits* anger. Now the notion of meriting a response seems peculiarly normative; indeed something's "meriting anger" seems the same as my "its making sense to feel angry" about it. It is hard, then, to see what the strength of the parallel is supposed to be. I think that it is supposed to lie in the feeling I am discussing, in our sense that our experiences are responsive to reality, that we see things as blue because they really are blue, and feel angry about things because they really are outrageous. Wiggins (1987, essay 5) takes up this 'because', and says it "introduces an explanation that both explains and justifies" (200). He calls the position he develops a form of subjectivism, but it departs in a number of ways from the straight pattern of secondary quality analyses I have been attacking. Some of the departures seem intended to account for features I myself think call for something like norm-expressivism: the concepts involved are "essentially contestable", answerable to criticism. We may "despair of letting the whole matter of correctness depend on the analogy between a sound, healthy sense-organ and a sound judge or organism" (199). I see myself as trying to say what this "essential contestability" consists in, and how we can think to assess a judge as sound or not without thinking that our criteria give what it *means* for a judge to be sound.

meaning, by saying that all my judgments claim for those feelings is that the feelings are normal. When I judge that it makes sense to feel angry, then however much I treat my anger as a response to outrage, my judgments are normative. I think it makes sense to be angry, and no story of sheer normality exhausts what that means. I am according authority to the normative judgments I make when guided by my feelings. Part of what makes conditions favorable for normative judgment, I am saying, is that in these circumstances, my judgments of how it makes sense to feel are guided by the feelings I really have.

10 · Parochial Judgment

A speaker who calls something 'rational' exerts a conversational pressure; he issues a conversational demand. He demands, in effect, that what he says be accepted. In the last chapter I introduced these conversational demands, and I explored them from the standpoint of the hearer. Should a hearer ever accede to such a demand? Some cases were unproblematical; sometimes the only authority claimed is contextual. In some cases, though, claims to authority go beyond all contextual rationale. The speaker relies on more than the norms the hearer already accepts. Even then, I argued, it may make sense to accede to the speaker's demands—to a degree, and with discrimination. Even with a rational audience, conversational demands need not be quixotic.

Turn now to the speaker. He treats what he is saying as objective, I suggested, when he makes conversational demands on its behalf. Now even if that is right, it says nothing about what objectivity means. We know what it is for a person to *treat* a normative claim as objective, let us agree, but what is it really to *think* the claim objective? The expressivistic strategy makes that the question to answer.

The speaker thinks his claim objective, we might say, if he can treat it as objective and do so sincerely. To complete the account, then, we need only explain sincerity. Sincerity must not be explained as saying what one thinks; the original question, after all, was what it is to think something objective. We need an independent characterization of sincerity. To think a claim objective is to stand ready sincerely to treat it as objective. To treat it as objective is to issue conversational demands on its behalf. We need to say what makes a demand sincere.

Legitimate Demands

In some situations, a speaker will persuade in any way he can. Cleopatra holds a sword over the messenger, ready to strike. The messenger will try to dissuade her and not scruple over method. In less desperate straits, though, he might well have scruples. He might want to speak honestly and sincerely. He might want to be open about the bases for what he is saying. He might want to be coherent in what he claims, and in the things he would say to back up his claims.

More than narrow sincerity comes in here. A person can be sincere as far as he goes, and still not be open. He can speak his mind but not all of it; he can hide his bases for what he says. Ptolemy knows he reasons from premises Cleopatra rejects. If he just asserts his conclusions and leaves her thinking he got them from things she accepts, he is sincere but not open. He says what he thinks, but misleads her about his basis.

In a minimal sense, we might say, sincerity is accepting what one asserts. Something more is needed, though, with conversational demands. Sincere demands should not simply browbeat. A person might accept a normative judgment and yet accept higher order norms that permitted the audience to do otherwise. If he is open about this and still makes demands, the demands constitute a kind of browbeating. He demands something of the hearer, even though he admits that, as applied to the hearer, the higher order norms he accepts place no such requirement.

That could be for either reason discussed two chapters ago: In the first place, the speaker might accept higher order norms that leave some slack. He then thinks that neither he nor the hearer is required to accept what he himself accepts. Alternatively, he may take the validity of what he asserts to depend on standpoint. He may think himself required to accept what he asserts, but the hearer not.

In both cases, either he must hide his bases for what he is saying, or he must engage in a kind of browbeating. We can ask, then, whether he can place his conversational demands on everyone, openly and without browbeating. He is open if he hides nothing about the bases for his demands. He browbeats if, openly, he makes a demand without thinking his audience need accept it—if he makes the demand without accepting norms that tell his audience to accept it. Can he make his demands on everyone with purported basis, while hiding nothing?

To do so, I am saying, he must accord the judgment a standpoint-independent validity: the highest order norms he accepts must tell everyone to accept it. True, they need not require accepting the judgment in light of the facts available to the audience. The speaker could be sincere even if he thought his audience lacked the facts to warrant what he was saying. He must think, though, that given the facts, his audience ought to accept what he is saying.

My questions are about ideally coherent thinkers. The goal is to display the logic of acceptance, the logic of thinking a normative matter objective. When does a person think a normative claim objective and do so coherently? He does if with full coherence he can demand of all that they accept his judgment, and if he can make the demand openly and without browbeating. We now have a synthesis of the theory of higher order norms and the theory of conversational demands. The conversational demands involved in calling something rational are not backed by force; they are made "in the name of reason". The speaker demands that his audience accept what he thinks it rationally must accept. That, at least, is what he presents himself as doing, and we can ask whether he does so coherently, openly, and sincerely. He will be sincere if he thinks that his audience rationally must accept what he is asserting: if the higher order norms he accepts, as applied to the circumstances of his audience, require this acceptance.

Conversational Standards

For a coherent speaker, sincerity is the possibility of openness without browbeating. Browbeating would consist in demanding acceptance of what one says, though one admits that the higher order norms one accepts, as applied to the audience, prescribe no such thing.

Why, though, should browbeating consist in just this? Other standards can be imagined. I browbeat you, we might say, only when I openly demand that you accept something I do not. Alternatively, we might say, I browbeat you whenever I claim an authority that is more than contextual. I browbeat you if I demand you accept more than follows from premises you already accept plus my observations.[1]

---

1. This line of thought could be put in terms of a coherence picture, in which what I can demand you accept is a matter of various pressures working on the things you find independently credible to various degrees. I can demand you accept what I say if, with my observations added to your stock of beliefs, what I say is part of the most coherent extension-plus-revision of your beliefs.

The question is one of conversational inhibitions and embarrassments. A speaker is normally inhibited from browbeating his audience. He is inhibited from making conversational demands, when being open about his grounds would force him either to withdraw the demands or engage in browbeating. A challenge that shows him to be in such a position will embarrass him. True, the inhibitions can be surmounted and the embarrassments borne, but they shape normal discussion. Our question is what standards to attach to these inhibitions and embarrassments. What demands are legitimate, in that no such qualms should be attached to them?

Should I be loath to claim any authority that is not contextual? Should I hesitate to assert anything that does not follow from facts and the norms you already accept? Should I be embarrassed if you show I have done so? These standards would subvert much of the point of normative discussion. If we limit assertions in this way, we rule out the kinds of demands from which fundamental normative consensus may emerge. We do make demands on each other that go beyond this, and we are each to some degree susceptible to these further demands. In the last chapter, I argued that some of these further demands are legitimate. These conversational demands serve to move discussion forward when the issues cannot be resolved contextually, when only mutual influence can lead toward consensus. We should not dismiss them as insincere or incoherent.

If this is right, then the legitimate bases for conversational demands are not confined to the speaker's observations and the things the audience already accepts. A speaker may legitimately claim authority that goes beyond the contextual.

Turn, then, to the other extreme. Perhaps any conversational demand for acceptance whatsoever is legitimate, provided only that the speaker is consistent, and he himself accepts what he demands others accept.

To accept this would deprive us of an important device for working toward consensus. Consider again the ideally coherent anorexic. I say that it doesn't make sense for her to starve herself to death for the sake of a trim figure. She says it does. We each make our conversational demands. Is there anything left to say?

What she can do now is to raise an epistemological challenge. She can ask me how I know. Now that we have arrived at the point simply of pitting my normative authority against hers, she can ask me what makes me think that I am the better judge. I of course can issue the same challenge to her, and the mutual challenges may do nothing at all to advance the conversation. They may be met with mutual dogmatism. Or instead they may undermine the confidence of both of us, leaving us normative skeptics. They may, on the other hand, allow for some further assessment of our opposing normative claims. She, after all, can lay claim to one special source of normative authority: it is she who is living her life; it is she who experiences what it is really like to be in her circumstance. I must answer this epistemological argument with one that favors my own normative authority, or else I must give up the claim I have been asserting. This may in the end not resolve our fundamental disagreement, but then again it might.

Our standards for conversational embarrassment should allow such challenges. A speaker should be embarrassed if he has no reply. That means that if conversational demands are to count as legitimate and ideally coherent, they must be backed by an epistemic story. The speaker must accept higher order norms that tell the hearer to accept what he is saying. These higher order norms form his story of why he is in a position to judge, of why his audience should accord him the authority he claims.

Considerations of discursive role, then, support the earlier proposal. If a person is fully coherent, then he accepts something as an objective matter of rationality only if the higher order norms he accepts ascribe it a standpoint-independent validity. The line of reasoning was roughly this: a speaker treats what he is saying as an objective matter of rationality if he can demand its acceptance by everybody. More precisely, the test is this: could he coherently make his demands, revealing their grounds, and still not browbeat his audience? What makes for browbeating in this test is a question of conversational inhibitions and embarrassments—of the inhibitions and embarrassments that should normally steer discussion. We might have attached these sanctions to all claims to authority beyond the contextual. Then, however, we would brand as illegitimate the conversational demands through which we can move from fundamental disagreement to agreement. Alternatively, we might have allowed any conversational demand, so long as the speaker himself accepts what he is saying. That, however, would rule out the epistemic challenges that sometimes resolve an impasse. For discussion best to foster consensus, demands should count as fully legitimate only when they are backed by a coherent epistemic story. The story will consist in higher order norms, and these norms must ascribe standpoint-independent validity to what is asserted.

Content-Fixed Qualifications

As part of normative rehearsal, we think through possible epistemological challenges. Parts of philosophy consist of normative rehearsal and discussion pushed far. As part of a philosophical inquiry we can ask what is required to respond to such challenges. That may help us to discern the kind of objectivity that is being claimed when a person makes a normative assertion. In daily life we are far from demanding an extreme, philosophical coherence. Still, even in ordinary discussion a speaker makes implicit demands, and these demands can be criticized. Among the possible criticisms are epistemological ones. The speaker, it may be said, is not in a good position to judge in the matter, or the audience is in a better position. The speaker is not blatantly incoherent so long as, when challenged, he either withdraws his demands or thinks the challenge answerable. It is an embarrassment not to have the answer himself, but it is not a scandal. For the most part in normal discussion, only incoherence that is blatant can force a speaker to change his mind, on pain of utterly disqualifying himself as a discussant. Even without an answer, the speaker can stick to his guns. In doing so, he has opted out of full discussion, but not out of all discussion. He may still think a good story could be told. He does not offer the story, though, and so he is not fully defending his claim to objectivity.

Return, then, to standards of ideal coherence. If an ideally coherent speaker claims objectivity, he needs an epistemic story. The hearer may reject what the speaker says, and then the speaker needs to say why he is competent to judge and the hearer is not. The story may be one the hearer rejects; indeed the hearer may accept an opposing story, a story that says why he himself is competent to judge and the speaker is not. In that case, the hearer will resist the speaker's influence and reject his demands. Still, the standards that allow the demand are useful. They allow both for mutual influence and for epistemological challenge. Mutual influence works in part through the conversational demands these standards allow, and epistemological challenges appeal to these standards. The standards, then, can help resolve some disagreements even if others remain unresolvable.[2]

If I am in the better position to judge, that must be in virtue of some of my characteristics. Perhaps I am an adult and my hearer is a child, or I have experience in these matters and he does not. Perhaps I make inferences quickly and in close succession which he makes so slowly that he forgets what he has already inferred. Perhaps I have been trained to question the beliefs of those around me, whereas he has been trained to suppress doubts and accept the beliefs of his culture with reverence. These epistemological stories are admissible; what is not admissible is the bare story that I can judge because I am I and my listener is not.

If the story need not be one that the hearer accepts, can we place any requirements on it at all? Qualifications for good normative judgment, we might want to say, cannot be doctored to give particular substantive results. Without this restriction, after all, a speaker can play dirty tricks. He can take anything he accepts and entrench it, simply by disparaging all those who fail to accept it.

Call the properties ruled out by such a restriction *content-fixed* and other properties *content-neutral*. A content-fixed property of a normative judge will be (1) any disposition to make some particular set normative judgments, or not to make them, or (2) any property that logically entails such a disposition. Other properties of normative judges

2. In my stress on discussion and reaching consensus, I follow Habermas (1973), who talks of a "communication community". To claim normative validity for something, Habermas says, is to think "it could be discursively redeemed—that is, grounded in consensus of the participants through argumentation" (105). He lists requirements for "discourse"—roughly, that "all motives except that of the cooperative search for truth are excluded. If under these conditions a consensus about the recommendation to accept a norm arises argumentatively . . . then this consensus expresses a 'rational will' " (108). Habermas might be read as telling an epistemological story: that competent normative judges are those who have achieved consensus in a cooperative search for truth. On that reading, nothing I am saying is in disagreement with Habermas; I commit myself neither to his story nor to an alternative, though my stress on the legitimacy of mutual influence seems to fall in well with Habermas's picture. I am proposing, in effect, what he might mean by his claim that a consensus of the kind he pictures expresses a "rational will": in claiming this, on my interpretation, he is according authority to the consensus judgments that would emerge "argumentatively from a cooperative search for the truth". He might, though, be offering a theory of what 'rational' means: that 'rational' just means "following from the consensus that would arise argumentatively from a cooperative search for truth". On this reading I disagree: a person might, without confusion, think something rational but have a story of what makes for competent normative judgment that is not Habermas's.

are content-neutral.[3] The proposed restriction on epistemic stories, then, is this: if one person possesses a normative authority another lacks, that must be because of some content-neutral property in which they differ.

Even if we accept this restriction, we can still treat making bad judgments as evidence of having bad judgment. Caligula judged it makes sense to admire gratuitous cruelty. I might think that no one could accept such norms if he fully and vividly understood what was involved in suffering cruelty. Vivid understanding, I might hold, is a chief qualification for good normative judgment—a content-neutral qualification. Caligula's endorsement of gratuitous cruelty, then, I would take as a sign of poor normative judgment. I would take it as a sign that he lacked a content-neutral property competent normative judges must have. True, I probably could not convince Caligula of this, but I could coherently think it and perhaps convince others. The requirement, then, still lets us dismiss someone as a competent normative judge because he has shown bad judgment. What it forbids is dismissing him while admitting that he lacks no content-neutral property a competent judge must have.

This may seem a reasonable restriction on epistemic stories, but we should nevertheless reject it. Take Caligula again. On confronting him we would at first, doubtless, take his admiring gratuitous cruelty as evidence of some content-neutral defect. Suppose, though, we investigate and find no content-neutral qualification he lacks. Would his normative authority then be vindicated? Perhaps not: could we not reasonably dismiss him, simply on the grounds that his normative judgments are monstrous? The alternative is to leave all our normative judgments at the mercy of a freak normative sensibility.

Content-neutral properties, after all, logically entail no particular normative judgments. If content-neutral qualifications rule out wild judgments, they do so in virtue of contingent limits on the ways people are constructed. These limits need not stem from happenstance, to be sure; we are shaped in systematic ways by natural selection and by life. Still, the limits are in no way guaranteed to protect what most needs protecting. Caligula, it might turn out, is superb as a normative

---

3. There will be tricky ways of defeating this characterization of content-neutrality. Properties that are each content-neutral, on this characterization, might in conjunction come out content-fixed. The real question will be whether one's entire epistemic story is content-fixed: whether it entails a disposition to make some particular normative judgment.

judge by every content-neutral test. If his judgments are monstrous, though, we shall not give them weight. If only content-fixed qualifications will rule Caligula out, then we cannot renounce them. We shall dismiss normative judgments if, in various substantive ways, they are egregious.

Normative Dogmatism

Tentatively accept, then, that some of the qualifications a competent normative judge must meet are content-fixed. Where does that leave us? Requirements of epistemic coherence ground an important move in normative discussion, a move that may sometimes lead to agreement. When the parties are otherwise coherent and their disagreement is otherwise fundamental, a party may be challenged as to why he thinks his own judgments the more to be trusted. If he has no answer, he suffers a conversational embarrassment. Now, though, it seems that answers come too cheap. He can simply cite the fact that he judges as he does, and say that that itself makes him the better judge. He can simply claim good judgment dogmatically. Epistemic coherence, it seems, has lost its teeth. What now is it doing for us?

The answer lies in prices. Dogma has a price. Ordinarily it ends discussion. One can be baldly dogmatic toward someone only if one is willing to dispense with him as a discussant. It is this price that gives the requirements of epistemic coherence their teeth.

When could a person accept that he is a poor normative judge, simply because he judges as he does? He might be highly influenceable. In that case, even blatant dogmatism might bring him to see things the speaker's way. Ordinarily, though, if a dogmatic claim to good judgment has any chance of being accepted, it will be gratuitous. Such claims will be accepted only when there is some great asymmetry between speaker and hearer: the speaker is socially dominant, perhaps, or speaks with some special background of expertise. In any of these cases there are content-neutral differences between speaker and hearer which might be used as the basis for a claim to a special authority.

In most cases, then, dogmatic conversational demands are self-defeating. We cannot often expect a person to consider himself a bad normative judge, for no identifiable reason except the content of the judgments he makes. Why, then, ever allow a person to be disqualified on the stark grounds that he makes bad judgments? It is not because we can expect to include him in normative discussion on that basis. It is rather because we need, as a last resort, to be able to exclude him. It may well be futile to tell the person himself that he is a bad judge of normative matters. We may, though, need to tell each other. Otherwise we leave our normative convictions unduly hostage to the possibility that others—a few quirky people in our midst or many strange people far away—will see things differently. We are unlikely to be able to engage many people in normative discussion in groundlessly subordinate roles, but we can refuse to give full weight to the judgments of people we are willing to exclude. We pay a price, but the price may be worth paying.

The price explains why fundamental disagreement should be so disturbing a prospect. Think of my telling the ideally coherent anorexic that it makes no sense to starve herself to death for the sake of a trim figure. I make a conversational demand: I demand that she accept what I say, that she share the state of mind I express. If I am coherent and sincere, the higher order norms I accept objectively require her to do so, given the facts as I take them to be. The facts, suppose, are agreed between us, and so our difference is entirely normative. I know that the higher order norms on which I base my demands are not the ones she accepts. She, of course, can make corresponding demands on me: she can demand that I accept that it does make sense to starve oneself to death for the sake of a trim figure, and she will be sincere in virtue of the higher order norms that she accepts.

The impasse I sketch is of course highly artificial, a philosopher's construction. Flesh-and-blood normative impasses may occur, but no party to them will be ideally coherent, and certainly neither party will be confident that the other is. Still, as we all know, cases do arise when Socratic influence and contextual authority seem to have given out, and these cases shake us; we say they threaten to degenerate into shouting matches. These cases can leave us asking whether such a thing could happen if everyone involved really were ideally coherent. To investigate this, we need a tractably idealized case.

Why, then, should fundamental disagreement be disturbing? The history of philosophy is full of attempts to prove that coherent thinkers cannot disagree. These attempts fail, it is widely acknowledged, but they address a human need. Our normative life seems challenged by the very possibility of fundamental disagreement, and I think I have displayed how. Shared norms protect us and give us a sense that our thought has moorings. Part of having a normative conviction is to think one could win an argument over it—or at least, this is part of the naive psychology of accepting a norm. We rehearse arguments as a part of refining our normative convictions, and we accept a claim when we think we could get the arguments right. We want to think we could win an argument with anyone who fully entered into normative discussion, with anyone who does not egregiously sacrifice all claim to normative authority. Even thinking about the possibility of a fundamental challenge may shake this confidence (see Sabini and Silver 1982, chap. 3).

We may, then, both need to include a person in normative discussion and need to exclude him. We need to include him because it is in discussion that we lead our normative lives. Fully to respond to him as human is to be prepared to discuss with him. On the other hand, if we do include him, pressures toward coherence may lead us in normative directions we are sure it makes no sense to take. Formal requirements on epistemic stories will not resolve these conflicting pressures.

Grandiose Objectivity

I have been speaking grandiosely. A person treats his judgments as objective matters of rationality, I have been saying, only if he can make demands on their behalf, and make them of everyone. He must be able to demand of everyone that they share his judgments, and to make the demand sincerely and openly. Who, though, is this "everyone"? All of humanity? All conceivable rational beings? He leads his discursive life in smaller groups. Perhaps he can make demands on his fellow discussants, even when he could not make them on all in a wider group. In that case he can still claim all the objectivity that matters for purposes at hand, even though he is not claiming objectivity in the most grandiose sense.

How useful is grandiose objectivity? A normative judgment is objective in this grandiose sense only if it would be accepted by any conceivable ideal normative judge. An ideally coherent thinker treats a judgment as objective, in the grandiose sense, if he can demand its acceptance, sincerely and openly, of all conceivable rational beings. He can demand acceptance sincerely and openly just in case he thinks his hearers would accept the judgment if they were ideal normative judges. An ideally coherent thinker therefore treats a judgment as objective, in the grandiose sense, just in case he thinks that any conceivable ideal normative judge would accept it. What he takes to constitute an ideal normative judge is a matter of the epistemic story he accepts. He treats a normative judgment as fully objective if, according to his epistemic story, the judgment would be accepted by any conceivable ideal normative judge. In my earlier terminology, he treats it as fully objective if he accords it a validity that is standpoint-independent, among all conceivable rational beings.

This is a stringent requirement. Indeed, it can be satisfied only by two kinds of norms, along with their logical consequences: first, the norms of minimal rationality, the norms that must be imputed to a person if he is even to be found intelligible; second, whatever content-fixed requirements there are for competent normative judgment.

To see this, imagine a set of content-neutral qualifications for competent normative judgment. (We might think here of kinds of requirements that have been typical. Brandt in effect takes the view that a person is in a position to judge in normative matters if he has been through "cognitive psychotherapy"—if he has had vividly represented to himself, repeatedly over a substantial period of time, all considerations extended, vivid consideration of which would affect his acceptance (Brandt 1979, esp. chap. 6). Rawls's theory of "broad reflective equilibrium" is similar (Rawls 1971, 46-53). Now in the case of actual human beings, these content-neutral qualifications might genuinely restrict the kinds of normative judgments people who satisfy them will make. There might, say, be a substantial range of matters on which all human beings would agree if they had undergone cognitive psychotherapy. Our present question, though, concerns not actual people but all conceivable beings. We are asking about all conceivable beings who meet these qualifications, and the qualifications by themselves entail no restrictions on content. How could any normative judgment be ruled out as one it was inconceivable for any such being to make? The being must be interpretable as making normative judgments. The judgments we impute to him, then, cannot be utterly wild. In interpreting a being we impute to him a logic and perhaps some substantive banalities. Beyond that, however, any coherent pattern of judgment will be conceivable. Content-neutral properties in themselves place no further restrictions (see Chapter 8).

Now take a being who meets not only these content-neutral qualifications but a set of content-fixed qualifications as well. He is required to have certain normative opinions and to lack others. In addition he is ideally coherent under our interpretation: he accepts whatever follows logically from the required substantive judgments and the banal-

ities needed for intelligibility. That is all, though. No specific judgments beyond these are mandated by the three kinds of requirements
we can place on a competent normative judge: that he be interpretable
as intelligible, that as interpreted he be fully coherent, and that as
interpreted he make certain specific normative judgments.

How restricted can we reasonably expect this set of normative judgments to be? Consider norms for guilt and anger. Some judgments
may be required for intelligibility. If enough of these judgments were
missing, we would not be able to interpret the person's mental state
as one of accepting norms for guilt and anger at all. There may be
certain judgments such that if a person did not make them, we would
take that very fact as disqualifying him as a competent normative
judge. These, then, could be taken as matters of objective rationality
in the grandiose sense.

If, though, we are really puzzled about when it makes sense to feel
guilty, these things will not help. The banalities required for interpretation are not the things that puzzle us. If we are really puzzled, moreover, we shall not write a person off as a normative judge simply
because of the way he judges on that particular matter. For our real
normative puzzles, we do want answers, but if we found them we
could not treat them as objective in the grandiose sense.

In short, then, for some normative judgments we can claim a kind
of maximal objectivity. We can claim, for such a judgment, that any
conceivable ideally competent normative judge would accept it. This
grandiose objectivity, though, may not be vastly important. It covers
sheer coherence and the requirements of coherence. It covers what one
must accept to be interpretable. If accepting a judgment is part of what
makes a person a competent normative judge, it covers that too. It
covers nothing else but the consequences of these things. Our real puzzles lie elsewhere.

Modest Objectivity

What matters chiefly is not what we can say to strange beings who are
merely conceivable, but what we can say to each other. We discuss
together how it makes most sense to live, what it makes most sense
to believe, and how it makes most sense to feel about aspects of life.
We can ascribe maximal objectivity to a rich set of judgments on these
matters only by foreclosing discussion: by placing those judgments
beyond challenge, automatically denying the normative competence of

anyone who rejects them. It is weaker kinds of objectivity that chiefly matter.

In the first place, we could weaken our claims to objectivity by restricting them to beings that exist. Our claim for a judgment would then be that any actual rational being would accept it in ideal conditions. A rational being will be one who would be ideally competent if he had the right properties, and for whom it makes sense to ask how he would judge if he had those properties. A full epistemic story will say what kinds of beings those are.

By limiting the demands we stand ready to make to actual beings, we shrink our claims to objectivity—slightly. Our claims are still too broad to be of much importance. They leave us a choice that should not matter to us, a choice between dogmatism and vulnerability. Suppose we make a judgment that is important to us: say, that honest dealing matters for its own sake. How can we claim objectivity for this judgment? On the one hand, we can simply be dogmatic. Honest dealing matters for its own sake, we can say, and if a person fails to see that it does, this failing in itself constitutes incompetent normative judgment. Thus if one of us disagrees on the matter, we rule him out of the discussion. On the other hand, we can keep our epistemic story free of any such content-laden qualification. We can then hope that all actual rational beings agree with us potentially: that they would agree if they were in the circumstances our story calls epistemically ideal. We can have no *a priori* guarantee this hope will be met; so I have already argued. If we take this course we are leaving our judgment vulnerable.

In some ways, to be sure, our judgments should be vulnerable. Indeed the problem with sheer dogmatism was that it leaves our judgments automatically proof against any disagreement. In this case, though, the vulnerability is extreme: the judgment is left vulnerable to the possibility that somewhere, far away, some rational being is so constructed that if he were in ideal epistemic circumstances he would judge otherwise. Should we leave our judgments hostage to the normative sensibility of beings in a far galaxy?

We form our judgments partly in community, and the claims we make should be vulnerable to the judgments of other discussants. Sheer dogmatism will not do. How they judge in the next galaxy, on the other hand, need little concern us. How they might conceivably judge can be of interest; it tells us what the possibilities are for normative judgment. Those possibilities, though, are too broad to matter.

Actual rational beings might all judge as we do, but if they are far enough away, why should that matter? Once we restrict our attention to actual beings, why not consider actual beings in the vicinity, the ones with whom we might discuss and interact?

We might stand ready to make our demands on all humanity. For any purpose we are likely to have, a judgment is as objective as it needs to be if it passes a human test: that any human being, if he had all the properties of an ideal normative judge, would accept it. From the point of view of the universe, the judgments that matter to us must be parochial. Perhaps, though, we can take all humanity as our parish.

We must be prepared, however, to find that we cannot. For our central normative judgments, we must be prepared to give up the claim that any human being whatsoever would accept them, if only he were ideally placed for normative judgment. Perhaps we must confine our judgments to a smaller community that is indispensable to us or nearly so. We have little idea on what things all actual human beings agree potentially—on what things all human beings would agree if they met certain specific standards for competent judgment. At the same time, we must lead our lives in the communities we engage in discussion. Shall we give up everything central to our normative life unless we can be reasonably convinced that all qualified humanity would agree?

For crucial parts of our normative thought, then, conversational demands will be confined to a group: perhaps to all of humanity or perhaps to some part. Let me call such a judgment—a judgment demanded of a group smaller than all conceivable rational beings—*parochial* to that group. Normally, of course, questions of parochiality will not arise. All parties to a discussion will form a single community of judgment and ignore outsiders. With ideal clarity, though, we would have to recognize our judgments as parochial. That does not detract from their importance.

11 · Rationale and Warrant

We press each other toward coherence, and these pressures help nudge us toward consensus. We are pressed in other ways too: We need cooperation and mutual restraint, and normative discussion helps us get them. In discussion we find human fellowship. We depend on normative discussion for a sense of meaning in life. We need stability in our views of life and our surroundings. How might we accommodate these many other pressures with the pressure toward coherence? How complete can the accommodation be?

That is what I want to ask in the end. My immediate strategy, though, is to idealize. Imagine a universe of two groups; call them the Greeks and the Scythians. Each group is ideally coherent and ideally informed. Each can achieve full consensus on matters that leave the other out of account. The two groups are not isolated enough, though, to ignore each other. They think about one another, and they clash if they are not governed by common norms in some range of matters— or if they do not clash, at least they lose various opportunities for cooperation. Each group is ideally coherent epistemologically; it has a coherent story of whose normative judgments are to be trusted when, and why that is. They disagree in some of their normative judgments, and since they are each ideally informed and ideally coherent, none of their disagreement is contextually resolvable; it is all fundamental.

How might the two groups regard each other? They might take a stance of parochiality: "We cannot engage in normal discussion with Scythians," a Greek might say. "On some topics, we can only browbeat them, try to manipulate them, or change the subject. It is not— or not only—that they are poorly qualified to judge. They don't think as we do, and we can't rely on their reasoning. We have to think matters through for ourselves." Groups should hope they can avoid regarding their neighbors this way, and often there will be alternatives with better promise. Greeks might have a story of why Scythian normative judgments are unreliable, or think that such a story could be told. Perhaps better still, they might engage Scythians in serious normative discussion, and try to work toward a broader community of judgment.

One possible basis for broader community is a kind of relativism. "Our way of life is not yours," a Greek may tell Scythians, "and the ways of thinking that suit you do not suit us. When we understand each other fully, we shall both see that, for the most part, your ways of thinking are right as they bear on your lives, and ours as they bear on ours." A deeper rationale, the relativist thinks, supports disparate everyday ways of thinking about disparate ways of life.[1]

Parochialism is not relativism in this modest sense. The parochialist gives up on full discussion with outsiders, and thinks with his group. The relativist looks for a basis that could unite the everyday thought of different groups. We need to explore both. Are they really distinct? Are both coherent?

Parochialism

A Greek treats a judgment as *parochial*, vis-à-vis Scythians, if he confines his demands on its behalf to a group that excludes them. He must so restrict his demands, I argued briefly, if he insists on denying all authority to Scythians and lacks any story of why. Or at least he must do this if he is to be sincere and ideally coherent. On with the story, then: The Greeks think that an ideally competent normative judge is one who has reached *dialectical equilibrium:* who knows enough that no further true beliefs would lead him to change his mind on normative matters, and who has engaged in dialectic to the point where no further dialectic will show him incoherent or make him give up normative judgments he now holds. They insist, however, that the normative judgments of Scythians carry no weight. Even were a Scythian to reach dialectical equilibrium, they say, his fundamental normative judgments would bear no credence. A normative claim is acceptable if, in

1. What I am calling "relativism" is the view that I find in the writings of some anthropologists—or perhaps that I read into them. See Benedict (1934), Herskovits (1948, chap. 5), and Firth (1951, chap. 6). Philosophers tend to find relativism in this sense trivial and uninteresting, and explore other, more radical forms. See, for instance, Taylor (1954) and Brandt (1959, chap. 11). I intend parochialism as a coherent, more radical form of what philosophers might count as relativism.

dialectical equilibrium, Greeks would accept it. Scythians provide no test.

Now the Greek who says this must treat his normative judgments as parochial vis-à-vis Scythians. He must treat conversational demands on Scythians as illegitimate. How, after all, does he pick the Scythians out? He thinks of them as non-Greeks, or as "not one of us". He picks them out not by any generic property they share, but through a proper name "Greek", or an indexical term "us". He might have dismissed Scythian judgments on generic grounds, and that would not make his judgments parochial. He might have written Scythians off as savages, lacking the advantages of a refined urban life. That would give him an epistemic story he could tell the Scythians, and he could use the story to back his conversational demands. In that case he would think urbanity a qualification for competent normative judgment.

The parochial Greek dismisses Scythians simply as non-Greeks, or as "not one of us". Nothing stops him from making demands on Scythians, or from being open about their basis. If he does so, though, his demands will have a strange feature. He has braced himself against Scythian influence, and for a reason he could put to them only in the terms "You are not a Greek" or "You are not one of us." Neither reason translates to the Scythian's perspective.

For not being "one of us" the point is obvious. To a Scythian, Greeks bear no such relation, and so a Scythian cannot accede to what the Greek demands—or at least, he cannot accede for the Greek's reason. The demand "Believe this because we believe it" cannot be accepted quite in its own terms. Scythians cannot take as their reason "that we believe it", or if they do, they are not according authority to Greeks. Suppose, then, they acquiesce to the Greek's demand in the only terms they can: "We'll believe it because you do." If this is a good reason, it can be filled out, and it could have been filled out by the Greek. What is it about the speaker that should give him authority with the audience? What is it about him generically, or about his relation to the audience? If the Greek's story about "us" can be accepted by non-Greeks, then he could have filled out the story and dropped the "us".

Turn, then, to not being Greek. For a Greek, that can be a reason for denying a person authority—but we have to ask why. What, for him, is the significance of being Greek? What is the full story of why being Greek matters? It may hinge on some generic qualification Greeks alone meet. In that case he has an epistemic story he can put in generic terms; he does not need a proper name in the story. He may, on the other hand, be taking his grounds for according normative authority to rest, ultimately, in some relation to himself—on being "one of us". Scythians then cannot translate the full story to their perspective. They cannot treat not being Greek as in itself a disqualification for competent normative judgment.[2] Suppose, nonetheless, he makes his demands on Scythians. He need be hiding nothing, to be sure. He can tell the Scythians on what basis he is making his demand. He can tell them what he accepts as generic qualifications for ideal normative judgment. He can tell them that even if they met all these qualifications, they would still not accept what he is saying—and he, moreover, would still give no weight to their judgments. All this may subvert the conversational pressures he can apply, but he can still shout and threaten to take offense if they reject what he says. In that case he is being fully open and still making conversational demands.

Are these demands insincere? They are not based on pretense, but they do have an air of browbeating. The Greek is asking Scythians to accept what he says, but for no reason he and his audience could share in the same terms. We are inhibited, normally, from making such demands. We are embarrassed if we are shown to have made them. To be inhibited in this way, to be prone to embarrassment in this way, are the marks of a good discussant. These traits help us work toward consensus. To call a kind of demand insincere is to attach these inhibitions and embarrassments to it.

A Greek, then, can treat his judgments as parochial vis-à-vis Scythians, but he thereby cuts himself off from ordinary normative discussion with them. He rejects their influence on his own thinking, and in return treats any demands he might make on them as illegitimate.

He can still apply his judgments to the lives of Scythians. To do so to their faces is incoherent, devious, or browbeating, but he can do so with other Greeks. Greeks can make conversational demands on each other, and they can demand acceptance of norms that apply to Scythians as well as to themselves. The Greeks need to think within their own community about what it makes sense to do, to think, and to feel in a variety of circumstances, and they need to think about the grounds for the things they accept. What they conclude will often have consequences for the case of being a Scythian, even if they do not

2. Proper names, I am saying, get their significance from a relation to the self. This would need more working out, and much of the working out is in the philosophical literature. See especially Lewis (1979a).

think the Scythians themselves to be good normative judges, even potentially.

We might, then, have characterized parochiality as follows: a judgment is parochial to the Greeks if, on the story they accept, only Greeks constitute potentially competent judges in the matter. A potentially competent judge is someone whose judgment would carry weight if he had all the properties a competent normative judge must have. These properties must be generic, not matters of being a particular person or in a particular group, or of bearing a special relation to the speaker. What qualifications a competent normative judge must have is specified in the epistemic story the Greeks tell each other. The story consists, in effect, of norms for according authority, and it picks out two things: a set of *potentially competent normative judges*, and a set of generic *qualifications for ideal normative judgment*. When a Greek makes a normative assertion, he accepts a supporting epistemic story—that is part of what it is to be sincere and ideally coherent. His judgment is *parochial* to the Greeks vis-à-vis the Scythians if he thinks that a Scythian, even if he met all generic qualifications for ideal normative judgment, would still be a poor judge.

He must then think it illegitimate to demand that Scythians share his normative judgments, though he can still apply the norms he accepts to the lives of Scythians, in discussion with other Greeks.

Relativism

The Greeks' normative judgments were parochial, and claimed to be no more. Now as Greeks' awareness of the Scythians broadened, they might come to restrict their normative claims in a different way: they might recognize many of their normative judgments as applying only within their own community. They would then stop using them, even in discussions with each other, to judge the lives of Scythians. To do this with full coherence, they would need a new kind of epistemic story: a story of how the norms that apply to a person depend on features of his community.[3]

One such story would give a leading role to commitment. A person can be committed to his community in a variety of ways, and these commitments might have normative import. Suppose the Greeks now think communitarian commitments valid. They accept higher order

3. Such stories are implied in the writings of such anthropologists as Benedict (1934), Herskovits (1948), and Firth (1951).

norms that say to abide by one's communitarian commitments. For someone committed to life as a Scythian, the Greeks now think, what it makes sense to do is quite different from what it is for a Greek. Through communitarian commitment, whatever norms emerge by consensus within the community come validly to apply within that community.

Once the Greeks accept all this, they ascribe a new status to their norms of daily life. Before, they may have found some of these norms self-evident, and so accepted them for no further reason. Now they hold them for a reason: "It is part of our ethos, the ethos to which we are committed." That, they say, gives validity to the norms they have come to accept.

Outsiders might reject these norms of commitment. Greeks, the Scythians say, regard themselves as committed. The Greeks themselves think it makes sense to conform to the ethos of their group, and that it makes sense because they have committed themselves to the community and its ethos. No doubt Greeks think their thoughts and feelings succeed in committing them to the Greek ethos. Really, though, the Scythians say, it makes no sense for Greeks to conform to their ethos—feelings of commitment notwithstanding.

The Greeks think that certain everyday norms apply validly to them, simply because those norms are part of an ethos to which they have each committed themselves. The Scythians see other, incompatible norms as valid independently of anyone's commitments. The Greeks now treat the norms they live by as matters of communitarian commitment, whereas the Scythians think them invalid even as applied to Greeks. Neither group need be incoherent.

Like things can be said of existential commitment. Existential commitment is like communitarian commitment, but confined to a community of one. Like communitarian commitment, existential commitment is possible only for a person who accepts higher order norms of a special kind. These norms are voluntaristic: they direct one to be governed by whatever norms one designates to oneself by thinking or feeling in certain ways about them. Whether we too think the person committed will depend on whether we too accept such norms.

Back now to the later Greeks of the fable, whose stock is in communitarian commitment. They take as basic a higher order norm that says communitarian commitments have certain normative results. Whatever norms make up the consensus in one's community, they think, apply validly to life in that community. In daily life they need think no such thing, but this is where a quest for justification leads if pushed to the end.

What is the status of this ground itself? The Greeks might treat it as parochial, or they might treat its acceptance as a qualification for competent normative judgment. What they cannot do is accept it simply because it is part of their ethos—valid for them but perhaps not for others. "It is part of our ethos" cannot be an independent reason for accepting the norm "Accept one's ethos."

Relativism as I am sketching it, then, is partial. The highest order norms of a relativist must have some non-relative status. However attractive may be a relativism bottom to top, it faces the old riddle of how relativism itself can be relative. What we can have bottom to top is parochialism, and parochialism should give us what we wanted from a thorough relativism.

A partial relativism is logically unproblematical. Everyone will agree that the application of norms must be adapted to circumstances. The difference between a relativist and an absolutist is not a matter of how each treats all norms, but of how each treats the everyday norms central to his way of life. The absolutist sees these everyday norms as universally applicable; the relativist takes them to have a deeper rationale that could apply differently in different cultures.

If others reject relativism, the Greeks' best first move is to claim special authority. They can maintain that others reject relativism only because they have not thought hard enough and in the right ways. They have not confronted the possibility of fundamental normative disagreement and the ways local norms give a sense of meaning to life. They have not mastered the relevant philosophical alternatives and their implications. Hard thought, the Greeks can say, is needed for competent judgment.

At least conceivably, though, others have thought hard and still reject relativism. Then the Greeks have the same options as non-relativists: they can work for a broader community of judgment in normative epistemology, or they can treat their relativism as parochial.

The relativism I gave the later Greeks is by no means the only kind. They might think that the norms of one's home community apply validly, whatever one's commitments, public or private. Or they might think that norms apply validly to a person when recognizing them would make life most meaningful for him—and for the most part these will be the norms of his community.

In all these cases the abstract logic is similar. To accept a version of relativism is to accept higher order norms of a special kind: norms that, as applied to different communities or different individuals, require the acceptance of different more everyday norms. These higher order norms are substantive, in that one could reject them without sheer incoherence. Nothing in normative logic forces them upon us; we can construct coherent alternatives. Still, when we reflect on the part norms play in our lives and the lives of others, we may come to see relativism, in some form, as forced on us as the most cogent and sensitive view to take.

Widening Communities

We talk in small communities, and ordinarily we forget outsiders. At times, though, we are confronted with them, and their ways of thinking can seem bizarre. We then want to know what to say to outsiders, and what to say about them among ourselves. At this point, we have choices. We can treat our local judgments as parochial to ourselves, and so have no story of why other groups should accept them. We can become relativists, and tell a story of why their way of thinking suits them and ours suits us. Alternatively, we can tell a story of why we are in a position to judge and outsiders are not, and use that story, if we wish, to back conversational demands on them. Fully coherent people can disagree because their epistemologies clash. Or, finally, we can drop exclusivity and work to expand our community of judgment.

Bring Persians into our myth. The Greeks think the Persians potentially competent as normative judges. If a Persian were in dialectical equilibrium, they think, his judgments would carry authority. No Persian, though, has been trained in dialectic. Hence every Persian lacks a generic property the Greeks think good normative judges must have.

The Persians think that no one becomes competent in normative judgment until he has dwelt upon a mountaintop. Persians do from time to time dwell on mountaintops. Greeks do not, and so the conversational demands Greeks place on Persians are ineffective—unless the Persians are influenceable in ways they think irrational. The Persians cannot be got to accept what the Greeks say by contextual argument. They treat any fundamental Greek influence on their thinking as illegitimate, and so to be resisted. The Greeks and the Persians think each other potentially competent as normative judges, and yet find it fruitless to converse. That is how things are likely to go on, so long as there are not many dealings between the groups.

Still, whatever conversational demands a Greek does place on Persians may be coherent and sincere. Conversational demands purport to have a basis. The requirement of sincerity is that the speaker think he has such a basis for his demands. The Greeks have such a basis; they offer Persians a reason for disqualifying themselves as normative judges: Persians are not trained in the dialectic. The Persians reject this reason, but there is nothing insincere about putting it to them.

A Greek, then, can exclude outsiders from his normative discussions in either of two ways: He can treat his norms as parochial. He still judges the lives of outsiders, but he cannot place demands on them—he cannot do so coherently and openly. On the other hand, he may have a story of why the outsiders' judgments carry no authority. In that case, he can demand that outsiders accept his judgments. These demands may be futile, but he can make them coherently and sincerely.

Instead, though, he could work to expand his community of judgment, treating outsiders as competent normative judges. Later, say, in normative discussion with Romans, the Greeks came both to claim fundamental authority and to accord it. They placed conversational demands on the Romans and acceded, to some degree, to like demands the Romans made on them. They insisted on influencing Roman thinking, while accepting Roman influence on their own thinking.

At the outset, Greeks could not think themselves ideally competent as normative judges. They had not yet been influenced by Romans. An ideal judge must assess authority rightly; he must accord equal authority to all ideal normative judges, and due authority to imperfect judges. Until Greeks and Romans have each weighed the others' judgments in with their own, their judgments fall short of ideal competence. So the Greeks now think, for they count both Greeks and Romans as competent.

A wider community of judgment will likely settle on various strands of relativism. A relativist may build a wide community of judgment around his relativistic stories, and thereby fuse smaller communities into a wider one. The wider community delegates some aspects of normative discussion to more intimate communities, and everyone holds the results valid within the communities that generate them.

Not that a relativist is forced to work toward wide community: His relativism may be parochial. He may confine his conversational demands on its behalf to his own group. His relativism may rest on a deep rationale for accepting norms, a rationale he does not leave vulnerable to the judgments of outsiders. One virtue of relativism, though, is that it can be used to widen communities of judgment. In certain versions it can appeal to a diverse variety of groups.

The choice between relativism, parochialism, and wider community impinges little on everyday life and everyday discussion. We may find no real cases of fundamental disagreement, or find them only with faraway people we can ignore. For the most part, discussion goes unchanged whatever status we accord the judgments we avow. The psychology of accepting local norms depends very little on what we say about people far away. Whether a judgment is parochial is not a chief psychological aspect of making the judgment. It is a matter of the epistemic story the person who makes it might tell.

Rationale and Warrant

It might seem that parochialism collapses into relativism. When our judgments are parochial, we trust the judgments of members of our group but not of outsiders. What can we say to ourselves about why that is? If we cite some generic property outsiders lack, then we are claiming normative expertise, not treating our judgments as parochial. What is left, it seems, is some relation to ourselves, the fact that they are not we. But why should that be a basis for rejecting their influence? Is it some special bearing our own judgments have on our own lives? That seems to push us back into relativism. The special bearing, after all, is only on our own lives, not on the lives of outsiders. How can we claim, even among ourselves, that our norms govern their lives?

To answer this, we need to distinguish two kinds of higher order norms: norms of warrant and norms of rationale, let me call them. Epistemic norms are *norms of warrant*; they say how to recognize a good judgment. The earlier Greeks' norms of dialectical equilibrium are an example. The Greeks said, in effect, to trust the judgment of people who have fully engaged in dialectic. The Greeks thought that normative judgments are ideally warranted by surviving dialectic. Contrast this with a higher order norm of a different kind: "Accept a norm if its acceptance, in one's community, would most enhance a sense of meaning in life." This we can call a *norm of rationale*; it implies a rationale for the norms we should accept. If someone accepts this norm, it will be because he thinks the chief thing about norms is their contribution to felt meaning in life. The everyday norms we should accept, then, have a deep rationale. Dialectical equilibrium theory, in contrast, is neutral on the rationale for the norms it says to accept. It just tells us how to recognize them.

Relativism concerns rationale: the deep rationale for accepting everyday norms as applying to us. The relativist accepts a special kind of higher order norm—say, for how to treat the ethos of one's community, or for how to treat one's commitments to one's community. This norm will not simply tell how to find out what norms are acceptable. It will be backed by a story of the importance of normative ethos, or the importance of commitments. This story will give a deep rationale for the acceptance of everyday norms, and this rationale will support different everyday norms for people in different communities.

For the hypothetical case of belonging to a different community, the relativist sticks to his rationale and applies it. The rationale supports various everyday norms for his own community, and he takes these norms seriously. He takes them to apply, though, only for the cases he and his neighbors face, cases of being a member of that community. He has a story of why it might make sense for others to think differently from him, and this story consists of a rationale with different implications for communities of different kinds.

Parochialism, in contrast, is a matter of warrant. The parochialist restricts the normative authority he will accord; he gives up on treating some people as good normative judges, even potentially. He refuses to include some people fully in the discussion, even if they meet his generic requirements for normative competence. This, however, can be a matter of how he thinks acceptable norms are to be recognized, and not at all what he thinks their rationale might be. The parochialist need have no story of how alien commitments parallel his own in their normative import. The rationale he accepts can be shallow and nonrelative: it can give everyday norms to accept whether Scythian or Greek. He is parochial in that he dismisses outsiders' assessments of the rationale—with no story of what, generically, disqualifies them.

Innocent Mistakes

Imagine that the Greeks are thinking how to apply their norms to the case of being a Scythian. The circumstances are intricate: In the first place, the Greeks are dialectical equilibrium theorists. Their norms of warrant, in other words, say to accept the judgments that would emerge from dialectic within one's cultural group. In the second place, the Greeks hold that one's normative judgments should be parochial to one's cultural group. Now among the Greeks, as it turns out, the norm of rationale that emerges from dialectic is perfectionistic: "Accept norms whose acceptance, in one's group, would lead to the greatest development of the human capacities of members of that group."

This perfectionistic norm can be applied to the Scythians too, and the upshot is this: Of the Scythians' human capacities, the bellicose ones are the most highly developable. Therefore for them perfectionism endorses bellicose norms. On the other hand, we can imagine the Scythians themselves engaging in dialectic. If they did they would settle not on perfectionism, but on a norm of rationale that is hedonistic: "Accept the norms whose acceptance, in one's group, would produce the greatest total net happiness." Now war, it turns out, makes Scythians miserable, and they are capable of living a happy and decadent life in peace. As applied to the Scythians, then, hedonism endorses pacific norms. Perfection is advanced by militarism; happiness by pacifism.

My puzzle now is this: are Greek norms consistent? They seem to prescribe conflicting things for a Scythian who must choose between war and peace. The Greeks accept perfectionistic norms of rationale, and these prescribe, for Scythian circumstances, bellicose norms and war. On the other hand the Greeks accept norms of dialectical equilibrium, and these, as applied to Scythians, say to accept a hedonistic norm of rationale. A hedonistic rationale supports pacific norms. Greek norms, then, tell a Scythian to accept norms that prescribe peace, but to choose war. Is this coherent?

The Greek in effect thinks the Scythians misled by circumstance. He distinguishes two questions: what judgments are warranted in Scythian circumstances, and what judgments are correct for them. Indeed, we might say, making such a distinction is another part of treating normative judgments as objective. Epistemic norms, after all, ordinarily allow that a person can be innocently misled. The Greek treats the choice of war, in Scythian circumstances, as correct, but he treats Scythian circumstances as misleading. Because, alas, Scythian dialectic would lead to the acceptance of a hedonistic norm of rationale, the Scythians could be innocently misled into accepting such a norm. The correct norm of rationale, even for Scythian circumstances, is perfectionistic, but if they achieved dialectical equilibrium they would be warranted in thinking otherwise.

Is this a consistent view for a Greek to take? It is not like usual cases of thinking someone innocently misled. The Greek has a story of sorts as to why it is the Scythians who are misled, but the story cannot be put in generic terms. It invokes the bare fact that the Scythians are not of his own group. The story therefore cannot be translated to a Scythian perspective; it is not one Scythians could accept. This case differs, then, from the clearest cases of innocent mistakes, in a way we could treat as crucial or not. The requirements of coherence will have to be settled not by appeal to analogy, but some other way.

Try thinking of our needs in discussion. To push disagreement off dead center, we may need to raise new considerations. Two kinds are especially useful. We can ask for a deeper rationale for the judgments discussants avow. Even then, however, the disagreement may resolve into a sheer clash of judgments, so that further conversational moves are needed. A further way of working toward agreement is to examine the judges' credentials. We need, in short, to allow two kinds of challenges to a normative position: a challenge to its rationale and a challenge to judgment. The two kinds of challenges involve higher order norms of different kinds.

There are two ways, then, to restrict a normative judgment to a community. On the one hand, we can invoke a deep rationale that applies differently to different communities. Then we are relativists. On the other hand, we can trust our own judgment in a special way. If we do that simply because we are we, that makes our judgments parochial.

One way to refine norms is to apply them to cases far from our normal experience—say, to a sharply different culture. If we come to accept a deep rationale for our local norms, we may find it applying differently away from home. If, on the other hand, we mistrust distant judgments, we can still apply our own judgments to distant circumstances. That is the difference between relativism and parochialism.

Still, why are we restricting our trust in human judgment? Do norms of warrant rest, in the end, on norms of rationale? The important thing about norms, we might say, is the sense of meaning in life that comes from accepting them. Deferring to alien influence leaves one accepting norms that make life seem less meaningful. Therefore we must accord no fundamental authority to those who do not share our way of life. If we say this, we are grounding norms of warrant on norms of rationale. To be coherent, we must accept the same rationale for exotic circumstances. If one is part of another culture, we must say, then one is to accept the norms whose acceptance would make life seem most meaningful there.

Perhaps we should take this conclusion as reason for denying that a parochialist could give a rationale and be coherent. The person who genuinely treats his norms as parochial, we might say, cannot do so with a rationale, for if he had a rationale, the question would shift to its status. What he must have is a special view of what he is doing in making normative judgments. He thinks of himself as working out, partly in community, the most fundamental aspects of how to think.

A better answer, though, would allow that a parochialist can have a rationale for his parochialism. The Greeks indeed can have a rationale for thinking for themselves and resisting outside influence. Thinking together in one's narrow community, they might say, is the best way to develop one's human capacities. That is what recommends it, and this perfectionistic rationale, Greeks can admit, gives Scythians, too, good reason to think for themselves. Alas, though, if Scythians think for themselves they come to reject perfectionism. Scythians are right to think for themselves and warranted in accepting the results. They are also mistaken—innocently. They have applied the right norms of warrant, norms supported by a good rationale. In so doing, they have come to reject that very rationale. In this they are mistaken, though by no fault in the norms of warrant they applied.

Authority as Voice

It is a shock to converse with someone and find discussion with him useless. Even picturing such a person can be unsettling. The illusion grips us that we must be able to resolve disagreement contextually, or that if we cannot, that must be because one of us has simply refused to engage the issue seriously. This must be an illusion—or at least it must be an illusion that agreement is forced by the demands of bare coherence. The speculative evolutionary story I have told, though, explains why the illusion should grip us. Much is at stake in trusting that all disagreement can be resolved discursively. It gives urgency to the discussion. Where there are disagreement and good will, we need to think, one of us can be shown to be mistaken in his own eyes. Much in discursive life depends on a bent to treat dispute as a crisis. We are discussants by nature, and this trust and this will to press for agreement are parts of our equipment as discussants.

These things have a price, though, and in some cases the price might be far too steep. We then have to take a stance that rules out normal discussion. Sometimes we may write a person off as a discussant, and decide that we simply cannot reason with him. We might even write off whole groups. I have been worrying about how we might do this and be coherent.

Normative judgment mimics the search for truth. That is what I have been arguing throughout this part of the book. Parochialism, though, limits the mimicry. That another judge has nothing to do with me could not by itself disqualify him as an indicator of truth, and so it could not undermine his factual authority. To treat a judgment as parochial is to stop treating authority for it as indicating truth. Instead, we might say, one treats authority as voice—as voice in judgments of how it makes sense to act, to think, and to feel.

Norms of warrant tell how to see which norms to accept; norms of rationale say what gives those norms their point. Parochialism consists in norms of warrant, whereas relativism consists in norms of rationale. Broad vision will move us to deep rationales that apply differently in different cultural circumstances. That makes us relativists. In order to keep our normative moorings, though, we must preserve a kind of narrowness: we must limit the influences we will accept. That makes us parochialists. These two pressures might resolve, at times, in strange and elaborate ways.

12 · Pragmatic Support

With norms as with facts, we can tell stories of what makes a person a good judge. From time to time we have to ask whether a person is silly or sagacious, whether his judgment is worth heeding and why. In response to demands for coherence, we might elaborate our answers and systematize them. We might inch, then, toward a full-fledged normative epistemology, a coherent story of what constitutes being a better or a worse normative judge.

An epistemic story might work to banish some people from our community of judgment. It might accord their judgments no weight. Sheer coherence places few constraints on who can be left out and why; the constraints with teeth are ones of cost. Excluding a person has its costs, and including him may too. Costs bear on what norms to accept, and they bear over the widest range of topics. Even with ideal coherence, even in epistemic conditions each thinks ideal, different communities might come to different normative conclusions. Trust different groups and you end up with different opinions. Whom a person includes in his community of judgment, then, may help settle what other normative judgments he accepts. If costs bear on what community to take as his, they may bear on normative issues of all kinds.

At the outset, though, I rejected crude pragmatism. Invoking Cleopatra and the messenger, I stressed a distinction between what it makes sense to think or to feel, and what it makes sense to *want* to think or to feel. Costs bear on what it makes sense to want, and so in particular on what it makes sense to want to think and to feel. What it really does make sense to think or to feel is not directly a matter of cost—or at least so we normally think, and our account should treat this thought as intelligible.

Can we explain what costs might have to do with the warrant for norms, and yet how warrant stays independent of costs? Can we find an explanation, moreover, that applies not only to judges who are ideally coherent? Our own coherence is far from ideal, but we are pressed in various ways toward more coherence. These pressures can make us examine our judgments and their status. They may lead us to choose a parish, to pick a group to which our judgments shall be parochial. Doing this may be the best way to save our norms from challenge as incoherent, when we find it costly to give them up. Costs thus do seem to bear on the choice of a community of judgment, and so too on the norms we can accept with passable coherence. Can we explain how all this could be so?

Pragmatic Rationales

Thinking about costs sometimes appears the only way out of a quandary. Sometimes norms resist further contextual discussion, and we find ourselves at a loss. How shall we decide among ways of thinking that attract us, and what account shall we give of their attraction? We might become convinced that incompatible alternatives are genuinely coherent, and so cannot succumb to internal criticism. Perhaps we are at a loss because we are really in fundamental disagreement with each other, and need new ways of advancing the discussion. Or perhaps we are simply contemplating the possibility of such a breakdown, having realized there could be coherent alternatives. Then we may turn to costs as arbiters, embracing a pragmatism of last resort: we may find ourselves forced, for want of any better way of settling matters, to a pragmatic standard. We may decide that what it makes sense to think and to feel is at base a matter of the costs of the broad alternatives.

There would be nothing incoherent about rejecting all pragmatism even at this point. Questions of warrant, we might say, are pragmatic only when the question is what it makes sense to *want*, to *intend*, or to *do*. To ask whether it made sense for Cleopatra to be angry at the messenger is not to ask whether it was desirable. Likewise with the acceptance of norms: even at a point of normative impasse, when we ask what norms it makes best sense to accept, our question is not even broadly what ways of thinking would most enhance our lives. Good thinking may bring its rewards and good thinking may be its own reward. What constitutes good thinking, though, is not at all a question of reward—apart from the very reward that one is thinking well. So we might still maintain.

Perhaps, though, there are pragmatic grounds for these very dicta. There might be a deep pragmatic story of why we should not treat ordinary questions of warrant as directly pragmatic. Ordinary, shallow antipragmatism might have a deep pragmatic basis. If so, we could go on distinguishing whether a way of thinking is desirable and whether it is warranted. We could go on making the distinction, and still think the story boils down in the end to one of desirability.

Belief makes for a good case in point. Think how a deep pragmatic story of norms for belief might go. Survey a few truisms: beliefs help us in many ways. They comfort us, they give life a sense of meaning, they strengthen personal and communal bonds, and they can be fun. One contribution, though, is especially pervasive and systematic: beliefs guide action. Roughly, with correct beliefs we get what we want and with incorrect beliefs we do not. If it is going to rain and I think it will, I carry an umbrella and keep dry; if I think it won't, I get wet. If it is not going to rain and I think it won't, I save myself bother. Correct beliefs make for the best decision. We can talk, then, of the rules of belief formation that contribute to success in this systematic way, and treat these as rules of warrant.

The full story is of course more complex. Its possibilities are explored in the theory of subjective probability and expected utility (see Ramsey 1931, Savage 1954, Jeffrey 1965). Still, in this more complex story there is a core, systematic way in which degrees of belief—subjective probabilities—contribute to success. In a miscellany of ways other factors can enter too, but these are idiosyncratic. Even the isolated thinker, then, will be helped by distinguishing the degrees of belief that work in this core, systematic way. In talk together the distinction will help even more, for other ways that beliefs promote aims will often vary greatly from person to person.

Pragmatically grounded rules of thought and discussion will give a special status to a core, systematic way that beliefs can promote success. Call the beliefs that work best in this way *systematically apt*. Many things recommend rules of thought and discussion that treat these beliefs in a special way. Ordinary thought mostly finds systematically apt beliefs the congenial ones. Normally, moreover, prescriptions for success in action will support systematically apt beliefs. Finally and chiefly, the pragmatically best norms for discussion will require factual claims to be systematically apt, and will allow challenges only to their systematic aptness. These rules will say, in effect, to treat a belief as credible if and only if it is systematically apt. They will rule out wishful thinking and safe thinking and ingratiating thinking. Of course, we are not always best off accepting what is systematically apt, but the exceptions give us no basis for shared standards. We are normally best off taking systematic aptness as the only standard of credibility.

Here, then, is an indirect pragmatic story of why we should be unpragmatic with belief—of why we should distinguish between what it makes sense to believe and what it makes sense to *want* to believe. Norms can govern believing directly, and they can govern wanting to believe. Norms for belief figure in discussions of what to believe, and the best rules for discussing what to believe will give heed to systematic aptness, and to that alone. We can also work discursively toward wants, and wanting to believe is a special case. Ground rules for discussing wants must allow the widest variety of considerations; otherwise the rules can impoverish our aspirations. Wanting to believe is no exception: the best rules will treat it as sensitive to the same wide range of considerations as other wants. Grounds for belief are sharply restricted; the best grounds for wanting in general are catholic. With belief, indirect pragmatic thoughts support a direct antipragmatism.

What then of feelings? Norms for feelings coordinate, as we saw with anger and guilt. A case-by-case pragmatic evaluation, though, would coordinate poorly; advantage pulls us apart. Then too, directly pragmatic standards would often tell against the responses things seem to demand. Bereaved, we ignore the advantages of sadness; we just feel sad, convinced it makes sense to do so. Direct pragmatic standards could not govern effectively, then—and to whatever degree they did, they would threaten our sense of the point of things. To think "Grieve only when it does you good" would drain grief of significance. None of this tells against an indirect pragmatism for emotions. Rather, it gives us pragmatic grounds for rejecting a direct pragmatism: what it makes sense to feel may not be what it has best consequences to feel. There are gains to be had from accepting non-pragmatic norms.[1]

For norms governing beliefs and feelings, then, we could accept the ordinary distinction between pragmatic support and warrant, and still ultimately ground warrant pragmatically. Perhaps like things go for accepting norms. What it is most desirable to accept, what it makes

---

1. This is the pattern of rule utilitarianism. See, for example, Brandt (1963) and Brandt (1979, chap. 15).

most sense to *want* to accept, may not be what it really makes most sense to accept. Still, we could say, the ultimate basis for what it makes sense to accept lies in the value of broad ways of thinking.

In short, we seem to face a perplexity: Ordinarily we insist that pragmatic support is not warrant, but at times we feel impelled to think in broadly pragmatic ways—especially when other ways of thinking no longer advance matters, when they no longer help us decide among competing systems. The perplexity, though, may be less cutting than I have been making it seem: pragmatic considerations may support this very antipragmatism. With beliefs and feelings, at least, there is pragmatic support for the very distinction between pragmatic support and warrant. Perhaps like things go for higher order norms, for norms for accepting other norms.

Pragmatic Influence

With norms, a puristic antipragmatism would be debilitating. Suppose we rejected all pragmatic stories of why it makes sense to accept the norms it does. What it is advantageous to accept, we said, is one thing; what genuinely warrants acceptance may be something quite different. If we thought this, we would have to despair of our normative competence—at least if the dynamics of normative discussion are at all as I have sketched them. In normative discussion we are influenced by each other, but not only by each other. Mutual influence nudges us toward consensus, if all goes well, but not toward any consensus whatsoever. Evolutionary considerations suggest this: consensus may promote biological fitness, but only consensus of the right kind. The consensus must be mutually fitness-enhancing, and so to move toward it we must be responsive to things that promote our biological fitness. We should expect, then, that in fact the judgments that emerge from normative discussion will be responsive to pragmatic considerations: to the sorts of things that tended, among our ancestors, toward reproductive success. If we were to reject all such influence as distorting, we would have to reject all our normative judgments as products of distorting influences.

In consistency the antipragmatic purist could stay unmoved by all this; it is, after all, a pragmatic argument against antipragmatic purism. The pragmatic stakes, though, turn out to be great. Antipragmatic purism, combined with the evolutionary story I have been telling, brings with it a complete skepticism of the powers of human judgment. Once we absorb the influence of this pragmatic consideration, we may judge that antipragmatic purism is unreasonable.

Let us refuse, then, to correct indiscriminately to counter pragmatic influences. When we recognize that pragmatic considerations have influenced us to see things as we do, we might consider those influences to be illegitimate and try to correct for them. I advocate that we do not. If we take this advice, we are according pragmatic influences a kind of legitimacy. We are not treating pragmatic considerations as evidence directly, but we are granting them sway. It is this kind of modest pragmatism—a *pragmatism of legitimate influence*—that we cannot reject without renouncing all our normative judgments.

Once a person accepts this modest pragmatism for his own current judgments, it is hard to see why he should not extend it to cover the judgments of others. He can extend it, moreover, to cover the judgments he himself would make if he were exposed to further influences. He needs a general account of what kinds of pragmatic influences make normative judgments more reliable and what sorts make them less.

Some kinds of pragmatic influence, we think, skew normative judgments. Say that I am convinced I could lead an opulent life as a propagandist for the rich—if only I had faith in the standards that favor them. My normative judgment, I now think, would be debased if I were greatly influenced by considerations like these. If pragmatic matters influence us legitimately, they must be ones that bear on human life broadly.

Suppose, then, I have an account of what broad pragmatic influences make for good normative judgment. I am willing to accord authority to the judgments of people who are subject to the broad pragmatic influences the story endorses. Then I can think about what our judgments would be if we had been optimally exposed to such influences. In this indirect way, pragmatic considerations will bear on which normative judgments I accept as warranted.

Not all pragmatic support gets endorsed by this route. For one thing, some pragmatic considerations will influence us and others will not. If a consideration would not, then I need not think it bears on which norms are warranted—even in the indirect way I have been sketching. A good judge exposed to it would not be influenced, after all. Then too, I have already said, not all pragmatic influences improve judgment; temptations can distort. In two cases, the kind of indirect pragmatic support I have sketched fails: first, when exposure to a consideration would leave a person's judgments unchanged, and second, when exposure would change his judgments but not improve them.

Take again the thought that believing in strong property rights could enrich me, by making me an effective propagandist for the rich. Whatever things might tell in favor of strong property rights, this is not one of them. How can I say this? Perhaps I think that even vivid exposure to this consideration would leave me uninfluenced. Perhaps, on the other hand, I allow that vivid exposure might influence me, but think that the influence would leave me a worse judge of norms of property, not a better one. In either case, I coherently deny that this consideration favors strong property rights. Not all pragmatic support counts as real support.

Still, we do have a route by which pragmatic considerations can bear on issues that seem nonpragmatic, on issues of what it makes sense to think and to feel. Take a pragmatic consideration C that bears on a norm N—say, that accepting N would enhance our lives. Suppose both of the following hold:

> *The influence condition:* A person fully exposed to consideration C would come to accept N.
> *The improvement condition:* Exposure to C would improve him as a judge of N.

Then together, these two conditions tell in favor of N.

Throughout the book I have stressed that normative discussion coordinates, and that coordination yields benefits. Normative discussion works partly by mutual influence, and so the story has been one of benefits from mutual influence. What happens, then, when we absorb this theory of normative discussion into our thinking? We might well come to accept norms that endorse mutual influence—norms for according fundamental authority to each other. Whether we do is a fact of our psychic makeup, but if we do, the influence condition is satisfied. Perhaps another result of absorbing the theory is to make us better judges of norms for according authority. Whether it does is a normative matter, and whether we think it does is a matter of the epistemic norms we accept. If it does, the improvement condition is satisfied. Suppose both conditions are satisfied: taking the story in does influence us, and it thereby makes us better assessors of norms of authority. Then the benefits of normative discussion tell indirectly in favor of a normative claim: that it does make sense to accord each other's judgments some degree of fundamental authority.

Whether the influence condition holds is a matter of psychological fact. Whether the improvement condition holds is a normative question, a question of normative epistemology. Whether a person coherently accepts the improvement condition will depend on the normative epistemology he accepts. I have argued, though, that sometimes a person must think the improvement condition holds—at least if he is not to be driven to an extreme normative skepticism. We have all in fact been influenced by pragmatic considerations, and influenced deeply, if my evolutionary speculation is on track. If such influences do not make for good normative judgment, we are hopeless as normative judges. Sometimes, then, both the influence condition and the improvement condition hold, and pragmatic considerations legitimately bear on what it makes sense to think and to feel.

Plausibility

Costs sometimes bear on normative issues, but I have not shown that they always must. Besides finding some judgments salubrious and others not, we find some things plausible and others absurd. Plausibility makes for pressures of its own.

We might envision a kind of pragmatic accord in the norms we accept. In pragmatic accord, we would accept an underlying rationale for all our judgments, a rationale in terms of ways of life worth leading. This rationale would apply to judgments of how to think and how to feel. (We might, among other things, appeal to benefits that stem from being able to find our way around in the world, and from the congeniality of ways of thinking and feeling.) The norms of warrant that were endorsed by this deep rationale would tell us to accept that very rationale. If we accepted the rationale and the norms of warrant it recommends, our thoughts would be in pragmatic accord.[2]

Nothing I have found to say, though, requires such a full pragmatic accord, even as an ideal. In the first place, pragmatic accord is no requirement of sheer coherence: we might coherently accept norms as overwhelmingly plausible, as self-evident, and still think we would be better off rejecting them. Then too, pragmatic accord or anything close might be a psychological impossibility. It might turn out that we

2. Taylor (1961), as I read him, seeks a pragmatic accord when he speaks of "vindicating" a value system to a person: we ask the person whether living in accordance with the system is part of "a whole way of life which, on reflection, he really wants to live" (1961, 132). See Chapters 5 and 6.

simply find implausible the ways of thinking it would serve us best to find plausible, and that nothing can change our minds.

Finally, for some ways the world could be, norms in pragmatic accord would be absurd. They would be absurd even if we could bring ourselves fully to accept them. Imagine a stock philosophers' fantasy: a demon who wants us to think an excellent suntan is all that matters in life. He threatens ruin unless we come to accept this, and bounty if we do. We have strong reason, then, to want to think as the demon commands. Perhaps with heroic effort we could succeed—and then, of course, it would not seem absurd to us that a good tan is all that matters. Still, we can now say, a tan is far from all that matters, and to think otherwise is absurd. Under the circumstances, it would be fortunate if we could talk ourselves into this absurd view of life, but the view is still crazy. If instead we went on thinking reasonably, that would be unfortunate but correct.

Less fantastic stories too might discredit pragmatic accord. The powerful have more influence than the rest of us. Now, it promotes coordination if our norms of authority move us wherever normative discussion naturally tends. Otherwise, the dynamics of normative discussion pull us one way, and our norms for authority pull us another way. Therefore if normative discussion tends toward whatever helps the powerful, then perhaps the norms that best foster consensus will say to defer to the judgments of the powerful. Suppose we filled in this rough argument and found it convincing. We could be in pragmatic accord, then, only if we thought it makes sense to trust most the judgments of the powerful. Would that make us accept power-sensitive norms of authority? Would it not rather make us reject the goal of pragmatic accord? Clearly, we can say, power in itself does not make normative judgments more reliable. If we would be better off thinking it did, so much the worse for pragmatic justifications. When ways of thinking with pragmatic support seem absurd, we shall reject pragmatic accounts of how it makes sense to think. Plausibility and costs may pull us in different directions.

Still, various things draw plausibility and desirability together. Plausibility itself bears on costs: there is cost in rejecting what we find plausible. Rejecting plausible judgments can make for a costly instability. Take the extreme of plausibility, self-evidence. To find a thing self-evident is to accept it confidently and for no further reason. At the moment of finding it self-evident, I do not accept it on the authority of anyone—even myself. Like things go for the partial self-evidence that must figure in a well-formulated coherence theory: being found plausible, to some degree, independently of the considerations for it or against it.

Suppose I find a thing self-evident, fully or partly: say, that vengeance is worth nothing in itself. Suppose also that the people I find good normative judges think otherwise: they think that vengeance matters even apart from any further good it does. The weight of the authority I accept is against me, and so my judgment is unstable. When I think directly whether vengeance is worth having in itself, I say no. When I remember what I have thought, and weigh that against what others think, I change my mind. My judgment shifts as I go back and forth between two ways of making it: facing the question directly, and relying on competent judgment.[3]

Some instability of judgment is unavoidable. Paradox makes for instability. We keep discovering that things we find evident clash. In the face of this, we must reshape our thoughts: we must learn to see some of the things we have found evident as illusions. For instability that stems from paradox we seek cures, and part of the cure is philosophical. Philosophers may find ways of thinking that cohere and that we can learn to find plausible. Philosophers' cures, though, are often not full successes. We are left with some instability even apart from questions of authority.

Where instability stems from authority, another kind of cure may be had. If others' judgments seem wild, we can discount them. We can rule people out of our community of judgment. After that we can shift back and forth between insight and authority, without overturning whole ways of thinking.

Plausibility bears on whom to trust in more direct ways too. If something is obvious, then anyone who rejects it tends to discredit himself. I may be more sure of a judgment than I am of the competence of anyone who rejects it. If someone rejects the judgment, I discount his competence; I edge him out of my tentative community of judgment. To do so has its pragmatic costs and rewards, but my reasoning may bypass them. What he accepts is so implausible, I can say, that he cannot be a good judge of such things. Such an argument from plausibility is not itself pragmatic, even indirectly: It does not proceed by

3. Compare Sidgwick on disagreement: "If I have no more reason to suspect error in the other mind than in my own, reflective comparison between the two judgments" will result in "an alternation and conflict between positive affirmation by one act of thought and the neutrality that is the result of another" (1907, 342).

way of the judgments we would make if the right pragmatic considerations had influenced us.

Norms of parochiality are not themselves likely to seem plausible or implausible. They say what status to accord our judgments. They say to treat our judgments as parochial to certain groups. That may have consequences that are plausible or implausible. Whom we include in a community of judgment settles whose judgments to heed, and thus what to accept on authority. It is not directly plausible or implausible, though, that our everyday judgments have a certain status. It is when discussion goes especially badly, or when we pursue ordinary questions to extraordinary lengths, that norms of parochiality might be made explicit. Then they must be tested by their implications for a whole coherent system of normative judgments.

I have been looking at ways plausible judgments tend to be advantageous. Deep pragmatic rationales may be discovered, rationales that support our standards of plausibility. Then too, plausible judgments have advantages that stem from their sheer plausibility: we can keep to them stably. At the same time I have insisted that plausibility and advantage need not coincide. Demon stories hold them apart.

Still, why care what it makes sense to think and to feel? Shouldn't our normative ways of thinking have a point? Shouldn't they enhance the worth of our lives?

The response must be complex. First, if our normative ways of thinking were a burden to us and there were a cheap cure, then of course we would do well to take the cure and drop the ways of thinking. We would do well, though we might then be thinking in ways that are absurd. Nothing guarantees that if we took the cure we would be thinking reasonable thoughts. Should we trust the thoughts we would have if we took the cure? That is a normative question, a question of norms for authority. The answer might perhaps be yes, but demon stories keep us from thinking that always, in any conceivable circumstance, the answer must be yes.

Still, it is reasonable to hope that as things are we are lucky: that we ourselves could attain pragmatic accord or something close, and that moreover if we did, we would be thinking in the ways it makes most sense to think. Plausible ways of thinking serve us well, in a rich diversity of ways—though not perfectly. I have been laying forth a number of reasons for thinking that advantage and plausibility might coincide fairly well.

If they do, that can be no evolutionary surprise. Our normative propensities constitute rough heuristics for promoting biological fitness, and our notion of benefit coincides roughly with biological fitness—through no accident. None of this guarantees an exact match between plausibility and advantage, but it makes a rough coincidence no surprise.

Ideal Judges and Us

Suppose my talk of ideal coherence is right. What does that have to do with us as we are? What does it tell us about the normative judgments we ourselves can make—we who are coherent only imperfectly? In real, non-ideal discussion, we take normative positions, and work out what norms to accept. We work it out partly in community. As we do, we hold each other loosely to standards of consistency: mistakes exposed make for embarrassment. These pressures are part of a psychosocial mechanism by which discussion tends toward consensus. Does ideal discussion tell us anything about how all this proceeds?

Real discussion starts with a scattering of tentative judgments. We begin tentatively judging what to accept, and also tentatively judging whose judgment to trust. We have tentative thoughts about what would put us in a position to make better judgments. These tentative judgments may confront each other in discussion, or in internal rehearsal for discussion. Sometimes firm judgments of substance make us revise our story of whom to trust: I may be more sure of a judgment than I am of anyone's competence. Sometimes judgments of competence lead us to revise judgments we started out accepting.

These scattered thoughts form nothing like an ideally coherent theory. They will, though, expose us piecemeal to demands for consistency. Among other things, they expose a speaker to epistemic challenge: if a dispute seems to boil down to sheer differences in judgment, a speaker can be asked why his own judgment is most to be trusted. Others see things differently from him; what does he say about that? Or he can be issued less blanket challenges. He himself is a poor judge of the matter, it can be claimed, because of bias, say, or lack of experience.

Stories about ideal coherence tell us where responses to piecemeal challenges could lead. Inferences that seem attractive one by one can be strung together to reach suspect conclusions. If we have some idea of what might be ideally coherent, that can guide our responses to piecemeal challenges.

What lines in normal thinking are supported by this talk of ideal epistemic coherence? One thing it supports is discussion. It supports thinking in groups, at least under favorable conditions. Discussion, of course, does many things: It spurs people to sort out issues. It exposes inconsistencies and suggests lines of thought. I have been stressing a further benefit: the mutual influence discussion brings. Sometimes, to be sure, this influence must be resisted. Influence can be manipulated to bad ends. A whole discursive milieu can put people in a bad position to judge, and distort their judgments in systematic ways. Exposure to such milieu can make one a worse judge and not a better one. When group conflict gives rise to strong passions, for example, intensive discussion with one side alone hardens bias. It leaves one a poor judge of the quarrel. Still, in circumstances we think favorable, part of what we can seek in discussion is mutual influence. We do not think any person an ideal judge, but we tentatively think some people better judges and some worse. Provisionally we can weigh their judgments accordingly.

One picture of how this might work seems false: I first note how things look to me and how they look to others. I tentatively assess how well the judgment of each of us is to be trusted. Then I accept, by my tentative lights, the preponderance of qualified judgment. To think this way would threaten my stability. How things appear to me might little fit what, on balance, the authority I recognize supports. I might then switch from finding things independently credible to finding them poorly backed by authority.

A better picture is this: We do take disagreement as cause for doubt, especially if we cannot explain it away as stemming from someone's epistemic fault. A conviction based on authority alone, though, is unsatisfactory. It is disquieting, especially if one suspects it goes against the way one would think matters through oneself with enough information. That is puzzling: why should it matter any more how I would see things—with enough thought and enough information— than how others would? The answer is that a kind of self-trust is needed for stable thought.

What can we seek in discussion, then, besides such things as consistency, the facts, mental exercise, and suggestions for ways of thinking? What more we can seek is to influence and to be influenced. Things are out of order in discussion until insight matches authority. The conclusions supported by the weight of tentatively accorded authority should match the ways we each see things when we think about them. Disagreement is occasion to check one's coherence, but it is also occasion to seek mutual influence.

To how big a group, then, should our judgments be parochial? How wide should be the influence we seek? Here we must be hesitant: we do not know where further thought and broader discussion might lead. The theory of ideal epistemic coherence, though, provides us devices for thinking about these things.

13 · Communities of Judgment

The crucial puzzles in life are more or less local. What we need from day to day is not a global rationality, not a rationality all conceivable discussants could recognize, if only they were coherent. Our problem is what to treat as rational among neighbors and other conversants. A person needs to ask what to treat as rational or irrational within the small communities that most engage him. He needs also to ask how to regard the awkward large groups that bear on his life and the lives of those around him. Sometimes cooperation with them is vital. Sometimes he can enjoy other groups and learn from them. With them he can hope to enjoy a partial community, and so to reap some of the benefits of normative consensus. He cannot, though, hope for anything like the full community of judgment he can look to with fellow spirits.

We live in fuzzy, overlapping communities of judgment. Some are large and some small; some are intense and others diffuse. With different groups, we come to tell different stories, and my question in this chapter is what those stories can have to do with each other. In a small, intense community we can talk through many things. One thing we can talk about is the lives of outsiders and our dealings with them. That helps us to develop our thoughts about life in our own community: How shall our norms extend to exotic circumstances? What does that tell us about those norms, and about our reasons for accepting them? In addition these intimate discussions can help us live with the outsiders we are discussing. They can help us to figure out how to work toward more widespread communities of judgment. Our larger groups will go on disagreeing on some matters. Still, we can talk other matters through, and we need to. On a restricted range of topics, agreement may be possible and worth pursuing. Agreement on restricted topics keeps peace. It helps groups cooperate. At its best it enriches people's lives, by broadening their understanding, their sense of humanity, the richness of their friendships.

My point in running through these truisms is this: The character of normative judgments is partly a matter of their role in discussion. Different discursive roles should make for normative judgments of different kinds. We need to ask, then, about avowals we make differently from one group to another. Some judgments we avow with intimates, but leave aside as diverse groups work toward a consensus on other topics. Acceptance, I have been claiming, has something to do with avowal. What, then, of these judgments we avow in one group but keep off the table in others? Do we fully accept them? Are they judgments of rationality, or do they have a specially modest status? What too of judgments we avow on their own terms in larger groups, but tell special stories about in smaller groups? How does my story look when communities of judgment form a collage of loose public groups on the one hand, and on the other hand intimate fellow searchers for truth and meaning in life?

We choose our communities of judgment, in a sense, and gains and losses bear on the choice. Life in a messy and dangerous world depends on being able to form widespread communities of judgment on a restricted range of norms—norms that enable us to live together. To thrive, though, we need more intimate communities as well. In these communities we can exercise our normative capacities and try to make sense of life and its possibilities. There is a complex story to be told here of practices and prices, of coherent possibilities and the pressures that bear on them—and I can tell very little of it. In this chapter I try to broach some of the things that need to be explored.

Isolation and Repression

In many realms of thought, feeling, and action, groups do not need to agree one with another. Some topics they do not need to discuss. They can work toward separate communities of judgment, and no group loses much. It used to be that faraway groups were isolated fully; now isolation is a matter of topic and degree. Groups can have separate norms, say, for how they treat their own members. They may be mutually indifferent as to how people in each other's groups are treated—though this indifference may have its limits. Likewise groups can accept separate norms for belief, separate norms for feelings, and separate aesthetic norms. If their interactions are sparse enough, that may mean no great loss for anyone.

I am characterizing isolation in terms of loss: groups are isolated on a topic if they can disagree on it without much loss—as they count losses. Whether much is lost by their lights depends in part, of course, on how the groups can interact or avoid interacting. It depends too on what they see as a loss, and judgments of loss can change. It might, for instance, cost a religious group sorely, by its own lights, to have infidels as neighbors. The lack of common religious norms would then cause them to lose something they valued. With revised standards of cost they might no longer find having infidel neighbors costly. If having infidel neighbors is not in itself a cost, then groups even in a single neighborhood may be able to think separately about religion, and do so without great loss. Then, they have achieved isolation on points of religion: they still have infidel neighbors, but that is no great cost.

People need intimate groups and not only widespread understandings. Isolated thinking is disorienting. On any topic a person needs other people with whom to think, but for many topics he has some choice of who those others shall be. He can seek out fellow spirits, people whose judgment rings true. He can work with them to develop his normative views. Within the chosen group discussants can brand views of outsiders irrational. They can do so without confronting these outsiders whose judgments they dismiss.

On other topics a group is imposed by circumstance. Without the right community, a person may lose chances at cooperation. He may face ruinous conflict or war. Or the price may be that he is alienated from people he could value. In some cases, for some purposes, isolation is costly or impossible. People must agree or pay.

The range of matters on which we need agreement will, of course, be greater with people close at hand than with those far away. Different relations will demand agreement on different matters, with varying urgency.

I take up isolation chiefly to set it off from other ways one group can exclude another from its community of judgment: costly conflict, repression, a modus vivendi, and full toleration. When disagreement hurts, groups can cope in various ways. They may just accept the costs. They may talk further and work toward a community that has so far escaped them. They may turn to repression. Or they may work for tolerance or a modus vivendi, agreeing on ways of coping together with their disagreements. Much of life, of course, entangles these strands.

Groups are isolated on a topic when none of them loses much from thinking about it in separate ways. Then they face little pressure to work toward a single community of judgment on the topic. Now we can ask what status the judgments of an isolated group will have if they are coherent, and I have already offered a menu of possible answers: The group may have a story of why the other group are poor judges of the matter. They may make their judgments parochially. Or, finally, they may accept a relativistic story. A group can always find a story of one of these kinds, a story that excludes others from the discussion. Still, it may not want to. The constraints with teeth on accepting such a story are ones of gain and loss—and where groups can conduct their discussions in isolation, even those constraints lose their bite.

What, then, when isolation is not to be had? Sometimes one group can repress another, and so still need not work toward common norms. By repression let me mean coercion of a special kind: coercion held illegitimate by the people coerced. Repression in this sense is possible only when people accept norms of legitimacy, norms governing complaint. Egoists can compete and they can bamboozle, but they cannot sincerely complain of each other. Normative agreement can coordinate, but egoistic norms coordinate poorly. Egoistic coordination is intricate and unstable.[1] A more effective device is to agree on norms for complaint. People then expect complaint if they cross certain lines, and the complaints are no longer at the mercy of intricate reckonings of what they will cost and what they will yield. If, though, people are at odds over what norms for complaint to accept, then trouble looms. Some may then be coerced and find this coercion grounds for complaint. That is repression in the sense I shall adopt: coercing people in ways they themselves find illegitimate.

Not all coercion is repressive in this sense. People may welcome coercion. They may want the discipline: military schools and rigorous sects have their draw. They may accept coercion to act as they would anyway; few of us object to being forced not to murder and not to steal. They may each accept being coerced so that others will be coerced; taxes work that way. Then too, even when people do not welcome

---

1. Schelling (1960, chap. 2) is the classic discussion of egoistic coordination.

coercion, they may think it legitimate. An egoist may think it fine to try to steal, and all right for others to try to keep him from stealing. Neither stealing nor threats against it are ground for complaint, by his doctrine. Threats against him then are coercive but not repressive: he treats both the threats and their evasion as legitimate.

Coercion, repressive or not, is no fixed result of thinking a person irrational. Even if we have the power to coerce him, we may think him irrational and yet leave him to make his own mistakes. His freedom, we may think, is a good thing, in itself or for its likely results. Leaving him free may stabilize social arrangements that leave others free, and we may value the freedom of those others. Conversely, we can think someone rational and still coerce him. We need not be convinced that a Mafia hit man has demanded too low a price, or misfigured the conflict between self-interest and morality, before we will stop him or punish him.

Repression in a narrower sense is repression of opinion, or of its expression. Here I am using the term more broadly. A person is repressed in my sense not only if he cannot express his opinion, but if he cannot act on it. More precisely, he is repressed if he is coerced in a way that, in his opinion, is ground for complaint.

So much for what repression is—or for what it is as I am using the term. Can we avoid it, then, and should we? Even in this wide sense of the term, repression is always a bad. It shifts the basis of normative discussion, and it subverts a valuable kind of respect we may have for each other. Normally we talk as if each is free to choose as he is persuaded. Threats are out of the picture; they do not apply to the alternatives anyone treats as eligible. In the background, to be sure, there will be limits, but none that anyone finds cause for grievance. When repression threatens in earnest this sense of autonomy is lost, and that is a cost. Respect itself is perhaps a feeling or attitude, but there are kinds of behavior that show it. There is a kind of respect that is shown by leaving people free to act in the ways they think it would be illegitimate for us to prevent. Acting on it consists in avoiding repression.[2]

Still there is a limit to what anyone will tolerate in others, given the choice. A thug might insist he had a right to his thuggery, but we shall

---

2. I discuss respect as a feeling in the next chapter. Scheffler (1979, 295) and Rawls (1985, 226) speak of "cooperation on a basis of mutual respect" as something we want, the desire for which explains our concern with justice. I am not at all sure whether they mean by 'respect' what I am proposing to mean, but their usage does seem to fit. In any case, their discussions prompted mine here.

repress him if we can. We want to extend this kind of respect, but not at all cost.

Sometimes, then, alternatives are bleak. On various topics for various groups, no community of judgment can be had, at least at a decent price. Groups then may think in separate ways, perhaps at no great cost. At times, though, the costs are substantial or even appalling— above all when groups are at odds over norms for complaint. Then one group may try to repress another. Repression is sad: tolerance shows a kind of respect, a willingness to treat people in ways they themselves find legitimate. It is part of our discursive nature that we find this respect important. We repress only at a price.[3]

Repression may be out, of course, even apart from this. A group may lack all power to repress, or repression may be possible only at the cost of ruinous struggle or costly effort. Then groups either bear the full costs of thinking their separate ways, or find ways to accommodate their differences.[4]

It is schemes of accommodation that chiefly interest me in this chapter. First, though, I have taken up ways of doing without them. Sometimes groups can stay isolated, at least on certain topics. Sometimes one group can repress another. I looked at repression for two chief reasons: partly to point to a cost that schemes of accommodation can avoid—the loss of a valuable kind of mutual respect—and partly to get away from the easy assumption that repression must always be rejected. Repression always has sad costs, but sometimes the costs of alternatives are greater. Schemes that avoid repression at lowered cost, then, are well worth seeking out.

Covenants with Hell

William Lloyd Garrison, the abolitionist, denounced the United States Constitution of his day as a "covenant with death and an agreement with Hell". The Constitution accommodated slavery, and slavery was Satanic. Now, we can agree with Garrison about slavery, and still not

3. Scanlon proposes "the source of motivation that is directly triggered by the belief that an action is wrong is the desire to be able to justify one's actions to others on grounds they could not reasonably reject" (1982, 116). This appeals to something like the discursive motivation I am invoking. In Scanlon's version, what we want to avoid is "reasonable" rejection; he leaves it open what 'reasonable' is to mean. I am suggesting also a broader, defeasible motivation not to repress at all, even when we think others unreasonable.

4. My discussion of accommodation in the rest of the chapter draws heavily on Rawls's explanation of a political conception of justice. See especially Rawls (1985).

think that all who accepted the Constitution had bargained away their souls. We can concur that the Constitution was an agreement with Hell, and think that men of goodwill can need to make such agreements. Abolition, after all, stood no chance in the South, and even a full lifetime after the Constitution was adopted, the North was hard put to end slavery in a bitter war. During that lifetime economic power had shifted toward the North. Until the end of that lifetime, the North could only have lived with slavery or lived apart. Hell would burn on, covenant or no, but the Constitution might one day prove an engine to quench it.

Between right-thinking people and slaveholders, there could be no community of judgment on slavery. For a time, though, I am saying, right-thinking people could share a constitutional order with slaveholders. On what basis? The Constitution allowed a modus vivendi: shared norms for cooperation in the face of deep disagreement, where one side at least would repress the other if it could.

The two groups could have developed completely separate communities of judgment on how to deal with each other within a constitutional order. They could each have treated norms of cooperation purely as instruments for advancing their separate goals. A more widespread community of judgment on constitutional arrangements, though, stabilized those arrangements—and stability at first was a good thing. People could not be brought to agree on the morality of slavery, but they might develop, in discussion with each other, ways of living together under norms that were the best anyone could expect. That would constitute a modus vivendi.

Here our puzzles begin. The psychology of accepting norms runs deep in us. Normative discussion, if I am right, can elicit the syndrome I have called accepting norms. What, then, if the topic is sharply delimited, and talk proceeds against a background of grave disagreement? What if each side would repress the other if it could? The psychology of accepting norms at these special times may still resemble the ordinary psychology of accepting norms.

When Satan is familiar and cannot be wrestled down, we may come to live with him on familiar terms. The potential for accommodation is in us, and its realization can be appalling.[5] We can turn too easily

5. Sabini and Silver discuss how naive and more or less decent women hired as guards at Ravensbrück turned to inhuman monsters (1982, 83–84). Zimbardo and coworkers simulated the brutality of prisons with Stanford students screened for psychological normality (Haney, Banks, and Zimbardo, 1973).

into instruments of oppression, or come to tolerate oppression we could have overcome at due cost. At times, though, it is good that we can form limited communities of judgment even with people who are evil. At times there is no acceptable alternative to a workable compromise. Compromise may then be stabilized by developing norms of accommodation: common norms on sharply restricted topics. These norms may need all the psychic support that better norms can have in better times (see Luban, 1985).

Part of the puzzle is when to accept norms of accommodation and when to stand firmly against them. The puzzles are most difficult with questions of war and peace with horrendous regimes. Peace depends above all on stable expectations, and here as with other bargains, expectations are steadied by normative commitments and normative appeals (see Schelling, 1960, chap. 2). Peace rests on a rough worldwide quasi-moral consensus on rules for states' dealing with states.

The rules take on a moral aura, even when by normal standards of decency they look absurd. Think of non-intervention: states must not intervene in each others' internal affairs. Breaches of this rule jump to mind, but the rule governs much of what states do, and it is embraced with fervor and cant. The people, we are told, have a right to decide their own way of life—though the ones who decide may turn out to be a dictator and his henchmen, or a small, determined party, or a large group that oppresses other groups. Why should such talk grip us? That is a socio-psychological question, a question of the dynamics of norm acceptance.

Another question is how to regard this grip, this moral aura. Is it an illusion to be resisted? The case for accepting a norm like non-intervention is strong. Norms of non-intervention are stabilizing, and they are more or less attainable. They are not the best possible norms for world affairs, but they may be the best on which a rough consensus of governments can be reached. On grounds like these we could accept norms of non-intervention in a coolly pragmatic, non-moral frame of mind. A moral aura, though, fortifies the norms. Their hold on actions then comes not just from pallid considerations of what makes for a workable modus vivendi. It comes from norms prescribing guilt and anger if rules of non-intervention are violated. Principles so fortified can stand against immediate pressures in the conduct of nations.

None of this is to say that non-intervention is the best of regimes. We can try to nudge the world toward a better consensus. Minimal standards of human rights hold out some hope, and we should press for their recognition. In a better world there would be machinery for enforcing them. International standards of democratic control would be even better; they would allow the people truly to decide. In the meantime, we are stuck with non-intervention: we need to cultivate respect for the principle, even when states violate human rights, and even when they are far from democratic.

My chief question, though, is not when to accept norms of accommodation, but what we are doing when we do accept them. What status do we give the terms of a covenant with Hell? In a sense we accept the terms; we embrace them in more ordinary normative discussion, and they work toward the same kinds of ends, mutual restraint and—within tight limits—cooperation. We see arrangements as fair or unfair, equitable or inequitable. By our normal standards, though, talk of fairness here is wildly out of place. The norms of accommodation we cling to and defend have little to do with the way we think things really ought to be. Can this be a coherent state of mind?

As groups work toward joint agreement on norms of accommodation, members need an account of what they are doing. Within each group people need to say what status the norms have, and what the norms have to do with the norms they accept within their own group. It should be clear what the best account is. Norms of accommodation, people can tell each other locally, are norms for circumstances of a special kind, the circumstances in which a modus vivendi is needed. They are norms for groups living in deep disagreement, when one group would repress the others if it could but no group can do so at a price it finds worth paying. In a modus vivendi, then, norms of accommodation are norms of the second-best: divergent groups can work toward a community of judgment on these norms when they see that no agreement is in the offing about what is best.

As they work toward widespread agreement on norms of the second-best, people can tell different stories within their own groups and between them. A local group must keep track of what really matters, and of how a better world would be arranged. That is part of making sense of life and of members' dealings with each other. Their norms of accommodation, they must say, are the right norms for coping with the stubborn disagreements they face with other groups. In the wider world, on the other hand, they must avow the norms of accommodation everyone needs, the norms whose global acceptance is in the offing. They must insist on these norms or accommodate their views to the views of others. They must enter into a widespread normative discussion on its own terms, engaging their ordinary normative equipment. Perhaps also they can tell the story of second-best virtues, for there may be enough agreement between groups on how to measure the benefits that flow from the norms of accommodation. Let me invent a speech by Jason to the Scythians: "We disagree irreconcilably on what political life should be accomplishing, in our own communities and in each other's. We agree on the need to keep peace, and we can work toward agreement on the norms that might help to do that. None of us would accept these norms in a world where our own political conceptions could prevail. In the world as it is we accept them or die." Whether or not people can tell this story globally, they must tell it locally or live with norms that clash. In the global discussion that develops norms of accommodation, this story of second-best virtues may play little part. Norms of accommodation come to be accepted by being avowed in their own terms.

As for the local norms, perhaps they too can be avowed coherently by one group to another. They can, I proposed earlier, if the group thinks a story can be told of why it can judge—a story that does not boil down to saying that we are we and others are not. Even if this intergroup avowal is coherent, however, it cannot be insistent. Groups must distinguish between urgent business and eventual business. Of some things a group might eventually hope to convince others, whereas there are other things that urgently must be established. In this sense discussants must bracket their views of what is most worth achieving, so as to carry on the urgent discussion of how it makes sense for groups to accommodate each other in the face of deep disagreement.[6]

Life with a modus vivendi, then, requires two things: First, in urgent discussions between groups, it requires setting aside norms on which no accord is in the offing. These norms can still be pushed locally, with fervor and conviction; between groups they are not seriously on the agenda. Second, it requires avowing norms of accommodation wholeheartedly to everyone. The avowal can be backed by a story of why these norms are valid as second-best norms, but it is the avowal, not the story, that does the chief work. For the most part, discussion will work by direct appeal to the norms of accommodation themselves. Norms of accommodation, after all, get their hold on us in the same

6. Ackerman (1980) imposes elaborate restrictions on the claims that can be made in discussions that work toward a liberal political accommodation. He argues that far-reaching conclusions can be derived from these restrictions.

way as other norms, through the psycho-social dynamics of normative discussion. The story of why they are valid as second-best norms does something else: it reconciles the norms of accommodation with local norms—norms that express a fuller view of life and what matters in it. The story thus makes for coherent local discussion with norms of both kinds in play.

Let me review. Living together is often a matter of bargaining, but raw bargaining is unstable. Human bargaining is pervaded by moral claims; even when the claims are transparently self-serving, bargainers feel called upon to make them. So it is with bargaining to a modus vivendi: the norms that emerge take on a broadly moral aura—even when each party finds evil in the others.

My earlier account of normative discussion explained these phenomena. Bargaining involves normative discussion: working out, partly in community, what norms to accept as applying to a situation. The psychic mechanisms in play have a biological function of coordination, and that includes the coordination that stabilizes bargaining. Even when moral disagreement runs deep, these mechanisms can work us toward a partial community of judgment on delimited subjects. They work to create some intrinsic attachment, some real normative governance for the norms that emerge.

My question was whether we could understand our resulting state of mind as coherent, and express it in a coherent normative story. We can, I proposed, if we explain norms of accommodation as norms of the second-best, as norms for coping with deep and perilous disagreement. We can then tell consistent stories locally and globally. We can develop norms of accommodation in global discussion, invoke them, and rely on their intrinsic appeal. Still we can admit openly, on occasion, that these norms are not directly the ones that matter. We can admit that we appeal to them for want of a better alternative.

Toleration

Real toleration is more than a modus vivendi but with similar structure. A modus vivendi is accepted only because the alternative is ruinous conflict, and all groups find the scheme preferable. Mutual toleration too involves a scheme of accommodation that all groups prefer to its alternative. What binds them to the scheme, though, is that it allows them to live in a kind of mutual respect.

Repression has its limits: not every group can repress all the others, and it may be that no group can. It has obvious costs, from war, to expenses of policing, to lost cooperation. Where trying to repress would provoke ruinous conflict, an accommodation may be what I have been calling a modus vivendi: one group would repress another if it could without ruin, but since the alternative is ruin, all prefer accommodation.

Some costs of repression, though, are more subtle. They are matters of what we can mean to each other, and so of what life can mean to us. I have spoken of a kind of mutual respect lost by repression. Respect is a feeling or attitude toward others that, among other things, prompts a person to try to rely on honest persuasion in his dealings with them. It prompts him to try to treat others in ways they themselves will find legitimate. This holds especially for coercion: respect keeps a person from coercing others unless they themselves find the coercion legitimate.[7] Respect, so defined, is not something one can show toward everyone always, no matter how they are prone to respond. More could be said about what treatment does show it, but the notion can be loose for my purposes, since respect on this reading is not to be shown invariably. It is wrenching to act toward a person against his protests, voiced or silenced. It is wrenching to turn away from a normal stance of heeding protests and working toward mutual consent. Lamentably it is not wrenching enough, and men too easily turn to battle with full heart and blind fervor. Still, in peace we can find that if we did take such a stance toward each other, we would have lost something worth preserving.

The problem is not one for delicate liberal sensibilities alone. Tyrants repress opinion, and so do whole social groups. Their very determination, though, suggests a drive for accord. If the real thing cannot be had, at least a forced semblance is wanted. We are discursive beings who thrive on discursive respect for each other. Even when we switch off the respect, as soon as we look for anything more than blind enmity, we feel the loss.

Toleration is a scheme to achieve this kind of mutual respect in the face of disagreement. In favorable conditions, groups at odds can work toward a community of judgment on restricted topics, and develop norms of accommodation. The initial pressures may be those of a

---

7. We feel compunction about treating people in ways we ourselves think illegitimate. That compunction too might be labelled "respect". It is not this kind of treatment, though, that is at issue with toleration, and so I shall leave it out of the attitude I am calling "respect" for purposes here.

modus vivendi, and those pressures may continue to help sustain the arrangement. Part of the reward of accommodation, though, is this kind of mutual respect. In time that itself may seem enough to justify the accommodation. Groups then have achieved toleration.

Again we can puzzle what status could be claimed, coherently, for norms of mutual tolerance. An answer is ready at hand. Norms of mutual tolerance, we can say, have roughly the same status as the norms of accommodation involved in a modus vivendi. They too are norms for a special circumstance of living in disagreement. They are norms whose acceptance might be in the offing in a wider group, a group stuck in disagreements on other norms. Again, a local background story can be told about why the norms are valid. The story reconciles these norms with the more local norms through which life and its significance are understood. Here, though, the story rests not on the overt costs of conflict, but on the importance of a kind of mutual respect. As with other norms of accommodation, these norms gain their hold in the usual way, through the socio-psychic mechanisms that make for normative discussion and normative governance.

Between mutual tolerance and a modus vivendi runs no sharp line. The costs of repression are of many kinds. Some are not matters at all of the value of mutual respect: groups may face danger and struggle; they may face economic pressures. Others are parts of the psychological package that comes with repression: hatred, resentment, incivility. In what I am calling mutual tolerance, people find this package bad enough that all prefer common norms of accommodation. They prefer these norms to the triumph of their group, even if it could be had.

People can come to delight in their variety. Then the problem of tolerance disappears. At that point groups no longer hold back from repression because it shows disrespect; they welcome what they might have repressed or tolerated. Still, for everyone there will be things he wishes no one did. If others do these things anyway and claim the right, he may want to be tolerant. He may wish, say, that there were no believers in astrology, and yet want such beliefs tolerated. He does not delight in the variety astrology adds; if he allows the beliefs even so, perhaps he is tolerating them. He *tolerates* something if (1) he prefers people not to do it; (2) the people who do it would think it illegitimate for others to stop them; and so (3) he refrains from coercing them, out of a wish to live in mutual respect.

At least since John Stuart Mill, a chief ambition of political philosophy has been to develop a test for legitimate coercion. It is urgent that some such test draw wide adherence, or at least that we agree case by case. Norms promote coordination in the broadest of senses, and shared norms of legitimacy and complaint do so most of all. For a particular kind of society, there may be a standard for legitimate coercion that almost all can accept. Of course, once again consensus and stability are not everything, but we may hope for even better: a formula that draws adherence and furthermore merits it.

We should not think that we can simply oppose all repression, or that the right formula is easy to decide. Almost inevitably we shall disagree, and some of this disagreement will make for hard choices. In what range of ways are parents to be free to treat their children as they think best? Shall we act against headhunting in distant places? Against discrimination? Against blood sports and other forms of cruelty to animals?

We may refer these questions to a decision mechanism, and treat as legitimate the outcomes, say, of voting or of trials. Within such procedures, complaints are heard and assessed. That leads to a multi-tiered conception of legitimacy, with its familiar puzzles. Parties make opposing claims on the mechanism, and some of those claims are denied. If all were pleading sincerely and hold to their views, then the losers still think the decision wrong, but they accept norms for acting in the face of wrong decisions. These must prescribe some acquiescence in wrong decisions, or the mechanism does nothing toward solving the problem of mutual respect. Still there may be limits, and what those limits are is a perennial question of political philosophy.[8] Mechanisms can help, but they make for quandaries of their own.

Schemes for mutual respect may be on terms we find scarcely acceptable. Then the choice is hard. There is value in relying on persuasion,

8. This sweeps past central themes in the political philosophy of the past few centuries. Both Hobbes and Rousseau argue, in effect, that a political system can be tolerably stable only if there is widespread acceptance of norms of unlimited acquiescence—norms that require acquiescence in all decisions that issue from a unified mechanism (Hobbes, 1651, part 2, chap. 29; Rousseau, 1762, book 1, chap. 6). Hobbes releases a person from acquiescing only in decisions to kill, imprison, conscript, or enslave him. Locke and the liberal tradition have favored a wide range of acquiescence, but with limitations (Locke, 1690b, chap. 19). Doctrines of civil disobedience allow for limited, open, and costly refusal to be bound by the outcomes of decision mechanisms, as a way of protesting decisions that are grievously wrong (see, for example, Rawls, 1971, 350–391).

Rousseau eliminates repression, in his ideal state, by educating all to conclude that if they lose, then they were mistaken in their original claims. People vote opinions that are to be revised in light of how the vote comes out (1762, book 4, chap. 2). Votes thus eliminate disagreement as to what is legitimate. I am assuming that this will not happen, so that some repression, in my sense of the term, remains even with common adherence to a decision mechanism.

in not coercing people in ways they find illegitimate. This makes for the normal free interchange on which we thrive. To achieve the widest mutual respect, though, we may have to give up too much. It may be hard to say whether gains from repression are worth a loss in mutual respect. We are stuck with a complex survey of what is gained and what is lost from particular attainable schemes.

Our problem then is to decide how wide a community to try to achieve on a basis all accept as legitimate. Our community of tolerance may not be the widest we could have achieved, for some things we may still find intolerable. We may, though, end up tolerating things we would repress, if only we could and achieve respect for each other in a wide enough group.

Suppose a system of tolerance is in fact in the offing. How shall we regard its norms of accommodation? An accommodation may be tolerant and still be unjust. There is nothing incoherent about thinking both that we shall achieve accommodation—that we shall come to coerce each other only in ways we have also come to think legitimate— and that some of the coercion will really be illegitimate. Once we have achieved toleration, once we regard our accommodation as a reasonable price for living in mutual respect, we then shall think our norms of accommodation just. In advance of the consensus, though, or before we ourselves form a part of the consensus, can we agree?

Again here the question is one of normative authority. We and others, talking in the widespread group, will be affected by the talk and come to accept certain norms of accommodation. The usual sociopsychic dynamics of consensus formation will have worked on us. Eventually we will be prone to avow those norms, and those norms will govern our sentiments. The question is, do we now in advance think that all this will make us good normative judges? Do we now accord authority to ourselves as we shall be as a result of discussion— a global discussion in which we work toward accommodation? The question again is what epistemic norms to accept, what norms for according authority. If we think we shall be good judges, then we think the norms we shall come to accept are valid.

As before, it would be extravagant to deny all normative authority to ourselves as we shall be as a result of discussion. It would be extravagant to think that widespread discussion worsens us as judges of the norms of accommodation that apply to our circumstances. Our normative sensibilities as they are now have been shaped by discussion and accommodation. If we think that further discussion and accommodation would deprave our judgment, why trust our judgment now?

That does not mean that we take any accommodation widespread discussion might produce as valid. We start with tentative judgments of what is fair and reasonable, as well as tentative judgments of what would make us good normative judges—of what would make us good assessors of norms of accommodation. Tentatively we must accord some authority to ourselves as we would be after global discussion. We think in advance also, though, that any such authority would be vitiated if the judgments we came to make were palpably wild. For some stories of how discussion might go, we are sure in advance that we would have gone astray. For others we shall be at a loss in advance to know what to say. Still, if we are to keep our normative moorings at all and stay coherent, we need to accord some authority to ourselves as we would be after global discussion. Valid norms for accommodation to our circumstances—valid norms for accommodating the disagreements that will survive discussion among different loose groups—are to be known in part by the hold they will have on us as a result of discussion among those groups.

Taking Stock

What are we doing when we make normative judgments? We know well enough without asking, in a way. We lead our normative lives, taking up questions as they confront us and discussing them in their own terms. From time to time that leads to puzzles, as any hard inquiry will. A new and special bafflement may come, though, when we try to shift views. We think normative thoughts, and we think we are part of nature. I have been looking at human normative life, and sketching how that life might be a part of nature. My question then was how the two pictures fit together: a naturalistic picture of norms in human life, and the rich picture of a normative world that develops as we push our normative inquiries.

I bridged the two pictures with a lightly regimented normative logic. Think of normative judgments as combining psychological notions with one simple normative notion—expressed by the words 'it makes sense to', or perhaps 'rational'. Many normative judgments are about the feelings or attitudes it makes sense to have toward things. To say it "makes sense" to have such-and-such an attitude is roughly to express one's acceptance of norms that permit the attitude. Expressing one's acceptance of norms is something we can understand in psychological terms, as a part of the natural world. That in outline is how

I proposed that our normative life could be a part of nature. To fill in the outline, I told a long story of normative discussion, normative avowal, and normative governance. These are the workings of psychic capacities whose chief biological function is coordination.

With the two pictures bridged, my hope is, normative inquiry can go better. Nothing guarantees straight out that it will: in strict logic, the facts of our normative lives leave unsettled the normative questions themselves. Still, bridging the pictures gives us a new view of what we are doing.

In my long treatment of normative objectivity, the point again was to bridge the two pictures and see where that took us. We treat our normative judgments as objective, and when we look at ourselves as part of nature, we can see how that might be. Normative judgments tend toward consensus—shakily but not by accident. With some other judgments consensus is automatic: we easily agree on the layout of surrounding rocks and trees, and those judgments are our prime examples of objectivity. We nudge each other to agree on norms too. We do this in a cluster of ways and, agreement achieved, we treat norms like rocks and trees, more or less. Our naturalistic story says how human normative life produces agreement when it does. First, of course, we each respond to similar pressures from circumstance: we want security, food, shelter; we want children who thrive; we want the rich multitude of natural-cultural signs that have promised these things. A person's sense of what is plausible responds to these wants. The wants conflict in part, though, within a single person and among people. Normative discussion works to accommodate them. In normative discussion we influence each other through conversational invitations and pressures. We demand consistency one of another, and try to meet these demands. These socio-psychic mechanisms combine, at times, to make norms as interpersonal as trees.

Norms present themselves as objective when they have the right structure—a structure that adds to the pressures to agree. I examined this structure: Norms can be unconditional, applying even to those who reject them. Higher order norms may leave no choice of what lower order norms to accept. In addition, higher order norms may be standpoint-independent, requiring acceptance of the same norms by everyone, or by everyone around. These higher order norms make in effect for a normative epistemology, a story of how to tell the right norms. The person who thinks there is such a story can be challenged: he can be asked what puts him in a position to judge. The challenge makes for new demands for consistency, and responding to it puts a person in a position to make demands himself. These demands and challenges move discussion forward.

Conversational demands themselves can be governed by norms. Norms can govern inhibitions and embarrassments, and they can govern responses to conversational demands. Here, then, was a further sense in which a person may treat his judgments as objective: the norms he accepts may permit demands on their behalf. If the norms he accepts let him be influenced by others, then in a sense he treats their judgments too as objective—as having some claim to objective validity. Higher order norms can endorse the influences that make for consensus, and their structures then constitute pretensions to objectivity.

Part of my goal has been to analyze these normative structures and place them in nature. My hope also has been to get help in normative inquiry: armed with a story of ourselves in nature, and armed too with philosophical analyses, we might see better how to assess normative claims. To that end I myself entered normative discussion. I took up normative questions about normative discussion itself. Conversational demands are legitimate, I claimed—not always, but at times. The norms I advocated allow some of these demands, and they say not always to brace oneself against normative influence from others. They endorse pragmatic rationales for norms, in a limited way, and those pragmatic rationales may apply differently in different places and times. Finally, these norms say something about how to live in a world of partial, overlapping normative communities, big and small. They tell us how, in normative terms, to understand what we are doing as we work toward a variety of communities of judgment: on the one hand, local, intense communities, and on the other, widespread communities on narrow topics.

Those were the ambitions of the book. In the final part, I turn fleetingly to morals again and to moral inquiry.

IV · MORAL INQUIRY

14 · Moral Concern

Morality is one normative topic among others, but in some ways specially baffling. Thoughts of morality lie behind much of what I have said, and much of the lore that sparked my discussions and guided them is the lore of moral philosophers. I now want to explore how normative inquiry might look to a norm-expressivist, and I take morality as a prime example.

If my analyses are on the right track, the resulting picture of moral inquiry ought to be familiar. The analyses, after all, were supposed to give an account of ordinary moral thought and talk, and to paint large parts of moral philosophy as ordinary moral inquiry refined. We can be happy, of course, for any quick new insights the analyses might yield, but my chief goal will be to glimpse old scenes in a new frame. The frame, I should add, does not generate the scenes by itself. Nothing much follows from a norm-expressivistic analysis alone; someone else who accepted such an analysis might go on to tell quite a different story from mine.

I spend two of the remaining chapters on how to conduct moral inquiry, and then the final two on how things might work out. To get a far-ranging moral inquiry started, we might ask why care about morality? Answer this and we can then proceed to look for a morality that best speaks to our cares. First, though, I ask why we do care—why in fact we are concerned with moral questions. I put off the moral questions themselves, and look at us, the inquirers. I venture a quick survey of broadly moral sentiments and ask whether these are sentiments that evolved, highly social beings might have, and why. I look to the rationales these sentiments seem to invoke. Our moral concern has many sources, often clear enough in their import and pulling in unison. Often too, though, our different sentiments pull apart from each other, and even a single sentiment can shift in its rationale.

That leaves us to go from psychology to morals. Once we have a messy story of why in fact we do care about morality, how shall we get from there to a good normative story, a story of why *to* care? To pass from why we *do* care—from our broadly moral sentiments and other sources of moral concern—to why *to* care means assessing feelings. We must assess which feelings, if any, to take as guides.

Now if we had one master source of moral concern—benevolence, say, or respect—things might be straightforward. We might find a clear rationale in that source of concern, and just adopt the rationale. As it is, though, no such straight path of self-trust is open. We have to ask how to assess feelings as moral guides when the feelings at times conflict, and feelings one by one come with no unique clear rationale. The problem is not simply to weigh our various feelings against each other and accept their preponderant urgings. We need to settle what norms to accept as governing these feelings.

I then return to structural questions about morality: Is anything ever morally wrong? Would we be best off without morality? Does it sometimes make sense to do things that are wrong? Earlier I boasted that a narrow construal of morality yields interpretations for these questions. I now glance at these questions against a background of norm-expressivism and the complex moral psychology I have been claiming. Finally I look at prospects for moral system. Even if our moral concerns pull us one way and another, critical moral inquiry might guide them into coherent formation. I ask how aspiration to system might look to a norm-expressivist.

This final part of the book scouts lightly: I spy out a few lines of approach to some questions in moral theory. The rough plan is to start with a naturalistic view of ourselves, beginning to appreciate some of the variety of our shifting moral concerns and sentiments. Ask then how to assess broadly moral sentiments: What bases can we have for thinking a feeling apt or not? Try out applying the answers to perennial structural questions of moral thought. Finally, cast an eye at the possibilities for moral system. The aim is to illustrate how one crucial kind of normative inquiry might look in norm-expressivistic light.

Broadly Moral Sentiments

What are the sources of our moral concern? There seem to be many: We wish others well, and we care about fairness. We want to deal with others in mutual respect. We carry a sense of our own moral value. Sometimes we are filled with moral inspiration, with devotion to highest goals—and doubtless the list could go on. Perhaps these putative sources all boil down to the same concern in the end, or perhaps only one of them stands up to criticism. At first glance, though, each of them appears to have its own claim on us.

When I ask after sources of moral concern, that suggests at least three kinds of questions. As I put the matter just now, the issue was psychological: I asked what the sources of our moral concern are in fact. The question was why we do care about morality, not why we should. A good answer, though, might hinge on a second, conceptual question: what makes a concern moral? Once we discover a source of concern in ourselves, how shall we decide whether it counts as moral or non-moral? Finally, the question suggests a cluster of normative questions: what moral concerns to have; how to assess the sources of moral concern we find in ourselves; which ones to embrace, and how to shape them, refine them, and reconcile them.

In this chapter I take up the first, psychological question, and put off normative puzzles. On the second, conceptual set of questions I shall be careless. I want to look at sources of concern that have some broad claim to being moral, whether the claim would stand up to challenge or not. The crucial question, after all, is what concerns to embrace, whether or not they count as moral. Indeed I look too at self-interest, not because it makes claim to being a moral concern, but as helping to shape and direct our moral concerns.

Moral concern involves feelings. Feelings have a rationale, or so it can seem, and often the rationale looks moral. Think of pity: it points to a rationale, and so we might speak of a pity-based morality.[1] Pity impels one to relieve suffering and to prevent it. A pity-based morality, then, is one grounded on relieving and preventing suffering. Such a morality is pity-based in a cluster of senses: First, feelings of pity prompt adherence to the morality. Second, the things the morality commands are the actions pity prompts. Third, the rationale for a pity-

---

1. I allude to Nietzsche, who speaks of "the morality of pity" and rails against it (1887, preface, secs. 5–6).

based morality is the rationale feelings of pity seem to carry. Pity is elicited by suffering and tends toward succor; thus the rationale it seems to carry is that suffering calls for succor. In general, a feeling tends to be elicited by certain circumstances, and it tends toward actions of certain kinds. Its rationale, then, will be that those eliciting circumstances call for the prompted actions. (A rationale might be found too in norms for the feeling, but for now I put norms aside.)

In the narrowest sense, I have kept insisting, the moral emotions are anger and guilt—though I smiled too on broadening this to include feelings of moral approbation. Other feelings, though, offer a rationale for giving the narrowly moral emotions some particular shape. They induce us to govern anger and guilt with one set of norms rather than another. Benevolent feelings, for example, push us toward benevolent norms for guilt and anger—norms, perhaps, whose acceptance would foster benevolent goals. Norms for anger and guilt, then, may be shaped in response to other feelings. These other feelings constitute sources of moral concern, and many of them we can count as broadly moral sentiments: benevolence, a sense of fairness, respect, feelings of worth, and the like.

I want some idea of the shape of these sentiments. I want especially to begin to understand them as sentiments an evolved, highly social being might have. Why want such a picture, though? I am curious about human moral nature, of course, but as always the things I say will be speculative. My main object is philosophical: to experiment with joining a naturalistic view of humanity to moral inquiry. My question is hypothetical: if our moral nature is as I speculate, how might that bear on questions of right and wrong?

Evolutionary considerations provide a check on psychological hypotheses—a fallible check to be sure, since we ill understand our own evolution. Even unreliable checks, though, can be useful if suitably mistrusted. It is easy to miss patterns in our thought and feelings, and seeing whether one view of ourselves fits another can help us find the best streams to pan. Try fitting together evolutionary theory and an account of common experience, and we may develop better maps of both.

We talk about morality and ponder it not with a single, pure objective in mind, but engaged by a host of overlapping concerns. A naturalistic picture of humanity suggests why this might be so, and our normative problem is then how to cope with competing pulls. Some of our strongest moral sentiments, moreover, carry no clear directives even one by one; they need to be filled in. Fairness impels us one way or another depending on what we think fair; the urgings of respect depend on what we take respect to demand. A naturalistic picture explains why we might have firm opinions on these matters, and also why these opinions might differ. As moral inquirers, we shall then need to ask what could make one such opinion better than another.

Benevolence

One reason we care about morality is that we care about others; we want life to go well for them. Benevolence competes at times with hatred or rancor, with envy or jealousy, with indifference or rivalry. Still at times good wishes for others sweep widely. Diverse traditions found morality on benevolence made universal: in one formulation, morality has won us when we love neighbor as self.

This conception of morality is widely embraced but widely challenged too. We go from day to day attached more or less to morality, but probably not overflowing with benevolence toward all. At times another's plight stirs sympathy, if it is vividly portrayed, but vivid portrayals can evoke other reactions too—hatred, for example, when the things portrayed are hateful. Everyday benevolence has its conditions. Even so, does a special, unconditional benevolence account for the force of morality? Benevolence is preached and not taken for granted. It is urged on us by tying it to other concerns and motivations. Worthy are the benevolent, we tell each other—and if that spurs us to benevolence, it was worthiness and not benevolence that first pricked us.

Still, benevolence is important to us, and that should be no surprise. A person wants benevolence from others, and often he finds it. The puzzle is why benevolence is to be found: why might an evolved being wish others well? The being will look, after all, as if it were designed to reproduce its own genes, whereas benevolence tends to enhance the reproduction of others. Why might that appeal to a product of natural selection? Or is human benevolence after all an illusion?

It need not be, Darwinian theory suggests, so long as we do not take it for more than it is. Benevolence would often be the best reproductive strategy, and so evolution does well to incline us to benevolence under certain conditions. We do well to be benevolent, so long as benevolence will be repaid and so will its lack.[2] Is what pays, then, unconditional benevolence or an eye to reciprocity? Sometimes one will do as well as the other, and plain benevolence can be cheap and reliable. A person may do well to act with no thought of reward, so long as the right cues put him in this benevolent frame of mind. The right cues will be ones that tend to crop up when benevolence would bring returns and selfishness not. It would be surprising indeed if we found among human beings a widespread benevolence unaffected by circumstance—but then we don't. It should not be surprising if we find widespread benevolence without thought of return. Often returns come unthought.

How much unconditional benevolence is there in our lives? Most of us avoid harming people—war and other extremities aside. We avoid cheating and fraud, more or less. On the whole we probably gain more from these plain scruples than we would from close, egoistic calculations that probed the limits of what we could do with impunity. We develop unconditional scruples, perhaps, in response to cues that playing fair is a good bet. Then too, we are friendly to people of many

2. A more prominent evolutionary explanation of human altruism invokes kin selection, or inclusive fitness maximization. If an organism acts in a way that enhances the reproductive prospects of its close kin, it thereby promotes the reproduction of the genes it shares with its kin. Genes favoring such acts tend therefore to multiply in succeeding generations. See Hamilton (1964), Wilson (1975, 1978), and Dawkins (1976). I ignore kin selection in this discussion because I doubt that it explains much of current human benevolence toward non-kin. True, the bare logic of evolution allows that it might. Psychic mechanisms that caused our ancestors to promote the reproductive prospects of close kin might be triggered among us by non-kin. If, say, our hunting-gathering ancestors associated intimately only with close kin, then any benevolent feelings triggered by intimate association would have been directed toward close kin, entirely or for the most part. Those same feelings would now be triggered in us by intimate associates who are not kin.

Various clues suggest, though, that our hunting-gathering ancestors must have associated with people who were not close kin—associated extensively, and at least as intimately as do we. Current hunter-gatherers camp temporarily in small groups, with about twenty adults. The groups keep splitting into smaller groups and reforming in new ways, depending on such things as season and social tensions. As a result, kinship within a camp is not always close, and yet people in the camp share food and cooperate extensively. Intercamp relations are cultivated, perhaps as a kind of insurance. Ties of kinship are important, but they need not be ties of close kinship. See discussions in Lee and DeVore (1968, part 3) and Lee (1976, esp. 75–79). Distant kinship, I suggest, is important not chiefly because of weak forces of kin selection, but because it organizes strong ties of reciprocity. Gulliver (1973) is suggestive on this score. If today non-kin trigger psychic mechanisms among us that distant kin triggered in our hunting-gathering ancestors, then the selection pressures that shaped those mechanisms must have stemmed from the advantages of reciprocity. See Trivers (1971) on reciprocal altruism.

kinds. We can be provoked, but while feelings stay friendly, they can move us to efforts great and small on others' behalf. We may act without thought of return, much of the time. Still, perhaps these feelings tend to arise where return is in the offing. Friends evoke benevolent feelings and actions far more than strangers or acquaintances. These truisms suggest that unconditional benevolence—benevolence without thought of return—might be evoked by special cues. The cues suggest, in effect, that the prospects of return are good.

Even if all this goes in the right direction, the story must be less direct than I have been making it sound. We should not imagine a sly, unconscious general-purpose calculator, assessing advantage and then producing the most advantageous feelings for a person's circumstance. The picture should rather be one of specific psychic mechanisms, some of them emotional. Each mechanism responds to special sorts of cues in special ways. Natural selection itself is the prime general-purpose calculator, but it calculated long ago, blind to current novelties. It produced a set of heuristics, a set of useful rules for reproducing as a hunter-gatherer. Some of these rules make up the shapes of particular feelings. Think of snakes and terror; the rule might go something like this: "If presented with a snake, feel terror, and if terrified, hold still." The rule gives a cue for the feeling, and an action tendency that stems from the feeling. What I have given, of course, is a caricature, even for snakes and terror. Emotional rules will be more complex. They deal in tendencies, and emotional tendencies compete. They are deeply affected by culture, in ways we little understand. The prime heuristics may be developmental, saying what emotional makeup to develop as some function of cues in early childhood. The two broad pictures I sketched in Chapter 7, of adaptive syndromes and ascriptions, give two rough possibilities of what this developmental function might be.

Back, then, to benevolence itself. Many familiar kinds seem more or less to track the likely returns. People may act with no thought of return, but their benevolent impulses can be stilled by indications that no return is in the offing. There is no great evolutionary mystery why we might be like that.

Other kinds of benevolence do not easily fit this pattern. Think of charity, blood donation for example. What reproductive heuristic would lead to giving blood, for no apparent personal reward? Perhaps such acts pay off reproductively in subtle ways, or similar acts did long ago. Being known for charity might somehow have tended indirectly to promote one's reproductive chances—especially if one was not seen as parading it. Why, though? Here there should be scope for fairly well grounded speculation. We have ethnographic accounts of giving, and we know that wherever charity is important, there is an art to evoking it. Much of the art, it seems, has to do with turning the charity into a group activity, or with cultivating the large donor. The large donor is given an honored position within the group that benefits. These observations suggest that we should look for some of the impulses behind charity to strangers in the ways common goals enhance possibilities of reciprocity within a group.[3]

What can we conclude, then, about impartial, unconditional benevolence? Rawls claims the impulse is weak—too weak to support a socially effective morality, and too weak to account for our strongest moral judgments (1971, 501). Most of our moral concern has other bases. In this quick survey I leave Rawls's claim undecided. Clearly we do feel benevolent at times, often without thought of return. Still, a cool observer might conclude that our benevolent feelings come when cues suggest they will pay, and we act on these feelings when cues suggest the actions will pay. Genuine charity is a puzzle: charity may have no apparent reproductive payoff. The lore of the things that evoke charity suggests that much more is involved than sheer awareness of a situation where good can be done. In short, nothing I say disproves the claim that all our moral concern stems from wishing everyone well. We do not always wish everyone well, but then too we are not always overflowing with moral concern. Still at best, impartial, unconditional benevolence blossoms with the right cues. When it is felt, it may still not lead to action unless the right cues are there. And much of life suggests that when benevolence does spur action, it does so with the help of other sentiments.

3. Singer (1981) discusses systems of unpaid blood donation as "working refutations of the contention that altruism can only exist among kin, within small groups, or where it pays off by encouraging reciprocal altruism" (134). Alexander (1987) offers an explanation in terms of indirect reciprocity: the blood donor shows himself altruistic, and so he "may receive his 'payment' from the members of society who accept him in social interactions or treat him deferentially." This raises a number of questions. Why will others specially accept the unconditional altruist or defer to him? In hope of gain? An unconditional altruist would be one who showered goods irrespective of whether others accepted him or deferred to him. Blood donation must signal something other than this, but how? Then too, there are puzzles about signals in general. Why not signal the usefulness of accepting me or deferring to me, and then save myself the trouble of delivering the expected reward? And if everybody does that, why should anyone take blood donation as a sign it will pay to cultivate me?

Reciprocity

Many of our chief moral sentiments are reciprocal overtly: a sense of fair dealing, feelings of gratitude, urges to retaliate. No surprise here for Darwinians: A sense of fair dealing prompts one to cooperate, and that elicits cooperation from others. Gratitude prompts the kinds of actions that will draw more favors. Retaliation deters. These sentiments pay, on the whole—or at least they pay in the central case, in an ongoing interaction between oneself and someone else. Tit-for-tat is then a marvelous strategy, and reciprocal feelings prompt the needed actions.[4]

Other cases are more puzzling. On a last move, reciprocity can draw no payoff. Perhaps, then, it will not be evoked by a gracious next-to-last move.[5] There lay one of Hobbes's central problems: his Foole would violate a covenant even when others had done their part—and perhaps then no fool he (1651, part 1, chap. 15). Would others be fools to have counted on him? Then too, third-party reciprocity may have no apparent payoffs: we do resent harms and injustices to others, but what explains our being so constructed? Puzzles abound in the theory of self-interested reciprocity, and these puzzles have their evolutionary analogs. Still, in the ongoing two-person case, the biological function of reciprocal sentiments is clear enough. We evolved social beings should have these sentiments abundantly—and we do.

Reciprocity needs terms of trade. Judgments of fairness may work to set the terms and to stabilize them (see Rawls 1971, sec. 75–76; Gibbard 1982). Once some things are seen as fair and others not, anger and guilt will attach to dealings seen as unfair. We find such dealings unreasonable, and not only in the sense that they go before a fall.[6] We loathe being cheated, often far more than our overt losses explain. What constitutes being cheated, then, and why? What makes for fair

4. See especially Axelrod (1984) for a many-sided investigation of the advantages of tit-for-tat and the circumstances in which it is likely to emerge. Trivers (1971) gave the seminal treatment of the evolution of reciprocity. Axelrod and Hamilton (1981) cite many biological examples. Rawls argues that reciprocity is a strong motive and sympathy a weak one (1971, 501).

5. See Luce and Raiffa (1957, 97–102) for the notoriously baffling "zip-back argument" for a prisoner's dilemma iterated a known number of times.

6. Rawls (1980, 528–530) marks off this sense of "reasonable" as distinct from "rational". He speaks of "fair terms of cooperation" as "terms each participant may reasonably be expected to accept, provided that everyone else likewise accepts them" (528).

dealing? The answers can be elusive: sometimes there are obvious symmetries or obvious rules to apply, but still there can be heated disputes about which symmetries are germane and which rules natural. Strong sentiments attach to disputable standards.

What explains all this? Judgments of fairness stabilize bargaining, I speculate. They do this by guiding moral sentiments of anger and outrage, and by weighing directly on action. These judgments are shaped in normative discussion: discussion tends toward agreement, and agreement is needed if the judgments are to stabilize. In a bargaining situation, there are gains to be had from cooperation and mutual restraint, and these gains might be distributed in any of various ways. Smooth progress to an outcome depends on establishing common expectations about the terms of cooperation, restraint, and distribution. These expectations can be stabilized by feelings, so long as the feelings mesh—so long as the feelings of everyone attach to the same arrangement. That is what it is for the arrangement to be seen by all as fair, as giving each his due. One prime stabilizer is provocability. The person who finds an arrangement fair will be angry if others insist on taking more at his expense. He will feel cheated; he will want to get even. This deters others from pressing over the boundaries the arrangement sets up.

Social practices of course are not always the outcomes of overt bargaining. Still, they share a structure with bargaining. Gains from cooperation and restraint could be distributed in many different ways. Common expectations are stabilized by common standards of fairness, with their potential for anger and retaliation if the standards are violated. That, perhaps, is a large part of why it is tempting to invoke a social contract, even where none has been signed.

No unique standard of fairness is wired into our brains, if my story is right. Judgments of fairness are shaped in part by complex workings of normative discussion. In the discussion and the judgments it shapes, symmetries will be important, and so will precedent. A person's interests may affect which possible standards he finds compelling, and one person's judgments will influence another's. The upshot may indeed be widespread agreement on what makes something fair— widespread agreement within a group. If there is agreement, though, it will not be because anyone was preset to see those particular standards as correct in the first place.

This is not to deny that some schemes for judging fairness are innate, or perhaps deeply ingrained by early acculturation. We latch

onto symmetries, favoring equal division or proportionality. We identify entitlements and protect them. We attach ourselves to schemes of
reciprocal insurance, and these respond to intensities of need: I might
reciprocate not for anything you actually did for me or will do, but for
something you would have done for me. I make no claims as to how
much of this is a matter of innate predisposition, or of how much is
fixed against reshaping by mature experience and discussion. I do
stress the indeterminacy of judgments of fairness, the ways different
groups come to see different standards as obvious and just. Indeed a
single person may feel pulled different ways in his judgments, and feel
at a loss as to how to resolve the conflict. Perhaps we have not too few
fixed predispositions but too many: what we find fair may depend,
radically, on how we look at things.

Tversky and Kahneman speak of *framing effects* (1981). The same situation may be seen in different ways, with a different gestalt so to
speak, and different judgments follow. That goes for judgments of fairness: a blizzard surcharge on snow shovels is seen as unfair, whereas
a high price that would be discounted in good weather is seen as fair—
even if the blizzard prices are the same in both cases and so are the
good-weather prices (Kahneman, Knetch, and Thaler 1986a, 1986b,
slightly extrapolated). Judgments of fairness thus reverse, according to
whether the same price difference is framed as a discount or as a
surcharge.

Judgments of fairness, in short, respond to many things: to custom
and familiarity, to symmetry, to interests, to protests. We may be pre-
disposed to make judgments on special patterns, to pick out certain
symmetries as relevant. Different framings, though, will evoke different of these predispositions, and then the predispositions may
clash. All these things will influence the course of normative discussion, and normative discussion in turn will tend toward consensus.
Then the norms people come to accept together will play back on their
judgments of fairness—in part through the ways they frame situations.
Agreement will stem in part from the play of interests and influences
and experiences in a series of normative discussions. It will coordinate
because, among other things, everyone has been suitably influenced.

Hume speaks of two separate virtues, fidelity and justice (1748).
Fidelity, he says, is "the observance of promises", and justice "a
regard to the property of others." Let me seize these terms to label the
two crucial aspects of reciprocity. Promises are often reciprocal, and I
have stressed how much of familiar moral life is reciprocal—how many

of the motivations are to give back in kind. That is what biological theory suggests, and it is what we see. Moral sentiments from gratitude to fairness to rancor each move us, one way or other, to give good for good and ill for ill. We support schemes for common advantage, each trading support for a share in the benefits. Call these motivations of fidelity; they work against the impulse to cheat.

Now it can seem that fidelity is all reciprocity needs: that giving like for like is a plain, straightforward matter, and the sole obstacle to reciprocity is poor motivation. A moral weakling's temptations outweigh his fidelity, and a con man's fidelity is missing entirely. What reciprocity takes, it can seem, is a strong and honest heart. But it takes more: reciprocity needs terms of trade—and hence the place for justice. If justice narrowly is regard for property, allowing each his own, then a chief part of justice is determining what constitutes each person's own. Trade requires terms, and often there is slack in what the terms might be. Reciprocity comes in bargaining situations, or situations with a like structure: more than one possible arrangement would be mutually advantageous, but some more for one person and some more for another. Somehow, one scheme must be selected from among this whole set. Standards of justice select one scheme, and thus shape and regulate motivations of fidelity. What standards people accept is influenced by normative rumination and normative discussion.

Respect

Some moral philosophers place their bets on respect, for others and for oneself. Respect is a tricky notion, though. Suppose morality does have one basic commandment, to respect persons. What will that tell us to do, if anything?

We do say that to treat people some ways is to treat them with respect, and to treat them other ways is to show disrespect. That suggests we might succeed in codifying respect: We might develop rules for which kinds of actions make for treating people with respect, and take these rules as a distillation of morality. Some philosophers have tried to do just that.[7] Earlier I myself tried in part: respect in one sense, I said, consists in not coercing people in ways they think illegitimate. Respect in that sense, though, is no invariant command of morality.

---

7. Donagan (1977) tries to build all of morality on a requirement of respect for rational beings, though not as a closed set of rules.

Sometimes we find we cannot agree with someone and cannot forgo coercing him. Murderous fanatics and unrepentant criminals offer the starkest examples. Most philosophical treatments of respect send us elsewhere in moral theory to learn what actions are demanded by respect. Rawls speaks of a "duty of mutual respect" that includes being prepared to offer reasons "in the belief that they are sound reasons as defined by a mutually acceptable conception of justice" (1971, 338). The duty is to give others reasons one thinks they should accept, not reasons they in fact will accept. To decide what they should accept one has to work out one's moral views. It seems unpromising, then, to try to find in respect some clear set of requirements on action, deducible simply by contemplating the nature of respect.[8]

Most talk of respect, indeed, best fits respect not as a feature of actions but as a feeling. We talk of respect as something an action can show, not a property it can have. We speak of expressing respect, of conveying respect, of evincing respect. We talk of signs and gestures of respect. All this fits talk of a feeling—and indeed if respect is a feeling, that explains the tie of respect to action. A feeling tends toward action as well as expression. To treat someone with respect, we can say, is to fulfill an action tendency of the feeling.

What kind of feeling could respect be? Can we understand it as a feeling that evolved social beings would have? To work toward a rough hypothesis, start with expressions: what might signs of respect portend, or signs of disrespect? Courtesy expresses respect, and slights and insults express disrespect. So too with gestures, demeanor, and tones of voice: some kinds express respect and others the reverse. Are these expressions just wheels spinning free in the works of our social dealings, attached to nothing else? That seems unlikely. What links these expressions to action is something like this: from abuse in manner and words, it may feel no great step to move to abuse in action. Our greatest inhibitions are often on evincing disrespect in the first

8. Kant speaks of respect (*Achtung*) for the law as grounding morality (1785, 400). He struggles to explain that respect is a feeling, but a special kind of feeling, "the consciousness of the submission of my will to a law without the intervention of other influences on my mind . . . All respect for a person is only respect for the law . . . of which the person provides an example" (401). Elsewhere (1797) he treats respect as the ground for a whole set of moral requirements, and many current writers speak of "respect for persons" as the basis of morality. Frankena concludes, "The principle that we are to respect persons in this sense says only that there are morally right and wrong, good and bad, ways of treating or relating to persons, as such or for their own sakes. It does not tell us which ways of treating or relating to them are right or wrong, good or bad" (1986, 157).

place. Whom one would destroy one must first demean, or so people widely seem to feel.[9]

Signs of respect, this suggests, signal certain kinds of treatment, certain kinds of restraint. Signs of disrespect signal that normal restraints are off. What kinds of treatment, though, and what kinds of restraints—and why must they be signaled? Words like 'abuse' apply both to speech and to actions, but to what kinds of actions? Some abuse is sheer physical assault, but in a complex social life, other kinds of abuse can be deadly too: pillage, cheating, exclusion, hard dealing. What unites all these, and why should signals attach to them as a package?

Think again of bargaining and the social contract, and consider what dispositions help stabilize social arrangements. What patterns of feeling mark the boundaries social arrangements set up, and what patterns deter incursions? I have talked of provocability, a tendency to resist incursions beyond arranged boundaries. Something else would help too: a special, intrinsic motivation not to cross the boundaries. Here, then, is a place for respect, with its special cluster of expressions and motivations. Feelings of respect attach to social arrangements and stabilize them. If one feels respect for someone, the feeling motivates one to accord him his place in social arrangements, with all its protections. Expressions of respect signal this willingness and elicit trust.[10]

Stable social arrangements, after all, need both provocability and restraint. Provocability consists in part in a sense of one's due: a sense of what would constitute being cheated, along with a tendency to lash back on feeling cheated. As for restraint, it will stem in part from respect. Respect for others tends toward according them normal pro-

---

9. Sabini and Silver (1982, 71–80) argue that the incredible brutality and degradation the Nazis visited on their death camp victims before killing them worked to undermine the normal inhibitions of those who did the killing. They did this by making it impossible for the victims to present "the immediate, compelling appearance of a worthy self." Indeed one camp commandant explicitly cited this as the reason for the policy of systematic degradation.

10. More needs to be learned about expression and signaling. If respect involves tendencies toward certain kinds of restraint, why might there be natural and social signals of such restraints? Here work needs to be done, with mathematical models among other things. Can we tell a fully coherent story where signals pay if true and cost if false? We find signals of restraint among non-human animals as well as among us, and they seem in turn to elicit restraint and cooperation from others. How might this be? Roughly, it seems, to be part of a scheme of cooperation and mutual restraint, one must signal one's adherence in various ways. Signs of respect for others in the scheme are part of this signaling. They evoke trust.

tections. Two patterns of feeling—a sense of one's due and respect for others—join in marking social boundaries and preventing incursions.

What makes for these boundaries, what gets felt as an incursion, must be a complex story. I have spoken as if respect and a sense of one's due simply attach to current social protections, whatever they may be. Social protections, though, are vague and contested. We may dream of a hypertraditional golden age, when everyone was in clear, confident agreement. Ethnographic reports suggest, though, that even in highly traditional societies, arrangements are ever in flux. Much of human talk even there consists in implicit renegotiation (see esp. Marshall 1976). In less stable conditions, current arrangements may lose their adherents and other models gain them. Always, respecting a person will motivate one to certain restraints, to according him certain protections. The content of those protections will normally have much to do with whatever social arrangements have been familiar; those arrangements will seem natural. Other things too, though, will affect what respect seems to demand. Respect comes to be felt as entailing certain things, but the socio-psychic dynamics of what those things are must be complex.

Respect is tied closely to dignity. Some people carry themselves with dignity, we say, and we speak too of the dignity of an office. Dignified bearing seems to express something, perhaps a claim to position and to certain kinds of treatment. Morality, we say, is respect for human dignity, and to speak that way is to accord humanity a special position. We claim protections for that position and extend the position to everyone.

As a first try we might say this: dignified bearing signals a confident claim to respect and the protections that go with it.[11] This rough hypothesis may help explain why sometimes a dignified bearing protects a person from tormentors, whereas losing his dignity opens him to dangerous abuse. This goes for dealings not only with other people, but sometimes even with stray dogs. The rough hypothesis helps explain too why dignity attaches to office as well as to people. It also helps explain, perhaps, why standing on dignity is sometimes ridiculous: dignity maintains barriers that may be unneeded; their protections may be superfluous. Then the barriers can get in the way of more important things.

Much as it explains, though, this first try does not quite capture what

11. Goffman (1959) offers a classic study of self-presentation and its importance.

it means to call a bearing dignified. Inspector Clouseau signals a confident claim to respect, but his dignity, we might say, is false. We are unmoved, or moved to contempt. The signal must be received in its own terms if observers are to speak of dignity. The signals must move observers toward respect. Suppose Calpurnia calls Caesar dignified; she thereby not only describes his manner, but expresses a response. His manner, if she is right, expresses a confident demand for respect, and moreover she expresses being moved toward respect by his manner.

Respect often means esteem of a kind. Darwall offers helpful terminology; he distinguishes "recognition respect" and "appraisal respect", where appraisal respect is a kind of esteem.[12] It is recognition respect I have been discussing, and respect in this sense seems quite different from esteem. Our legal system, we say, must treat even a heinous criminal with respect, though he lack all claim to esteem. Now that makes sense if respect involves protections, for protections need not be grounded on esteem. Still, we need to explain why recognition respect gets blurred with esteem, and the tie is not hard to find: Recognition respect accords protections to a position, and often people think a position should be merited. They may then accord protections of the position only to someone they think merits it. In that case, recognition respect depends on esteem of some kind. Indeed if these

12. Appraisal respect, Darwall says, is "a positive appraisal of a person or his character-related features" (1977, 41). To have *moral* recognition respect for something is "to regard it as requiring restrictions on the moral acceptability of actions connected with it," and to regard the restrictions as "not incidental, but as arising because of the feature or fact itself" (40). It involves "a regard for a fact or feature as having some weight in deliberations about how to act" (41). As for the feeling of respect for a person, it is "the one which is occasioned by the positive appraisal which constitutes appraisal respect for the person." I accept much of this, but I want to treat feelings as more central, and characterize them in part by their action tendencies. Darwall ties recognition respect closely to action, through a person's views about moral acceptability and its grounds. I want a looser, less reflective kind of tie, so that one could even have feelings of respect and think them unwarranted: Feelings of respect could hold one back from treating a person in ways that one thinks, on reflection, are morally acceptable. Still, I could take most of what Darwall says into my own picture, by reading him as elucidating the kind of rationale feelings of respect will seem to have for us.

The kinds of treatment respect inhibits or arouses are hard to specify. Not all "restrictions on the moral acceptability of actions" connected with a feature of character are a matter of respect. It may be morally unacceptable to loose a dangerous rapist-murderer on the community, but we don't keep him in jail out of respect for his viciousness. Moral recognition respect, Darwall says, "includes a component of regard"; it will be important to explain this component.

assumptions are common knowledge, signs of respect may also be signs of esteem.

Respect is not the same thing as benevolence, and the account I have given explains why an evolved social being might have both these sentiments. Respect moves a person to heed accepted rules of protection, whereas in some cases benevolence might move a person to ignore protective rules as superfluous. Impulses to kindly interference may then meet feelings of respect, and be held in check. If benevolence wins, the beneficiary loses some protections. Certain barriers collapse, and he is left to depend on free benevolence. To desire that, he must have great trust in his benefactors.

Respect, in short, may seem the crucial moral sentiment, but its content is elusive. At times it is unclear what actions are demanded by respect, and when the demands of respect do seem clear, it may still be quite unclear what rationale unites those demands. I have speculated why an evolved social being might be equipped with such a sentiment. Respect is a feeling, I suggested, and as a feeling it tends both toward action and toward expression. Its biological function is to stabilize the results of bargaining—bargaining understood broadly. Respect, then, is an aspect of reciprocity. It motivates toward constraint; respecting someone includes being moved to accord that person important social protections. Signs of respect signal this motivation. Feelings of respect, though, come with no particular wired-in standards, or too few to settle our moral quandaries. Feelings of respect will attach themselves to various social constraints, actual or possible, but which arrangements will draw the feelings must be a complex matter of psycho-social dynamics. We enter moral inquiry, then, feeling that respect makes strong demands. Still, we can expect confusion and disagreement about just what the demands consist in.

Other Bases

I have speculated about human benevolence and human reciprocity. Under reciprocity I included a sense of fairness: provocability along with respect for others. Other sentiments too need mention—sentiments that are not reciprocal, at least overtly. Let me rush through a few of these, without claiming to have found them all. A person carries a sense of his own moral value, a value that he can affirm by worthy deeds. Some circumstances evoke a feeling of moral inspiration, a feeling that can spur great sacrifice. Disgust supports taboos and a thirst for moral purity. No doubt there are other bases for broadly moral concern, although some of them, I shall be claiming—adherence to rights, the need to justify one's actions—boil down to things already discussed.

"When we present examples of honesty of purpose, of steadfastness in following good maxims, and of sympathy and general benevolence even with great sacrifice of advantages and comfort, there is no man, not even the most malicious villain . . . who does not wish that he also might have these qualities." So said Kant (1785, 454). Nozick speaks of "some individuals whose lives are infused by values, who pursue values with single-minded purity and intensity, who embody values to the greatest extent. These individuals glow with a special radiance" (1981, 36). The special cost of immoral behavior "is a *value* cost. The immoral life is a less valuable life than the moral one, the immoral person is a less valuable being than the moral one"(409). A taxonomy of these feelings of worth must be difficult: pride seems the wrong term for them, and so does self-esteem. Self-assessing feelings will take culturally varied shapes, no doubt, and so on some narrow readings a sense of moral worth may be peculiar to cultures like ours. Still, concern of some kind with one's standing is probably universal, and it would be surprising if there were no underlying biological adaptations at work. The selection pressures that shaped our capacity for a sense of moral worth must have had to do with the rewards of good will, with the qualities that call forth love and glad cooperation. A sense of worthiness or self-esteem of some kind, it seems, makes much of the motivational world go around.[13] These motivations are deep and central to human existence.

13. Steele (1988) argues that the extensive phenomena that were long explained by a drive to reduce cognitive dissonance can be better explained by "self-affirmation processes . . . activated by information that threatens the perceived adequacy or integrity of the self" (262). In Salt Lake City, a man posing as a telephone pollster told women in one random group that pretty much by common knowledge they were "uncooperative with community projects." Other women were scolded as careless drivers. Two days later, in an ostensibly unconnected call, a woman asked for some burdensome help toward developing a food co-op. Of women who had not received the initial call, about half complied, whereas almost all the women who had been scolded two days earlier complied—whether they had been scolded relevantly or irrelevantly, as uncooperative or as careless drivers (264–265). Then too, consider the "lab coat effect": people tend to rationalize choices they have made, so that when, for instance, they choose between alternatives they rank closely together, they subsequently tend to think that the one they chose was substantially better. They want, it seems, to be able to tell themselves a good story of why they chose it. Steele and coworkers selected science-oriented students for

Moral inspiration is another striking phenomenon. It can be felt as overwhelming and purifying, yielding visions of a special sanctity one might hope to attain. The vision may then be hard to square with more everyday motives and habits. Here above all is a broadly moral sentiment that can place itself at odds with other broadly moral sentiments. What, after all, has inspiration to do with careful reciprocity, with civility, tolerance, and balance? Inspiration can bring disappointment, then; it can fail to sustain us, but we should recognize the power it does sometimes have. Why would evolved beings have such strong and selfless motivations? Sometimes it is ritual that inspires, and sometimes preaching. Perhaps, then, we should look for a biological function of inspiration in group spirit. Part of the story may lie in militancy and the ecology of primitive warfare.[14]

Some cultures, it would seem, elaborate disgust as a prime emotion shaping communal life. They expand cleanliness, metaphorically, into an elaborate code, and then the rules of the code can serve as a group badge. This fixation on purity might seem rather different from morality, but we could expect the feelings involved—disgust and cravings for purity—to influence clear cases of moral judgment: we want clean hands and moral purity, we say. Morality's hold on us tightens if morality helps us affiliate, if it anoints us as members of the company of the pure and righteous. We may find ourselves drawn to elaborating moral standards that will provide a test of moral purity.[15]

The things I have been discussing might all be called broadly moral feelings, but another basis of moral concern is straight self-interest. Morality is useful; it offers protection. We fear what might happen if its protection is undermined; we fear it as we fear any great calamity. Self-protectiveness might not count as a moral feeling even broadly, but it will influence our moral judgments. Fear indeed shades into a feeling of reverent dread, fear of a deity or a stern parental figure, and

---

whom "a lab coat symbolized their personal goals." For these students, wearing a white lab coat almost eliminated this tendency to rationalize, whereas for business-oriented students it had no such effect. Putting on a white lab coat, it seemed, affirmed these subjects' sense of worth, and then they had no need to rationalize (275–277). Unfortunately too, it appears, being made to feel in control of a situation can render a person insensitive to some kinds of new information (see 285–288).

14. Rappaport (1979) discusses extensively, among other things, ritual, "numinous" experience, a ritual cycle of primitive warfare, and the ecological significance of warfare.

15. See the *Oxford English Dictionary* citations for early recorded uses of the English term "pollution"; these were religious and moral, and dominant images were filth, excrement, and pigsties.

fear may attach too to all nature: even without gods, we may feel the world as morally ordered, as standing watch and punishing transgressions. In ethnographers' reports, fear can figure in the best equivalent of morality, as fear of God can for us.[16]

I have said nothing about some of the other bases philosophers find for morality. Some ground morality in rights. Perhaps rights are discovered by intuition, and intuition guides something similar to case law, with analogies and intuitive tests of principles. Or perhaps rights can be discovered by appeal to a further rationale. In any case, judgments of rights, it should be clear, are closely tied to the sentiments aroused when rights are violated. These sentiments are retaliatory, sometimes on one's own behalf and sometimes on others'. The sentiments are kinds of anger, with a first-person counterpart, guilt. I have tried to say what the tie is between these sentiments and rights: a judgment of rights consists in norms for anger and guilt. What a person's rights are is a matter of what is just or fair, and to judge fairness is to accept norms for anger and guilt, norms adjusted as part of the dynamics of normative discussion. We already have a naturalistic picture of why we should see people as having rights.

Scanlon, on the other hand, grounds moral concern in a need to be able to justify one's actions to others.[17] This need, though, constitutes no separate moral impulse; it is a part of the workings of guilt and exoneration. Not all justification is moral, after all. One can justify a claim in mathematics, say, and that is no part of narrowly moral life. One can justify a business move as smart, against the non-moral claim that it was stupid. What makes justification moral is a tie to guilt and anger and the like. Parents scold and children justify or cringe. Friends remonstrate and meet justification or apology. Like sentiments extend to more public forums. The need to justify is the need to be held blameless—and also really to be blameless, whether blamed or not by others. What constitutes blamelessness, in a person's eyes, adjusts according to the dynamics of normative discussion.

Moral concern is not all straightforward benevolence working to constrain self-interest. Other concerns too are broadly moral: they are not

16. Ladd (1957, 226–227), for instance, reports that one important ethical term of the Navaho means roughly "dangerous"; the appeal seems to be to fear and dread. Navaho speak of "mistakes", not of guilt (272).

17. Scanlon (1982, esp. 116–118). More precisely, the motive he invokes is "the desire to be able to justify one's actions to others on grounds they could not reasonably reject." He adds, "reasonably, that is, given the desire to find principles which others similarly motivated could not reasonably reject" (116).

straight matters of self-interest, and they affect which norms for guilt and anger will look plausible to us. I have been asking about the actual shape of these broadly moral feelings, taking up various truisms and common observations, and trying to fit them to evolutionary possibilities. A highly social species like ours might well evolve to have the set of broadly moral sentiments we seem to observe in ourselves. These sentiments fall into no neat system: different ones at times push different ways, and even one by one some of them lack clear content. Sentiments of fairness and respect in particular come with a definite form but issue no fixed directives; their seeming content emerges from an intricate social dynamic.

15 · Assessing Feelings

In the last chapter I tried for an ecology of broadly moral sentiment. Now suppose I succeeded with it, beyond my fondest hopes: suppose I got the shapes of our broadly moral feelings just right. What would the feelings have to do with a justified morality?

We could decide they are no part of it—no part of any morality we should accept. That might be what we ought to say, for instance, about a thirst for vengeance. The impulse is broadly moral, but perhaps it never makes sense to want plain vengeance just for itself. How, then, could we assess an impulse like vengeance, or a more genial feeling? How can we go from the actual roots of our moral concern to rationales it makes sense to accept? What do feelings and good rationales even have to do with each other?

This chapter has two somewhat disjointed parts. First I grapple with two ways we can view our feelings, as we think what norms to accept as governing them. One way is to take the feelings as guides; the other is to ask how best to put them to work. In deciding what norms to accept for a feeling, we can consult our sense of plausibility, accepting norms that fit the rationale the feeling seems to carry. Or we can look to the good the feeling can do, and accept norms that promote that good. Each way leads to the other: feelings make poor guides unharnessed, and yet we can put them to work only by taking them as guides. Norms for feelings are to be tested both by their plausibility and by their pragmatic point.

That leads to the second topic. The two prongs of normative inquiry—plausibility and point—are held together by requirements of consistency. Philosophers strive for rigorous consistency over a wild range of cases. This is no part of normal thought and discussion; should a norm-expressivist go in for it? The question, of course, concerns normative inquiry in general; I am using inquiry into feelings as an illustration. The case of feelings confronts us with a question about normative inquiry of all kinds: what, in a norm-expressivistic picture, is special about consistency?

Nothing in this chapter will seem astounding, and in a way that is sad: it would have been good if norm-expressivism could offer us new keys to normative inquiry. In a way, though, it is fortunate: the theory gets some confirmation if norm-expressivistic musings yield familiar precepts.

Trusting Feelings

My question is what authority feelings carry: shall we endorse the feelings we tend to have? When earlier I asked about the authority of normative judgments, I spoke of self-trust, and here we may need to invoke it again. Moral inquiry, we might say, demands that to some degree at least we trust the moral sentiments we have. Moral judgments say how it makes sense to feel about actions. Acts, though, evoke feelings anyway, somewhat apart from whatever norms we accept. Shall we trust those feelings? Shall we use them as a guide to the norms that should govern them? In other words, we feel certain ways about things, and we feel them even apart from the norms we accept. Does that in any way go to show that it makes sense to feel those ways? Does the fact that we do feel some way support norms that say to feel that way?

It does, we might try arguing, because we have to trust ourselves as inquirers, and our feelings are bound to steer our inquiries. Try this first on a non-moral feeling like sadness. "No use crying over spilt milk"—maybe so, but something strange is being hinted. The message seems to be that it makes no sense to be sad about things one can't help. Crying is not only useless; the feeling behind it is senseless. That seems off base: sadness *is* about losses. A more useful feeling might spur one in time to ward off dangers, but that isn't sadness. With sadness usefulness is not in question; it makes sense to be sad over losses when they come. It is when a loss can still be avoided that sadness would be perverse—or so we find.

Some things do make me sad, then, and that moves me toward accepting norms that say to be sad about those things. If I find myself sad and think it makes no sense to be sad, that makes for strain. The norms I accept work to muffle my sadness, but the sadness works in return to subvert the norms. When sad I am pushed to think it makes sense to be sad.

Other things may work against this push, buttressing the norms I already accept. I may ruminate, in effect rehearsing my avowals, and so hold to norms I am prepared to avow. I may discuss and be influenced by what others avow. Even here, though, sadness works on the norms that govern it; the workings this time are social. Others too, when they have been sad over something, will tend to accept norms that endorse the feeling. Normative discussion will smooth out emotional quirks, but still it will respond to the broad shape of the kinds of things that make us sad. It will tend to sanction the broad form our emotional capacities take.

What I think it makes sense to feel, then, responds to the kinds of things I do feel, and it responds also to the kinds of things people around me feel: their feelings are contagious, and their feelings work on the norms they accept and avow, influencing me. We can expect, then, that in fact—in socio-psychological fact—my feelings will move me toward accepting norms that endorse those very feelings. So will the feelings of people around me.

Recognizing all this, shall I resist? In fact I will not utterly yield to these tendencies. Other things too will affect the norms I accept for a feeling like sadness. I will respond to pressures for consistency. I may be moved by thoughts about the social role of sadness and its benefits, or the costs of sadness repressed or unacknowledged. I will not, then, always accept norms for feelings that endorse the feelings I and the rest of us have. Still I will tend that way, and the question is whether to resist the tendency wholesale.

Now at this point we might try arguing that blanket resistance means blanket skepticism. It makes sense to feel sad, we think, about the various kinds of things that typically do make us sad. We must accord some authority to ourselves as we are—we who are influenced, in the norms we accept for feelings, by having had those feelings. Otherwise we renounce all claim to being tolerably good judges of how it makes sense to feel about things.

With norms for feelings, though, we could mistrust our natural bent even radically without sheer disaster. Other views pull us. On feelings we could well be skeptics: There can be no real question of what it makes sense to feel, we might conclude. A person just *feels* what he feels. He may accept norms about feelings, and that will affect what he does feel—but not rightly or wrongly. It may be important in his life, and in human life in general, to think it makes sense to feel some ways about things and not others. Still, that is an illusion, and its importance does not keep it from being an illusion. So we might say, and no clear disaster looms.

Puzzles About Feelings

Morality consists in norms for moral sentiments. I am looking for a way to assess moral sentiments, asking how to decide what norms to accept as governing them. I tried an argument from self-trust, but it failed to discredit the alternatives. With feelings we might be skeptics. True, with each new happening in our lives, we think it makes sense to feel some ways and not others. As philosophers, though, aiming at system, we might reject these thoughts as illusions.

Alternatively we might test feelings by results. Feelings can be advantageous or disadvantageous, good or bad. A pragmatic test need not be direct; perhaps we should ask about whole capacities for feelings, or about whole programs of reforming them. At times, for instance, what recommends a feeling is the cost of repressing it. Still, the test in the end is one of cost. A death is sad, but only if somehow, directly or indirectly, the benefits of the sadness outweigh its costs.

Neither of these—skepticism or direct pragmatism—is a normal frame of mind. We think feelings can be apt or off the mark, and we do not settle which by counting costs. We experience injury as dismaying, we experience achievement as welcome; we experience the deaths of those we love as searing. We accept norms that endorse these ways of experiencing things. The norms tell us, roughly, to celebrate the things it made sense to want to happen, and regret the things it made sense to want not to happen. They say nothing about the costs and benefits of regret itself, or the costs and benefits of the training that would change the feeling.

Of course, normal frames of mind are not always correct. Commonsense physics is wrong; why not our common norms for feelings? How can we even decide? A norm-expressivistic analysis offers no quick answers, but I want to try a somewhat inconclusive line of thought.

In normative inquiry in general, we begin with tentative views. These views are of many kinds: of substance, of form, of authority. We think it makes sense to be sad at a death; that is a substantive view. We think that if it makes sense for me to feel sad about something, it makes sense for you to feel sad about like things in like cases. That is a view about form. We think that if we pondered more about when it makes sense to feel sad, our opinions would be better founded. We might think carefully, say, about when it makes sense to feel sad about bad things from long ago. Whatever opinion we would come to, the fact that we would tells in its favor. That is a view about authority. We start with opinions like these, though we allow that inquiry might change our minds.

What happens with feelings when we start on this course? There will be some tendency to endorse the feelings we have. As we push matters further, though, other things might tend to undermine our normal views.

Some aspects of the ways we feel about things we are willing neither fully to endorse nor fully to reject. Sadness responds to place and time, but we are not clear whether it should. The plight of a stranger can make us sad if it is depicted vividly, and indeed we seek out sad stories and are moved by them—and yet we could not possibly respond vividly to much in the world. We are clear enough about when it makes sense to be sad as opposed to happy, but not about when it makes sense to be sad as opposed to emotionally detached or matter-of-fact. If we tried really to work out norms for a feeling like sadness, would we get a system we could take seriously? We may despair of getting anywhere with the job, and think there is no genuine question of how it makes sense to feel about things.

Serious inquiry into norms for feelings would have to look across cultures too. Now perhaps it makes sense for us to feel one way about things and for peoples far away to feel differently—but if we take norms for feelings seriously, we shall have to ask why. We shall have to confront the diversities in human feelings as well as the likenesses, to puzzle through the ways feelings in other cultures can seem bizarre, the things that make for culture shock. We shall have to ask if our own norms for feelings are ethnocentric, whether there is anything about us that puts us in a specially good position to judge feelings. It is hard to see what there might be, except perhaps when other peoples' feelings are tribalistic and ours are humanistic, or theirs are grounded in superstition and ours are not. Indeed, we need to ask whether our norms are vestiges of superstitions we have cast off, so that we would accept quite different norms if those old superstitions had been different. Whatever may be special about our scientific standards and our critical methods, it is not clear they have much to do with our views on how it makes sense to feel about things.

To the extent, then, that we are not happy to be quite narrowly parochial, we shall be forced either to skepticism about norms for feelings, or to some kind of relativism. If we are not to be skeptics, and if we are to endorse the general shape of the norms for feelings we started with, we shall have to come up with a story of why those norms are all right for us in virtue of some of our cultural peculiarities. It will have to say why quite different norms are all right for other peoples with different cultures. The story will have to get to this point without relying on features of our culture that are special and arbitrary—special as seen among all human cultures, and arbitrary in that we cannot honestly see them as putting us in a better position to judge feelings.

Detached Observers

How might a plausible story for feelings go? Why ought one set of norms to govern our own feelings, and other sets to govern the feelings of others far away? I can think of at least two live possibilities. First, we might try a pragmatic story: a story of how norms for feelings contribute to a life worth leading. They do so, we might say, partly because the norms fit ways we do feel about things. We experience life through our feelings, and so norms that endorse our feelings enhance our experiences. Still, why accept norms for feelings instead of just reveling in the feelings themselves?

Consider a second kind of story. Adam Smith thought that the proper emotions are the ones a detached observer would have. The proper degree of an emotion is its degree in a detached observer.[1] Now as an account of meaning, I have rejected this (see Chapter 9). To make such an account precise, I argued, we would need to specify further what the test observer is to be like. He must be informed, alert, sober, and the like. Once we fill out the specification, though, a speaker could think it mistaken; he could think that a somewhat different kind of observer provides the right test. Then he could agree, say, that any

1. Smith (1790, esp. I.1.5 and II.1.5). According to Smith's theory, the proper degree of grief for a bereaved parent, say, is the degree of grief into which a detached spectator can enter (see V.2.5). Still, "There are some situations which bear so hard upon human nature, that the greatest degree of self-government, which can belong to so imperfect a creature as man, is not able to stifle, altogether, the voice of human weakness, or reduce the violence of the passions to that pitch of moderation, in which the impartial spectator can entirely enter into them. Though in those cases, therefore, the behaviour of the sufferer fall short of the most perfect propriety, it may still deserve some applause, and even in a certain sense, may be denominated virtuous" (I.i.5.8).

observer of the kind we had specified would feel angry, and still deny that it really made sense to feel angry. He could do all this without logical or linguistic mistake—or so I claimed. What qualities make an observer a good indicator of proper feeling is itself a normative question, not a question of meaning alone.

Still, perhaps Smith's theory or something close to it is good as a substantive account of what makes feelings proper—of when it does make sense to feel some way about something. It makes sense to feel the way a detached observer would (with specifications added about the test observer).

Left at that, the account does not answer why we should care how detached observers feel. Smith himself has a story: A person wants sympathy, he wants others to feel as he does. His best hope for that is to feel himself as a detached observer would (1790, I.1.5).

This story gives the account a pragmatic twist, and that is good. We are asking what, in general, a feeling must be like for it to make sense to feel that way—what general property makes some feelings apt and others not. A good answer will tell us not only what the property is, but why that property should matter. It need not define the property normatively, in terms of what it makes sense to want, but if it does not draw some tie with what it makes sense to want, it passes over the questions we really need answered.

Now if Smith's pragmatic story supports his detached observer theory, it supports the theory in a relativized form. The proper feelings for a person, Smith must say, are those of a detached observer who belongs to that person's own culture. The feelings people have, after all, depend greatly on their acculturation. A person wants others' feelings to match his own, the story goes, and that presumably means people who matter to him—typically people of his own culture. He matches his feelings to those of a detached observer in order to have feelings he can hope his fellows will match. If his fellows, the ones who matter, are of his own culture, the detached observer should be too. It is the detached observer belonging to the person's own culture, after all, whose feelings others who matter to the person might share. Smith's theory, then, should be put in the form its rationale supports. The proper feelings for a person, the things it makes sense for him to feel, are the ones a detached observer who shares his culture would feel.

Smith's rationale clearly has truth to it, up to a point: one thing we want from others is fellow feeling; we want our fellows to confirm us in what we feel. We need to look beyond this desire, though, and ask why. The desire plays a social role, I have been claiming. It serves to mesh feelings. Meshed feelings coordinate actions, and coordinated actions make for cooperation and keep conflict from being ruinous. In part this is a matter of what caused us, evolutionarily, to be the kinds of beings who crave fellow feeling. It appeals also, though, to things it makes sense to want in life. Not only do feelings give life its savor; sharing our feelings not only does give us much to cherish in human fellowship. In addition, a person who cannot share feelings will be socially lame. He will be moved to act in ways that mesh poorly with the actions of others—even in terms of things it makes sense to want, all fellow feeling aside. Capacities to coordinate feelings are part of normal human equipment, like the capacities to walk and to run. To be without them is to be crippled.

On Smith's theory, the proper feelings for everyone in a group are the same. On ordinary views, the ways it makes sense to feel about things can depend on one's position. It makes sense for intimates to grieve in a way it does not make sense for strangers.[2] Triumph makes sense in the victor but not in the vanquished. The feelings and degrees a detached observer finds proper will not always be the ones the observer himself shares.

In the end, then, the detached observer theory is inadequate by two standards. It falls short as an account of ordinary views of apt feelings. Sometimes it gets things right and sometimes not. It falls short also in terms of the point of shared feelings: we need to ask why sharing feelings should matter, but the points we can find are not always best served by sharing. Shared feelings are not always the ones we crave: triumph craves submissiveness from the vanquished, and hurt may crave comfort. Finally, if we think that part of what matters in shared feelings is coordination, that too is not always best fostered by sharing. With meshed pairs of feelings, the matter is clear enough: think of anger and guilt, disdain and shame, triumph and submission. When a person grieves, friends may help most not by grieving too but by feeling concern for the person who grieves. In short, Smith's theory leads us to look for a point, and the points we can find lead away from

2. Smith admits we indulge grief even when we cannot fully share it, but that does not mean the degree of grief is proper. We may pardon excessive grief, because grief is so hard to master (I.iii.I.5). In Camus' *L'étranger*, much is made of the narrator's lack of a normal show of grief at his mother's funeral. It seems to be taken not only as a sign of a character bad in other ways, but as damning in itself. The same would not go for mild grief at the funeral of a distant acquaintance.

Smith's theory. The feelings of a detached observer are not always the ones we normally think it makes sense to feel. Like feelings, Smith's claims notwithstanding, are not always what we crave. Like feelings are not always the ones that best coordinate.

Two Prongs

Let me review. In normative inquiry, we start with tentative norms and work from there. Some of the norms are substantive, some are formal, and some are epistemological—norms for what makes a normative judgment most reliable. Now with feelings in particular, I have been claiming, normative discussion must move or collapse; we could not end an adequate discussion with our starting opinions just lightly smoothed out. Our initial thoughts form nothing close to a coherent system, and they give poor heed to the diverse judgments and feelings of other peoples. If we are not to be too narrowly parochial, and if we are not to come out skeptics on norms for feelings, we need a story of how the feelings it makes sense to have depend on one's culture.

I tried one such story: Adam Smith's with a relativistic twist. The story fails but it is right in its appeal to gains from coordination. Smith looked to why it helps if we share each other's feelings. He then proposed matching the feelings of a detached observer, as a person's best hope of sharing the feelings of those around him. At times, I objected, people coordinate best with distinct feelings that somehow mesh. Still, we can follow Smith in spirit by looking to the kind of meshing that has most point. We can look for norms that promote the best kind of meshing. Smith's treatment points us in a hopeful direction. It leads to questions about why it matters, at times, that we share each other's feelings, and when it is that, for like reasons, different people might best have different feelings.

We need to push these questions directly, then—keeping in mind how things we say might apply in distant cultures. We need to think radically about the pros and cons of alternative norms for various feelings. We might still end up fairly conservatively, endorsing the broad shapes of the feelings we do tend to have. Even if we do, though, we need to generalize. We need to think about cultures with different starting points and different emotional tendencies. Here at the very least, gains and losses will bear: thinking about them may help us in generalizing, and it may even point to ways to change our initial views.

The relevant considerations are of many kinds. They include the feelings we crave in each other. They include the coordination that stems from meshed feelings. They include more generally the value of the kinds of actions various feelings prompt. They include also something that is harder to discuss, the sense we make of life through our feelings.[3] MacIntyre speaks of the narrative structure of a life, how important it is to see oneself as unfolding a significant story. To grasp this talk and its implications, we would have to understand more about narratives: what gives stories their bite, what makes for a good story or a bad one. Still, we can see already that MacIntyre is pointing to something important, to something that bears on the feelings it makes sense to want. Stories have to do with feelings; in part, we might say, they are training for feelings. Part of what we might want from feelings, in turn, is a promise to make life—even a hard life—into a good story.[4]

I told Smith's story of the virtues of matched feelings, and repeated his proposal for how to get the match. I then moved on from Smith to mention a wider range of values that can stem from feelings. Norms can be chosen to enhance the balance of gains over costs, where some of the gains stem from coordination and some from other things.

Still gains and costs, even glossed this expansively, might not be final arbiters. Pragmatic accord might elude us. We might think fully about norms for feelings, work out which ones come out best for us—and simply find those norms incredible. Suppose, now, that after full inquiry, we indeed would reject the norms for feelings we see it would be best for us to accept. If we know already that this is how matters would come out, and we now trust ourselves as we would be then, we must reject pragmatic standards already. We must agree even now that the norms that would be best for us are not the right ones. This, of course, is not our real case; in fact we do not know where the best inquiry would lead. We do not know whether, on full and ideal inquiry, the most beneficial norms would seem credible. We do not know in advance, then, whether pragmatic tests for feeling norms are good ones.

If all this is right, we need each of two prongs for assessing feelings. One is the pragmatic one I have been pushing, emulating Smith: bring

3. Benedict (1934) portrays the sense we make of life through our culture in general, and places this at the heart of an appeal that an undisturbed culture, even with atrocious features, is better for the people who share it than a disturbed culture. See also Turnbull (1962).

4. MacIntyre (1981, 190–209). MacIntyre himself has much to say about what makes for a story of the right kind.

to bear gains and costs, broadly understood. The other we might call loosely intuitionistic: take up the inquiry, think through examples, discuss together, confront puzzles and inconsistencies. Then see directly which norms for feelings strike us as plausible. We do not think we can peer into a special realm of normative fact, but we can act as if we thought we could.

Neither prong stands alone; the first brings along the second, and also serves as a check on it. First I argued that loosely intuitionistic thoughts lead to pragmatic tests. Normative thought about feelings must be far-reaching. Our thoughts as they are lead us into quandaries, even if we stick to familiar circumstances. Other peoples hold different standards, and we have no quick story either of why we are right and they are wrong, or of why we are each mostly right for our own circumstances. Since for feelings we could be normative skeptics, any thought about norms for feelings will soon lead to thoughts about what point there might be to having such norms.

On the other hand, I am now saying, thoughts about the point of norms can settle matters only if they lead to norms we find credible. One thing pragmatic considerations endorse is some of our normal ways of thought and discussion. They endorse thinking together about how it makes sense to feel about various things. Many of these ways of thinking verge on the Socratic: push some of our discursive tendencies, and the discussion begins to seem loosely intuitionistic. There are gains to be had, then, from thinking these ways, and setting out to think involves putting some trust in one's powers of judgment—in the things one will accept as a result of the thinking. Pragmatic considerations endorse a loosely intuitionistic check.

Norm-expressivistic thoughts about assessing feelings, in short, can lead to a picture that should be familiar enough. Intuitionistic refinement leads to thought about gains and losses, and any conclusions we draw from thinking about gains and losses need to be checked in loosely intuitionistic ways: thinking about the widest range of circumstances, pushing for clarity and consistency, and seeing what, on the widest view of things, we can find plausible. Both prongs are needed: loosely intuitionistic refinement and pragmatic assessment.

Normative Consistency

As we press normative inquiry with these two prongs, we must not leave the prongs loose to poke any which way. The prongs must be

welded together by consistency. Ideal inquiry achieves consistency—
or so we assume. Consistency alone is far from enough, to be sure.
There are too many possible consistent systems, some of them horrid.
Still, ideal inquiry would achieve ideal consistency, along with other
good things as well.

We need to ask, though, why consistency should matter with
norms. To be sure, part of our normative equipment, as I keep saying,
is a responsiveness to demands for consistency. That responsiveness,
though, has limits. Socrates tried to press consistency to an extreme.
Is there anything special about full consistency, the kind philosophers
seek, a kind of consistency that has no place in our normative life from
day to day? The problem of course is for norms in general, not just
norms for feelings. Let me first, then, turn away from norms for feelings, and take up the question for norms that bind action.

Rigorous demands for consistency can have far-reaching consequences. Harsanyi showed this spectacularly: from a few sparse premises he derived an entire theory of morality. His premises one by one
seem compelling and innocuous, but from them there follows a full-
blown utilitarianism. If we hold ourselves to consistency, it seems, we
can be led from clear and obvious premises to disturbing conclusions.
With extreme demands for consistency, Socrates misled youth and
made the worse appear the better cause—or so it was charged. We
need to scrutinize the demands for consistency that threaten normative
ruin. Harsanyi's derivation provides one occasion for this scrutiny.[5]

How can alternative policies be assessed? asks Harsanyi. We can
look at their impact on the lives of the people they affect, but the
results of any policy are uncertain. We should think, then, not of sure
impacts, but of the prospects each person would face if a policy were
adopted. A compelling principle of evaluation is the *Prospective Pareto
Principle:* Suppose we are faced with a choice of two policies, and under
policy *A* the prospects of everyone are better than under policy *B*.
Then, the principle says, policy *A* is the better one from an ethical point
of view. Harsanyi combines this principle with standard, equally compelling strictures on the rational ordering of prospects, and shows that
a kind of utilitarianism follows. Policies are to be ranked, from an ethical point of view, entirely by a (possibly weighted) sum of the values
of the prospects they hold out for the people affected.

Utilitarianism, though, is notorious for consequences that fly in the
face of judgments we make with great confidence. Now, things can be

5. What follows is roughly the theorem of Harsanyi (1955, 312–314).

said to attack Harsanyi's postulates, and things can be said to attack the contention that utilitarianism has such wild consequences. If, though, Harsanyi's postulates do seem compelling and the consequences of utilitarianism do seem unacceptable, then we have to recognize ourselves as inconsistent.[6]

I want to ask not whether this is so, but what we should think if it is. The situation has parallels; think of subjective probability. We can take its theory as normative: it elaborates norms for belief and for partial credence. Debates on the foundations of subjective probability, so conceived, are a kind of normative discussion—in this case epistemological. Now Tversky and Kahneman, in an exciting series of experiments, seem to show that people are not only subtly inconsistent in their probability judgments, but blatantly so (Tversky and Kahneman 1983). Almost anyone will agree that the probability of a conjunction *A and B* cannot be greater than the probability of one of the conjuncts *A*. Yet if we make Linda sound sufficiently intelligent and free-spirited, then the overwhelming majority of subjects will judge it more probable that

> Linda is a bank teller who is active in the feminist movement

than that

> Linda is a bank teller.

Again, there are debates about this, but Tversky and Kahneman make a strong case. We judge probability, they suggest, by heuristics: quick rules that are generally useful, but that cannot be made consistent with each other under pressure. Now with subjective probability theory, not many people who think about it are in serious doubt about what norms to accept and what norms to reject. Arguments have been devised about the books that can be made against a person who bets on the basis of probabilities that violate the standard axioms. Unorthodox probabilities leave us expecting the wrong frequencies. For most theorists of probability, these arguments seem to settle the matter.

Normative ethics, on the other hand, has been much more obdurate. To the extent that there is a consensus, it seems not to include any one story of what is wrong with arguments like Harsanyi's. Not that

---

6. See also Parfit (1984) for a superb collection of arguments that press demands for consistency in ethics and the theory of rational choice to surprising conclusions.

searching critiques of Harsanyi's axioms are absent from the literature (see Gauthier 1982 and Griffin 1986, 111–113). Still, the sureness with which his conclusions are rejected is not at all matched by the sureness with which these critiques are accepted.

All this raises a puzzle for any non-cognitivist: why should ideal consistency matter in normative judgments? Traditional cognitivists face their own embarrassments, but at least they have something strong to say about consistency. Normative judgments are true or false, and if our normative judgments are inconsistent, they cannot all be true. We may not care about avoiding falsehood, but if we do, we cannot have achieved our goal if our judgments are inconsistent.[7]

Earlier I spoke at length of "normative objectivity", and we should get it straight what that has to do with consistency. Objectivity is a matter of ways a kind of judgment mimics certain paradigms: judgments, say, of the layout of sticks and rocks in one's surroundings. In my discussion of objectivity I simply assumed consistency—for I could say most clearly what it is to treat one's judgments as objective or not against a background of consistency. A person could be perfectly consistent, though, in a set of judgments he treats as non-objective. Conversely, there are sides to objectivity that we can well understand apart from perfect consistency. I am sure—to say the least—that one shouldn't amuse oneself by torturing people. It takes no great consistency, on my part, to think this holds whatever one's feeling and convictions. It takes no great consistency for me to think that everybody should accept this judgment, and to think myself warranted in demanding that they do so. Purported objectivity and perfect consistency are separable features a set of judgments might have.

Why, then, seek consistency in normative matters, on the kind of account I have been giving? The account says why it is in our nature

7. Some of the newer views of the nature of normative ethics share my puzzle. If a theorist's goal is to work our considered normative judgments into consistency, we need to ask why he should bother. (Rawls has talked in this vein; see 1971, 46–47.) Some current writers argue that the putative contrast between normative judgments and descriptive judgments is based on a misconception about the nature of the prime supposed examples of descriptive language: ordinary judgments of surrounding objects, judgments in the sciences, and ordinary psychological judgments. The contrast, they say, is based on a naive empiricism or a naive correspondence theory of truth. For arguments roughly along these lines, see Putnam (1981, chap. 6), Rorty (1982, Introduction and Essay 11), and Sturgeon (1985b). If these arguments are right, then the usual, naive stories of why consistency matters will have to be reexamined. In my puzzle, then, I have company—but it remains a puzzle. The very concept of truth, we might try saying, carries with it a requirement of consistency. In that case, though, we need a story of why truth, conceived so as to include this requirement, should matter so much.

to seek consistency: doing so is part of the mechanism by which normative discussion can lead to consensus. That something is in our nature does not endorse it, for horrifying things too are parts of our nature—in particular, an easy slide into group hostility and fervor to do battle. The explanation, though, does carry with it a kind of pragmatic endorsement: the goods fostered by normative consensus are real, and being responsive to demands for consistency helps foster consensus.

Caring as we do about consistency, moreover, we can say in part why to care about consistency just by expressing this side of our nature. We can insist that consistency matters for its own sake. To say this is to express a confident acceptance of norms of consistency—a confident acceptance that stems from nothing else we accept, and that survives normative discussion. Finally, we can use the search for consistency as a prod to sort out what matters and why. Faced with an inconsistency, one can try to think through what one cares about for its own sake, and what for other reasons that might adjudicate the conflicts one discovers. This kind of examination of life can be part of what makes it worth living.

Turn, though, to the pragmatic part of the story, that responsiveness to demands for consistency fosters consensus. Like other stories of the pragmatic value of caring about the things we do, this one will leave us ambivalent. Even if the story is convincing, it will not straightforwardly give our reason for caring about consistency.

In addition, there is a special problem with the story: it gives consistency no special status. Consistency, for all the story tells us, is simply an instrumental good that competes with others, and sometimes competes poorly. In the first place, the goods that stem from consensus are not all the goods worth caring about; it matters what the consensus is. A consensus that we should devote our lives, say, to flagellating each other would not be worth having. It is part of the mechanism of normative discussion that we think it matters which consensus we achieve.

Furthermore, even if consensus were all that mattered, responsiveness to demands for consistency would not always promote it. If some are especially consistent, that might drive them away from consensus with the rest. Jointly inconsistent norms may each have a strong natural appeal. When that is so, there may be more consensus to be gained by sweeping inconsistencies under the rug than by exposing them and trying to root them out.

The Special Value

Is there anything special, then, about normative consistency? If there is, it does not straightforwardly lie in the ways responsiveness to demands for consistency promotes consensus. We can be glad, on these grounds, that we are somewhat responsive to demands for consistency, but also glad, perhaps, that we are not more responsive than we are. Is there a special way, then, in which inconsistency is bad? No one thinks that consistency is all that matters, but cognitivists at least can say it matters in a way that is special: inconsistency is a guarantee of falsehood. Can a non-cognitivist say anything corresponding?

I think he can, and indeed what he can say is familiar. Inconsistency lays us open to a special kind of self-frustration. Take procrastination: I reject today in favor of tomorrow, tomorrow in favor of the next day, until I am months overdue. I do not find being months overdue acceptable. Had I resolved these preferences I might have acted on a policy I could live with.

The parable is a rough one. Decision theorists have tried to work it out exactly, and controversies over their work have been lively and illuminating (see Ramsey 1931 and Savage 1954). Let me go on treating the parable roughly, though, and try to say what it might have to do with normative life. Accepting a norm makes for kinds of local commitment. In the first place, norms involve tendencies to action: if I judge it makes sense to reject today for tomorrow, then I tend in fact to reject today for tomorrow. In the second place, norms involve tendencies to reason and discuss in certain ways: if I claim to you that it makes sense to reject today for tomorrow, then I am under strong pressure in normative discussion to accept things we all see as following from that. Otherwise I have opted out of normative discussion, to some degree at least. Both these kinds of tendencies come inevitably with accepting norms, and indeed I have been using both to pick out what kind of thing accepting norms is supposed to be. These aspects combine to serve a function we can endorse.

Our problems come when we string together these local commitments. We may string them together in action, as with procrastination, and find ourselves stuck with terrible results. We may string them together in reasoning, under the lead of sophistic, self-serving arguments or more innocently. As a result we find ourselves under pressure to accept what is clearly unacceptable. Now the two kinds of chaining are different: Chains of action bring their results unbidden;

after disastrous procrastination I cannot reject a disaster. With a chain of inferences, on the other hand, I can accept each link and then baldly reject the whole. The problem is how to do so without opting out of normative discussion altogether, or discovering that I can no longer get others to take my claims seriously. There is room for skilled fudging, but the skill may be more than we can muster. We need some local responsiveness if we are to engage each other in normative discussion at all, and global inconsistency shows we can get to local inconsistency. If, on the other hand, we did achieve a global consistency, we would have confronted the pitfalls in the path we can be led along by local demands for consistency. Without opting out of all normative discussion, we have made ourselves proof against sophistry, and proof against the push of logic to fanaticism.

This argument is pragmatic, but it is different from the earlier pragmatic argument. The pragmatic element is this: We need the benefits of normative discussion. Gleaning these benefits requires two things, a tendency to be governed by what one avows, and a tendency to avow other things as a result of what one avows—what I have been calling a responsiveness to demands for local consistency. That leaves us open, though, to a special kind of danger: local commitments chain into more far-flung commitments. Some consistency is a good thing, but it did not follow that extreme Socratic consistency is even better. I still needed to argue that a little consistency is dangerous, and dangerous in a special way. It can lead us, I said, to sequences of actions that are jointly unacceptable, and it can leave us with the hard choice of following a chain of inferences to unacceptable conclusions or opting out of normative discussion.

How, then, does all this apply to norms for feelings? We do reason about how it makes sense to feel. This reasoning matters, as I keep arguing, and not just for the insight it yields. Feelings tend to action in a complex variety of ways, and it is important, often, to have feelings that mesh. Meshed feelings lead to meshed actions. Now with feelings as with actions, once we reason, we have accepted some local demands for consistency. Again, local consistency can have far consequences. With feelings, in short, there are strong pragmatic reasons for not being normative skeptics, and once we drop skepticism, we buy into normative reasoning. Buying in halfway is a shaky and delicate business.

Still, with feelings, consistency is not always urgent. How urgent it is will depend, in part, on what norms we accept tying feeling to action—tying the things it makes sense to feel to the things it makes sense to do. With a feeling like sadness the tie might be weak. Shared sadness makes for bonds, to be sure, and the bonds can be felt as important. They may lead to special ways of treating each other. Still, perhaps fellow feelings of sadness need not be closely negotiated. We may get along fine sharing our sorrows without any delicate reasoning about when it makes sense to be sad. Guilt and anger, though, may be different. We might tie them much more closely to action. We might decide that what it makes sense to do depends (among other things) on what sorts of things it makes sense to be angry at people for doing, and on what sorts of things it makes sense to feel guilty about having done. Whether we should I ask briefly in the next chapter. If we do, though, that gives special urgency to consistency in norms for these narrowly moral feelings.

Both with norms for action and with norms for feelings, I have told how pressures toward local consistency are part of any reasoning, and how local consistency can have far-reaching consequences. These are by no means the only problems we face in life, and efforts at global consistency are not the only effective remedies. The struggle for consistency has costs. If inconsistency has costs too, it may be best to mitigate them with fudges, obtuseness, hypocrisy, and good inarticulate judgment. There is a special way in which inconsistency matters, both with norms for action and with norms for feelings. Still, it will not justify seeking consistency at all costs.

It may, though, justify a division of labor: wanting some people to press demands for consistency in normative discussion with special rigor. The specialist's goal should be not to attain consistency at the expense of everything else, but to work especially hard and effectively at seeing how far extreme consistency can be reconciled with other things worth wanting. That seems to me to describe much of philosophy.

Glances Back

This chapter and the previous one are preface to a few glances at narrowly moral inquiry. Moral inquiry develops norms for guilt and anger. Diverse things will affect which norms for these two feelings we find plausible; some of them will be other feelings—feelings with broadly moral import, such as benevolence, respect, fairness, a sense of worth, reverence, moral inspiration. These count as moral sentiments on any but the narrowest reading. For each we can see why an evolved social being might have it, or something close, and each feeling carries with it a kind of rationale. These broadly moral feelings will help shape our norms for action, and for the narrowly moral feelings of guilt and anger. So too will crucial non-moral wants, especially our need for the protections morality can bring.

Our broadly moral feelings, though, offer no unified guide to living. Different feelings may draw us different ways, and different framings can enlist even a single feeling on different sides of an issue. This is the way we are, if I am right, and it sets us our normative problem: starting with a whole array of crucial wants, broadly moral sentiments, and tentative normative views, how shall we proceed with moral inquiry?

To proceed is to develop norms for the morally relevant feelings, and in this chapter I have discussed the problem of criticizing feelings in general. We see people and their acts through a host of feelings, and we accept incoherent fragments of norms for these feelings. Norms for feelings are crucial to human life, I keep insisting. Even if we accept all this, however, we could easily find ourselves baffled about how to decide on norms for feelings. I have been claiming that we do have ways to begin. For philosophers the ways are familiar—indeed familiar rivals. One way looks much like utilitarianism; the other much like intuitionism. My claim is that norm-expressivism makes sense of both these familiar ways.

Once we begin to think and discuss normatively, we have already bought into demands for consistency, locally at least. Then it is dicey to know where to stop. Extreme, global consistency, if we can combine it with other inquisitive virtues, lets us see where local demands might lead. With feelings that matters chiefly if we tie action closely to feelings: if we tie what it makes sense to do to ways it makes sense to feel about things people do.

Narrow moralizing does just that, and we need to ask whether it should. In the next chapter I look at the narrowly moral sentiments, and I look at them pragmatically. I take up guilt and anger, and their tie to action. In the final chapter, I glance at moral theory in general: how we might pursue it, and what the prospects might be.

16 · Structural Questions

Throughout the book I have read morality narrowly. We can mark it off, I proposed, through its connection to narrowly moral sentiments, guilt and resentment. Morality on this narrow reading looks to the kinds of acts for which a person can be to blame. A person is to blame for an act if it makes sense for others to be angry at him—from a standpoint of full, impartial engagement, I added—and if it makes sense for the person himself to feel guilty for what he has done. Morally wrong acts are not always acts a person is to blame for; there can be excuses. Still, the connection is tight. Wrong acts, roughly, are acts a person would be to blame for if he chose them in a normal state of mind.

I proposed this not as the only way of picking out morality. Morality, as we normally think of it, involves a cluster of features. In advance we are not at all decided which parts are central—which parts we should still count as belonging to morality if we come to think the cluster breaks apart. The tie to guilt and resentment is a chief part of the cluster, and I proposed using that tie to sharpen the concept of morality. That yields a conception that corresponds fairly well to the rough one we started with.

This proposal will be helpful if it leads to important questions. In Chapter 3, I mentioned a few staple questions of moral theory, and said what the questions came to on the analysis I was proposing. With these questions, it can be puzzling even what is being asked. The norm-expressivistic analysis offered interpretations, and the interpretations will be useful if they make the questions clear, tractable, and significant.

First, why be moral? We can ask this with a particular substantive conception of morality in mind, a set of ideas of what sorts of acts are morally permissible and what not. So conceived, though, the question seems misleading. If a person rejects abiding by certain restrictions, is he challenging morality, or is he revising his idea of what morality is? Is it not part of the idea of morality that its reasons count above all others? To ask why be moral, it can seem, is just to ask what reason there is to do what one has most reason to do.

I proposed we should think the question genuine, and read it as a question about action and moral sentiments. It asks about the tie between what it makes sense to do and what it makes sense to feel about things people do. Does it ever make sense to do something one would nonetheless be to blame for having done? In other words, first, does it ever make sense to do something it also makes sense to feel guilty for having done? Second, does it ever make sense to do something it makes sense for others to feel angry at one for having done—angry from a standpoint of full, impartial engagement? Put this way, the question has to do with the shape of the moral sentiments it makes sense to have, the connection of rational action to rational moral feelings about actions.[1]

We can ask too about guilt and anger, and the fit between them. I have been assuming that guilt and anger will be governed by the same norms: the things it makes sense to feel angry about in others are the things it makes sense to feel guilty about in oneself. If it makes sense for someone to be angry at me for something, it makes sense for me to feel guilty over it. Or at least this goes for anger that is impartial. We can ask, though, why this should be so—and indeed if it is so.

Finally, I asked whether morality is of value. As I am glossing morality, there seem to be cultures that get along without it. Might we best do likewise?

I now take up these questions as a group, hoping one line of inquiry can help with them all. In this chapter, though, I can only suggest a few directions for thought. What I say will be quick and sweeping. Much of it will be familiar to moral theorists; some of it will be obvious, and most of the rest, I fear, dubious. Here and in the final chapter I want not to establish conclusions, but to illustrate how a normative inquiry might begin. Moral inquiry, I have proposed, is normative inquiry into moral sentiments. My aim now is to take a few halting

---

1. The question in this version is, roughly, whether morally required conduct is always rationally required. We could also ask whether morally required conduct is ever rationally forbidden. I have not found anything much different to say about the two questions. My formulations also ignore questions of excuse—cases where an act is wrong but the agent is not to blame.

steps at illustrating how the kind of inquiry I have pictured might proceed—how it might proceed if it is informed by the picture itself.

The Question of Guilt

Turn first to the narrowly moral sentiments, guilt and anger. Are they rightly subject to normative governance? Does it sometimes make sense to feel them and sometimes not? In part the question is pragmatic: might we do best without these particular feelings, or without norms to govern them?

One enticing vision is to replace the sanctions of narrow morality by something more endearing. Could we replace guilt and anger with love and attachment? Attempts to rely fully on these positive sentiments have failed; but perhaps we can accomplish more with good feelings than we do. Guilt and anger are costly; they can be excessive; they can crush us to no good purpose. The excesses, though, seem excesses of engagement, and not matters of feeling ways it makes no sense to feel. The mistake of overmoralizing is not like Cleopatra's mistake with the messenger. It is that we dwell on some things more than makes sense. Sometimes we are too fully engaged in misdeeds, our own and others'; we may need to treat them as water over the dam. Take, though, the acts we do contemplate with full engagement: could we get rid of costly bad feelings even for them? It seems doubtful that we could and rely on warm feelings to do enough. When love fails, bad feelings about bad things we might do can still restrain us.

If that is right, then the serious question is not whether to do without bad feelings about actions entirely, but what place to give them. Shall we treat them as governed by norms? What bad feelings about actions shall we endorse and regiment?

Guilt and anger are by no means the only such feelings. For one's own actions, I find at least these: guilt, shame, fear, disgust, embarrassment, and humiliation. All are reported in the anthropological literature. Guilt itself may be special; it looks as if many cultures ignore it.[2] Even if we do need bad feelings about one's own actions, and even if we do need norms to govern them, perhaps guilt is not the feeling to choose.

---

2. Shame cultures are an anthropological staple; see Singer (1953). Benedict (1934, chap. 6) depicts humiliation to be the dominant motivation among the Kwakiutl. Singer (1953) discusses why the anthropological data might be difficult to interpret in clear terms of "guilt" or its absence.

Among all such bad feelings, though, guilt has strong advantages.[3] Above all, it is tied to the voluntary, and it meshes in a special way with anger. Take first the tie to the voluntary. One can easily be ashamed of something one cannot help, one can fear its consequences, one can find it disgusting or embarrassing or humiliating. Can one feel guilty for having done it? Yes, of course, but there does seem to be a special strain. First, the norms we already accept tell against it; they say not to feel guilty over things we could not have helped. These norms, though, we must now treat as initial and tentative; they are what we are assessing. Even apart from norms, guilt is tied to the voluntary—or so I argued earlier, in the chapter on moral emotions. There I considered two alternative kinds of accounts of moral sentiments, and in particular of the difference between guilt and shame. One account treated guilt and shame as adaptive syndromes; the other was attributive.

On the adaptive syndrome story, guilt is tied genetically to poor cooperative will—to a special way a social being can fail to be a good candidate for inclusion in cooperative schemes. It is tied to insufficient will to play one's part in a scheme and to share its fruits—and so is anger. Anger is punitive and punishment deters; what can be deterred most directly is the voluntary. Guilt placates anger, and the threat of guilt averts acts that would evoke anger. Thus guilt too is tied to the voluntary.

On an attributive account, there is no genetic programming for guilt in particular. Rather, there is programming for broad abilities to pick up the emotional scripts one's culture provides and to play them through. The script for guilt is to be found in some cultures and not in others. Still, where it is found, what makes it a script for guilt is, in part, a tie to one's own voluntary actions. On either kind of account, then, guilt applies specially to one's own voluntary acts.

Likewise, on both accounts guilt meshes with anger. On the adaptive syndrome account, guilt evolved to mesh with anger, to prompt acts that will placate anger. On attributive theories, the mesh with anger is part of a cultural script. Both accounts, in short, tie guilt to one's own voluntary actions, and both mesh guilt with anger.

---

3. Here again, I do not distinguish guilt and remorse. Taylor (1985, 85–107) insists there is a crucial difference: that guilt is an emotion of self-assessment, whereas remorse is not. Guilt concentrates on oneself, and involves feeling disfigured by a transgression. In remorse, the thought concentrates on the deed, seen as one's own action.

Our normative question, then, is whether to elaborate norms for a bad feeling of self-assessment that has two special characteristics: it concerns one's own voluntary actions, and it meshes with anger from others. Tentatively we accept such norms, and we need to ask whether pragmatic considerations, on balance, weigh toward rethinking them.

Guilt: First Inquiries

Begin with the tie of guilt to the voluntary. The tie can mislead us: we can push questions of voluntariness beyond normal limits, asking about free will in general, or flirting with exalted standards for how directly willed an act must be to merit blame. Our normal morality has elements of strict liability; we think there can be fault in sleeping through one's alarm. Folk morality laughs away pleas of involuntariness when they get too delicate. Still, it does keep a rough tie between guilt and anger and what one could have helped. It aims these sentiments at the kinds of acts they might deter.

Now because of this, we can argue, guilt hits where it can do most good. Guilt does not always reform a person, but it does confine itself fairly well to the things he can be motivated to do or not to do. Other self-directed bad feelings—shame, fear, disgust, embarrassment, humiliation—are less discriminate.

That makes guilt an especially good candidate for norms. Norms for guilt can attach a bad feeling to things bad feelings can move us to avoid. Norms for shame, fear, disgust, embarrassment, and humiliation hit less discriminately. Take norms for shame: either they allow shame over things that would not have been different even with different motivation, or they tell the feeling to take a whole new shape. Now norms that say to reshape one's feelings radically must govern ineffectively; they set out not to channel feelings, but to work against their entire force. Normative governance is too weak for the job. Norms for guilt, on the other hand, not only can steer a bad feeling to where it will make a difference; they can do so without departing far from what already seems more or less right and acceptable to us.

Shame is not tied specially to things one could help. Of course at times what shames a person is something he could have helped—a petty action, for instance—but often not. Shame motivates in useful ways, but not by sticking to things where motivation could make a difference. Primarily it motivates ways of coping with disdain: it prompts withdrawal, deference, and willingness to accept poor terms in cooperative schemes when better terms will not be forthcoming.

Shame can also motivate a program of redemption. The things that prompt shame are often not things one can help directly, but they may be things one can attack indirectly, over a long period. Poor family, say, one cannot help, but perhaps one can compensate in time, with wealth or position. All this suggests why the lore of virtue tends to go with pride and shame rather than guilt. When bad deeds seem not momentary flaws of motivation but fruits of a character that needs rebuilding, then motivations that stem from shame may be most apt. The prospect of guilt works primarily at the moment of action. Shame motivates toward more indirect programs, whether to cope with bad motivations or with some other problem.

Back now to guilt, and its mesh with anger. Shall we elaborate norms for guilt and anger, and shall the norms be the same for both feelings? What are the pragmatic considerations?

Anger, it seems, will be with us whatever we decide. Guilt may be culturally peculiar, but anger or something close to it seems to crop up in all cultures. We need to ask two things, then: First, whether to have norms for anger—given that we will be angry at times either way, and that the consequences of anger are bound to be serious. Second, whether to have norms for a first-person emotion to mesh with anger, an emotion that prompts acts to placate anger.

A pragmatic start at an answer is now fairly clear. First, for anger: The emotion is powerful and inevitable, and it often helps regulate actions in desirable ways. Anger is subject to normative governance, to some degree. Why not, then, shape the feeling with norms, and so capture its advantages and mitigate its harms?

Next, guilt: Guilt may be culturally peculiar, and perhaps we could live without it, or our grandchildren could. Still, being capable of guilt and governing it by norms can pay. Indeed the tie of guilt to anger makes guilt an especially fine candidate for governance by norms. Guilt and anger together can help regulate social life. If norms for guilt and anger are well chosen, they will motivate people in desirable ways, and they will diminish the conflicts that can arise from anger. The prospect of rational guilt will motivate people not to do the things that will make others rationally angry. That speaks for having guilt and anger governed by the same norms, and by norms whose governance can be effective. When one person angers another, meshed norms can reconcile them—so long as the norms govern effectively. Either the norms will tell the one not to be angry, or they will tell the other to feel guilty and work to placate the anger.

Much more needs to be said, but let me suppose that guilt and anger have some place in our normative life, and that it makes sense to feel them discriminately. We still might use the term 'morality' pejoratively, for systems that make too large claims for guilt and anger. If all rational choice is supposed to be moral, if it all is to rest on guilt and anger, that is too much; the things I have been saying give no reason for wanting anything like that. My own question has been whether morality, on my narrow reading, has any part in our norms—not whether it can take over practical rationality.

The considerations I have swept through, then, bear on each of the three questions I posed at the outset. Would we be best off without morality? Would we be best off, in other words, without norms for guilt and anger? No: Meshed emotions coordinate, and norms mesh emotions. Norms for guilt and anger can do so especially well, for two reasons. First, guilt and anger are tied to the voluntary, and to motivations at the time of action. They are costly, but they work discriminately where motivation makes a difference; thus they can be cost-effective. Second, we are stuck with anger, whatever our norms. Guilt can placate anger, and norms for guilt and anger can help shape the feelings so that they mesh.

Shall our norms for guilt and anger be the same? Shall we think it makes sense to feel guilty exactly when it makes sense for others to feel angry? Pragmatic considerations stem from the things I have just been saying. A chief advantage of having norms for anger and guilt is that norms can help these emotions mesh, which fosters peace and cooperation. That requires norms that call for guilt on one's own part when they call for anger on the part of others.

Next, are moral demands always demands of reason? Or can it sometimes make real sense to do things that are morally wrong? At first glance it seems it may: we can condemn a person morally, after all, without complaining that he has been irrational. An act may be outrageous without being foolish or crazy. The question, though, is about a more full-blown rationality, one that goes beyond shrewdness. Full rationality includes good judgment of what it really makes sense to work for in life, all things considered. To judge that it fully makes sense to do a thing is, in effect, not to rule out doing it oneself, if in exactly like circumstances. Now, anger seems incoherent when joined to the thought "If I am in his shoes let me do the same." Likewise with guilt: it seems incoherent when joined to the thought "With the same opportunity, let me do it again." Anger and guilt seem indefensible at the very moment of embracing the act condemned.

So much for intuitive judgment. Quick pragmatic considerations give support—but the question will take more thought. Norms for guilt and anger work to coordinate these feelings, and that can tend to coordinate actions to the benefit of all. Our actions, though, are motivated not only by our feelings, but by the norms for action we accept. If our norms for action do not fit our norms for guilt and anger, that works against coordinated action. Norms for anger and guilt coordinate actions most effectively with help from norms for action. Allied norms for action will say not to act in ways that call for guilt and anger. They will say not to do things our norms for anger tell others to be angry over, and they will say not to do things our norms for guilt say to feel guilty over.

There is pragmatic appeal, then, to norms that mesh guilt and anger, and match action to the feelings they say to have. If these were the only pragmatic considerations, then all would support having guilt and anger governed by the same norms, and having norms for action constrained by norms for guilt and anger. Anger is inevitable, and can be steered where motivation can be most effective. Guilt is perhaps not inevitable, but it has the advantages of anger, and the advantage of meshing with inevitable anger. The pragmatic point of norms for guilt and anger is to work in an indirect, especially effective way on actions. There are strong tendencies in our prior thinking that go this way too, and so pragmatic considerations, so far, support our prior thoughts.

The Private Ruminator

I have been asking whether to elaborate norms for anger and guilt, and if so, how. What fit shall we require between norms for guilt and norms for anger? What fit shall we require between norms for these feelings and norms directly for action? The considerations I put forth were pragmatic: they concerned advantages and disadvantages of various alternatives. But whose advantage? Nothing was very precise; the standpoint I took, we might say, was one we could work toward jointly in normative discussion. In effect I took the standpoint of a psychic engineer charged with designing our norms for an advantage we recognize together.

That is not the only standpoint for pragmatic assessment. A private ruminator might have his own. His standpoint could be secret, or it might come into the open in normative discussions on which little hinges. When much does hinge, the private ruminator keeps his counsel; he must enter into the common standpoint or feign it. The common standpoint I have been taking, then, is the one we develop in most normative discussion. Still, a person may also ruminate from his private standpoint, and we need to ask if he can be satisfied.

From the standpoint of common discussion, things have worked fairly well, but the private ruminator will have doubts. His allegiance to the common standpoint is uncertain. From the common standpoint, he can see, there is much to be said for impartial norms for anger and guilt. There is much to be said for meshing norms for action with norms for anger and guilt. Still, the private ruminator will want to know whether to accept meshed, impartial norms for himself. Why not be angry whenever anger is advantageous, and avoid guilt whenever he can do so with advantage? Freed of guilt and anger when they don't help him, why not act for his own advantage apart from all consideration of guilt and anger?

Each of us at times becomes a private ruminator, more or less. He wants to settle for himself how to regard morality and the demands it makes on him. Now thinking can be good or bad, he is convinced, and he wants the conclusions that stem from good thinking—if he can settle what good thinking on the subject amounts to. He might think about good thinking, then, and look to an ideal of good private thought. Any one of us, as private ruminator, will not only start out with tentative views of what is worth seeking in life; he will start with tentative views of what makes for good private thought. He trusts informed thought over ignorant thought; he trusts consistent thought over inconsistent thought. These procedural views, and others, he might elaborate into an ideal of the private thinker, a thinker whose conclusions he could take as proxy for his own.

The private ruminator questions moral demands: is anything convincing to be said on their behalf? His question is not quite whether we could convince him, for he fears he might be taken in. He wants to decide what to think, and decide well. Equivalently, he wants to know about the ideal private thinker—call her Athena. What might we say together, on behalf of morality, to this ideal private thinker Athena? How convincing could we be?

To answer this, we need to fix the ideal. It must be an ideal that speaks to the private ruminator's puzzles. That is to say, it must speak to the puzzles each of us privately faces. What will Athena be like?

We might picture her a committed egoist. That would not speak to us, though, even in private. With us, after all, generous motives count: we prize goodwill, decency, concern, fairness; shall we reject them when our thoughts turn private? Sometimes we may, but in a sulk and with some regret. We feel put upon; we find our generous motives exploited; we wonder whether anyone else really acts on them. We act on contrary motives and then wonder if we would seriously wish to do otherwise. Generous motives count with us, but other motives compete. We want to know how to adjudicate, and whether to throw one set of motives out of court.

The task the private ruminator sets, then, is not to convert the thorough egoist by force of reasons even he must recognize. That would be a neat trick, but it would speak only to one important side of us. We do not start out blithely wanting to take on the mentality of a con man, a man who feigns morality and exploits it, but feels no moral pull himself. We do start out wanting things moral scruples might keep us from getting. We feel both the pull of egoism and the pull of goodwill, decency, concern, and fairness.

To address the private ruminator we address ourselves. We do not address a pure, committed egoist. The selves we address, though, are full of suspicion. They are in a specially wary mood. We need to identify the suspicions and construct an ideal of private thought that speaks to them. The private ruminator suspects that when he responds to moral demands, he is being taken in. He is too much subject to persuasion, to the pressures of others who gain from his moral commitment. Athena the ideal private thinker, then, will be someone who could not be taken in in this way.

Call the private ruminator Thrasymachus, or Sym for short. How does Sym think he might be taken in? The morality that he eyes with suspicion, after all, is not an arbitrary one—so we are supposing. It is one he can embrace from a standpoint we develop together. Now, from that public standpoint we do not lack information. We do not lack sensitivity. What could be wrong?

Sym's suspicion must be that he has been too much taken up with the public standpoint. He cannot defend himself adequately against demands others place on him. A striking feature of public discussion is its conversational demands. In discussion we accede to each other's influence. Sym's suspicion is against the standpoint we thereby forge together. His charge turns out to be one of undue influence. In his suspicions, he thinks he responds too much to the interests of others—more than makes sense.

What ideal speaks to this suspicion? Athena must, among other things, be shielded from the force of conversational demands. Glad she may be that people make demands and others respond—morality depends on that, and their morality protects her. She responds to no such demands herself, though. Or if she needs conversation to keep her bearings, it is the chat of a bull session: those who place conversational demands on her are not those who stand to benefit from her moral commitments. Their standpoint is hers. Sym, after all, suspects undue influence from others on their behalf, and so an ideal that speaks to his doubts might be a thinker on whom no self-serving conversational demands are placed. In his suspicious, private frame of mind, Sym is going to want to make sure that Athena's conditions are free of conversational influence on behalf of anyone else.

In short, we address a private ruminator Sym, who is social but ambivalent, and we develop an ideal private thinker, Athena, whom he can trust. To Athena we can put considerations of fairness, decency, and welfare, but we put them pallidly, without the conversational demands that bombard Sym. Sym, after all, suspects he is being taken in. Part of what he suspects may be that he isn't considering everything there is to consider. Another part of his suspicion, though, will be that he is too exposed to influences on behalf of others, that if he learned to defend himself from these influences he would change his commitments. In many ways, then, ideal private thinking will be like ideal thinking together, but in one crucial way it will be different: Athena does not face conversational demands from anyone specially attached to the interests of others. She is cut off from their social influence. What Sym wants to know is this: would he accede to moral demands if he saw things clearly, uninfluenced by conversational demands others make on their own behalf?

Imperious and Diffident Moralities

How will Athena treat moral demands? That must depend on what those demands are. Moral demands are demands we might work toward in normative discussion together. They are demands to be backed by guilt and anger, with these feelings in turn governed by norms—the norms we would come to accept in ideal discussion. The discussion, I have been supposing, would look to goods that norms can achieve. It would respond to the ways common acceptance of norms can foster good things, things worth wanting from a standpoint we develop together.

How, then, design a morality to foster good things? First we need to know our powers; the good designer knows what he can manage and what he cannot. Can we decree together how everyone shall act? Little good that might do; decrees do not work by magic. Our hopes from morality must rest on the ways norms can get their hold on us and affect what we do. We need to decide together not what to have people do, but what norms to instill. The norms will then have to prod on their own. The demands of morality, we can say, are the ones we would want morality to make if we kept in mind both the strength of moral motivation and its limitations.[4]

Not everything norms say to do gets done. Not every norm once accepted stays accepted. As designers of norms, then, we must look to stratagems. We must think how to get norms to elicit the actions we want, expecting that not all is possible.

At one extreme we might be imperious in our stratagems. Knowing we cannot have all we want, we might demand far more than we think we shall get—in hopes that that is the way to get as much as we can. At another extreme we might be diffident: we might trim our moral demands to what, for the most part, we think we can get. Our stratagems as moral inventors may be more or less imperious, more or less diffident.

Suppose we demand that the rich give the bulk of their wealth to the poor. As a purely moral demand, that would be imperious. Even if the rich accept that they ought to give up their wealth, few of them will. Absent coercive enforcement, mere norms for guilt and anger make for too little motivation. Suppose, on the other hand, we demand that people not steal, and we back this moral demand with substantial legal enforcement. That demand might well be fairly diffident. Even

---

4. Rule utilitarians try to make this vague dictum more precise; see especially Brandt (1963; 1979, part 2, esp. chap. 10). Hare pursues the dictum, in effect, with his treatment of "intuitive level" morality (1981, part 1, esp. chap. 3). Brandt and Hare are both utilitarians, but the spirit of the dictum guides some non-utilitarian treatments as well. Rawls assesses principles of justice for the appeal they would have to parties behind a veil of ignorance. The parties try to advance a broad set of interests, and they choose in light of general knowledge of the ways public acceptance of principles of justice can motivate, and of limitations in the ways it can motivate. See especially Rawls (1971, chap. 8).

when someone thinks he could get away with stealing, so long as he is not desperate the moral norms he accepts may swing the balance. There may be sufficient other motivation not to steal that it plus moral motivation prevails. Imperious demands take on strong contrary motives, and take them on unaided. Diffident moral demands prevail with the help of other motives. The social designer can choose to be imperious or diffident, and to what degree.

Perhaps on this choice will hang Athena's response to morality. Take first imperious design. Imperious norms may be hard to accept, privately. Even if instilled, they will be widely violated—that is what earned them the label imperious. Athena may well find some of these violations rational. The demands may be more than she finds it makes sense fully to grant.

As designers, we chose the imperious strategy—so I am imagining. We chose imperious moral norms to instill in ourselves. Inevitably from the common standpoint, we want more from morality than we could get. Morality places demands on each of us for the sake of each other, and it backs these demands with norms for anger and guilt. We are imperious designers if we demand, in this way, everything we want done. We proceed as if our demands would be obeyed whatever they were. Of course we know they will not be, but we demand all to get as much as we can. We direct guilt and anger toward everything we wish, from a common standpoint, that all of us would shun. Much, we realize as designers, we agents will go on doing despite the moral norms we come to accept together. Pelting actions with norms for anger and guilt, we have aimed farther than we could expect to throw, in order to throw as far as we could.

What, though, when public discussant turns private ruminator? Can he still say yes to imperious morality? Athena the ideal private thinker is, as I have said, a social being. She feels the pull of goodwill, of decency, of concern for others. Still, as she eyes the demands of morality, she will have private reservations. She wants things for herself, sometimes intensely. Imperious morality says to give some of them up. In a way, to be sure, it caters to her wants marvelously. Though it makes strong demands on her for the sake of others, it also makes strong demands on others for her own sake. Unless her position is unusual, she profits on the whole if all the demands are met. She profits still more, though, if she can have it both ways: if others meet moral demands for her sake, but she herself evades some moral demands. Sometimes this trick will be hard to bring off without reprisal—but sometimes not. Her sense of fairness may tell against the attempt, but then she has to decide how much else it makes sense to give up for the sake of being fair.

In any case, fairness does not tell for imperious moral demands; it tells against them. Imperious morality asks more than it thinks it can get. If Athena alone gives it all it asks, she takes on an unfair share of morality's burdens. She may accept demands of fair reciprocity, and still ask herself how much there is to reciprocate (see Rawls 1971, 242, and sec. 76).

In short, then: With an imperious morality, it would be good for all of us if all its demands were met. For each of us it would be better still if everyone else met the demands, while he himself evaded some of them. Unavoidably, if we instill an imperious morality in ourselves, we end up evading a large bulk of its demands. Now as discussants together, I am supposing, we come nevertheless to accept an imperious morality. We conclude that its somewhat ineffectual hectoring still works better than the alternatives—works better to promote things we recognize together as good. We accept together imperious norms for guilt, for anger, and for action. As private ruminators we each then review matters. Can I accept in private the demands I accept when we work things through together? And here I may balk. The demands are great. I care about others, and I care about doing my part, but shall I care that much? Even if I am drawn by an ideal of moral heroism, I am drawn by other things too, and I may conclude in the end that it makes more sense to pursue those other things. Then too, even if I stand fiercely determined to do my part if others do, I know others won't. The imperious morality draws my allegiance, but other things work to subvert it. I try to decide what norms to accept privately, for myself, and I may decide that often it just doesn't make sense to accede to the imperious demands of morality—even if others do, and in any case they won't.

Diffident Moral Design

With diffident moral design, the chances of drawing Sym along look stronger. As diffident planners, recall, we try for crafty schemes. We moderate the demands of morality to a point where they might be effective, where those demands will be met for the most part. We take care not to leave morality to fend for itself against strong opposition. We seek allies; we look to other motivations to reinforce the proddings of narrow morality. Whenever strong motives are in play, our morality works to channel and coordinate them, not to push against their full weight. Diffident morality coordinates exchange; it coordinates bargaining; it coordinates enforcement. Where allies for morality are not to be found, it cautiously withdraws.

A diffident morality may still be socially imperious. It may make strong demands with strong social enforcement. It is diffident only in that it does not rely too heavily on internal moral motivation. That way it keeps from being subverted by disuse; its demands are widely met. Morality is not made to be its own reward; rather it coordinates effective approval and disapproval, tied perhaps to a stringent scheme of social enforcement.

Where will that leave Athena? A diffident morality is advantageous on the whole, at least when stakes are high. It appeals to her generous motives, just as does imperious morality, and it also draws strength from the benefits of keeping on friendly terms with others—commanding their respect, goodwill, and cooperation. It helps one stay out of trouble. It is mostly to Athena's advantage, then, not only for others to act on morality's demands, but for her to do so too.

Still, the coincidence of morality and advantage will not be perfect. And even if it were, we can still ask, would being moral for the sake of advantage really be accepting moral demands? How does a diffident morality go beyond sheer egoism?

In the first place, generous motives count in the kind of morality Athena will accept. To be an ideal for us, Athena must be a full human being leading a human life. She thinks privately, but she is also part of a normative community. She feels the appeal of a jointly recognized good; she supports the things morality is to foster. The morality is hers as well as ours: it strikes her as right and proper, it promotes things she wants for herself and for others. Because its demands are reciprocal, it draws support from her sense of fair reciprocity. She is an intensely social being, and she accepts moral demands partly out of generous motives. A diffident morality can call on these motives; what makes it diffident is that it does not call on them for radically more than they can accomplish. Athena can accept diffident moral demands in part out of decency, goodwill, concern for others, and a sense of fairness. The content of the demands need not be fully egoistic, and still Athena may well accept them.

At the same time, of course, she has other concerns. In resolving her ambivalence between generous concerns and these others, she will be immune to conversational demands. She will be immune to influence from others who benefit when she acceeds to moral demands. Her allegiance to a diffident morality is bolstered by a fair parallel between moral demands and her own advantage. Moral decency often pays, after all. One might, then, take up cold, self-interested calculation about when acts of moral decency will pay. Calculation, though, is a taxing motive and a flimsy one too at times, when vivid temptations compete. Even assessed egoistically, moral motives may be cheaper and more reliable than cold, self-interested calculation (see Frank, 1988). That will matter to Athena.

Suppose this were all that mattered to her. Suppose her generous motives played no part. She might still want herself to accept diffident moral demands as moral demands. She might want herself to care about the demands themselves and their moral basis, not just to find it convenient to comply. The diffident morality makes many demands one would want to comply with apart from any moral concern. Moral concern will often be the most reliable motive promoting self-interest. To have moral concern, though, is not to be purely self-interested. An intrinsic concern for morality is useful from other points of view. Even if Athena is egoistic, she may want herself not to be.

How does this matter to the private ruminator? Sym the private ruminator is not a pure egoist; he is ambivalent and suspicious. His generous motives support morality, but he suspects them. If allegiance to morality is the best way to promote his more egoistic goals, then his ambivalence is resolved. With an imperious morality this is unlikely; with diffident morality, it seems more plausible. If a diffident morality has enough egoistic appeal, that will resolve Sym's ambivalence. He wondered whether his generous motives would survive the right kind of scrutiny. Egoism tells him to want to be as he is, generous motives and all.

Morality traditionally demands more than that one accede to reasonable terms when one is being watched and sanctioned. It pictures the grandeur of genuine sacrifice; it appeals to heroism. More to the everyday point, it appeals to goodwill, friendly feelings, decency. These are all things that matter to Sym. Other things matter to him too, though, and so the worry is what will happen in his private ruminations if these other things clash head-on with goodwill, fellowship, decency and the like. With a diffident morality, the clash might be largely averted.

Not that I have shown it would be. What makes a morality diffident is that it allies itself with enough other motives to prevail, for the most part—to prevail with actual people, with all their jointness and separateness, with their normative motivations and their appetites, feelings, impulses, and yearnings. Athena the ideal private thinker is not us. First, she is stripped of some of her sociability: she is unresponsive to conversational demands on behalf of others. Second, her motivations work only through norms. She differs from us in both these ways, and there is no guarantee that a morality that prevails with us, for the most part, will prevail with her. Whether it does is a complex question, largely socio-psychological. There are reasons, though, for thinking that a diffident morality might do fairly well with her.

That still does not tell us whether, in discussion together, to go for a morality at the diffident end of the spectrum. Imperious morality might still be the best strategy of moral design. If, though, Athena would reject such a morality, that is cause for worry. It means that imperious morality cannot withstand the scrutiny of ideal private thought. What hold can it have on us, then? In our everyday reactions to life, to be sure, we are not controlled by anything close to ideal private thought: our thought is neither ideal nor private. Perhaps, then, it will not matter greatly if morality fails with Athena; it may still keep enough of our own allegiance to serve. Still, in that case, the morality will suffer a special kind of instability. Not only will its strictures be widely violated—we already knew that, and as social engineers we made allowances. In addition it fails a kind of scrutiny that is bound to have a pull on us. The grip of the morality will depend, if not on things we consider defects in our thought, then on the power of conversational demands by which we support it in each other. If we choose an imperious morality, we pin our hopes on our mutual influence. We hope our conversational demands can keep us each from slipping too far into private thought.

I have not shown either that an imperious morality fails with Athena, or that if it does, it must lose its hold on us. Nor have I shown that a diffident morality can succeed with Athena. Rough considerations suggest, though, that matters tend in these directions, and that supports diffidence in moral design. Where morality places heavy burdens, it must mobilize strong social monitoring and control. Then, we can hope, the intrinsic moral motivations it invokes will bear private scrutiny.

17 · Moral System

Narrowly moral inquiry is only one kind of normative inquiry. Some say we should do without it, and live together on the basis not of moral norms but of norms of other kinds. In the last chapter I championed morality: I spoke from a point of view we develop together, and found virtue in meshed norms for guilt, anger, and action. I then confronted Sym the private ruminator.

Now as I worried over Sym, I spoke as though it were clear enough how to think when we think together. I spoke as if when we discuss morality with each other, it is clear enough what considerations to weigh. I worried about private allegiance to these public conclusions, but I spoke as if the public conclusions themselves might be unproblematical. Moralities, I assumed, will be assessed by how they promote the good, and this good is to be understood from a standpoint we work to together.

Notoriously, though, the good and the right both draw controversy. Philosophers dispute what things are intrinsically good, and they dispute too whether that is the best first question to ask. Some think it is, that morality depends at base on what is good and what is bad. Still, these philosophers argue delicate questions of what the dependence is. Others reject starting with the good at all, and try to ground right and wrong independently of the good.[1]

Of course, none of these controversies could be settled by a sweep

---

1. The dispute is whether to start with goods other than morally good character: intrinsically good experiences, and perhaps such things as knowledge as well. Utilitarians like Mill, Sidgwick, and Brandt want to. Kant (1785) insists that morally good character is the place to start. He starts out arguing that the only thing good in itself, without qualification, is a good will—a morally good will, it turns out. Others, like Prichard (1912) and Ross (1930), start not with good of any kind but with duty. They argue that duties are of many kinds, and there is no one relation to the good that all duties share.

of the hand or a sharp argumentative blow. In this book I have steered clear of trying to settle them at all: I have not asked what makes some acts right and others wrong. I have asked what moral inquiry is, but not much engaged in it. Still, various things I have said suggest ways controversies over these questions might go. How will moral inquiry look if it is what I say it is?

At its most grandiose, the question would be just this: Suppose we managed to conduct our moral inquiries ideally. What conclusions would we reach? I start the chapter by taking this grand question and trying to get clear what it means. It is not a pure question of where moral inquiry does lead in psycho-social fact, but where it would lead at its best. I ask how a norm-expressivist would understand the question, and I ask too how the facts—of human psychology and group dynamics especially—bear on it.

For the rest of the chapter, I steer clear of facing the grand question directly, and ask instead about the form answers to it might take. Moral philosophers tend to press toward moral system. The forces that push us toward system are at work in everyday moral discussion, but so are other forces that might push us away. If philosophers pursue system with a special relentlessness, is that a good thing to do? How should a norm-expressivist look on hopes for system? Could we expect his moral inquiries to look like moral theorizing as philosophers have practiced it?

It seems not. An expressivist does not think there is a realm of moral facts that might turn out to be systematic. Morality is not like physics. Instead, I have insisted, moral inquiry consists in deciding what norms to accept as governing moral sentiments—and also how norms for moral sentiments are to bear on norms for action. Now this means according some authority to our broadly moral sentiments and to other sources of moral concern. These sources of moral concern, though, offer uncertain guidance. Some, like fairness and respect, are open to reworking: the social arrangements they latch onto will depend in part on what is familiar, and on what people around us say and how they react. Different views of a problem will give rise to different feelings about it. One feeling may compete with another. From all this, can we expect anything to emerge bearing a comprehensive and unified rationale?

I try to say why, even so, a moral system might be well worth trying to get. Moral philosophers have worked to see how system might be attempted, and devised tools and methods; many of these should work just as well in a norm-expressivist's hands. I worry about coping if, nevertheless, system is not to be had. My overall claim is that in the picture of morality I have been patching together, we can see the point in familiar philosophers' practices. We can see the point in devices philosophers have found for pressing their moral inquiries, and we can see the point in familiar worries too.

Ideal Moral Inquiry

Moral inquiry is a kind of normative discussion, voiced or ruminated. Part of this book has been a rough tale of how normative discussion works—a theory of normative discussion as part of nature. I spoke of mutual influence and demands for consistency. There must be more, though, to how we come to see certain norms as plausible and others not. Influence and consistency alone might lead us to agree on any consistent set of norms whatsoever, helpful or baleful. Other things must play on our receptivity to norms; otherwise our normative capacities would never have been adaptive. I had some vague suggestions of what these other things might be. Partly our judgments respond to wants and advantages. Perhaps we innately see things particular ways, though it appears these ways are sensitive to the way a case is presented. Partly, too, our normative judgments respond to feelings—feelings that are themselves adaptively shaped.

Narrow morality consists in norms for guilt and anger, or so I have proposed. The shapes these feelings take play back on our norms for the feelings: feeling angry about something, we tend to think it makes sense to feel angry about such things. Gains and losses too help settle which norms for guilt and anger will strike us as plausible. In addition, a variety of other feelings will bear on our norms for the narrowly moral feelings, and I tried listing some of them: concern for others, pride, shame, respect, moral inspiration, a sense of one's own moral value, along with reciprocal sentiments of obligation, gratitude, and rancor. These broadly moral feelings may affect which norms we find plausible for guilt and anger. We begin hard moral inquiry with many kinds of concerns; we start out responsive to diverse feelings—and a naturalistic view of people explains why that should be. All these concerns and feelings will play on which moral norms seem plausible to us.

Now I might try going on to elaborate all this, observing how moral inquiry goes and explaining why it would for beings like us. Another question, though, is how moral inquiry would go at its best. What kinds of inquiry shall we trust, and how would such inquiries come out?

These questions are normative in part; they are not questions of psycho-social fact alone. What properties of a moral inquiry would constitute its being ideal? To ask that is to ask what norms to accept for moral inquiry, and for accepting moral judgments on authority. How would ideal moral inquiry go, and what would be its results? This question has two sides. One is the purely normative question of a moment ago: what constitutes ideal normative inquiry? The other side depends on what we are like: given some particular account of what constitutes ideal moral inquiry, how will such an inquiry go? What would we think if we had engaged in moral inquiry of this kind? When we ask how ideal moral inquiry would come out, the answer depends not only on the dynamics of moral inquiry, but also on the properties that would make an inquiry ideal. This last is a normative matter.

Does this question—how moral inquiry would come out if ideally conducted—have determinate meaning? We know what would be sufficient for accepting an answer: First, accept norms that say to rely on inquiries with such-and-such features. Second, have a view as to how inquiries with those features would come out. In Chapter 5, I worked to a more elaborate way of saying what the question is.[2]

Still, on what facts does the right answer hinge? Here there is nothing to say that everyone must accept—must accept, that is, on pain of mistake in logic or meaning. That is how it is with any normative question: its meaning does not by itself determine how facts would settle it. To come to a view on what facts would settle it is, at least in part, to decide what norms to accept. We start not with rules of meaning that settle, all by themselves, what counts as better or worse positions for moral judgment; we start with tentative opinions. We sharpen our answers not only by sharpening our meanings, but also by sharpening our epistemic norms. The views we start with fall well short of a full system of moral epistemology, a full doctrine of what constitutes ideal

---

2. Take the question "Is there a unique set of moral norms that would emerge from ideal inquiry?" We explain it by explaining what would constitute accepting that there is—a state of factual-normative belief. We explain the state by saying what factual-normative possibilities it rules out. It rules out all pairs of norms and facts with this feature: the norms include norms for accepting or rejecting moral norms, and those norms, as applied to the facts, either permit definitely accepting more than one incompatible set of moral norms, or forbid accepting any set of moral norms whatsoever.

moral judgment. Still, we can begin with our tentative opinions and work to improve them.

In saying this last, I assume a normative judgment, a judgment of authority. I accord authority to moral inquiries that, as with Neurath's boat, start from our tentative judgments and advance from there. That suggests a program of investigation: Take our initial views of what constitutes trustworthy moral inquiry. Add our best theory of the influences that shape moral inquiry, the things that help determine which moral norms will strike us as plausible. Then ask where these influences would lead in ideal conditions.

Proceeding this way might help with central controversies of moral theory. It might help with the bearing of good on right and wrong; the question now becomes how gains and losses would affect our thoughts if our moral inquiry were at its best. Thinking this way might help too with feelings, with how feelings bear on right and wrong if they do. The question becomes how feelings would affect moral thinking at its best. Asking these questions might let us bring positive social theory— a theory of the psycho-social dynamics of normative inquiry—to bear on normative quandaries.[3]

Such a program, of course, comes with no advance guarantee. Perhaps the questions it raises are less tractable than the questions it was meant to help resolve. Perhaps if we saw where seemingly ideal inquiry leads, we would change our minds about what makes inquiry ideal. In any case, if such a method works it must work slowly, with painstaking effort along many lines.

Let me now take stock. In earlier chapters I developed a picture of how moral inquiry actually works, and of what moral judgments amount to. This chapter looks at how moral inquiry might go ideally. I have tried to say what this question is, and how the facts bear on it— especially the facts of psychology and the group dynamics of moral inquiry. On a view I reject, rules of meaning settle what counts as ideal moral inquiry, or they would if they were precise and complete. Instead, I am saying, we start with opinions, and these tentative opin-

3. We might try reframing some of Brandt's views in terms of this un-Brandtian psychology and metaethics (Brandt 1979). The ideal position for normative judgment, on this reframed view, is one in which one has undergone cognitive psychotherapy, and accepts norms that endorse whatever desires one then has arrived at. Rational desires, it follows, are the desires one would have after cognitive psychotherapy. We can figure out which desires are rational even without undergoing cognitive psychotherapy, then, if we know enough psychology to know what the results of cognitive psychotherapy would be.

ions are not only matters of meaning. They include rough thoughts on what kinds of moral inquiry are to be trusted. Now, one thing we can do is just start with these opinions and proceed, with a special philosophical determination. To sail in Neurath's boat is to place some trust in the outcome. Another possibility is a more self-conscious investigation, an inquiry that exploits the facts of our moral proclivities. We can think what would constitute ideal moral inquiry, and develop a socio-psychological theory of its dynamics. I try neither kind of project here, but I do take a glance at versions of the first. Can we hope to sail Neurath's boat into a port of moral system?

The Value of System

Broadly moral feelings of many kinds affect which moral judgments we find plausible, and conflicting possible standards guide these feelings. The pressures may work differently on different people. How would sources of moral concern work themselves out if we conducted our inquiries ideally?

More specifically, moral philosophers (or some of them) take system as their aim, and I am asking whether a norm-expressivist should share these aspirations. Partly these aspirations are to consistency, and partly to objectivity. I have explored at length what marks of objectivity a norm-expressivist can recognize. Still, part of the aspiration goes further, to finding a deep background rationale. Systematizers look for the point behind everyday moral convictions, a point that could be invoked to criticize and correct those convictions. Now a background rationale is partly itself a matter of consistency and objectivity; it can serve as a device for achieving them. It can tell us what to do when precepts clash. It might help us achieve the interpersonality that is one of the chief marks of objectivity. We can try to use it as a basis for agreement; we can appeal to it, with some hope, to ground widespread conversational demands. Yet, the drive to a unified background rationale is more: the goal is a kind of normative understanding, a unified, comprehensive vision of how, normatively, things fit together.

We should want all these things if we can get them. Consistency and objectivity I have already praised: Global consistency steers us around pitfalls that local demands for consistency can lead us into. Claims to objectivity—not perfect objectivity, but parochiality over the widest parish—help toward consensus, at least if a person stands ready to revise his judgments to make his claims defensible. Would the rest of finding an articulated, comprehensive background rationale for morality have value too? Consistency and objectivity are important and hard to attain, and a systematic rationale could foster them. Do we have further reasons, though, to press for system?

We reason with norms, and part of reasoning is to look for reasons. Reasons give out at some point, but not too soon or we are not fully thinking. To think normatively is to be drawn toward accepting norms for reasons, reasons that we can accept fully as reasons. This matters to us for its own sake, and our very proclivity to think normatively makes us into beings for whom it would. We are creatures who ask why, with norms as in other domains. We want to take morality not blindly as a set of taboos but as something with a point—or perhaps with more than one point, but then we want to think out what those points might have to do with each other and how to reconcile them.

The goods of system are real goods, then, and a norm-expressivist will so regard them. They are special goods; they connect in a special way with our thinking normatively at all. Still, they are goods among others. The costs of going for system, along with dim prospects for getting one, can sour us. How might we hope to get a system worth wanting without giving up too much? How could we press for a systematic resolution of the many pressures on our judgment? With two prongs, I said earlier: general philosophic refinement of our norms, and the search for a pragmatic rationale. The same two prongs help us work toward the marks of objectivity, if the refinement of norms works across a broad enough community. They help us work toward deeper rationales.

Some classic moral inquiries employ such a strategy, and we can look to them to glimpse how, in the face of diverse and changing pressures on our judgments, moral thinking might be systematized or resist system.

Debunking and Reconciling

Sidgwick in his great treatise *The Methods of Ethics* shows some of the chief ways moral inquiry might go. At times he debunked, at times he reconciled, and at one crucial point he retrenched. He debunked when he found that a source of moral concern yielded no systematic rationale that could withstand scrutiny. To a large degree, though, he thought he could reconcile diverse moral impulses: he found that one source of moral concern provides a rationale for the shape of others. The morality of common sense expresses a diversity of moral impulses and adjudicates among them, but in a way that is unconsciously utilitarian. Considerations of benevolence settle conflicts among the other moral impulses. On one point, finally, Sidgwick had to retrench in his claims for practical reason. He found practical reason ambivalent between egoism and universal benevolence, unable to declare for one or for the other. As we pursue moral inquiry we should be prepared for elements of all these kinds: debunking, reconciliation, and retrenchment.

Sidgwick's own inquiry was intuitionistic: his question was whether we might be able to discern the normative facts, to see the truth of moral axioms. We could reinterpret his investigation, though, in norm-expressivistic terms. Are claims to moral objectivity tenable? If we could pursue our moral inquiries in the best way, what marks of objectivity would our moral judgments bear? How close would we get to a systematic, comprehensive background rationale for our moral judgments?

Sidgwick recognized diverse moral impulses that seemed to carry their separate rationales. Many of these he debunked. He looked at justice and fidelity; he examined honesty, prudence, purity, courage, humility. He debunked not these virtues, but pretensions that any of them might yield genuine moral axioms. These impulses seem to carry implicit rationales, and we might hope to elaborate their rationales into fundamental moral principles. Sidgwick tried, and found that he had failed. Each rationale, he concluded, yields rough maxims useful for daily guidance. For a maxim to serve as an axiom, though, it must pass severe tests. It must be stated clearly and precisely. So stated it must still be self-evident, to oneself and to others. The principles that pass these tests must be consistent with each other (Sidgwick 1907, 3.11.2, pp. 338–343). Suppose, then, we try to sharpen the maxims of common sense, and qualify them to make them consistent with each other. The precise, well-qualified principles we develop, Sidgwick argued, are then no longer self-evident. They no longer draw universal assent. To vague maxims everyone may agree with confidence, but we do not know how to move from there to agreement in detail.

Sidgwick held that moral thought must rest on intuitions, and so he set up tests for telling real intuitions from bogus. His four tests for moral axioms were that the principle be precisely formulated, self-evident in its precise formulation, accepted by the experts, and consistent with other principles that equally pass the first three tests. I say instead that moral thought consists in pondering what norms to accept. Still Sidgwick's tests apply. Self-evidence, to some degree, is inescapably a part of accepting norms. In so far as a norm is accepted not entirely on the basis of other things one accepts, one finds it self-evident. Clarity and precision help us apply norms to cases, and help us agree with each other on how the norms apply. We work toward them as part of meeting demands for consistency. Like things go for consistency among principles: demands for consistency help push us toward consensus, and with inconsistent principles we get different answers for the same case. Agreement, finally, is required if norms are to coordinate. Sidgwick's discussion is no ordinary moral discussion, but the pressures his tests embody figure in normal discussion too. Failing his tests can make for trouble: when moral thought fails one of the tests, that points to ways the thought can be undermined.

Now, debunking might lead in either of two directions: to a larger synthesis that reconciles different sources of moral concern, or to despair of treating morality as a genuine subject matter. For the most part, Sidgwick thought, the various sources of moral concern could be reconciled. Each in its place, modestly understood, has a rationale in terms of the good it promotes—where the ultimate good, Sidgwick argued, is pleasure. He debunked claims that each source of moral concern can be given its own rationale, coherent and independent. Each in its place, though, he argued, draws a rationale from a single source of moral concern, universal benevolence. The proper shape of each moral impulse is given by a single rationale.

Hopes for reconciliation have been prime drivers in moral philosophy. Think of Mill on justice. An essential ingredient of the sentiment of justice, Mill maintained, is the desire to punish, "the natural feeling of retaliation or vengeance." In itself, however, this sentiment of retaliation is nonmoral. "What is moral is, the exclusive subordination of it to the social sympathies, so as to wait on and obey their call" (Mill 1863, chap. 5, para. 21; see paras. 16–23). The sentiment of vengeance is thus trimmed of some of its claims and reconciled to the social sympathies.

Not only utilitarians debunk and then reconcile. Kant did too. All moral motivations that withstand scrutiny, he thought, can be boiled down to one: respect for the law, the law one gives oneself. Again, other sources of moral concern must be trimmed of some of their claims. Once they are, though, they become moral; they can be reconciled with respect for the law.[4]

Mill and Kant pick different feelings as basic to morality, but there is something in common to the structure of their treatment of moral concerns. Many impulses we discover we cannot trust as moral guides on their own. Still, in their place, they turn out to be endorsed by moral principles. They need some trimming, some debunking, and then they can be reconciled. That is how we can picture many philosophical treatments of the varied sources of concern with morality.

Retrenchment

Sidgwick thought that in the end his project had failed. Two different sources of practical concern each withstood scrutiny, and he had not fully reconciled them. "Even if a man admits the self-evidence of the principle of Rational Benevolence, he may still hold that his own happiness is an end which it is irrational for him to sacrifice to any other; and that therefore a harmony between the maxim of Prudence and the maxim of Rational Benevolence must be somehow demonstrated, if morality is to be made completely rational" (1907, 498). We can observe that prudence and benevolence do sometimes clash in this life; whether we can demonstrate them to be harmonized in a next life Sidgwick leaves open. At the very least, he thinks, it is a serious possibility that we must retrench on our claims for practical reason.

Sidgwick's project is not mine, but the upshots of the two might be alike. Sidgwick looked at practical reason in general, not at morality narrowly glossed. Still, narrowly moral inquiry too might end in retrenchment—perhaps in retrenchment far greater than Sidgwick's. Then too, Sidgwick treated what he was doing as a test of claims for a power of intuition. He tested the claim that we can see the truth of certain normative facts, much as we can see the truth of certain geometrical facts. I take the question to be different: how far would pressures toward system be accommodated in ideal moral inquiry? Still, my answer might have to be like Sidgwick's or worse. We may find there are severe limits to the power of reason in morality.

4. One might see Kant as simply debunking the claims of sympathy (1785, esp. 398, 442, 454), but he does think that sympathy is needed (423, 454), that it deserves praise and encouragement when properly directed (398), and that moral systems based on sympathy have some of the virtues of true morality (442).

I have already claimed that there must be some limits: that at best we can hope our judgments will be parochial over a wide parish. Inevitably our moral judgments fail an extreme version of Sidgwick's fourth test, consensus of the experts. Much more could go wrong, though. We might find that the moral precepts of common sense are incoherent, as Sidgwick argues, and still not find the deeper principles that will trim them and reconcile them—not discover principles that strike us as evident, as we put ourselves in what we think a better and better position to judge. We may confront inconsistencies in our thinking, and be pulled in different directions as we try to correct them. The choice among consistent systems may not become clearer as we proceed. Then too, even if each of us thinks he has got things right, we may find we do not agree, and that still we cannot brand each other incompetent judges.

Recent philosophical writings, indeed, have sharply questioned hopes for moral system. Perhaps no full system will suit us. Perhaps no systematic reconciliation supports our moral views, either as they are or as the best inquiry would make them. We must then learn to press our moral inquiries with more restricted aspirations. This recent discussion has not, of course, been norm-expressivistic—not overtly, at least—and it has a richness I must ignore. Still, I have been asking how moral inquiry looks if we see it norm-expressivistically. I have been saying why it tends toward system, and why it might not get there. We can see why to expect everyday consensus, more or less, but not why to expect agreement on a set of theoretical underpinnings and their consequences. Above all, we cannot see why to expect the kind of agreement that would bring different communities together.[5]

5. Prominent writings in this vein are Baier (1985, essays 11–13) and perhaps Williams (1985, esp. chaps. 5–6). Williams works to reach "an outlook that embodies a skepticism about philosophical ethics, but a skepticism that is more about philosophy than it is about ethics" (74). He attacks the search for an "ethical theory", which he defines as "a theoretical account of what ethical thought and practice are, which account either implies a general test for the correctness of basic ethical beliefs and principles or else implies that there cannot be such a test" (72). This he distinguishes from "a theory about the nature of ethical thought that *leaves open* the question of whether there could be such tests." His own account is of that kind; according to it, "there may be tests in some cultural circumstances and not in others". In the right circumstances "we can think in ethics," but "philosophy can do little to determine how we should do so" (74). (To my own eye, at least, that still leaves philosophy a big job: coming up with a theory of the culture-dependence of correct ethical thinking, explaining how the ways we *should* think in ethics are determined by our cultural circumstances. Williams may be proposing such a theory, especially in chaps. 9–10; I myself speak to it most in Chapter 11.) Is a "moral system" in my sense, then, part of an "ethical theory" in Williams's? Perhaps not,

Suppose all this is so: that we become convinced there is no such thing as the moral system we would accept if we inquired ideally. To give up system is not in itself to lose moral seriousness. We can still hold deep convictions and act on them. Consider torture as an obvious example. Extreme circumstances may puzzle us, but for ordinary cases, it is much more clear that torture is wrong than anything about moral system will ever be. Clearly it is wrong, to say the least, to torture people for amusement, or for revenge. We will not give up these claims because of the way a philosophical project is going. By the same token, though, a firm conviction that some things are right and others wrong is not enough to keep us from being skeptics of a kind. We can still doubt that ideal inquiry would lead to coherent moral system, a system with the marks of objectivity. We can doubt that the wrongness of torture is part of a comprehensive and satisfactory way of understanding the world normatively. If we can doubt the prospects of moral system and stick to our moral convictions, it follows, trivially indeed, that we can embrace clear moral truths and reject system.

Still—and here is the chief point—renouncing system limits the ways we can hope to discuss moral issues, and the difficulties are not just for philosophers. Ordinary moral thought mimics correspondence to moral facts, and that serves purposes it makes sense to want served. We are well prepared for debunking with reconciliation; we are not well prepared to retrench.

If nonetheless we must, discursive life goes on mostly as before. We already know we live with inconsistency, disagreement, and moral myopia. Quarrels can kill, and whether they do depends on many things—but never on the full success of a grand philosophical project. Philosophical failure means pitfalls for ordinary discussion, as I keep saying, and in morals we cannot give up discussion without great cost. We do have ways of coping, though, other than by resolving everything; we develop some skill in keeping clear of the pitfalls. If we must retrench, that means we cannot even specify fully what would count as having this skill. The specification, after all, would have to invoke some sort of rationale; it would have to say what the point or value is

---

strictly speaking: I look for a deep background rationale that is parochial to a wide parish, and the parish will be delimited by cultural circumstance. I read Williams, though, as holding that good ethical thinking, even at its most fundamental, will be much more finely dependent on cultural idiosyncracies than anything with appeal to a wide parish could be.

in skillful moral judgment. To spell this out would itself be to construct a system.

Socrates taxed his fellow Athenians with question after question; he forced them to try to give rationales for their unreasoned convictions. He went to extraordinary lengths in pressing them for consistent, principled answers. His targets knew what they thought, and their convictions helped them make sense of the world and to live together. We are all part righteous, muddled Athenian and part Socrates—and we need both parts of this equipment. We want a moral vision that is worth having. The Socratic part adjusts moral vision, but it can subvert it as well. Ideally we would find a scheme to satisfy both parts of our natures, but we may have to settle for a partly articulate skill in balancing them.

Prospects

System is a virtue in moral thought, but not because a system is implicit in our thought from the start. The prospects for moral system can look grim if our moral concern rests on the hodgepodge I have sketched, on impulses pushing in so many ways. All the worse if the shapes of crucial moral feelings vary with the ways we look at things, and with the influences that come our way. Our judgments then will shift from case to case in ways that do not jibe. For a single occasion they may switch. The judgments of different people will differ when they have been influenced differently, or different influences loom large for them, or different ways of framing the matter come to view.

We can hope that moral discussion and rumination will mitigate some of this. They draw us toward consensus. Consensus in fresh cases, after all, coordinates best if it comes without new discussion. Then we can act quickly. For that we need shared ways of assessing fresh circumstances—ways shared in advance. Normative discussion helps us develop these ways.

Still, nothing like explicit system is needed to get advance consensus, or to get it much of the time. We could develop coordinated responses to the bulk of new problems without formulating uniform principles, so long as the right habits mesh. We could cite a principle in one case and ignore it in another, so long as we all selected our cases the same way. If we did agree on each occasion, to be sure, there would be a pattern to our agreement. A clever observer could formulate principles that yielded our responses. The principles he could find, though, might have right and wrong hinging on things we find morally irrelevant—say, on who commands big guns or big money. Ordinary discussion, then, might elicit shared responses to most new cases, without there being any acceptable moral system that fits all those responses.

Actual moral discussion, of course, does not get even this far. Different groups form around different precepts and framings and influences and banners. Self-serving arguments work at times and clash at times. Even in small groups where moral life is working well, the complexities of life throw up new situations where new discussion is needed. Old habits are not enough to bring current agreement.

Now my question, I keep saying, is about not actual but ideal inquiry. Pare down our faults as discussants and judges, and extrapolate the trends. Would we then find discussion tending toward agreement on a system?

Take two groups locked in enmity. Discussion is intense within each group, with little discussion between them. Within each group, slights and harms and betrayals to insiders figure large, and harms to the other group count for little. All this keeps them apart, walled into separate communities of discussion and feeling. That gives us reason, we think, to mistrust the consensus either group achieves. Mix the two groups together, though, for a long, intensive discussion with peaceful ground rules, and a common set of judgments may be forged. That is a move toward our tentative ideal: we think the results of this joint discussion are more to be trusted than the results of discussions in separate groups. A move toward our ideal might bring more consensus.

Even reliable consensus is not system. Still, various parts of our normative makeup tend toward moral system, and better inquiry fosters these tendencies. We can come to regard some ways of seeing a problem as misleading, and others as giving a key to its solution. Perhaps morals are like physics: a student of physics learns new ways of thinking, and he learns too to discount as illusions some of the old, compelling ways of seeing matters. He learns to think within a system. In morals as in physics, we can try out many different ways of looking at things, confront inconsistencies, and learn a steady way of conceiving things through these changes of view. As we do so, we improve as judges—so our initial opinions would have it.

What is at issue, then, in these musings about system and its prospects? One question concerns the strategy of moral inquiry. Is the best bet to try for system? Or are prospects better with piecemeal inquiries? What should philosophers be doing, if anything? This question is partly normative: how to weigh systematic virtues against other virtues moral thought can have. Partly, too, the question is the likely result of inquiries conducted in various spirits. System builders oversimplify, and we learn more, the challenge may be, if philosophers renounce the dogged pursuit of system for other virtues, like insight and range of vision.

Another worry is what would happen if system won. Suppose we found a system that stood up rigorously to all challenge. Might that drive us away from a morality we can thrive on? Are the judgments we would attain ones that could sustain us in the flux of life? Could they give our lives the sense of meaning our old, messy prejudices gave it? Perhaps rigor in moral thinking must lead us down the paths of Sidgwick and Harsanyi (or perhaps, instead, of Kant), and those are not systems anyone could fully accept and still live a life most worth leading.

The issue, then, is partly what is needed to live with felt meaning and enriching commitments. Another problem also stands out in the picture I have been trying to draw. I have speculated that a chief bio- logical function of our normative makeup is coordination, and system can enhance coordination. The extreme systematicity of Harsanyi or Sidgwick, though, might put us out of step with everyone around. Reactions less tutored by system might well coordinate better.[6]

I mention these doubts without trying to put them sharply. Beautiful work has been done getting the questions clear and tackling them (see Railton 1984). Earlier I myself ran through various devices for giving moral system the right allure, ways to advance and accommodate the various concerns that draw us to morality. I spoke of surface judg- ments and deep rationale, of diffidence in moral design, of liberalism; I took up relativism and parochialism in various forms. Hopes for moral system must feed on devices like these. It is hard to see why our broadly moral concern should fit a neat pattern from the start. Get- ting to pattern takes invention. We have some flexibility in the kinds of normative schemes we latch onto, but we have strong tendencies as well—tendencies that can pull apart from each other. The challenge for system builders is to find devices to channel these eddies of broadly moral concern.

6. A vague worry I have about Parfit's intense and brilliant work (1984) is whether the thinking he can lead us to through a series of precise philosophical gymnastics can infuse our daily normative lives.

Good devices must do two things. First, they must win reflective conviction: When we think hard together, the devices must convince us to see most of our broadly moral impulses as guides with limits. The devices must give us a settled way of viewing our moral concerns when they conflict, a way we can accept together. They must transform our views on hard philosophical inquiry. Second, the devices must work in action: They must not put us so far out of touch with ordinary ways of thinking and discussing that we lose the advantages of a human normative makeup, the coordination moral discussion can bring. They must combine hardiness under scrutiny with daily moral power.

Sidgwick thought he had such a device in utilitarianism. Mill worked on subsidiary devices that would help us think and act together on liberty, forms of government, and the position of women. In our day, Brandt especially has worked on joining utilitarian rationales to an effective, learnable public moral code. Rawls, who denounces utilitarianism, has offered devices for coping with a problem utilitarians too must recognize: living in mutual respect in the face of sharp disagreements on what is worth wanting in life. Well-put challenges to system can at least show what current devices lack. When they do, then more invention is needed, and the prospects for moral system are prospects for these inventions.

Is there one systematic ideal, then, to which moral inquiry points? Would full idealization lead to full moral system? Is morality a determinate subject matter, with one set of right answers that would form a complete, consistent system if we could find them? These are not questions I can answer. I have tried to say what the questions mean, and then to mention a few things that point one way or the other.

If we do get a system worth accepting, it will not be because that system was always implicit in our thought. Too many sources of moral concern pull in too many ways. Rather, it will be because the right devices of thought were found: coherent devices that reconcile our concerns to a degree, and then referee with enough command to guide us.

Hopes

We could ill give up on normative thought across the board; a person who could and did would be worse than crippled. He would muff the intricacies of life with other people; his feelings and actions would mesh so badly with theirs that he would bump against them at every turn. He would lose multifarious benefits of coordination. Narrow morality itself, in contrast, may be optional. Perhaps we could come to live without guilt, or without norms for guilt and anger, or without norms for action constrained by these norms for guilt and anger. I argued, though, that we should not. We are probably stuck with anger, whether norm-governed or not. Bad self-directed feelings of some kind or other are needed to serve as a backstop when sweeter motives fail. Guilt, joined with anger, has great advantages for normative regimentation: the two feelings mesh, and both attach to the things a person can control. Norms for action constrained by norms for guilt and anger may, then, figure in the least baleful way of achieving a life together. That was how I defended keeping narrow morality.

How systematic, then, should our moral thought be? My own hopes are that hard inquiry can bring us toward a resolution of our broadly moral impulses, a resolution that adds to the richness of life. If we think both deeply and broadly about what can be had from morality, and about what really matters in life and to whom, we should find devices of thought that get us somewhere. On my own favorite picture, a resolution would come not from developing a sharp alternative to utilitarianism, but from a refinement of the basic utilitarian insight that morality can be a tool for the good.

A reader could accept the story in this book and not think my own hopes are the right ones. He could look for system where I do not expect it to be found: say, in a balance among independent claims of benevolence, fairness, legitimate endowment, and the like, or even in an overthrow of human thriving as any basis at all for moral system. Or he could think instead that system is not to be found—that the claims of fairness, entitlement, respect, and the worth of the moral agent will not be resolved with even the wisest conceivable general concern for human good.

I have tried chiefly in this book to join two ways of seeing normative life: as a part of nature, and as part of a world of norms—a world where it does make sense to do, think, and feel some things and not others. In addition, I hoped this would help with normative inquiry itself, and especially with morals. I glanced at some questions about the broad structure of moral inquiry: How shall we inquire into norms for feelings? How seriously shall we take consistency, and why? Shall we keep morality? Can we reconcile the good, as we think about it together, with the best private rumination? What are the hopes for moral system? I voiced some answers; I recommended methods of inquiry. In effect, though, I said why a norm-expressivist might do things as many philosophers already do. Nothing in what I said jumped out as a new key to moral system.

I do have further hopes, though, hopes to strengthen a vision that already guides many deep inquiries into morality. The rough line of thought is this: Human moral propensities were shaped by something it would be foolish to value in itself, namely multiplying one's own genes among later generations. Still, the kinds of coordination that helped our ancestors pass down their genes to form us are worth wanting—for better reasons. Darwinian forces shaped the concerns and feelings we know, and some of these are broadly moral. For the most part these concerns are for things other than one's own good or the common good. Still, we can see how having those concerns promotes a good we can recognize. Up to a point we can be pleased with ourselves as well as horrified, and we can try to do better.

An important part of reflective life is sorting out what really matters and why. With injunctions on how to live, to heed the letter without the spirit is to worship a false idol. With morals, though, we find many different spirits eager to lead us. Our puzzle is not quite which are the true ones and which the false, but what kind of truth each spirit carries. Which of them can we take as worth valuing and fostering because it proceeds, in the proper way, from a further spirit? Which can we take as something more: as giving us the eyes to see what other spirits in us merit devotion? What background vision, moreover, can we share with peoples who find our own spirits dull and others dazzling? Some of the central elements of our moral makeup are things it would make sense to want—to want in oneself and one's fellows— even apart from any value we see in their objects on their own. Seeing them this way, I hope, can work on our sense of plausibility in morals. It can help make fruitful ways of thinking seem evident and right.

References

Ackerman, Bruce A. 1980. *Social Justice in the Liberal State*. New Haven: Yale University Press.

Alexander, Richard D. 1979. *Darwinism and Human Affairs*. Seattle: University of Washington Press.

————. 1987. *The Biology of Moral Systems*. New York: Aldine de Gruyter.

Anscombe, G. E. M. 1958. "On Brute Facts," *Analysis* 18:69–72.

Arnold, Magda B. 1960. *Emotion and Personality*. New York: Columbia University Press.

————. 1970. *Feelings and Emotions: The Loyola Symposium*. New York: Academic Press.

Audi, Robert. 1986. "Acting for Reasons," *Philosophical Review* 95:511–546.

Axelrod, Robert. 1984. *The Evolution of Cooperation*. New York: Basic Books.

Axelrod, Robert, and William D. Hamilton. 1981. "The Evolution of Cooperation," *Science* 211:1390–1396.

Ayer, A. J. 1936. *Language, Truth and Logic*. London: Victor Gollancz. 2d ed., 1946.

Baier, Annette. 1985. *Postures of the Mind: Essays on Mind and Morals*. Minneapolis: University of Minnesota Press.

Baier, Kurt. 1958. *The Moral Point of View: A Rational Basis for Ethics*. Ithaca: Cornell University Press.

————. 1978. "The Social Source of Reason," *Proceedings and Addresses of the American Philosophical Association* 51:707–733.

Barnes, W. H. F. 1933. "A Suggestion about Value," *Analysis* 1:45–46.

Benedict, Ruth. 1934. *Patterns of Culture*. Boston: Houghton Mifflin.

Blackburn, Simon. 1981. "Reply: Rule-Following and Moral Realism," pp. 163–187 in Steven H. Holtzman and Christopher M. Leich, eds., *Wittgenstein: To Follow a Rule*. London: Routledge and Kegan Paul.

————. 1984. *Spreading the Word: Groundings in the Philosophy of Language*. Oxford: Clarendon Press.

————. 1985. "Errors and the Phenomenology of Value," pp. 1–22 in Ted Honderich, ed., *Morality and Objectivity: A Tribute to J. L. Mackie*. London: Routledge and Kegan Paul.

Bond, E. J. 1983. *Reason and Value*. Cambridge: Cambridge University Press.

Boyd, Richard N. 1988. "How to Be a Moral Realist," pp. 181–228 in Geoffrey Sayre-McCord, ed., *Essays on Moral Realism*. Ithaca: Cornell University Press.

Brandt, Richard B. 1946. "Moral Valuation," *Ethics* 56:106–121.

———. 1954. *Hopi Ethics: A Theoretical Analysis*. Chicago: University of Chicago Press.

———. 1959. *Ethical Theory*. Englewood Cliffs, N.J.: Prentice-Hall.

———. 1963. "Toward a Credible Form of Utilitarianism," pp. 107–143 in Hector-Neri Castañeda and George Nakhnikian, eds., *Morality and the Language of Conduct*. Detroit: Wayne State University Press.

———. 1979. *A Theory of the Good and the Right*. Oxford: Clarendon Press.

Bratman, Michael. 1983. "Taking Plans Seriously," *Social Theory and Practice* 9:271–288.

———. 1984. "Two Faces of Intention," *Philosophical Review* 83:375–406.

———. 1987. *Intention, Plans, and Practical Reason*. Cambridge, Mass.: Harvard University Press.

Brentano, Franz. 1889. *Vom Ursprung sitticher Erkenntnis*. Leipzig: Duncker & Humblot. Citations from *The Origin of Our Knowledge of Right and Wrong*, Oscar Kraus and Roderick Chisholm, eds., R. Chisholm and Elizabeth H. Schneewind, trans. London: Routledge and Kegan Paul, 1969.

Buck, Ross. 1976. *Human Motivation and Emotion*. New York: John Wiley and Sons.

———. 1985. "Prime Theory: An Integrated View of Motivation and Emotion," *Psychological Review* 92:389–413.

Buck, Ross, and R. Duffy. 1980. "Nonverbal Communication of Affect in Brain-Damaged Patients," *Cortex* 16:351–362.

Caplan, Arthur, ed. 1978. *The Sociobiology Debate*. New York: Harper and Row.

Carnap, Rudolf. 1947. *Meaning and Necessity*. Chicago: University of Chicago Press.

Carson, Thomas. 1984. *The Status of Morality*. Dordrecht: Kluwer.

Church, Alonzo. 1949. "Review of Ayer's *Language, Truth and Logic*," *Journal of Symbolic Logic* 14:52–53.

Darwall, Stephen L. 1977. "Two Kinds of Respect," *Ethics* 88:36–49.

Darwin, Charles. 1872. *The Expression of Emotion in Man and Animals*. London: Murray.

Davidson, Donald. 1980. *Essays on Actions and Events*. Oxford: Oxford University Press.

———. 1984. *Inquiries into Truth and Interpretation*. Oxford: Oxford University Press.

———. 1986. "Judging Interpersonal Interests," pp. 195–211 in Aanund Hylland and Jon Elster, eds., *Foundations of Social Choice Theory*. Cambridge, England: Cambridge University Press.

Dawkins, Richard. 1976. *The Selfish Gene*. New York: Oxford University Press.

Donagan, Alan. 1977. *The Theory of Morality*. Chicago: University of Chicago Press.

Dretske, Fred. 1986. "Misrepresentation," pp. 17–36 in Radu J. Bogdan, ed., *Belief: Form, Content, and Function*. Oxford: Clarendon Press.

Eells, Ellery. 1982. *Rational Decision and Causality*. Cambridge, England: Cambridge University Press.

Enç, B. 1982. "Intentional States of Mechanical Devices," *Mind* 91:161–182.

Ewing, A. C. 1939. "A Suggested Non-Naturalistic Analysis of Good," *Mind* 48:1–22.

Firth, Raymond. 1951. *Elements of Social Organization*. London: Watts and Co.

Firth, Roderick. 1952. "Ethical Absolutism and the Ideal Observer Theory," *Philosophy and Phenomenological Research* 12:317–345.

Foot, Philippa. 1958. "Moral Arguments," *Mind* 67:502–513.

———. 1959. "Moral Beliefs," *Proceedings of the Aristotelian Society* 59 (new series):83–104.

Frankena, William. 1939. "The Naturalistic Fallacy," *Mind* 48:464–477.

———. 1986. "The Ethics of Respect for Persons," *Philosophical Topics* 14:149–167.

Frank, Robert F. 1988. *Passions within Reason: The Strategic Role of the Emotions*. New York: Norton.

Frankfurt, Harry. 1965. "Descartes' Validation of Reason," *American Philosophical Quarterly* 2:149–156.

———. 1971. "Freedom of the Will and the Concept of a Person," *Journal of Philosophy* 68:5–20.

French, Peter A., Theodore E. Uehling, and Howard K. Wettstein. 1982. *Midwest Studies in Philosophy VII: Social and Political Philosophy*. Minneapolis: University of Minnesota Press.

Gauthier, David. 1982. "On the Refutation of Utilitarianism," pp. 144–153 in Harlan B. Miller and William H. Williams, eds., *The Limits of Utilitarianism*. Minneapolis: University of Minnesota Press.

———. 1986. *Morals by Agreement*. Oxford: Oxford University Press.

Geach, Peter. 1958. "Imperative and Deontic Logic," *Analysis* 18:49–56.

———. 1965. "Assertion," *Philosophical Review* 74:449–465.

Gewirth, Alan. 1977. *Reason and Morality*. Chicago: University of Chicago Press.

Gibbard, Allan. 1978. "Act-Utilitarian Agreements," pp. 91–119 in Alvin Goldman and Jaegwon Kim, eds., *Values and Morals*. Dordrecht, Holland: Reidel.

Gibbard, Allan, and William L. Harper. 1978. "Counterfactuals and Two Kinds of Expected Utility," vol. 1, pp. 125–162 in Hooker et al., eds., *Foundations and Applications of Decision Theory*. Dordrecht, Holland: Reidel.

Gibbard, Allan. 1982. "Human Evolution and the Sense of Justice," pp. 31–46 in French, Uehling, and Wettstein 1982.

———. 1985. "Reply to Sturgeon," *Ethics* 96:34–41.

Goffman, E. 1959. *The Presentation of Self in Everyday Life*. New York: Doubleday-Anchor.

Grandy, Richard. 1973. "Reference, Meaning and Belief," *Journal of Philosophy* 70:439–452.

Grice, G. R. 1967. *The Grounds of Moral Judgment*. Cambridge, England: Cambridge University Press.

Grice, H. P. 1957. "Meaning," *Philosophical Review* 66:377–388.

———. 1969. "Utterer's Meaning and Intentions," *Philosophical Review* 78:147–177.

Griffin, James. 1986. *Well-Being: Its Meaning, Measurement, and Moral Importance*. Oxford: Oxford University Press.

Gulliver, P. H. 1973. "Negotiations as a Mode of Dispute Settlement: Towards a General Model," *Law and Society Review* 7:667–692.

Habermas, Jürgen. 1973. *Legitimationsprobleme im Spätkapitalismus*. Frankfurt am Main: Suhrkamp. Cited in translation by Thomas McCarthy, *Legitimation Crisis*. Boston: Beacon Press, 1976; London: Heineman Educational Books, 1976.

Hamilton, William D. 1964. "The Genetic Evolution of Social Behavior," *Journal of Theoretical Biology* 7:1–52.

Haney, C., C. Banks, and P. Zimbardo. 1973. "Interpersonal Dynamics in a Simulated Prison," *International Journal of Criminology and Penology* 1:69–97.

Hanson, Norwood Russell. 1958. *Patterns of Discovery*. Cambridge, England: Cambridge University Press.

Hardman, Charlotte. 1981. "The Psychology of Conformity and Self-Expression among the Lohorung Rai of East Nepal," pp. 161–180 in Heelas and Locke 1981.

Hare, R. M. 1952. *The Language of Morals*. Oxford: Oxford University Press.

———. 1963. *Freedom and Reason*. Oxford: Oxford University Press.

———. 1964. "The Promising Game," *Revue Internationale de Philosophie* 70:398–412.

———. 1979. "What Makes Choices Rational?" *Review of Metaphysics* 32:623–637.

———. 1981. *Moral Thinking: Its Levels, Method, and Point*. Oxford: Clarendon Press.

Harman, Gilbert. 1977. *The Nature of Morality*. New York: Oxford University Press.

———. 1982. "Critical Review: Richard B. Brandt, *A Theory of the Good and the Right*," *Philosophical Studies* 42:119–138.

Harsanyi, John. 1955. "Cardinal Welfare, Individualistic Ethics, and Interpersonal Comparisons of Utility," *Journal of Political Economy* 63:309–321.

Heelas, Paul, and Andrew Locke, eds. 1981. *Indigenous Psychologies: The Anthropology of the Self*. London: Academic Press.

Heelas, Paul. 1984. "Emotions across Cultures: Objectivity and Cultural Divergence," *Philosophy*, supp. vol. 17, S. C. Brown, ed., *Objectivity and Cultural Divergence*, pp. 21–42.

Herskovits, M. 1948. *Man and His Works*. New York: Knopf.

Hobbes, Thomas. 1651. *Leviathan*. Amsterdam: A. Crooke.

Hollis, Martin, and Steven Lukes, eds. 1982. *Rationality and Relativism*. Oxford: Basil Blackwell.

Horton, Robin. 1970. "African Traditional Thought and Western Science," pp. 131–171 in Wilson 1970.

Howell, Signe. 1981. "Rules Not Words," pp. 133–143 in Heelas and Locke 1981.

Hume, David. 1739. *Treatise of Human Nature*, vols. I and II. London: John

Noon; vol. III, London: Thomas Longman, 1740.

———. 1748. "Of the Original Contract," in *Essays, Moral and Political*, 3d. ed. Edinburgh: Alexander Kincaid.

Jacob, François. 1977. "Evolution and Tinkering," *Science* 196:1161–1166.

James, William. 1884. "What is an Emotion?" *Mind* 9 (old series): 188–205.

———. 1897. *The Will to Believe and Other Essays in Popular Philosophy*. London: Longmans, Green. Cited edition, New York: Dover, 1956.

Jeffrey, Richard C. 1965. *The Logic of Decision*. Chicago: University of Chicago Press. 2d. ed. 1983.

Kahneman, Daniel, J. L. Knetch, and R. H. Thaler. 1986a. "Fairness and the Assumptions of Economics," *Journal of Business* 59:s285–s300.

———. 1986b. "Fairness as a Constraint on Profit Seeking: Entitlements in the Market," *American Economic Review* 76:728–741.

Kahneman, Daniel, and Amos Tversky. 1979. "Prospect Theory: An Analysis of Decision under Risk," *Econometrica* 47:263–291.

Kant, Immanuel. 1785. *Grundlegung der Metaphysik der Sitten*. Riga: Hartknoch. Trans. as *Foundations of the Metaphysics of Morals*, by Lewis White Beck. Indianapolis: Bobbs-Merrill, 1959. Standard page numbers from the Königliche Preussische Akademie der Wissenschaft edition. Berlin, 1902–1938.

———. 1797. *Metaphysik der Sitten (The Metaphysics of Morals)*. Königsberg: Friedrich Nicolovius.

Kenny, Anthony. 1963. *Action, Emotion and Will*. London: Routledge and Kegan Paul.

Kitcher, Philip. 1985. *Vaulting Ambition*. Cambridge, Mass.: MIT Press.

Kripke, Saul. 1972. "Naming and Necessity," pp. 253–355 in Donald Davidson and Gilbert Harman, eds., *Semantics of Natural Language*. Dordrecht, Holland: Reidel.

———. 1982. *Wittgenstein on Rules and Private Language*. Cambridge, Mass.: Harvard University Press.

Kuhn, T. S. 1962. *The Structure of Scientific Revolutions*. Chicago: University of Chicago Press.

Ladd, John. 1957. *The Structure of a Moral Code*. Cambridge, Mass.: Harvard University Press.

Lee, Richard B. 1976. "!Kung Spatial Organization," pp. 73–98 in Lee and DeVore 1976.

Lee, Richard B., and Irven DeVore, eds. 1968. *Man the Hunter*. Chicago: Aldine.

———. 1976. *Kalahari Hunter-Gatherers*. Cambridge, Mass.: Harvard University Press.

Leventhal, Harold. 1980. "Toward a Comprehensive Theory of Emotion," pp. 149–207 in L. Berkowitz, ed., *Advances in Experimental Psychology*. London: Academic Press.

Levi, Isaac. 1975. "Newcomb's Many Problems," *Theory and Decision* 6:161–175.

Levy, Robert I. 1974. "Tahiti, Sin, and the Question of Integration between Personality and Sociocultural Systems," pp. 287–306 in Robert A. Levine, ed., *Culture and Personality*. Chicago: Aldine.

Lewin, Kurt. 1947. "Group Decision and Social Change," pp. 330–344 in T. M.

Newcomb and E. L. Hartley, eds., *Readings in Social Psychology*. New York: Holt, Rinehart and Winston.

Lewis, David. 1974. "Radical Interpretation," *Synthese* 27:331–344.

———. 1979a. "Attitudes *De Dicto* and *De Se*," *Philosophical Review* 87:513–543.

———. 1979b. "Prisoners' Dilemma is a Newcomb Problem," *Philosophy and Public Affairs* 8:235–240.

———. 1986. *On the Plurality of Worlds*. Oxford: Basil Blackwell.

Lewontin, R. C., S. Rose, and L. J. Kamin. 1984. *Not in Our Genes: Biology, Ideology, and Human Nature*. New York: Pantheon.

Locke, John. 1690a. *An Essay Concerning Human Understanding*. London: Thomas Bassett.

———. 1690b. *The Second Treatise of Government*. London: Awnsham Churchill.

Luban, David. 1985. "Bargaining and Compromise: Recent Work on Negotiation and Informal Justice," *Philosophy and Public Affairs* 14:397–416.

Luce, R. Duncan, and Howard Raiffa. 1957. *Games and Decisions*. New York: Wiley.

Lukes, Steven. 1982. "Relativism in Its Place," pp. 261–305 in Hollis and Lukes 1982.

Lyons, David. 1976. "Mill's Theory of Morality," *Nous* 10:101–120.

Lyons, William. 1980. *Emotion*. Cambridge, England: Cambridge University Press.

MacIntyre, Alistair. 1981. *After Virtue*. Notre Dame, In: Notre Dame University Press.

Marcus, Ruth Barcan. 1980. "Moral Dilemmas and Consistency," *Journal of Philosophy* 77:121–136.

Marshall, Lorna. 1976. "Sharing, Talking, and Giving: Relief of Social Tensions among the !Kung," pp. 349–371 in Richard B. Lee and Irven DeVore, eds., *Kalahari Hunter-Gatherers*. Cambridge, Mass.: Harvard University Press.

Maynard Smith, John. 1974. "The Theory of Games and the Evolution of Animal Conflicts," *Journal of Theoretical Biology* 47:209–221.

———. 1976. "Evolution and the Theory of Games," *American Scientist* 64:41–45.

———. 1978. "The Evolution of Behavior," *Scientific American* 239:176–192.

———. 1982. *Evolution and the Theory of Games*. Cambridge, England: Cambridge University Press.

Maynard Smith, John, and G. A. Parker. 1976. "The Logic of Asymmetric Conflicts," *Animal Behaviour* 24:159–175.

Maynard Smith, John, and G. R. Price. 1973. "The Logic of Animal Conflicts," *Animal Behaviour* 24:159–175.

McDowell, John. 1978. "Are Moral Judgments Hypothetical Imperatives?" *Proceedings of the Aristotelian Society* (supp. vol.):13–29.

———. 1981. "Non-Cognitivism and Rule Following," pp. 141–162 in Steven Holzman and Christopher M. Leich, eds., *Wittgenstein: To Follow a Rule*. London: Routledge and Kegan Paul.

———. 1984. "Wittgenstein on Following a Rule," *Synthese* 58:325–363.

———. 1985. "Values and Secondary Properties," pp. 110–129 in Ted Honderich, ed., *Morality and Objectivity*. London: Routledge and Kegan Paul.

Milgram, Stanley. 1974. *Obedience to Authority*. New York: Harper and Row.

Mill, John Stuart. 1859. *On Liberty*. London: Parker and Son.

———. 1863. *Utilitarianism*. London: Parker, Son, and Bourn.

Millikan, Robert A. 1917. *The Electron*. Chicago: University of Chicago Press.

Millikan, Ruth. 1984. *Language, Thought, and Other Biological Categories*. Cambridge, Mass.: Bradford/MIT.

———. 1986. "Thoughts without Laws: Cognitive Science with Content," *Philosophical Review* 95:47–80.

Moore. G. E. 1903. *Principia Ethica*. Cambridge, England: Cambridge University Press.

Murphy, Jeffrie. 1982. "Forgiveness and Resentment," pp. 503–516 in French, Uehling, and Wettstein 1982.

Nagel, Thomas. 1970. *The Possibility of Altruism*. Princeton: Princeton University Press.

———. 1978. "Ethics as an Autonomous Theoretical Subject," pp. 198–205 in Gunther S. Stent, ed., *Morality as a Biological Phenomenon*. Berkeley: University of California Press.

Nash, John F. 1951. "The Bargaining Problem," *Econometrica* 18:155–162.

Nash, June. 1970. "Rhetoric of a Maya Indian Court," *Estudios de Cultura Maya* 8:239–296.

Needham, Rodney. 1972. *Belief, Language, and Experience*. Oxford: Basil Blackwell.

———. 1981. "Inner States as Universals," pp. 65–78 in Heelas and Locke 1981.

Neurath, Otto. 1932. "Protokollsätze," *Erkenntnis* 3:204–214.

Newcomb, Theodore M., Ralph Turner, and Philip E. Converse. 1965. *Social Psychology*. New York: Holt, Rinehart and Winston.

Nietzsche, Friedrich. 1887. *Zur Genealogie der Moral*. Trans. as *On the Genealogy of Morals*, by Walter Kaufmann and R. J. Hollingdale. New York: Vintage Books, 1967.

Nisbett, Richard, and Lee Ross. 1980. *Human Inference: Strategies and Shortcomings of Social Judgment*. Englewood Cliffs, N.J.: Prentice-Hall.

Nozick, Robert. 1969. "Newcomb's Problem and Two Principles of Choice," pp. 114–146 in Nicholas Rescher, ed., *Essays in Honor of Carl G. Hempel*. Dordrecht: Reidel.

———. 1981. *Philosophical Explanations*. Cambridge, Mass.: Harvard University Press.

Panksepp, J. 1982. "Toward a General Psychobiological Theory of Emotions" (with commentaries), *The Brain and Behavioral Sciences* 5:407–467.

Parfit, Derek. 1984. *Reasons and Persons*. Oxford: Oxford University Press.

Piers, Gerhart. 1953. "Shame and Guilt: A Psychoanalytic Study," pp. 15–55 in Piers and Singer 1953.

Piers, Gerhart, and Milton B. Singer. 1953. *Shame and Guilt: A Psychoanalytic and a Cultural Study*. Springfield, Ill.: Charles C. Thomas.

Pitcher, George. 1965. "Emotion," *Mind* 74:326–346.

Plutchik, R. *Emotion: A Psychoevolutionary Synthesis*. New York: Harper and Row, 1980.

Prichard, H. A. 1912. "Does Moral Philosophy Rest on a Mistake?" *Mind* 21:21–37.

Provis, Chris. 1981. "Reason and Emotion," *Canadian Journal of Philosophy* 11:439–451.

Putnam, Hilary. 1981. *Reason, Truth and History*. Cambridge, England: Cambridge University Press.

Quine, W. V. O. 1951. "Two Dogmas of Empiricism," *Philosophical Review* 60:20–43.

———. 1960. *Word and Object*. Cambridge, Mass.: MIT Press.

Raiffa, Howard. 1968. *Decision Analysis*. Reading, Mass.: Addison-Wesley.

Railton, Peter. 1984. "Alienation, Consequentialism, and the Demands of Morality," *Philosophy and Public Affairs* 13:134–171.

———. 1986a. "Facts and Values," *Philosophical Topics* 14:5–31.

———. 1986b. "Moral Realism," *Philosophical Review*. 95:163–207.

Ramsey, Frank Plumpton. 1931. "Truth and Probability," pp. 156–198 in *The Foundations of Mathematics and Other Logical Essays*. London: Routledge and Kegan Paul.

Rappaport, Roy A. 1979. *Ecology, Meaning, and Religion*. Richmond, Calif.: North Atlantic Books.

Rawls, John. 1971. *A Theory of Justice*. Cambridge, Mass.: Harvard University Press.

———. 1980. "Kantian Constructivism in Moral Theory," *Journal of Philosophy* 77:515–572.

———. 1985. "Justice as Fairness: Political Not Metaphysical," *Philosophy and Public Affairs* 14:223–251.

Roberts, Robert C. 1988. "What an Emotion Is: A Sketch," *Philosophical Review* 97:183–209.

Rorty, Richard. 1972. "The World Well Lost," *Journal of Philosophy* 69:649–665.

———. 1982. *The Consequences of Pragmatism*. Minneapolis: University of Minnesota Press.

Ross, W. D. 1930. *The Right and the Good*. Oxford: Clarendon Press.

Rousseau, Jean-Jacques. 1762. *Du contrat social, ou principes du droit politique*. Amsterdam: Marc Michel Rey.

Ruse, Michael. 1985. *Sociobiology: Sense or Nonsense?* 2d ed. Dordrecht: Reidel.

Ryle, Gilbert. 1949. *The Concept of Mind*. London: Hutchison.

Sabini, John, and Maury Silver. 1982. *Moralities of Everyday Life*. Oxford: Oxford University Press.

Sartre, Jean-Paul. 1946. *L'existentialisme est un humanisme*. Paris: Nagel.

Savage, Leonard J. 1954. *The Foundations of Statistics*. New York: Wiley.

———. 1972. *The Foundations of Statistics*. 2d ed. New York: Dover.

Scanlon, T. M. 1982. "Contractualism and Utilitarianism," pp. 103–128 in Amartya Sen and Bernard Williams, eds., *Utilitarianism and Beyond*. Cambridge, England: Cambridge University Press.

Schachter, Stanley. 1971. *Emotion, Obesity, and Crime*. New York: Academic Press.

Schachter, S., and J. F. Singer. 1962. "Cognitive, Social and Physiological Determinants of Emotional State," *Psychological Review* 69:379–399.

Schank, R. L. 1932. "A Study of a Community and Its Groups and Institutions

Conceived of as Behaviors of Individuals," *Psychological Monographs* 43, 62:1–133.

Scheffler, Samuel. 1979. "Moral Scepticism and Ideals of the Person," *Monist* 62:288–303.

Schelling, Thomas. 1960. *The Strategy of Conflict.* Cambridge, Mass.: Harvard University Press.

Searle, John. 1962. "Meaning and Speech Acts," *Philosophical Review* 71:423–432.

———. 1964. "How to Derive 'Ought' from 'Is,' " *Philosophical Review* 73:43–58.

———. 1969. *Speech Acts.* Cambridge, England: Cambridge University Press.

Sherif, M. A. 1935. "A Study of Some Social Factors in Perception," *Archives of Psychology* 27:1–60.

Sidgwick, Henry. 1907. *The Methods of Ethics.* 7th ed. London: Macmillan.

Singer, Milton B. 1953. "Shame Cultures and Guilt Cultures," pp. 59–100 in Piers and Singer 1953.

Singer, Peter. 1981. *The Expanding Circle: Ethics and Sociobiology.* New York: New American Library.

Smith, Adam. 1790. *The Theory of Moral Sentiments.* 6th ed. London: A. Strahan and T. Cadell.

Smith, Jean. 1981. "Self and Experience in Maori Culture," pp. 145–159 in Heelas and Locke 1981.

Solomon, Robert C. 1976. *The Passions.* Garden City, N.Y.: Doubleday/Anchor.

Sperber, Dan. 1982. "Apparently Irrational Beliefs," pp. 149–180 in Hollis and Lukes 1982.

Sperry, R. W., E. Zaidel, and D. Zaidel. 1979. "Self Recognition and Social Awareness in the Disconnected Minor Hemisphere," *Neuropsychologia* 17:153–166.

Stalnaker, Robert C. 1976. "Possible Worlds," *Nous* 10:65–75.

Stampe, Dennis W. 1977. "Toward a Causal Theory of Linguistic Representation," *Midwest Studies in Philosophy* 2:81–102.

Steele, Claude M. 1988. "The Psychology of Self-Affirmation: Sustaining the Integrity of the Self," pp. 261–302 in L. Berkowitz, ed., *Advances in Experimental Psychology*, vol. 21. New York: Academic Press.

Stevenson, Charles. 1937. "The Emotive Meaning of Ethical Terms," *Mind* 46:14–31.

———. 1944. *Ethics and Language.* New Haven: Yale University Press.

Stich, Stephen P. 1983. *From Folk Psychology to Cognitive Science: The Case against Belief.* Cambridge, Mass.: Bradford/MIT.

Strawson, P. F. 1949. "Ethical Intuitionism," *Philosophy* 24:23–33.

———. 1961. "Social Morality and Individual Ideal," *Philosophy* 36:1–17.

Sturgeon, Nicholas L. 1985a. "Gibbard on Moral Judgment and Norms," *Ethics* 96:22–33.

———. 1985b. "Moral Explanations," pp. 49–78 in David Copp and David Zimmerman, eds., *Morality, Reason and Truth.* Totowa, N.J.: Rowman and Allanheld.

Symons, Donald. 1979. *The Evolution of Human Sexuality.* Oxford: Oxford University Press.

———. 1987. "If We're All Darwinians, What's the Fuss About?" pp. 121–146 in C. B. Crawford, M. F. Smith, and D. L. Krebs, eds., *Sociobiology and Psychology: Ideas, Issues, and Applications.* Hillsdale, N.J.: Erlbaum.

Taylor, Gabrielle. 1985. *Pride, Shame and Guilt: Emotions of Self-Assessment.* Oxford: Clarendon Press.

Taylor, Paul. 1954. "Four Types of Ethical Relativism," *Philosophical Review* 63:500–516.

————. 1961. *Normative Discourse.* Englewood Cliffs, N.J.: Prentice-Hall.

Thagard, Paul, and Richard E. Nisbett. 1983. "Rationality and Charity," *Philosophy of Science* 50:250–267.

Trivers, Robert L. 1971. "The Evolution of Reciprocal Altruism," *Quarterly Review of Biology* 46:35–57.

Tucker, D. M. 1981. "Lateral Brain Function, Emotion, and Conceptualization," *Psychological Bulletin* 89:19–46.

Turnbull, Colin M. 1962. *The Lonely African.* New York: Simon and Schuster.

Tversky, Amos, and Daniel Kahneman. 1981. "The Framing of Decisions and the Psychology of Choice," *Science* 211:453–458.

————. 1983. "Extensional vs. Intuitive Reasoning: The Conjunction Fallacy in Probability Judgment," *Psychological Review* 90:293–315.

Van Fraassen, Bas. 1973. "Values and the Heart's Command," *Journal of Philosophy* 70:5–19.

Wiggins, David. 1987. *Needs, Values, Truth: Essays in the Philosophy of Value.* Oxford: Basil Blackwell.

Williams, Bernard. 1985. *Ethics and the Limits of Philosophy.* Cambridge, Mass.: Harvard University Press.

Wilson, Bryan R., ed. 1970. *Rationality.* Oxford: Basil Blackwell.

Wilson, Edward O. 1975. *Sociobiology: The New Synthesis.* Cambridge, Mass.: Harvard University Press.

————. 1978. *On Human Nature.* Cambridge, Mass.: Harvard University Press.

Wittgenstein, Ludwig. 1953. *Philosophische Untersuchungen/Philosophical Investigations.* New York: Macmillan.

Wright, Larry. 1973. "Functions," *Philosophical Review* 82:139–168.

Zajonc, R. B. 1980. "Feeling and Thinking: Preferences Need No Inferences," *American Psychologist* 35:151–175.

Index

339

Harvard University Press is a member of Green Press Initiative (greenpressinitiative.org), a nonprofit organization working to help publishers and printers increase their use of recycled paper and decrease their use of fiber derived from endangered forests. This book was printed on 100% recycled paper containing 50% post-consumer waste and processed chlorine free.